BEYOND MY DREAMS

BEYOND MY DREAMS

OLAJUMOKE ADENOWO

Prestige

Published in Nigeria in 2019 by Kachifo Limited
Under its Prestige imprint
253 Herbert Macaulay Way Yaba, Lagos, Nigeria
0807 736 4217
info@prestige.ng
www.prestige.ng

A catalogue record for this book is available from the National Library of Nigeria.

ISBN: 978-978-56969-3-6

All Bible quotations are taken from the King James Version and New King James Version unless otherwise stated.

Cover design and layout by Akeem Ibrahim
Cover image by Emmanuel Oyeleke

All proceeds from the sale of *Beyond My Dreams* go to Awesome Treasures Foundation.

Dedication

Beyond my Dreams is dedicated to the Holy Spirit, without whom marriage as God intended is impossible. To the many who have been hurt by those who should have been their role models for love as God intended – my sincere prayer is that as you read this book, you would find it in your heart to forgive and attain liberty and your journey to God's best for you would truly begin.

Love is God's idea – God is love.

BOOK ONE

Prologue

"Though He slay me, yet will I trust in Him."

Job 13:15A

The darkness was so deep that she could feel it, darkness - thick and black as tar, darkness she could almost inhale. A weighty black doom pressing down on her, layer upon layer of dense shadows - oppressing her. A darkness so deep that she could touch it, like a dark, steamy fog born out of the deepest night.

"This is death..." she thought. Only in death could there be such an utter absence of light. If this was death, then something was wrong. She had ended up in the wrong place. This can't be heaven.

Her foggy mind tried to make sense of her present state. Panic gripped her heart for a split second as she considered the only other alternative to heaven in her own understanding of destinations in the afterlife. If she wasn't in heaven then, "Why am I in hell?" she said aloud and her voice breaking the eerie silence shocked her.

Wondering gave way to a burst of panic. "What would I be doing in hell?"

She began to think but her mind wasn't cooperating and she couldn't stay focused. She began to sink back into the deep well of unconsciousness that had been her refuge hitherto.

"Morola." The familiar voice whispered her name and she felt herself being dragged out of her dark descent.

"Morola," she heard his velvety baritone saying gently, a little louder than a whisper now, with the peculiar accented drawl he gave every syllable of her name, as if he was willing her name to go on forever, as if caressing the name itself, cherishing her very name.

She shook herself. This was a delusion. It couldn't be his voice; she was losing her mind. Her mind couldn't deal with the recent horrors it had witnessed and it was fleeing to an alternative reality it could cope with.

But, could it be real? Was she really hearing him? Was he alive? This voice that pulled her back to consciousness, was it him? Hope began to rise uninvited in her soul, a surge of joy filled her heart. He was alive! He was close by! It was all a bad dream after all.

Just as swiftly as the hope seeped in, despair like dark waves rolled in and drowned out the short-lived joy. The rational part of her mind struggled to prevail and intervened with a cruel truth – he can't be alive.

In fact, he wasn't alive. She had heard with her own ears, she had hard evidence. He was dead.

If only he was still alive, if only things were different, if only he had turned down the role, if he had been less trusting, he would be alive and she wouldn't be here. Her thoughts began to drift again in spite of her circumstances, as if inexorably drawn to joyful times. Joy seeped into her heart like golden rivulets of pure honey. The feelings of impending doom began to ebb and fade. The dark curtain of darkness began to fall away like discarded layers of black drapes, light seeped into her heart at the thought of his smiles, his enigmatic smile, his smile lighting up his eyes, the genuinely sincere and engaging smile that made everyone trust him instinctively. The gentle smile he seemed to specially reserve for her; that smile that was never without a steady open gaze from those eyes that seemed to bore deep into her soul.

As the image of his face crystallised in her mind she felt the beginning of a smile come in unbidden response to her own face, but just as it started, the blossoming smile died an abrupt death - the pain! The nerve-jangling pain! She couldn't bear the pain. It stopped the growing upward curl of her lips. The numbing pain seared down her face and raced across her jawline. She gritted her teeth instinctively as her thoughts raced in all directions trying to make sense of it all. What was going on? How could it hurt to smile? Slowly the realisation dawned on her – the dead don't feel pain.

"Am I really still alive?"

Her analytical mind still tried to wrestle with her feelings and make sense of the confusion. How much suffering would suffice as a sacrifice, how much pain would it take to merit the reward of death?

If she was alive, how come she couldn't see? This thought crashed into her consciousness like an intruder. She moved what she felt should be her right arm slightly and the limb rose upwards in response as she lifted her hand to where her face should be, but she couldn't see the hand. She felt her face and stretched out a tentative finger to touch her eyes - her eyes were no doubt still shut tight by bruises from the blows she was now beginning to recall she had received.

Her hands were right in front of her face; she could feel the humid air against her face at the slight movement of her hands. But she could see nothing. Something was definitely wrong. She touched her face again tentatively, her fingers resting lightly against her cheeks. Then she probed further. Her fingers poked her right cornea and she winced sharply. Her eyes were open! Why then couldn't she see? Panic began to set in as it dawned on her that she had gone blind! Blind? Blind?

She wiggled her fingers. She still saw nothing but she felt her fingers move. It slowly dawned on her fevered consciousness that the darkness was so deep that she couldn't see her fingers though they were right in front of her face. Where would this nightmare end?

But what difference did it make? She would be dead soon any way. There was nothing to live for anymore.

The heat was intolerable, the kind of heat that was as laborious to inhale as steam. Rola, drenched in sweat and hovering on the verge of consciousness, let out a low moan; a moan that emanated from pain. Her head throbbed as if each nerve had been set on fire – from her neck up, all she felt was a ball of liquid pain.

She tried to breathe in deeply to relieve her pain, but a stench assaulted her nostrils. Something was rotting in the cell. A rodent perhaps? What smelt so foul? It hit her suddenly that she was the culprit - she stank. She stank from days of lying there on the floor unwashed. A maelstrom of emotions filled her heart – disgust at her own state, physical and mental pain. Volcanic rage surged through her, but the rage was better than the hopelessness and emptiness she had felt just moments ago.

How could anyone be treated so badly? How could anyone be left to rot in the filth in this dark hole?

It took what seemed like several minutes before Rola could calm her rage, breathe evenly again and piece her thoughts together.

Kaniz... she had just heard his voice or had she really?

That one name nudged Rola almost into full consciousness, as more memories flooded her rousing brain.

"Kaniz..."

"Morola..."

She must have spoken out loud because she heard the voice again, whispering back to her, answering her.

Rola's eyes felt heavy, as if a malevolent force weighed them down. But she opened them gradually.

"Kaniz... my Amir." She muttered his name from her cracked lips, struggling and slurring the words through a tongue swollen with dehydration, as if saying his name out loud could bring him back from the grave. As if she could invoke his resurrection by the force of her longing, as if his pet name would do the miracle if his given name didn't rouse him from death.

"Amir, you are the lucky one. You are resting. You are beyond the cruel hands of betrayal now." She was muttering, speaking her thoughts aloud. She didn't concern herself with the rationality of talking to the dead. It was better to speak to the dead, she reasoned; they were soon to be her companions. She couldn't last too long in the state she was being held anyway. Just a few more days, perhaps even hours. With the dehydration, the trauma, the weakness, the pain... her end was near and she welcomed the release from suffering.

Rola tried to make sense of her immediate environment. She was lying flat on a hard surface. She allowed her right hand to feel the ground. It was grainy and slippery, a dirt floor of sorts covered with something wet, sticky and slimy. Steadying herself first on her elbows and then with her palms, Rola attempted to sit up, in spite of the searing pain in her head that heralded her every movement.

At that moment, as she struggled to sit up - flashes of memory came unbidden. One after the other, images flickered across the screen of her mind. She could hear again the first gunshot from the anteroom, a groan in a man's voice as something heavy hit the floor with a thud. Then a second shot and Raliat's voice full of morbid urgency shouts, "Madam!"

Just that one word and Raliat was silenced. The gun went off and they heard another thud. She could see clearly in her mind's eye how the armed men had burst in through the anteroom door into her study, instantly surrounding her and her guest. It all happened so quickly, without warning. The second man to enter the study pointed his gun at Tega and without hesitation took the shot. That's all it took, one shot to Tega's head. She could still hear the retort of the pistol and smell the gunpowder. She could still hear the sickening sound as her friend groaned and fell face forward on the desk with a dull thud. As he was shot, his blood sprayed all over her face, her clothes, the papers on her desk they had been working on. Where his lifeless body now lay, a rivulet of blood oozing rapidly from his head wound like red molten lava, the papers soaking rapidly, his left hand jerking involuntarily in dissonance with the rest of his still form. She screamed and lunged towards her friend. From her peripheral vision, she saw one of the men move and then the cold nozzle of the gun was pressed against her throbbing temple, stopping her, daring her to move again.

She resisted, desperate to see if she could still help her friend. She could feel again the resounding crash of the butt of the gun on her right temple. Her assailant struck just once and her jaw jolted with the blow. She fell and heard a crack in her left ear as her head hit the cold hard floor. Her assailant crouched and moved in close to her face. She smelt his rancid breath as he barked, "Woman I will waste you."

His boot came down on her back with brute force and as his boot connected with her soft flesh, she felt pain explode through her lower torso as her midriff flattened painfully against the floor.

More strangers were speaking, all male voices. She could tell that at least three more men were in the room. She couldn't make out exactly how many they were now as the blood from the cut on her temple oozed into her right eye, blocking her vision.

Now more voices were barking commands at her... Then the handcuffs came on. Someone jerked both her hands behind her back and turned her flat on her face on the floor and the blood from her head smeared the floor. She struggled to hear what they were saying. It was important to know who they were and what their plans were. Were they going to kill her too? They had killed Raliat and Tega without hesitation. They would definitely kill her. She had seen their uncovered faces.

Why didn't they just kill her right now? If only her head was clear. What were they saying? She felt the desperation rise in her. The pain in her head was disorienting. She fought back against the restraint of the handcuffs and tried to turn to see her captors better. Down came the butt of the gun again and she blacked out, mercifully.

She came round with that smelly blindfold wrapped tightly around her eyes. She was in the back of a covered vehicle. From the jolts and jars as it bumped along the road, it seemed to be some kind of a truck. The blindfold smelt of petrol. Perhaps it was a rag that had been used to clean the back of the truck. They probably just improvised and tied whatever they could find around her eyes.

The swollen bruises around her eyes hurt as if they were set on fire. The ride went on for hours as she was thrown about at every twist and turn. With every jolt of the truck, her shoulders jarred as they hit the truck floor or the truck sides.

The truck stopped abruptly and the voices moved from the front of the truck towards the back of the truck. She was unceremoniously dumped out, tumbling to the ground as the tail gate was flipped open by one of her assailants; Rancid Breath it seemed... from his body odor. She was yanked to her feet and half walked, half dragged into a building. She could tell they were walking into a building because the acoustics changed and the warm night air gave way to a humid and hot atmosphere. More voices. Two? Or were they three or more? Everything at this point was now a blurred memory, everything was undecipherable, till she was un-cuffed. That caught her attention. It was a small relief. She could now move her numb wrists. The awkward angle at which her arms had been cuffed behind her had made her shoulders ache terribly. Her arms felt like they would come out of their sockets and her shoulder blades were sore.

With her hands un-cuffed, her captors seemed to think they had been gracious enough already and at that point, she had been briskly handled by what seemed like two sets of male hands. Rancid Breath's hands were not one of the hands, his hands were more calloused than these ones and larger, and his smell wasn't lingering in the air around her as these ones dragged her along. She was pushed roughly into this hole and what seemed to be a metal gate was shut with a loud clang of finality behind her. The sound seemed to seal her fate.

She remembered that the first thing she did as the door clanged shut was to struggle with the blindfold until she tore it off, but it was so dark in the room that it made no difference if the blindfold was off or on. It was at the point that the blindfold came off that her recollections began. It was almost as if the blindfold coming off her eyes also took the blinkers off her mind and the memories filed away by her concerted focus on survival trickled back into her mind.

She could again hear the gruff male voices in the cab of the truck, low undecipherable voices. She couldn't make out what they were saying but then, one of them must have turned on the radio and turned it on really loud. She could hear the radio above the noise of the truck's engine, above the sound of the clanging chassis, above the sound of the truck tires crunching against the asphalt. The voices on the radio were clear – broadcasters' voices carrying far – announcing the night's events, announcements that all deteriorated into a fuzz in her shell-shocked mind after she heard the one sentence that stopped her heart stone cold.

She couldn't bring herself to recall the awful words the male broadcaster had employed. All that mattered at the moment was the import of his words: Kaniz was dead! Shot dead at point blank range. One shot to the back of his head! He was executed. That was the import of the broadcast. Everything else was incidental.

"We interrupt our regular programming," that was how the ominous announcement that ended life as she knew it had started. "We interrupt our regular programming to announce..."

How true. The programming of her life had been interrupted forever by that singular announcement.

Kaniz was dead!

Kaniz was dead!

Rola sank back slowly like a crumpled rag doll, sliding to the dirt floor as she lay still in her prone position. The slippery substance on the floor smeared her hands. It was more viscous than aqueous and it appeared to become sticky as it dried on her fingers. Her skirt was stiff with it. What was it? She lifted her hands to her nose. She could smell even if she couldn't see in this darkness.

It stank.

It really stank.

Blood.

It was blood. Her hands flew to her belly as she grabbed her mid-section and remembered.

"Our baby..."

Panic filled her heart. What else could possibly have gone wrong? Was there to be no end to her loss? The life that had been growing inside her for the last four months till the tiny swell could just be seen below her navel – was it now dead with Kaniz? Was there nothing left of the hope of life that had begun to flutter within her? A pool of dried blood and pain?

What happened?

When had it happened?

How had it happened?

It all began to make sense. She had lost consciousness the first time when the severe pain in her abdomen and lower back started. Spasms racked her body and she had doubled over in pain on the rough cell floor. She had screamed, she had cried out loud but no one had come.

"I need a doctor!"

She screamed not because of the pain but because she had to save her child.

"I need a doctor! Help me!"

No one answered. The darkness swallowed her screams. No one came. She felt her thighs get wet and though she couldn't see, in that closed humid cell, the unmistakable smell of fresh blood filled her nostrils. Then even her legs got wet as the bleeding continued and she slipped into unconsciousness.

She now realised that the stench in the cell was from the dried blood she had lain in.

"Oh no," she gasped.

In the deepest anguish, she screamed, "My child!" Her voice rose but failed again in despair. Kaniz's child. Their child had been her only hope. It was the only reason she had got, through it all – the abduction, the long and tedious journey to the cell, the beatings. She had survived all because she knew she had to live. She knew that even on that night of death and dying, she had new life within her, their baby, and if she held on and carried this child to term, then Kaniz could have been murdered but he wouldn't be forgotten. Their dreams wouldn't be forgotten because he would live on in this precious child.

Kaniz had whispered to her that final morning, "My love now lives within you Morola." But now, all hope was finally and absolutely lost. It crossed her mind that since she had miscarried, she needed access to a doctor before infection set in. She needed to renew her efforts to get someone with medical training to take a look at her. But her sinking soul rejected any plans of survival. No, now there really wasn't any need to keep holding on. It was just easier to die.

Sobs welled up from deep within her as the full magnitude of the nightmare that she was in hit her.

Their joy was dead,
their dreams were dead,
all dead,
dead like Kaniz,
dead like their child,
dead!
Everything that mattered – everything was dead!

Rola's heart threatened to shatter to smithereens. She felt a black hole of anguish where her heart should be; such agony that she was certain she would implode. How much pain could a heart take before it failed? She began to sob and a sharp pain shot through her forehead, jolting her. Rola lifted her hand and touched the spot – it was a huge bump rising from her face where the butt of the gun had come crashing down on her head.

Kaniz...

He was beyond pain, beyond suffering. She envied his swift end. She knew he would gladly switch places with her now to save her from this horror but he wasn't here anymore.

"My Amir," she muttered into the darkness as love and grief collided in her soul. For the very first time, she felt envy.

"Oh Lord, if you still answer any prayer at all, grant a swift death for me too." She prayed from the very depths of her being. Perhaps God was still interested in her; perhaps He could still hear. If He could see her in this deep darkness, maybe He would answer. She could only imagine the horrors and torture lined up for her. This was just the beginning.

Suddenly, it was all too much for her and waves of agony too deep to articulate surged within her. Sob after sob wracked her body. She was oblivious of every other pain but the pain in her heart. As hot tears stung her eyes, she cried out in the dense darkness, "Why am I still here? Why am I alive? Why?"

She screamed into the darkness. "No! I can't be alive. I refuse to live! I don't want to live!" She could hardly speak through the sobs convulsing her being.

After what seemed like a lifetime, through the palpable darkness, a still voice whispered from what seemed like deep inside her, floating up from the recesses of her being, from the core of her existence.

"Grace."

Just the one word, "Grace," and inexplicably, peace greater than the darkness around her enveloped her profoundly and absolutely. The darkness ceased to matter.

Rola was suddenly aware that she was not alone. Someone cared. Someone infinitely powerful had calculated that these calamities would not overcome her. This present situation had a purpose. An uncanny peace and rest came upon her as the Voice lifted her out of the black hole she was in.

"Grace," she heard the voice say again and hope ignited in her.

"It will not all end here." She had this knowing settled with finality deep within her, too deep to be reached by the gnarled fingers of doubt, too bright to be dimmed by the oppressive darkness she laid in.

"This is not what I was promised. This is not why I returned," she muttered as the peace descended upon her, cocooning her in its safe embrace. She lay on the earth floor and found strange solace in its firmness. As her thoughts began to slide involuntarily to her return home, a deep sigh escaped her. It now seemed like an aeon had passed since that happy time.

Chapter One

"He hath made everything beautiful in His time; also He hath set the world in their heart, so that no man can find out the work that God maketh from the beginning to the end."

Ecclesiastes 3:11

The chirping sound of a Skype call from the laptop on her work desk, woke Rola up. She sprung out of bed and rushed over to the laptop. One tap and the screen came alive. An attractive lady in her forties was at the other end, while Rola's sleepy face appeared at the bottom left.

"Hi, Mo. Hey, poor soul, you look like you still need your beauty sleep—"

Rola cut in. "Thanks to Di and Synergy." Perhaps it was the reference to sleep that got to Rola but a huge yawn escaped her that moment.

"Aww my dear. Di is off to San Francisco for the meeting with the VCs on the new FocusWare. Well done Mo! You came through again."

"Bev darling, I didn't sleep for two days!" Rola moaned.

Her eyes were red with fatigue but though she was obviously worn out, she still mustered a smile, her tired eyes crinkled at the corners as she chatted with her executive assistant and self-appointed consigliere.

"I had better let you catch some rest Mo darling, but just a quick one about your apartment. We've had six responses already to the ad since yesterday, but can you really let it out for a year? Everyone wants a loft in Tribeca, it's a no brainer getting a tenant."

Rola thought for a moment. "Bev, let's do it. I will be back in New York often in the next year, but I think right now, I should sort out this youth service thing I told you guys about; not that I will ever serve in government or anything but who knows? One day I just might need to prove I served my country. We get asked for the weirdest documents at the weirdest times. I wouldn't be surprised if someone asks for your voters' registration card before you can get a marriage license." Rola chuckled softly at her really dry joke.

"Something just tells me I need to be here for now. Olaotan is super happy I am home. Mrs B and TK too. Please, let out the apartment. We can make Synergy work, one app at a time." She smiled. "It's a global village Bev, it really doesn't matter where I am working from, does it? New York is just twelve hours away and there are several flights a day I can take from Lagos. I can make any important meeting with forty-eight hours' notice."

"Yeah, but we miss you, the whole team does. You know you are the glue that binds Synergy. I promise you the interns are not the same when you are not here." Bev rolled her large eyes. "Tim is driving me crazy with questions—"

The sharp barking of a small dog could be heard on Bev's end.

"Aww that's Jay-Z," Rola cooed, her tired face breaking into a warm smile.

"Yes. He heard your voice and went gaga. Mo, I swear this dog thinks you are his mum," Bev said, reaching just below Rola's view and raising a lovely Lhasa Apso with the cutest face for Rola to see. The puppy let out a medley of excited barks, its tail wagging excitedly as it caught a glimpse of Rola.

"Hi, Jay-Z," she said to Di's dog. "I am not around so it's Aunty Bev's turn to babysit you. I miss you too Jay-Z. Is Di taking you for walks in the morning like I do? Is she getting your biscuits?" She was making cooing sounds to Jay-Z, speaking in that cheesy voice all adults seem to adopt when speaking to infants, smiling widely.

Bev broke into her repartee. "Mo, about Tim..."

Rola rolled her eyes and made as if to get up and end the conversation. "Beeevvv you are so ruining my plans right now. I had plans to sleep for the whole day!"

Bev became serious. "Mo the guy really seems to care about you."

Rola sighed. "I hear you."

A pregnant silence followed and Bev spoke again breaking into Rola's reverie. "Oh Dave, remember Dave? The Zimbabwean or was it Zambian? From Tricott? Tall, just a little grey at the temples? He has been calling incessantly..."

Rola rolled her eyes again and rose, blowing Bev a kiss. "Bye Bev. Bye darling." Wrapping up the conversation abruptly, Rola punched a button and the screen went dark again.

She stood up from the wing back chair, letting her hand linger on the plush velvet covering. As she rose, she let out another yawn and stretched. She walked over to her windows and switched on the socket hidden behind the drapes. Blackout blinds in opaque cream descended with a soft whirr and completely shut out all the sun light filtering in. Now the only light in the room was from the soft glow of the bedside lamp on her nightstand. She switched on the air conditioning and the room was instantly transformed into a cocoon of comfort. She moved over to her bed and sat and ran her right hand over the silver-grey sateen bed linen and slid under the covers.

Rola took a quick look at the dainty gold-toned clock on her nightstand to see what time it was. A gift from Tim, it was meant to stop her from looking at her phone screen to tell the time and waking herself up in the process. As she looked at the timepiece for one second, she thought of Tim. She had met him while pursuing her goal to sell her app to venture capitalists and they had become great friends. Rola's impossible schedule running a start-up made her cherish the times when she could relax and just have fun with her good friends and she had considered Tim one of such friends, till he started changing the script.

"I hate it when guys step out of the friend zone without permission." She shook her head and sighed as she took a look around her room.

Blackout blinds down? Check.

Bathroom door closed? Check.

Lights off? She flicked the master switch by her bedside and the soft glow of the bedside lamp went off. Check.

Air conditioning on? Check.

Remote control within easy reach? Check.

Phone on silent? She looked at her phone.

"What? Five?"

Rola was startled at the five missed calls from her best friend, Amaka. She took a deep breath and dialled Amaka's number and her friend picked up the call as if the phone was in her hand.

"Maccky baby." Amaka's response was mumbled.

"Amaka? What's up?" The sleep was fading from Rola's eyes. "Is everything alright? Femi? Your work?"

Amaka sniffed and Rola could almost see her wiping tears. "Tomorrow Mo, I can't really talk now."

Rola was concerned, but she knew better than to probe when her friend had spoken so definitely.

"Are you sure Maccky? I can talk now." No matter what she was facing herself, Rola tried to always be available for her friends and they knew. "What's the p?"

"Mo, tomorrow. You understand, don't you?"

Rola immediately knew her friend wasn't alone. "Tomorrow then, Amaka. Afternoon as we planned. I assume you still want to come from the office?" It was just 3:30 p.m. Amaka usually worked late hours at her own start-up consulting firm, so something was definitely wrong.

"I will come over to yours," Amaka said and ended the call.

What is wrong with her?

Like her friend, Amaka was so full of life, and always so optimistic. She was sure Amaka wouldn't stay down for long. She would tell her what it was tomorrow. Rola was sure she would. It couldn't be anything major – maybe issues with a client? From her own experience starting Synergy, Rola was keenly aware of issues start-ups could have. Or had a doctor given Femi and herself bad news? She had been married for almost five years now, but she had not shown any concern about a baby.

"Four and a half years," Rola's brain retorted, correcting her. She always had to be precise. Amaka was married now for four and a half years to the most wonderful, calm and gentle man. Femi was always all over Amaka; he loved her to bits. None of the silly stories about affairs or looking at other women were told about him. Amaka's photo was displayed prominently in his office – a huge photo in a huge frame in everyone's face. He was super proud of his wife and didn't hide it. Where some other guys shied away from public displays of affection, Femi was like a Latin lover, always hugging and kissing.

Amaka seemed to be the practical one who lacked romantic inclinations. Her friends were forever telling her off for not responding as ardently to Femi and Amaka's response would be, "I am not romantic please," with a laugh. Amaka seemed to live a charmed life.

"It's nothing. It has to be nothing," Rola whispered to herself.

She let her head fall gently on soft goose down pillows and sighed with satisfaction. Free to sleep at last.

Rola woke up much later than she had expected the next day. It was a Wednesday and the day passed by in a flurry of routine activities: exercise, catching breakfast and tidying up some work remotely at the office as New York woke up.

Work sucked her in as usual – conference calls with the interns and Di, who was still away in San Francisco, and a quick admin briefing with Bev.

Bev was Jamaican and had the warmest heart and the quintessential Jamaican accent and Rola just loved her. A single mother in her forties, she seemed sometimes more bent on getting Rola to choose from her coterie of suitors than any other official assignment she had. She was a natural mother hen and cared for Rola genuinely. This week, Bev seemed to have shelved her self-assigned "settle-down-Mo" mission temporarily because she had Mo's apartment to sort out.

Rola was attached to her loft and didn't want strangers in it, but she was also a pragmatic businesswoman and knew the money from the rent would come in handy. If her parents had not insisted she stayed at home with them, if she had chosen to live in her own place in Lagos, a couple of months' rent from her loft in Tribeca would sort out a nice little two-bedroom flat for the year. Perhaps in Ikoyi or close to her parents in a gated community similar to theirs in Lekki.

Olaotan was just not hearing anything about his SisMo staying anywhere else but home and he had said he would also move with her if she left home for even a day. He had missed her so much when they were apart. She never got to spend enough time with him. He was just a four-year-old when she left for her A levels and first degree in the UK, before she moved to the states for her master's degree in Information Management Systems.

The family tried to spend time together. She was home every Christmas and then they were all together, or they sent Olaotan to her in New York every summer and they all visited together every spring. Everyone said the siblings couldn't be close. They said the twelve years age difference between them was just too wide. Besides, she was female and he was male and they hadn't lived together at home for long enough. The naysayers gave so many reasons why the siblings couldn't get along as beautifully as they did, but the naysayers were wrong. Olaotan was the surprise child the Bolades had given up all hope of having. He was leaving for college in the UK in the summer, in just eight months. He would be sixteen then, just as she was when she left.

Beverly had finally come to terms with the fact that Rola was really not returning to New York immediately after this particular Christmas break. Now, she was genuinely concerned about her living arrangements in Lagos. How would she feel living at home after so many years of living by herself? She hoped the living arrangements wouldn't cause unnecessary tension in the family. What if it just didn't work out and she had to leave home? What were her options? Was it even safe?

"There are travel advisories on your country Mo," Bev remonstrated.

Rola tried her best to describe what the different areas she could consider living in Lagos were like to Bev. Beverley had moved from London to New York in her early 30s, so she could understand references from both sides of the pond.

"So Bev, Ikoyi is so diverse, from like a Belgravia high-end to a High Street Ken. We call that Awolowo Road. It's also where we have our own Hampstead, so perhaps in New York, Ikoyi could be the Upper East Side."

"So what's Victoria Island then?" Bev asked. "Was that actually named for Queen Victoria of Great Britain?"

Mo wasn't sure who Victoria Island was named after, but she took a wild guess.

"No Bev, it was named for the wife of a young head of state called Victoria." She hoped she was right, but no way was she going to admit to colonial mentality on behalf of her beloved country.

"So, in New York, Victoria Island would be the Upper West Side," Rola continued her comparative, cross-cultural, inter-urban neighborhood analysis.

"And your parents live in Lekki?" She pronounced it "Lekkai," but Rola let that go. Though she was always very particular about foreigners getting pronunciations right, this was Bev. "What's that like?"

"Lekki? The *real* Lekki? It's a mix. Lekki may be Finchley Road, Edgeware Road, Swiss Cottage or Golders Green in London. Relative to Ikoyi, it may be like Chelsea, Tribeca, the Village... hey maybe it's even parts of Queens in New York."

"There's a fake Lekki?" That phrase "real Lekki" didn't escape Bev. She was curious now and really wanted to know.

Rola laughed. She wasn't going to let Bev draw her out.

"Bev, let me be." She wrapped up the conversation to prepare for Amaka's arrival.

Working from home had its advantages but looking presentable wasn't one of them. She was still in her loungewear and it was afternoon already.

No more than an hour after her conversation with Bev, she was ready to leave the house and expecting Amaka to arrive. She stood in front of the full-length mirror in her room. Though she had changed her room's décor over the years – one of the advantages of being home often – some things stayed the same, like her mirror. Her mirror had seen the teenage tomboy blossom into a beautiful woman, or in her opinion, a passably pretty lady.

She was oblivious to the fact, but Rola cut a striking image. Like many beautiful but unassuming women, she had many features she would have gladly changed which were in fact just perfect. She caught a glimpse of her perfect bow shaped lips which she had hated growing up but were now apparently in vogue. Every time she thought of how she prayed hard as a child that her lips would shrink, she shook her head. *Thank God He doesn't answer our every prayer.*

She was an American size eight and curvy. And though not tall in her own estimation, she was definitely model height at 5'10". Even the most critical person had to concede that she was striking, but Rola herself sincerely didn't know the impression her looks had on others, perhaps because the Bolades had always reinforced academic achievements. Her academics and later entrepreneurship had been Rola's focus. Her mum had never praised her for her looks or guided her to make the most of those features. Mrs B was an achiever, a solicitor and advocate who didn't rely on her own looks to make headway and she didn't raise her daughter to depend on her looks or feminine wiles to get ahead.

Rola packed her dark, full hair well away from her face with a black velvet hair clasp. She had on a Mondrian inspired colour-blocked wrap dress with kimono sleeves in jewel tones. The colour blocks were separated with black accents in velvet and the same black velvet was at the edge of the kimono sleeves, forming a high mandarin collar. She complimented her dress with suede Miu Miu kitten heel sandals in a shade of burgundy.

She reached for her bag and took another look at it. She couldn't believe the price she had snapped up this lovely handmade gem. It was a black crocodile skin shoulder bag. One of her latest discoveries in Lagos were the fabulous exotic skin bags designers were making in the country. She never ceased to be amazed by the entrepreneurial and creative spirit of her country.

"Yet, all we get to hear about us outside is bad news. When are we going to be serious about projecting the truth about ourselves? Why don't those in charge seem to care?" she said to her reflection in the mirror and sighed.

Her phone started chiming from within the bag and she took it out.

"Mrs B," Rola said, her face lighting up with a happy smile.

"Good afternoon, darling. Just so you know, I was able to get on the afternoon flight, the 3.30 p.m. I have boarded now and I should be home soon." The Bolades had a habit of always letting each other know when they boarded a flight or landed. It didn't matter if the flight was taking off from Tokyo or Kano, the protocol was to reach a member of the family on ground and let them know what flight you were on and what time you took off. This was a habit developed in response to the avoidable air crashes the country had had in the past.

"Oh, lovely. How about dad?" Rola asked.

"Morolawe! If you hadn't asked about your dad, I would have been convinced I dialled the wrong number. He should be taking the last flight out, the 7 p.m. Atlantic Air flight. Joe will pick him up. He is having meetings in their Abuja branch. I have to be at a partners' meeting before 6 p.m. and you know Lagos traffic." No explanation was needed to describe the traffic that was the bane of Lagosians' existence.

"Rola, sometimes I just think that to you, I am just the woman who married your dad, right?"

Rola smiled. Her mum said provocative things like this tongue-in-cheek to wind her up so she could get affirmations of undying affection from a daughter she already knew loved and respected her immensely. Rola also knew the game and always played along.

"Aha. Mrs B, why are you jealous of dad now? How can you say that? I just asked since you both left home for Abuja together. Shouldn't I ask, Mrs B? You know I absolutely love you to bits. I tell you every time my one and only Mrs B, every other Mama Rola is a counterfeit."

Rola didn't need to see her mum to know she had a wide smile on her face.

"Love you too darling Morolawe. So you are going shopping with Amaka then hanging out with some friends?"

"Mrs B, you need to advise me to stop shopping. These Lagos designers. What?" she drawled. "I am spending all my future income now. I am just shaking my head for myself and you know it's not like stuff I can get on Fifth Avenue or Madison where everyone else has the same things too. Tempting stuff in this Lagos. Real conversation pieces – these finds. Good icebreakers at a networking event."

"Rola! Networking, icebreaker. Must you always be thinking about business?"

"Your reflection Mrs B," Rola retorted.

Rola could hear the safety announcement from the flight attendants on board her mum's flight. "Catch you later, Mum. Your phones are going off now. Uncle Sam is picking you up right?" Uncle Sam was the senior family chauffeur of sixteen years. "So you are arriving on the 3:30 Atlantic

Air and dad is on the 7 p.m. Atlantic Air? Copy that." She blew her mum a kiss and ended the call.

Rola looked at the time. Amaka would be downstairs by now. She rushed downstairs to the dining room and grabbed the key to the reliable Toyota Prado from where it hung next to the dining room shelf.

"Aunty Wumsy!" she shouted out a friendly greeting to their housekeeper who she could see in the living room.

Rola laughed heartily as Amaka regaled her with yet another hilarious story of her adventures. It seemed like there was always so much catching up to do.

If anything was wrong yesterday, Amaka wasn't letting on yet. Rola had asked as soon as they settled in the car and were set to drive out of Bolades' home, but Amaka had brushed her enquiry off with, "Later, let's chill first."

They had a protocol since Amaka got married and moved farther away. Since she would still be driving herself later, to save Amaka time at the wheel, Rola had with her characteristic kind consideration, volunteered to be the designated driver for times out in town.

Amaka always paid attention to her appearance and today was no different. Her wigs were always on point. She was "well-kept" as Olaotan would say in his rapidly expanding cheeky lexicon. Fair-skinned Amaka loved her brands, but she was surprisingly down-to-earth, sometimes to a fault. She was blunt like her friend Rola and because of such traits they shared, they were the closest of friends. They had stood with each other through so many challenges.

They had met when they had both lived on an estate in their primary school days. Though Amaka was three years older than Rola, she was just two classes ahead and they had gotten yet closer when they ended up in the same secondary school. When the Bolades had built their house in Lekki and moved, the two families had already been drawn close by the friendship between the two girls and their friendship only grew stronger as the years went by.

Amaka had waited a year before getting into the university, whereas

Rola had gone in straight from her A levels. Subsequently, they had gone to different universities in the UK, where Rola had studied electrical engineering and Amaka, international relations.

When Rola left for America to earn her master's degree, Amaka had gotten a job in London with a policy think tank - Global Solutions.

Amaka returned home five years ago to start her own consultancy and within six months of her arrival, had married Femi.

"Amaka! You know that cannot be true."

"So, I have now become a fake news channel," Amaka snorted as she strutted beside Rola on her 10.5cm Louboutins. She wore a navy stretch jumpsuit and her Chanel handbag swung on its gold chain on her left shoulder. Rola's first instinct when she saw the jumpsuit and towering shoes was to say, "Where are you coming from Amaka? Didn't you go to the office today?" but she bit her tongue. They were at the mall getting lunch at one of Amaka's favourite Italian restaurants. Rola didn't care for Italian food at all and she sincerely didn't know when Amaka developed a taste for Italian food. She could have sworn they both liked Thai food. She just wanted her friend to be happy and comfortable, then get her talking about whatever was getting to her so badly yesterday. So far, Amaka seemed ready to discuss anything else but that.

"Mo," Amaka lowered her voice to a conspiratorial tone. She stopped completely in her tracks and looked around theatrically. "What is going on in this country defies belief."

Rola mirrored her friend's posture and stopped walking too. She leaned in, her face a picture of keen interest.

"This matter with the judges is just the tip of the iceberg. Most of the system is corrupt."

All Rola could muster was a very engaged "hmm-hmm." The assertion seemed a bit preposterous, far-fetched at the very least.

"So the first judge was caught with three hundred million cash in his office and the second caught two days later with some amazing amount of dollars in his house, his house o. In all, about seven of them were exposed. Mo..." She paused and tapped her friend on the left shoulder with a finger. Rola couldn't help stealing a look at her own nails, neatly manicured but without a hint of nail polish. Amaka's were long and gel wrapped in royal blue. "Mo, I said why did it all die down?"

Rola's face was blank.

Amaka laughed. "Too many heads were going to roll! So to protect themselves, they started noise about due process and rule of law but when those who should uphold the law pervert it, what recourse does the ordinary man have?"

Rola recalled the events Amaka referred to, but she suspected Amaka was alluding to something much wider and deeper than the public knew about.

"It's actually a syndicate," Amaka said, "a nation-wide syndicate. You know my work exposes me to these things. I have to work with all sorts of people in sensitive positions. Mo, if the scale of these things gets into the public domain, the hue and cry could cause a revolution." She shook her head.

Amaka's work indeed exposed her to the inner workings of government. If Amaka gave anyone information on the nation, one was well advised to take it as the gospel truth.

The friends' shared passion for the country and for good leadership was one of the main reasons why despite the cosmetic differences a casual onlooker could observe between the two ladies, they had remained close over the years.

"Hmm. Mo the Motivator," Amaka whispered and winked as two men strolling into the high-end mall each turned in succession to stare at Rola.

"What?" Rola said, oblivious to the stares.

"You didn't see those guys?" Amaka rolled her eyes. "I told you about Tani Fairweather now. I said he just got an oil block, hush hush, not common knowledge yet. The other guy even I don't know."

Rola looked like she couldn't care less.

"Mo! You need to at least remember the gist I supply. Authentic info like mine doesn't come easily," Amaka chided. "I told you his best friend, Dayo Phillips, dumped his girlfriend of five years, Priye, and is about to marry one girl he just met three months ago."

"You called the guy a Yoruba demon, right?" Rola said, recalling part of the conversation.

Amaka gave her a nudge of approval. "That's my girl."

"And I told you that the guy is not a demon. He is just bored. Five years is too long for two able-bodied graduates, with good jobs to date. The guy was just waiting for someone who would sweep him off his feet to come along. The lady was convenient, but he wasn't convinced she was "the one" so he let her just hang in there. When a man is sure, really sure, he rushes the girl." She shrugged.

"True..."

"You also said she had been cooking and cleaning and was always at their family dos and I replied, 'that figures'."

"You remember!" Amaka clapped triumphantly. "So it's his friend Tani checking you out. See," she said in a whisper, "he is coming over."

Amaka turned ever so slightly to cast a surreptitious glance in Tani's general direction just to evaluate how much progress Rola's latest admirer had made and how much longer she would have to stand in these killer loubs till he could get to them, and just then, a huge sign caught her attention.

"Wait. Mo," Amaka interrupted herself and put a hand on Rola's right arm, pointing to a shop on their right, right in front of the mall. "Fergie's has a sale on." Tani was on his own. Any admirer worth his salt should be able to trail Mo into the shop right in front of the mall. Amaka began to make a bee line towards Fergie's.

Rola knew what would follow if she didn't nip this in the bud. She wasn't ready to engage with any dry pick-up lines and neither was she about to be stuck in a jewellery store. She grabbed Amaka's nearest arm, interrupting her trajectory. "Oh, no you don't. You are not buying stuff today. Today is for simply chilling. We agreed."

"Let me make myself happy o. Mo, let me make myself happy." Amaka was resisting verbally but wasn't making any physical effort to escape Rola's restraining pull.

It occurred to Rola suddenly that Amaka used this phrase a lot in recent times. "Let me make myself happy" or "I need to cheer myself up," she would say, shrugging off restraint and forging ahead with some slightly prodigal purchase. Rola subsumed the thought. Why did her friend need retail therapy? Perhaps, she was just imagining things. It was just a manner of speaking, nothing more.

Suddenly, Rola let go of her friend's arm.

"Wait. Wait, Amaka, hold on. How come all your own favourite restaurants are in malls where clothes and accessories are sold? Not the computer malls, just the fashion malls." She turned around and looked at the adverts on the mall's periphery. "In fact, malls where they are having blowout sales. I see now." Realisation dawned on Rola. "We are not even coming here to eat at all really, are we?" With her left hand on her hips, she looked at her friend with a look of mock disgust and shook her head. "419."

She looked at the "friend of the Yoruba demon" gaining ground, cast another look at the offending Fergie's and quickly grabbed her friend by the left arm, propelling her in the direction of the car. "I am choosing the restaurant. C'mon, let's go to a restaurant far removed from any mall."

Amaka muttered below her breath something unintelligible and Rola could tell she was speaking Igbo, which she always did when she had to vent, but Rola was driving, so if Amaka wanted to ride home without hailing a taxi or getting an Uber, she needed to toe Rola's line. Hurrying after Rola in her stilts, she caught up with her, opened the car door and sat in the front passenger seat. "Okay, madam," she said. "You rumbled me. No jewellery today o, you win. You just helped me save my money, that's all. Let's eat, let's get fat. Where to?"

Chapter Two

"Be not forgetful to entertain strangers: for thereby some have entertained angels unawares."

Hebrews 13:2

Rola was headed for their favourite Thai restaurant, Sattaya, which was just about fifteen minutes away. She drove along one of the major roads that would connect them from the RedStar mall Amaka had tried to trick her into going to.

Amaka wouldn't let sleeping dogs lie and Rola wasn't taking the bait. Finally, she conceded and spoke. "Maccky, you know I am not interested in who is going out with whom." She shook her head.

"That's not what I am saying Mo. You know I also don't gossip."

Rola chuckled. "Maccky! Maccky! You don't gossip but you gist. Right?" Rola knew Amaka enjoyed her "gist" with her other "gist friends".

"But Mo, why would you not support Priye? This Dayo guy is just evil. Five years of her life wasted! She is now thirty-four. From where does she begin again?" She spread her hands.

"The person he dumped her for is not even as fine as Priye o and she is even older. She is thirty-five!"

Rola laughed. She had expected to hear Priye's replacement was forty-five. "Just thirty-five? Amaka, you have drama. Okay, since you insist, let me give you my analysis. Going solely by what you have told me, Priye had issues because she had become a "wife" and she wasn't even married.

"Amaka, men like to hunt and they crave variety. It's hardwired into the male gender. That's why they can easily be polygamists. It's nature's way of ensuring the human race is propagated. So if one woman is going to hold his attention, then she needs to be different from season to season. Priye must have become predictably boring even without a ring on her finger. She was cooking for him and washing his clothes. Why would he need to marry her? She was already giving him all he would get in marriage before even marrying her."

Amaka's eyes were as big as saucers. She had heard only one phrase. "You said men are polygamists? Ewoo! We are all in trouble!"

Rola laughed.

"No o, Maccky. I said they can *easily* be polygamists. Let's understand the biology behind it so we know how to deal with it. It's nature Amaka. It's just physiological."

Amaka looked at her with an expression that clearly meant "I am in trouble" and Rola chuckled.

"So that's why those who misbehave do so? I wonder what is in Femi's physiology that keeps him in check."

"No o. It's not an excuse to mess around at all. That's why a serious man should be aware of his physiological propensities and guard himself against those tendencies. I am definitely not giving the guys an excuse to philander." Rola pulled a stern face. "So even you as a married woman Maccky, it's not over yet. You can't afford to become predictable." Rola looked at her friend, flashed her a smile and gave her a thumbs up. "I trust you Maccky Babe! Look at you. Your life is about much more than just Femi. If not, by now, your constant hanging on to him would be irritating him." She smiled.

"Men respect independent women, Mo, but sadly, they won't tell their partners o."

"They respect independent women, but they are not sure they can manage them. That's the paradox," Rola replied.

They fell into that comfortable silence; each lost in her own thoughts.

"So, Mo Babe, tell the truth, are you really, really, really home for one whole year? Are you happy with your decision?" Amaka broke the silence.

"What's all this fuss now Maccky? *You* returned finally five years ago. Are you not happy? You are a consultant in cahoots with intelligence agencies. Policy this, military that, all in five years."

"We are not talking about me Mo, we are talking about you. Is this what you really want to do?"

"Something tells me, Amaka, that I need to be home at this time. I really must confess that I don't have the full picture but just let me sort out this youth service stuff."

Amaka's lips were twisted in a smirk. "The service year thing. But I have told you so many times, you don't need to serve. Now or ever."

"You know that's not true, Amaka. I graduated before thirty. I must serve if I ever want to hold any public office or work in the public service or even take any paid employment right now. Goodness knows what it will be next in our country. They may ask my child to bring his mother's NYSC discharge certificate before he can get a blood transfusion. I don't know what next it will be and I am not risking it. Besides, I want to get it out of the way now that I feel like."

"Of course you must serve, Mo, that's normal. I served *nau*, in my own customised way," she added. "It's just that you can easily serve and continue to do business and make your dollars in the States."

Rola shook her head. "Chiamaka! I could honestly disown you for that rubbish you just said."

"Mo, everyone does it. You alone can't change the system. I have been here five years. If you can't beat them, join them. It's so demoralising when the actual lawmakers, the interpreters of the law and the law enforcers are the greatest outlaws. What is the citizen to do?"

Amaka had made a slight point and Rola wanted to think of a good comeback, so she reined in a spontaneous stock response.

"Hey, have we passed that fruit stall you told me about? The one on Jaja road?" Rola wanted to buy fruits for the house. Olaotan loved pineapples.

"Just a little ahead," Amaka replied and pointed to a stall with a green and white striped awning on the right. "That woman near the kiosk," Amaka said, pointing to their right to a lady in a T-shirt and a wrapper with a green apron over her outfit. She had a huge wide-brimmed raffia hat to shield her from the sun. She was standing and rearranging her produce with her back to the approaching car.

Rola slowed down and with her right indicator flashing, eased to the right side of the road. Thankfully, it was on their side of the road and she didn't have to change lanes. There was a layby, so it was safe.

On both sides of the road were passersby – men, women and children alone and in small groups.

"Madam!" shouted Amaka, after rolling down her window. "Bring pawpaws and pineapples."

Rola didn't see why the "madam" had to bring her produce to them in the car. She picked up her bag to get down and buy the fruits and in the process, she checked her phone for messages from her mum. She should have landed a while ago. Sure enough, a text message confirmed that.

"Let me get down quickly," Rola said to Amaka. "You sit in the car. If you come down and she sees this your jumpsuit, the price of these fruits will increase."

"Maybe she can't hear us," Amaka said, as she rolled down the car window on her side and shouted again, "Madam." No reply from her. "Na wa o," she rolled her eyes and wound up the window. Rola slung her bag on her shoulder and exited the car.

Just as Rola alighted, a loud shout ensued from across the road. It was a female voice. She was startled for a moment but soon realised that Amaka and herself were not in any immediate danger. Instead, on the other side across the four-lane dual carriage way, someone or something lay in a heap by the side of the road. She looked closer. It appeared to be a child. She couldn't see too well from this far away.

Rola watched from afar, concerned, as others stopped to look. A corpulent woman carrying a tray of plantains was the one raising the alarm. She didn't approach the figure on the ground, she just kept rotating around it in concentric circles. The woman was alternately flapping her hands and clasping and unclasping them on her ample bust. Quickly, people gathered, some crossing from the same side of the road that Rola stood by way of a pedestrian footbridge.

"Mo, what's going on there?" Amaka asked.

Rola didn't wait to answer her friend. She felt an inexplicable urgency in her heart to help the child. She knew she had to reduce the number of people crowding around the victim on the other side so the child could get fresh air. She made a beeline for the bridge.

"Mo!" Amaka called out but Rola didn't look back.

When Rola did not stop, a protective instinct nudged her friend's heart. They always looked out for each other and Rola might need her. Amaka grabbed her bag, looked uncertainly at her favourite nude Loubotins, put off the air conditioner, switched off the car engine and took the car keys. She stepped out of the car, locking the car door securely behind her and followed quickly behind her friend. On crossing the road though, Amaka still looked back to ensure that no one was lurking around the car.

Rola quickly descended the footbridge on the other side and started to push her way into the crowd of about a dozen people. She moved closer to the figure on the ground. What seemed like a young boy laid on the bare earth, the laterite rendered into mud by the rain. She could hear people saying, "Pour him water." Someone peeled away from the crowd, sprinting off to get water.

"Please, give him some air. He needs air. Air, please," Rola said politely.

No one moved.

"Please move back!" she shouted. Even the plantain seller looked at her quizzically as if "that's what you should have said initially." The plantain seller took charge immediately. She sprang into action. As the official first responder, she had appointed herself captain of the situation.

"Dress back," she shouted. "Shift!" Her paunch was visible through the fabric of her fuchsia T-shirt and the navy-blue skirt she had on, her generous belly rising and falling as she bellowed the commands. She added some copious hand gestures for those pretending to be hearing impaired.

The people moved backwards a bit. Another woman, in a maid's uniform, with palpable sympathy in her eyes and voice asked, "Na your pikin?" her hands with their palms facing up as if in supplication for this woman's child.

A wiry bespectacled man in a tired blue suit on the fringes of the crowd spoke up. "It's not her offspring. The boy was just striding along solitarily. Alas! He swooned and landed on terra firma."

Rola looked back to see who was speaking. She knew his type. More seen in the South West than any other part of the country, overeducated but under-optimised. She noticed Amaka had joined the crowd and was standing beside the wiry man. She turned her attention back to the boy on the ground. A man bent over the boy, slapping his face gently and shouting, "You fit hear me?" He seemed confused when he didn't get a response.

"Let me do that," Rola said.

"You be doctor?" the man asked. He was wearing oil-stained coveralls and Rola pegged him as a mechanic.

"No, but don't worry. I know CPR." Rola quickly knelt by the boy and put her handbag beside her. The mechanic moved a bit and watched as she tried to revive the boy.

At close glance, Rola realised that the person on the ground was not a child as she had thought earlier. He had the beginnings of a moustache, which, in her opinion, put him in his teens. Poor young man.

Rola felt strangely drawn to the slender, frail figure on the muddied ground. She felt a wave of compassion, something shifted in her and her mission now became more like rescuing her own brother. He had fine features: high cheekbones and fair skin that was now becoming ashy. He had well-groomed, low cut hair and it looked as if he had had a recent shape up.

This was certainly not a vagrant. His clothes were all wrong for taking a stroll and he certainly didn't look like the type of young man who took a stroll anywhere. In fact, if the maid who spoke earlier had been able to get a clear view of the young man, she wouldn't have asked if he was the plantain seller's child. He had on a hunter green Gucci polo neck shirt. Not Gucci polos emblazoned all over with the logo, but one with a discreet little bee. She knew this polo because it was released last summer for $650 and this colour was very rare. It was not one of the faux designer labels that Olaotan couldn't stop cracking jokes about.

"SisMo, guess what I saw today?" he would say.

Rola never could guess, so she would smile in anticipation and say, "Just tell me."

As he was wont to do, Olaotan would lower his voice and whisper something like, "Dadidas!" and start laughing at his own pronouncement.

No, this was the real McCoy and the dark brown calfskin drivers on his feet were real Guccis too. Mud was already on his trousers and his left hand was in a puddle. A gold identity bracelet was on his right hand, engraved in Arabic and English. The English letters read, "I-S-A".

Rola decided that the boy couldn't have been more than fifteen.

Having done a quick external examination of the young man, Rola's training kicked in. "Thank goodness for FGGC," she thought, as she remembered the secondary school she had attended with Amaka. At the school, they had all been compelled to learn CPR amongst other lifesaving skills they would need as first responders.

Rola tilted the boy's head backwards and as she reached out for his closest wrist in a bid to place it beside his body, he moved, muttering unintelligibly. Then, he went still again.

"Excuse me, please. Excuse... make una shift!" Amaka's familiar voice came from the crowd. From the corner of her eyes, Rola saw Amaka come to stand beside her.

After a few minutes of administering CPR, Rola turned to the mechanic who was still crouched by her side. "We need to get him to a hospital immediately," she said and stood up.

The man started asking those in the crowd which hospital was nearby. Apparently, he was just passing through. His assertion was credible as there were no mechanics enclaves in this upscale part of the city. The crowd was conferring on the best option for hospitals and those not in conference were muttering prayers. Others were listening to the wiry man who was holding court. "The symptoms conform precisely with epilepsy," he was saying.

"Epilepsy!" the plantain seller heard the diagnosis Bright Blue Suit delivered and her hands flew instinctively to her head, almost knocking over the tray of plantain balanced on it.

"Oh! It's not contagious," Bright Blue Suit continued. "Illiterate superstition posits that it is infectious or contagious, but it is not at all. There's a difference you know," he said to no one in particular, "contagion varies from infection."

The plantain seller gasped and began that peculiar waltz reserved for those who needed a bathroom break with all urgency. Back and forth, she hopped from one foot to the other. Bright Blue Suit saw the obvious distress his ill-advised spouting had caused the kindhearted soul and tried to quickly calm her down. "Madam, wetin I talk be say e no dey catch person, nothing fit do you, madam."

Amaka burst into laughter, looking over to catch Rola's eyes. Rola could only smile briefly in return. So Bright Blue Suit could speak pidgin? She crouched back down by the boy's head and restarted CPR, Amaka beside her.

Someone with a shrill voice shouted, "Abeg, which one be dis upandan for the boy *chaist*? Make we pour am small water, e go wake." It was the courier who had gone running to fetch water returning.

Before Rola could advise otherwise, a slush of water of questionable provenance came from a plastic bottle from above her right shoulder. Somehow, the spray missed the boy and Amaka got the worst of it. Amaka's wig was drenched, all thirty-six inches of the luxurious mane. Rola could see that it took all the self-control Amaka could muster not to lose her cool. She took the wig off, revealing her hair under the wig plaited *didi*-style. She couldn't resist scratching her scalp in sweet relief. Her gelled nails making any serious digging impossible, she dragged her nails across her scalp anyway making a rasping sound. She held on to the wig with her left hand and then, perhaps the relief of getting some air on her head made any further restraint stressful, she suddenly became aware that her calves and feet were on fire. She took off the Louboutins as she gave a sigh of relief.

"Ah, shakara get pain o," she said under her breath as she rolled up her jumpsuit pant legs which as she descended from the height of her shoes, were now dragging on the muddy ground.

"Is there a hospital nearby?" Rola asked no one in particular.

"The government health centre is few streets away," someone said and her thoughts shifted to getting the boy to the health centre. Instinctively, she reached for her car keys in her bag hanging on her left shoulder, it wasn't there. Nothing was on her shoulder. Someone had taken her bag. She scanned the crowd trying to calm her panic.

"We have done our best, Mo; we need to go," Amaka said, looking like a pack rat with Rola's bag and hers on her left shoulder, her wig and louboutins in her right hand and her rolled-up pantsuit. The car keys dangled in her left hand. Amaka scratched her scalp again, the cool air was therapeutic. If not for the gravity of the emergency, Rola would have laughed. "He is dead for all you know," Amaka intoned pessimistically.

Rola didn't bother responding. The boy had a pulse and he had muttered. His pulse was weak but certain, so he was alive but if they didn't get him medical attention soon, he could die. She turned to the mechanic and said, "I'll get my car from over there, then, you can show me to the health centre."

The mechanic shook his head, indicating his filthy overall. Before Rola could gather her thoughts as to what to do next, a huge man with a tough face, who had been standing quietly all along, spoke. "I go take you go hospital. Make I carry am?"

Before Rola could accede, Mr Tough bent over and picked the boy up effortlessly. Rola took her car keys from Amaka and pushed through the crowd which had now more than doubled in size. They crossed the busy road and she silently blessed the forward-thinking governors of Lagos for building so many footbridges. How would they have carried the boy across the busy road to her car? Mr Tough was right behind her, overtaking Amaka to get to the car.

Rola quickly opened the back door of the car. Mr Tough eased the boy into the car, putting him in a sitting position, his limp head against the backrest. Then, he entered the car, drawing the boy close to him for support.

Rola jumped into the driver's seat, started the car just as Amaka reached the car and clambered in. Rola made a U-turn as suggested by Mr Tough.

"This is going to lead us into trouble, Mo. This matter is not your problem. You don't even know this boy," Amaka said.

"And if it had been my brother? Have you thought of that?"

"Well, he is not. Ah, where do you think you are?"

A loud shout came from behind them just then and Amaka looked in the rearview mirror by the passenger door. "There are two men running after the car and they look dangerous. Mo! One of them seems to be waving a gun," she screamed. "What have you gotten us into? What's all this wonderwoman, superhero moves?"

"Madam, turn right," Mr Tough ordered from the back seat. Rola obeyed.

"I am not saying it is wrong to do a good deed, but it is never appreciated by the authorities in this country. If this boy is dead or dies, you know we are all in trouble with the police, right?"

"And what if he lives?" She glanced at Amaka for a split second then returned her attention to the road. "Amaka, please allow me drive."

Rola took a sideways glance at Amaka who was muttering under her breath. "Whatever. Just stop talking for now," she thought. She began praying in a low voice. "This boy must not die."

After a few more turns, they arrived at the health centre. The drive had taken under ten minutes but for Rola, it felt like ten hours. She had no clue as to the stability of her passenger.

Rola drove into the parking lot. There was a porte cochere by the front door, so she drove underneath it and parked.

Rola and Mr Tough came down from the car. Rola was confused when the man turned to her, looking genuinely apologetic. "Na here I go leave you, Aunty."

"But-"

"I fear police wahala. Aunty please, no vex."

He looked crestfallen but determined. Rola knew there was no point protesting and time was not likely to be on the boy's side.

"Aunty, wetin you do today for this pikin, God will bless una. Ah, Aunty you try for am, you try. Kai! Na person like you them suppose take do minister or governor for this country, but them no go hear word. Na so so thief thief them go they put." Rola thought perhaps he was lingering for a tip and motioned to Amaka, who had wound down the car window on her own side and was listening and watching them, to pass her bag. She had been honed by several encounters to understand that too much greeting sometimes meant that some money had to change hands.

At the sight of Rola dipping into her bag and holding out some notes towards him, Mr Tough's face fell and he looked sincerely wounded. With his right hand, he touched his chest. "Me? Aunty me? Money? Why I go want money? To help this pikin, Aunty? God forbid." At this statement he snapped his fingers above his head in a circular sweeping motion.

"Thank you, sir," she said, curtseying now and genuinely grateful.

Mr Tough was already on his way to the gate but he responded, "No mention, Aunty."

Rola turned to run into the facility.

"Hey, madam. No parking inside," a loud voice came from another direction. A gateman attired in a faded wine-coloured uniform came rushing towards them.

"Oga, emergency!"

"This is where we use to park our ambulance," the man growled.

"Please, help me with a gurney. Emergency!"

The man saw the immobile boy slouched on the back seat and his countenance changed.

"We need a gurney and nurses!"

"Gur... which one be—? See, go park outside first," the man insisted.

Rola cut in. "That boy must not die! I need—"

Before she could repeat her last sentence, the gateman rushed into the lobby. Hopeful that he had understood, Rola went over to check the boy, praying under her breath. Meanwhile, Amaka was standing by the other side of the car, looking confused.

"Is the man coming back?"

Rola ignored her friend. How was she to know? Instead, she reached into the car through the open window and tentatively touched the boy's cheek. It was a little cold. Rola's heart started beating fast. She was about to rush into the lobby to get somebody to assist when she saw the gateman, pushing a rickety wheelchair ahead of him.

Within moments, the gateman loaded the boy onto the wheelchair. The boy's limp body would have tipped forward if the gateman hadn't stabilised him with his left hand as he propelled the wheelchair forward with his right hand. Amaka rushed over to Rola and grabbed the car key from her when she started rushing in after the gateman and the wheelchair. Then Amaka suddenly realised that she didn't have shoes on, having ditched her louboutins on the floor beneath the car seat. Opening the car, she quickly grabbed the shoes, slung both her handbag and Rola's on her right shoulder, secured the car and followed barefooted.

The hospital lobby was small: a paying pharmacy to the right, cashier's office to the left and a hallway straight ahead. The cry of a child ushered them in. A large group of people occupied all the seats and some even stood. The queue in front of the lone cashier was long.

But there was no medical staff in sight.

"Where are the nurses?" Rola asked the gateman, her pounding heart pacing up a notch.

"Inside. Five emergency dey here. Motor accident."

Rola looked around and the only uniformed people she saw were cleaners and orderlies in faded green overalls. Nobody in a white uniform.

"And all the doctors are there too?" Rola asked the gateman, as she considered rushing down the corridor to one of the consulting rooms. However, she hesitated. There were also five other people there in need of medical help.

"No. One doctor dey Room Two, na him all the patient dey wait here. He fit answer you. But madam, you go collect card first," the gateman said, pointing towards the queue.

"This boy might be dying. Oga, please help us."

"Madam, get card and go Room Two," the gateman said impatiently. "Nobody dey my post."

"Um, I—"

"And, madam," the gateman was not through yet, "you know say na me dey help you since. Your motor sef dey our door—"

Amaka came to the rescue, truncating the lamentation abruptly. "Wetin you do sef? And the small you do, no be your job? Dey go!"

Rola looked at her friend in surprise. For a moment, she had forgotten her existence.

The man looked like he would say more, but the sneer on Amaka's face put paid to that. Ignoring him, she turned to Rola and said, "You get a card. I'll fetch a doctor."

As the gateman walked away, Rola quickly said to Amaka, "No. You get the card."

At that instant, a nurse came from the right, carrying files. A wave of relief flowing through her, Rola rushed over to the woman.

"Emergency! Emergency!"

Looking tired, the woman replied, "Take your turn. Madam, there's a queue here."

"It is an emergency."

"And how do you know that?"

"The boy is unconscious!" Rola said, pointing in the direction where the young man remained slumped on the wheelchair, watched by others around.

"Oh," the nurse said and then sighed. "Our hands are full. Bus accident." With those words, the nurse walked past Rola to an empty desk by the wall on the other side.

Rola glanced at the boy quickly, desperation buoying her as she rushed after the nurse. The latter was arranging some of the files on the table.

"Please, Sister. I'm begging you, help me!"

It appeared the nurse saw and felt the raw desperation, because she let out a deep breath. "Everyone is occupied, so you really must wait a little. Have you registered? I mean, paid for a card?"

"We are working on it."

The nurse picked up a file, opened it and started writing on it.

Rola wanted to say more but changed her mind. What had that gateman said? Rola turned and rushed towards the corridor ahead. She heard the nurse's voice from behind, "Hey, madam, where are you going?"

Rola did not stop. In just moments, she found Room Two. As she was about to enter the consulting room, a man in a white coat walked out. Rola guessed that he was a doctor from the stethoscope around his neck. He looked approachable – young, in his thirties, a little fair-skinned, of medium build and average height.

He stopped and smiled at her.

"Doctor! Emergency," Rola said. "A boy. Collapsed on the road."

What Rola said sunk in and the doctor's eyes became more animated than before. He was about to speak when the nurse at the lobby arrived.

"Excuse me, madam!" the nurse blurted.

"There's an emergency. Come with me," the doctor said to the nurse and rushed after Rola, who was headed back towards the lobby.

The doctor took charge of the wheelchair immediately and pushed it in the direction of the cashier's office. The awkward angle the gateman had propped the boy in had uncannily kept his body intact in the wheelchair. There was a door beside the office that Rola had not seen because of the long queue blocking it. The nurse from the lobby quickly pushed the door open for the doctor.

"Get Staff Nurse Lawan," the doctor said to someone inside the room.

"Yes, Doctor." A cleaner rushed out and Rola entered the room closely after the lobby nurse. They were in an observation room of sorts – or was it an emergency room? – which had one consulting bed. The bed was thankfully free.

While the medical personnel took charge of things, Rola looked around. The room was bare, without emergency equipment, unlike other emergency rooms that Rola had seen.

With synchronised movements, the nurse and the doctor lifted the boy and laid him on the bed. As the nurse removed the boy's T-shirt, the doctor said to Rola, "Madam, please, you really have to get him registered. But first, what did you say happened to him?"

"I was told he slumped while walking by a roadside."

"Was he ill before?"

"I don't know. I just rushed to him to administer CPR."

The doctor stopped. "You don't know him?"

"No, I don't, but CPR didn't revive him, so we decided to bring him here. Please, is... is he still alive?"

The doctor turned back to the boy and took his pulse, the boy's chest was now exposed. He placed his stethoscope on the boy's torso. After listening for a moment and checking his wristwatch, he said, "He is alive."

"Thank God!" Rola shouted.

A tall, thickset and harried nurse with a notepad in hand, rushed in moments later, once again heading straight for the doctor. "I'm here, Doctor."

The doctor asked the lobby nurse to return to her duties, while he reeled off instructions to Nurse Lawan for the care of the boy. His words sounded like music to Rola's ears.

The nurse removed a pen from the two attached to the pocket of her uniform and made notes.

Amaka chose that time to arrive with the card. "Mo, here's his card."

"You are together, I presume?" the doctor asked Rola. She looked at Amaka, seeing what the doctor saw. One of her mud stained pantsuit legs was down, while the other was rolled up. She had no shoes on, but rather carried them in one hand. A small smile touched the doctor's lips.

"Yes, we are together."

Amaka reached out to hand the hospital card over and Nurse Lawan took it, saying, "Thank you, ma. You will need to purchase some items for his treatment from our pharmacy. Please, come along so that we can do that fast."

"What? He is alive. Wow! Let's hurry."

"Nurse Lawan, quickly set up that line, keep a close watch on him and alert me when he wakes."

"Yes, Doctor."

Rola spoke to Amaka, reaching out for her bag on her friend's shoulder. "I have some money in my wallet. If it's not enough, please—"

"Mo," Amaka interrupted, "I got this." The boy was alive, it was time she played her part.

She left with the nurse, leaving the doctor and Rola with the boy in the room.

Amaka had given an oblivious Rola a worried look just as she exited the room into the stuffy lobby. Her friend seemed to be really emotionally involved in this. Thankfully, the boy was alive and the situation was not as critical as they had thought. Hopefully, Mo's heart would not be broken.

As Amaka walked into the lobby with the nurse, she heard a stir by the entrance and watched as two tall men with bouncer-like bodies walked in. The gateman they had seen earlier was talking to one of them, looking nervous.

Amaka thought their discussion could be about the black 4 x 4 vehicle parked next to the Prado, almost blocking the entrance. However, when the gateman pointed towards her direction and the men looked towards her, Amaka's antenna went up. As the two men walked towards her, she knew she and Rola were in grave danger.

Amaka turned and ran back to the observation room.

"Surprisingly, he is now in a stable condition," the doctor said to Rola. "He should be okay."

Suddenly, the door swung open violently and Amaka rushed to grab Rola. Both the doctor and Rola were alarmed.

"What—" Rola started, not resisting Amaka as she pulled her to a corner away from the door.

"Those men... They are here!" Amaka's eyes looked like two globes as she panted.

"Which men?" the doctor said, quickly looking at the door. He did not wait for an answer. Instead, with determined steps, he left the room, hanging his stethoscope back around his neck.

"It's those men I told you were following us."

Fright did a waltz all over Rola as her heartbeat paced up once again. "Oh! Who are they?"

"You see, Mo. I told you o. I said we should leave well enough alone, but no, you didn't listen."

"Amaka, let us find out what is going on first."

"Let me call the Commissioner of Police," Amaka said, dumping her shoes on the floor and reaching for her bag.

"Oh, no, you don't. What will we tell him?" Rola said. "Amaka, let's see these men and find out what this is all about."

With that, Rola grabbed Amaka's closest arm and started moving towards the door. She waited only when Amaka bent over to pick her shoes.

The two menacing-looking men were outside the door on the other side. They were tall, dark and well-built.

"Good day, sirs. How may I help you?" the doctor said, looking upwards.

"We have reason to believe that our ward is here," the bulkier man said.

"I saw the woman with the rolled trousers in the car that abducted him," the second man added.

The doctor ignored the last statement and said, "Kindly identify yourself and describe this ward of yours."

The first man looked impatient but gave their names, "I'm Tarfa. He's Bala."

The two men brought out identity cards and flashed them at the doctor, but the latter took them for inspection. While he did this, the men looked impatiently around. The doctor returned the I.D. cards shortly after.

"And our ward is a boy, a teenager," Bala added. In a few more words, he described the doctor's latest patient.

Rola stepped outside the observation room and the two ladies stood a little behind the doctor. Amaka's heart was cold with trepidation.

Almost immediately, Bala said, "That's the woman again! And the car they put Isa in is parked outside."

"And for that, we have to be grateful to these two ladies," the doctor said. "They found him collapsed by a roadside and brought him here."

"We want to see him," Tarfa said, brusquely.

The doctor shook his head. "We are still attending to him, but you will see him shortly. You realise though that as it is, I have only your word here that you know this boy. Can you please put me through to his parents? Just for confirmation."

Amaka realised then that she was not in any mortal danger and seeing Nurse Lawan waving from the pharmacy, walked towards her. The boy still needed to be treated after all.

The two men, obviously unhappy with the new instruction, looked at one another but they nodded at the doctor.

While Tarfa brought out a mobile phone and made a call, speaking in Hausa, Rola frowned as a tall thin man with a protruding belly incongruous with his skeletal physique hurried towards them, a determined look on his face. What next?

The new entrant on the scene stopped beside them and addressed Rola directly. "Madam, are you the suspected accident driver who kidnap a child?"

"S.O., kidnapped a child? What are you talking about?" The doctor was quick to intervene.

"Taiwo, on duty at the gate, just tell me."

"There was no accident or kidnap, S.O." said the doctor.

"But as *Chief* Security Officer in this health centre, I have—" S.O. started, superciliously.

"You may go," the doctor interjected in a quiet but authoritative voice.

"Doctor, the boy's father is on the line," Tarfa said just then.

The doctor took the phone, raising a hand to wave the S.O. away.

Rola saw the reluctance in the eyes of the security officer as he stared her down, but he left all the same. She turned her attention to the doctor's phone conversation. She heard him explain that some Good Samaritans had brought the boy in for treatment, that he was stable although still unconscious and it appeared that he was dehydrated and that the first dose of IV fluids should have started already.

Amaka and the nurse returned, as the doctor confirmed that he would let the boy's guardians know when he needed any other thing for his patient's care.

Nurse Lawan rushed into the Observation Room to start the process of reviving the boy, while Amaka stood beside Rola waiting for the doctor to end the call. Eventually, he did end the call - promising the man at the other end that he would do all he could to care for his son.

Once the doctor was through, he handed the phone back to Tarfa, who turned to Rola asking how much they had spent on the boy. She waved it off.

"I guess we are done here? Mo, let's go," Amaka said. The bags and her shoes now weighed a ton. She was tired and hungry to boot. How did this pleasurable afternoon turn all pear-shaped?

Rola turned to the doctor. "Thank you, Doctor."

The doctor smiled and Amaka frowned. Why was he looking at Mo like that?

"Once again, I will like to appreciate what you did today. If only we all were our brother's keeper, our country will be the better for it."

Amaka was not impressed, but Rola said, "It was nothing."

The boy's guardians moved closer to the door of the room where their ward was being treated, but didn't enter.

"Um, may I know you?" The doctor was speaking to Rola.

Amaka's eyes narrowed.

"I'm Rola. This is Amaka."

"I'm Dafe. Lovely meeting you." Dr Dafe reached a hand to shake Rola and an unsmiling Amaka.

"May I have your number, please?" he said to Rola.

"Not really," Amaka blurted, interjecting.

"Of course," Rola quickly corrected, smiling. "Thank you so much for coming to our aid."

Dr Dafe produced his phone from his pocket and took Rola's phone number.

At the car, after wiping some mud off the back seat with tissue from her handbag, Amaka offloaded both their handbags onto the seat. She sat on the front passenger seat again, dropped her shoes by her feet and let out a loud yawn. Rola, the designated driver, resumed her duties.

At the gate, the gateman waved, trying to get their attention as Rola drove out of the compound, but not vigorously enough to catch the attention of the tired duo.

Chapter Three

"The steps of a good man are ordered by the Lord:
and He delighteth in His way."

Psalms 37:23

"I'm famished," Amaka said. "But what I really need is a scrub from head to toe with antiseptic soap, not a shower. Once we get to yours, I'm headed home, Mo. Honestly. Walking on mud and then, barefooted into a government hospital is definitely not a picnic." Amaka shook her head.

"Oh, the floor in the health centre was actually clean. Didn't you see all those cleaners around?"

"That's true. You know, Mo, I don't think that we should make sweeping statements about the ineptitude in this country anymore. Some things do work in spite of all. The truth is that many are doing all they can, despite the meagre resources they have to work with."

"Hmm... I suppose. Imagine how smoothly things will work in this country if we had the appropriate infrastructure and support."

"You know, it's actually achievable."

"Someday, maybe. Once we choose the right leaders."

"Right leaders? Leaders are people, chosen from amongst us. Perhaps we actually don't have the right people."

"Hey, wait!" Amaka shouted. "Are those not slippers in that kiosk?"

"So, I am all ears. What happened?" Mrs B went straight to the point.

Rola sat in front of her open laptop by her desk while her mother sat on her bed, clad in a white dressing gown, Rola had been trying to round up her work with minimal success, when her mum had entered her room. She rose and went to sit next to her confidante, who had arrived home a few hours before her.

"There was no lovely lunch. Amaka and I ended up in a health centre."

"Health centre! What happened?"

"No, no, we are both fine," Rola said and then launched into the happenings of the day.

"Rola, that was a commendable and brave thing to do. And thankfully the boy is alive and this didn't get you into police trouble with the attendant horror."

"Oh, the security officer wanted to make an issue of it, but the doctor put paid to that."

Mrs B shook her head sadly. "It's what it is. I don't know why someone would prey on the misfortunes of others."

"You know, Mum, the health centre wasn't so bad. Not as bad as I expected. The emergency room didn't seem to have equipment, but the environment seemed neat. And the doctors and nurses seemed to know what they were doing." She paused a little and continued. "If what I saw today is what obtains, some people are still trying their best."

"Is it not unfair to give someone responsibilities and not empower them? You should hear the conversations out there. People are speaking out now against the inequity, the injustice, the nepotism..."

"My concern is that our conversations are not really about a solution. It is like the people complain everywhere and do nothing; effectively accepting defeat."

"Well, you are right. But it's a start. In Abuja, you should have seen how Paula and I had to stand our ground to get what we needed. Everyone wants to be settled before they do their jobs." Paula was her mum's personal assistant.

"And if you ask those extortionists why they do what they do, they will tell you that it is their share of the national cake." Mrs B continued.

She sighed. "I am thankful that Amaka was with you though."

Rola chuckled. "Mrs B, you should have seen your girl, Amaka. Oh dear! She ended up yanking off her wig and walking barefooted."

Mrs B frowned. "Barefooted? Even into the hospital?"

"Yes. She had on 10.5cm loubs. Luckily for her, the health centre was clean. On our way back, we ended up having to stop to buy a pair of flipflops, those laundry bar soaps and a huge bottle of water. You should have seen her scrub her feet by the roadside with her royal blue pedicured nails dangling out of the car." At the image, Mrs B burst into laughter.

Rola had to go through the day's happenings again with TK. Mrs B had hinted at some of the events but left Rola to give her father the full gist.

"You risked a lot but you did well Rola. I... we, we are extremely proud of you," he said. "You must be tired my dear. I was still going to say we should discuss where you want to serve and all. You can choose between Abuja and Lagos but we all know its Lagos, right? But let's talk about that tomorrow."

In spite of the drama of the day before, Thursday was surprisingly calm. Amaka had called Rola as soon as she woke up to reassure herself that the events of the day before had not just been a dream. After the call, Rola went back to her routine – exercise and a shower, then calls to the New York office and fine tuning some projects she was working on.

The chime of her phone snapped her out of work mode. She looked at her screen and Truecaller showed the name of the caller as Ishaya Mamane. She tried to recall the name of her bureau de change operator. It was Alhaji Galadima, not Ishaya. She switched the phone to silent and just let the phone ring. Two missed calls from the strange number were followed by a text message, then she took a look at her phone.

HELLO MADAM. THIS IS ALHAJI ISHAYA MAMANE, ISA'S FATHER. I WILL CALL AGAIN IN ONE HOUR.

She didn't know what to think but her curiosity got the better of her. When it was an hour on the dot the phone rang and she picked up.

"Good evening, madam. This is Alhaji Ishaya Mamane. May I speak with Mrs Morolawe Bolade?" His voice at the other end was that of a cultured middle-aged man who spoke like one of those national TV broadcasters of old.

"Rola Bolade speaking sir, good afternoon, sir."

"I am Isa's father. Isa, the boy whose life you saved yesterday."

"Sir, God saved his life. Those of us on the scene just tried our best to assist him, sir. How is he doing now, sir?"

"Oh, doing well at St Paul's hospital. We moved him a few minutes after you left the Government Health Centre. In fact, he was fully conscious an hour after he arrived in St Paul's. You see, he had been ill before yesterday and taking him to the mall to watch a movie was supposed to cheer him up. But he excused himself to go to the conveniences and his minders traced him to where he passed out just a few minutes after you had taken him to the hospital. You really acted very swiftly, that was admirable, madam. I was gravely worried when Bala and Tarfa told me that they had searched all over the mall and not found him. But I thank The Almighty for allowing you to cross his path."

Rola tried to figure why Isa, obviously from a privileged home, would abandon a movie to tramp around in the sun. He was obviously trying to escape his minders; but she certainly couldn't probe.

"So, I want to visit you to say thank you properly."

"No, no, sir. That will not be necessary." Rola was familiar with the norms and "saying thank you properly" usually involved some reward, usually cash.

Rola looked up to find TK standing beside her. She hadn't heard him come in.

"I insist," Alhaji Mamane said.

"Kindly hold on, sir." Rola said and hit the mute button.

"The boy's father. Alhaji Mamane."

"Which boy?" her father whispered.

"The one we took to the hospital yesterday. Apparently, he is Alhaji Mamane's son. Alhaji himself is on the phone."

"What does he want?" he mouthed.

"Dad, speak normally, the phone is on mute." Rola smiled.

"He wants to visit us."

"Well, let him come over."

"Really?"

"Yes."

After she ended the call, she found her dad looking at her with a pensive expression.

"My dear, let the man come. Something tells me there's more to this than meets the eye."

Alhaji sat in the Bolades' living room sipping from a crystal goblet that Wunmi, the Bolades' housekeeper, had served him water in. Rola watched him as he looked around the living room, taking in the furnishings done in shades of grey and aubergine with accents of silver and rose gold. Rola sat across from him with her mum on a two-seater love seat while her dad sat on Alhaji's right on another love seat.

After the initial pleasantries, Alhaji had assured them Isa was on the mend and would be discharged by Saturday. TK and Alhaji had engaged in small talk while Rola watched a talk show on TV from the corner of her eye. The panel was discussing how a civil servant had claimed a snake swallowed a parastatal's money in her care.

"No way," she said aloud without meaning to. "I'm sorry," she said to their guest and reached for the remote control to turn down the volume.

TK motioned her to leave it. "That's nothing compared to the seventy million law makers claimed monkeys stole."

Alhaji and her parents burst into laughter while Rola wondered if they all were just pulling her legs.

"Where? They claimed monkeys held up a bank?"

Mrs B shook her head. "No, the money was on the farm, and monkeys allegedly stole it from the farm." This drew more laughter from the older folk.

"Why a farm? How did money from the legislature end up on someone's farm?"

"They said it was there for safe keeping," Alhaji said and chuckled. "Farms are good locations apparently, better than banks and garages too. By the way, five exotic cars were found on a farm last week. Range Rovers, Mercedes G Wagons, five! All covered in grass and vegetation."

Alhaji shook his head and looked at Rola, smiling. "So, Rola – I got the name correct, right?"

"It is certainly a good attempt Alhaji, sir."

"What do you do?"

"I am about to sign up for my youth service, sir."

"Where are you serving?"

"I am still to settle on a place, sir."

"Oh! Then, you need to come and work with us. My group of companies always has a place for young talents like you! Um, what is your discipline?"

Rola looked at Alhaji properly as if for the first time. He had offered her a placement and yet he didn't know what she did? Did he have a place in his "group of companies" for everyone regardless of their discipline? Was he being serious?

Even sitting, it was clear he was tall, 6'1" at least. He had a slight paunch, his complexion was dark, not latte or mocha, or any of the other culinary-inspired colours black people called themselves. Alhaji was ebony. He had a long face and four long tribal marks across his cheeks like two number elevens, one set on each side, which gave the illusion that his face was even longer; and one central mark running down from his forehead to the tip of his nose. He seemed to be in his 60s but it was difficult to say exactly how old. She could only be sure he was not past his mid 60s. She couldn't get any help in pinning down his age from his hair because he was cleanshaven from the little she could see since he had a cap on. His eyes also weren't giving anything away. They were slightly obscured from the reflection in his really impeccable pair of rimless glasses. His dazzling white voile babaringa was paired with black ostrich skin sandals. When he was young he must have cut quite a dashing figure.

When she had walked into the room, she got a whiff of sandalwood and something else she couldn't quite place. Amber perhaps? Alhaji looked like someone who only wore bespoke oudh.

Why was Olaotan stuck in IGCSE tutorials when she needed a co-conspirator? This "GQ Alhaji" couldn't be dissected effectively without her brother's help. Olaotan would have picked up that watch brand immediately even from this distance. All *she* saw was a thick gold bracelet. Alhaji oozed wealth but he seemed like quite a pleasant man too, convivial with a really genuine laugh.

"I am a software engineer," she had to answer before Alhaji misinterpreted her silence.

His smile widened.

"You must work with us, Rola, you understand?"

"Er, I'll, er, think about it, sir. Thanks for the offer, sir."

"You can be assured that I will top up whatever the service corp gives you quite generously."

Alhaji reached for his black leather pouch by the armrest of the chair, unzipped it and from a smooth black leather card holder, brought out one of his complimentary cards. He wrote something on the card with a thick gold and diamond tipped Montegrappa fountain pen. Then he handed it to Rola.

"Let's see on Tuesday. I just wrote my cell phone number on the card. It's my direct line. Come in on Tuesday, see what you think of us. You will be given a choice of Lagos or Abuja. Since you studied abroad, you will be posted to either, that's not an issue. All we need to do is request for you and you will be deployed to Mamane Group. Does that sound like a plan?" He was serious.

"I will let you know what time on Tuesday I can make it, sir. This is so kind of you, sir."

Alhaji then brought out an off-white envelope and stretched it out towards Rola. It looked like dollars inside the slightly transparent envelope, the green tinge was visible through the paper. "A small token for you, Rola. For fuel."

Rola turned her palms up instinctively as she shook her head, and it was clear, she had no intentions of touching the envelope Alhaji was offering.

"I was doing what I should do, sir. If I didn't help him, someone else would have. I am glad I could help."

Olaotan bounced into the living room just then. He had greeted his mother with a hug and his dad with a loud, "Dad! How was your day?" Then he stooped low and greeted Alhaji. "Good evening, sir."

After Alhaji's departure, Rola briefed Olaotan as best as she could.

"It was an Audemars Piguet," Olaotan said.

"Huh?"

"The watch, Alhaji's watch. It was an Audemars Piguet."

Rola laughed. "Olaotan! You had better work hard and be rich with the way you know all these brands. If you can't afford them, it will be torture for you."

"I intend to work hard SisMo, I already started. See when I just got back from school?" He grinned. "But I intend to also collect dollars when rich people offer me. What was all that drama for SisMo, refusing money? I was praying he would just toss the envelope to me instead. If only he gave me a few notes. Sis, it was over $20k. I saw two wads." He put two fingers of his right hand up for emphasis. "Did you see that his Bentley?"

Rola knew the gist had just begun as Olaotan followed her into the kitchen to get an evening snack.

Chapter Four

"When the Lord turned again the captivity of Zion,
we were like them that dream."

Psalm 126:1

Alhaji reflected on his time at the Bolades with a smile. Such a pleasant family. Such polite offspring. The humility of the beautiful Miss Bolade was such a rarity these days, her future husband was indeed blessed. He couldn't shake the feeling that there was something familiar about Rola. He had her on his mind all the way home as Junaid drove him through the streets of Lekki and across one of the picturesque bridges lit with the colours of Lagos to his house in Old Ikoyi. His house was a sprawling edifice, a white building with soaring columns clad in white marble. After the Bolades' lovely manicured garden, he felt there was something amiss with his own garden as he alighted from his Bentley and walked to the front door. It struck him suddenly – there was too much concrete, hardly any grass.

His domestic servants greeted him with deference as he went straight up the sweeping cream granite staircase to his master bedroom wing. The six-bedroom house was quiet. The vast grounds held yet another two-bedroom guest chalet, meant in the northern tradition for older sons of the family; but his stood empty: empty as his heart stood empty. As he thought of the erstwhile inhabitant of the guest chalet, he sighed deeply.

"Rola." Alhaji tried the name out. There was definitely something familiar about her. He changed into a white cotton jalabiya and sat on his bed. For some inexplicable reason, he felt his loneliness more acutely than ever tonight. More than ever since Laraba had died. It would be twenty-nine years this October. Twenty-nine years with no one suitable to fill the void. He had tried and failed with Aminat. Aminat who had cost him everything he had left – everyone that mattered that he held dear. And with the tragedy that was Aminat came this problem that made it impossible to keep any woman by his side. How different Aminat had been from Laraba. How different Aminat was from Rola. The thought hit him suddenly. His eyes flew to Laraba's photo by his bed side. That was it. Rola looked uncannily like Laraba. He picked up the gold frame and looked at Laraba's photo closely. Yes, it was the same height, the same curvy figure, the same dark skin, the almond-shaped eyes, the high cheekbones.

If another person had been looking at Laraba's photo and comparing her to Rola, the similarity would have ended there, but Alhaji was seeing what no one else would see. No wonder he felt so strangely protective of the young woman. He felt his head go light with the realisation of what was happening. What had his marabout, Sekou Traore, said when he consulted with him in Senegal last August?

He had sat before Traore on the ground. At the marabout's mansion, everyone – president or proselyte – sat on the rugs in Traore's grand living room. All shoes were off outside the door and what an array of shoes it was: the Italian brands favoured by rich Africans, all manner of ostrich, alligator, python and crocodile skin shoes. It was like a zoo of shoes.

"This is not a strange thing, El-Hadj," the marabout said. "But you said it started as she left fifteen years ago?"

"Yes, Great One. It started when I divorced Aminat."

"Hmm." The marabout fiddled with his prayer beads and muttered under his breath. "What evil took, good will restore." He went silent and rocked slightly back and forth. "When the one that is gone returns, then, that which is lost will be restored."

He gave him no medicaments, no potions; nothing but that prophecy.

Sometimes, the marabout spoke in parables that only he could decipher, but this prophecy was as plain as day to Alhaji. Laraba had returned. *For Laraba to return through Rola, Laraba's death must have preceded Rola's birth.* His mouth went dry, Laraba died on 28 October 1990. As he took out his smartphone and typed in Rola's name into the search bar, he was surprised to see his hands were trembling. In seconds, the screen was full of references to Rola. He scrolled till he saw the reference he was looking for. He clicked on that link, not sure what to expect. There it was, her birthdate – 28 November 1990.

Alhaji felt his heart beating, thumping in his chest. His ordeal was over! Laraba had returned. He who had lost his sons in more ways than one, could now at last have sons. His mind raced. Once he was sure he was restored, he had to make up for lost time. Once Rola conceived, he would marry another, someone from his area ideally. One who knew their culture and tradition and who could see to his home and extended family here in the country the traditional way, like Laraba had. She, the second, would be here with him with her own children. Rola and her own children would live in one of his houses in London, the one in South Kensington most likely. That should be big enough - she could have all she wanted, there would no longer be any need to stress herself working. If all worked out well, then his third could be back home in the North, to see to his welfare when he was visiting home and hosting his clansmen.

He had been content with three and if not that he was starting again so late and had to catch up, two would have done. That would suffice. It was a bit much marrying four women, the stress would just be too much. He shook his head wondering how some men coped with four. Four? "That is just greed," he thought. If Laraba had lived perhaps, who knows? Maybe it would have been just Laraba. He had certainly never considered another woman for the ten years they were together, though she had challenges. They had waited two years to have their first son and had only the one son for so long, yet he persevered and stood with her. Even when she passed on, years went by before he could recover from the grief and agree to marry Aminat.

He had been willing to stay as he was for a while longer. The son Laraba had bore for him wasn't a child in need of care anymore, but he couldn't very well have just one son, could he? Everyone agreed that was odd, so he had married Aminat to raise more sons for the family name, and now, instead of a house full of sons, there was no one. His beloved son was gone, and Isa, poor child, Isa was all smoke and mirrors.

Chapter Five

"Who is this that cometh out of the wilderness like pillars of smoke, perfumed with Myrrh and frankincense?"

Song of Solomon 3:6

Alhaji woke up the next day elated, oblivious at first to the source of his good mood. When the revelations of the preceding day came rushing into his consciousness, he could hardly contain his joy. "When the one that is gone returns, then that which is lost will be restored." He had memorised that prophecy, chanting it since August, never knowing till now how it would be achieved. He hadn't slept so peacefully, so deeply in years. Finally, the reproach was over and life could start again; he could begin to recover from his loss.

Alhaji picked up his phone to check for his 7 a.m. update from Khadijat. Hajiya Khadijat, he corrected himself. He had sponsored her pilgrimage to Mecca after she had spent ten years in his employ and he had been paying Fatima, her daughter's school fees for the last fourteen years. She was in her final year.

Sure enough, as he picked up his phone, there was Khadijat's text message. Reliable Khadijat, what would he do without her? He smiled and read the email. A Group Captain Ishaya had stopped by to see him at 4.05 p.m. The officer must have just missed him as he left the office at exactly 3:55 pm. Alhaji had no appointment with anyone in the air force but with all the defence contracts his company was running in their position in the country's defence industry, it wasn't strange for personnel from all the armed forces to visit the Mamane Group from time to time.

A noise from outside distracted him from his phone. It sounded like Samson, shouting. Alhaji looked out his window and saw his long-time cook yelling something unintelligible at the gatehouse. He was holding on to a tall man in a uniform, with a cap on. Alhaji couldn't see the man's face from this angle, just his broad shoulders from the back and his long legs. He was tall though, even taller than Alhaji's 6'1". Samson had his face buried in the man's chest. For someone who had been with him for over thirty years, Alhaji typically just looked the other way when Samson received personal guests during working hours, but this was just too bad. The noise was too much. He decided to have a word with Samson at an opportune time. Isa was going to be discharged today and Alhaji had decided to go and pick him up himself. He needed to have breakfast first, though. He walked out of his bedroom into his private living room on the first floor and dialled the kitchen extension. The line rang out just as he heard Samson's unmistakable footsteps on the stairs. A second set of feet were also coming up.

"No. Samson isn't really bringing his relative into my house and up the stairs? He knows he can come up and ask for whatever money he wants for his people and I would send it through him? So why bring this one up here, to my own private wing?" he thought to himself.

Samson was now before Alhaji. He stooped down low on one knee and he seemed quite overwhelmed by emotion. He had been crying. He kept shaking his head as if in awe and looking down, unable to utter a word.

It was most odd. The *relative* stood behind Samson. He had a presence, a comportment that was so familiar. He was tall, dark, broad shouldered... this was a familiar face. Alhaji's heart stopped for a moment. He felt lightheaded and the blood drained from his face. The prophecy was true! Scarcely one day after he met Rola, those presumed dead were resurrected, the lost was being restored. This was Kaniz standing before him. A taller, broad-shouldered muscular Kaniz, but it was Kaniz. A scar that hadn't been there before ran in a jagged line from his left temple to his left brow. Still, scar or no scar, it was definitely Kaniz.

Alhaji didn't know if it was possible to have a heart attack from joy, but if it was, this would have been his last moment on earth. Alhaji sprang up from the sofa and moving swiftly, embraced his son. Now it was Alhaji's turn to cry. Quietly, without warning, the tears welled up and spilled out of his eyes.

Father and son were silent but the tears kept coming unbidden. Apparently, men could cry and men who had their dead brought back to life actually did cry. Sons who fled from home and didn't know what to expect at their return but were met with joyful tears and a warm embrace not only cried but wept! Samson arose from his stooping position and gently withdrew to the kitchen. Father and son would need to eat together and he needed to get a worthy celebratory breakfast ready.

Alhaji eventually stepped back and looked at Kaniz. He was taller than Alhaji, perhaps by about four inches. He was dressed in fatigues and his name tag read "Ishaya". Was this the Group Captain Ishaya who came to the office yesterday and narrowly missed him?

"Kaniz? You are Ishaya? You took my own first name?" He looked at the fatigues. "You are in the air force? Where have you been? Why didn't you call home? Why didn't you return?"

"Shehu. Can we sit, sir?" Conflicting emotions filled Alhaji's soul on hearing his beloved son call him that name. No one else called him by his clan title.

"Yes! Yes, yes of course," Alhaji said. He kept a hand on Kaniz's shoulder as they sat beside each other, perhaps subconsciously ensuring that he wasn't an apparition subject to vanishing on a whim. Alhaji kept staring at Kaniz. When he had first disappeared seventeen years ago, his initial reaction had been fear as he searched high and low for his son, then anger when it became apparent from the fact that his passport and critical documents were gone, that his son had been deliberate about his hurried departure. Anger soon gave way to disbelief and then a defiant nonchalance. Alhaji reasoned Kaniz was the offender, he could go to blazes for all Alhaji cared. At the worst, he had Isa and would soon have other children; so, if one patently evil son decided to dissociate himself from the family, he was welcome.

Nonchalance soon gave way to a slowly encroaching and crippling grief as months turned into years and all efforts to find Kaniz proved abortive. Despair took over as Aminat's exploits were revealed and he realised the gravity of his loss in Kaniz's departure.

"What happened Kaniz?"

"After the incident," Kaniz began to speak – his father didn't ask what incident he referred to, he simply gave a knowing nod – "I laid low in Lagos for two days, then bought a cheap ticket and went off to the States. I landed in Atlanta. I am sure you noticed I took my passport—"

"Then the air force? How?"

"I moved to Florida later and spent almost two years just doing whatever my hands could find to keep body and soul together. I made some money and decided to return home and start some type of business but I joined the air force soon after I returned from the States. Thankfully, I got a scholarship and they sent me back to the States."

At the thought of his son needing a scholarship to pay for his university education, Alhaji's countenance fell. His own son? Needing a scholarship? While he was alive and sponsoring dozens of others he had never even met?

"What did you study? At which University?"

"What I always wanted to study," Kaniz said, smiling.

"Aeronautic engineering?" His father stared in disbelief. "You actually still went ahead and studied aeronautic engineering?" He shook his head in disbelief and pointed at Kaniz as if to say "you?", tilting his head to the right, his eyebrows arched in wonder and pointing the long index finger of his right hand at Kaniz, "aeronautic engineering?" he repeated to himself again like he couldn't comprehend his own voice.

"Bachelor's and master's," Kaniz replied.

All this while, he had thought his son was a cokehead or running around with a gang of robbers, he actually had attended university? He obtained a first and second degree? All those years he hadn't heard from his son, Alhaji did not in his wildest dreams imagine Kaniz was making the slightest headway with his life. Not with all Aminat had been telling him for years about his son and not with the damning evidence of "the incident".

He had run this reunion through his mind several times but never came up with this scenario. Being called to identify his body in the morgue, *that* he had replayed several times in his mind. The commissioner of police calling him to say his son was amongst suspects rounded up at an armed robbery; that too he had been prepared for.

Alhaji finally found his voice. "Where? Which university?" His voice was almost a whisper.

"Both degrees at Georgia Tech."

Georgia Institute of Technology. That was a good school. "Your children, your wife, where are they?" Kaniz was thirty-six now. Every year on his son's birthday, Alhaji ordered special prayers for him. Though in recent years, it was more for the repose of his soul than in any hope that he would still be alive. In Ishaya Mamane's mind, if his son was still alive, he couldn't conceive of a scenario in which his son would not contact him as the years went by, no matter the gravity of events that had led to their parting.

"I am not married yet, sir."

The icy fingers of fear clutched Alhaji's heart. He had imagined this possibility once but thought it preposterous. Had the curse afflicted his son also? Was it generational? How could he find out from his son what the real state of affairs was? How could he broach the topic? He would proceed with caution till he uncovered the truth. He took another tack.

"Your girlfriend then Kaniz? Where is she? It doesn't matter if she is an American - white or black, she is welcome. All those sentiments are for the unexposed."

"I am still waiting for the right person. Marriage is an issue with a divine dimension. I am sure you agree, sir."

"No girlfriend? No wife? No child? You are thirty-six now. I know we have been, should I say, 'disconnected' for almost two decades, but I am your father, open up to me." He cleared his throat. "Is everything alright? There are solutions to these matters you know."

From Kaniz's quizzical expression, it was clear he was finding this trend of conversation really weird but he rallied as he finally caught his father's meaning. He laughed aloud and something about his mirth assured Alhaji Ishaya Mamane that his son was being sincere.

"Where is your luggage? Where are your things?"

"Shehu, I am only visiting you; I have just been transferred to Lagos from Colombia." Alhaji frowned and Kaniz felt the need to elaborate. "I was defence attaché at our embassy there."

"Ah. Defence attaché." Alhaji nodded his approval. "But what's this about visiting? Visiting your own home? Nonsense!" He reached for the intercom. "Let Junaid go and get your things."

Kaniz placed his right hand gently on Alhaji's right forearm to stop him from dialling on the intercom to alert Junaid in the drivers' lodge.

"Shehu. I am comfortable. I am settling down. I have been in Lagos now for three days. I arrived on Wednesday. I am staying in my place at the air force base in Ikoyi. Not far from you here. You know it, sir, Tadan Barracks."

"Barracks? My son is living in the barracks?"

"Sir, it's not bad. The group captain's quarters is actually decent. I have been through much worse. This is living in the lap of luxury for me," he said dryly.

Alhaji couldn't imagine the Kaniz who grew up in this palatial mansion now living in a barracks and referring to his living arrangements as "decent". Kaniz always had that streak though. He could be strangely ascetic though he still valued and appreciated the finer things in life. Just like his mother, Laraba. "Who would have married me fresh out of polytechnic when I had no prospects except Laraba?" Alhaji thought.

Kaniz had arrived on Wednesday? Alhaji was processing the information. He was in Lagos when Isa's escape and collapse was unfolding. Alhaji didn't even know what to make of this strange week.

As if he could hear his thoughts, Kaniz asked, "Where is Isa? He is a young man now, Shehu. I follow him on Instagram. But anonymously, of course."

Alhaji wondered how much Kaniz knew. Isa was just a baby and a few months old when Kaniz left. If Kaniz knew anything though, it wasn't obvious. The younger Ishaya Mamane adjusted his posture and his demeanour signalled that he was about to broach a serious subject. "Shehu, what happened... it wasn't what Hajiya Aminat said. It was not true that—"

Alhaji cut Kaniz off mid-sentence. "Kaniz, events have proven you right. I should have believed you. There's a lot for us to discuss." This was as close to an apology he felt he could give. He sighed. "Kaniz, there's just too much we have to discuss. But first, let's eat. God be praised! He has spared your life, I am not—" Alhaji bit his tongue on the word "childless". Time enough to discuss all that with his son.

He took another look at the fine gentleman opposite him, his back straight even as he sat. He, Ishaya Mamane, was the father of Group Captain Kaniz Ishaya, Btech Mtech Aeronautic Engineering? He, Ishaya, was the father of the living and not the dead? The Almighty be praised. How could his fortunes have been restored so dramatically? He, who had clung to Isa in spite of all to cover his shame.

"Kaniz, you are never leaving again. I will never again let you go," he said with finality. "Whatever it takes, I will never let you go."

Chapter Six

"Thou has ravished my heart, my sister, my spouse; thou hast ravished my heart with one of thine eyes, with one chain of thy neck."

Song of Solomon 4:9

Kaniz couldn't believe the warm reception his father had given him. To be honest, he hadn't known what to expect. He only had faith and went with his deepest inward inclination and the perception he had within him that it was finally time to return. By the time Alhaji had told him the events of the last years, he knew he couldn't have returned at a better time and returning too early would have been counter-productive.

His taciturn traditional father had changed radically. He was more open, he spoke and conversed with his son more like an equal and he didn't seem to be able to get over the fact that his own son was at thirty-six, the youngest group captain in the history of the country's air force. Alhaji was positively bursting with pride as he introduced Kaniz to his business associates at the Knights Club, a gentlemen's club, on Sunday evening.

"Kaniz is a decorated war hero. How many sorties did you fly over Darfur for the joint forces?" He was cueing Kaniz to speak, but the self-effacing Kaniz wasn't taking the bait. He nodded politely, smiled but kept quiet. Darfur held dark memories he didn't want to revisit on such a bright day, memories that sent him down a dark spiral. He had banished those dark memories beyond the realms of speech.

Alhaji had gone on about Kaniz's exploits like the proud father that he was. Others had been boasting about their scions for years as Alhaji kept silent, but tonight his fortunes had been restored, it was his turn to shine; he had not just a son, but a truly worthy son.

The weekend had been a blur of accompanying Alhaji everywhere possible. Kaniz got a glimpse of the trauma his departure had caused his father, a trauma his father could not speak openly about. He was of the stock of warriors that had built great northern empires, a stock that had known no defeat, not even when conquerors had swept through the country from the north to the south to be eventually halted at the fringes of the Oyo Empire at Ilorin, not even then did his people yield in defeat.

Alhaji was a true son of the soil just tempered by living in the South West. Kaniz remembered his father's clansmen visiting them at their homestead in happier times when his mother was alive. The dark fierce-looking men with the prominent scarifications on their faces came in - each with his dagger strapped to his upper arm and would be welcomed in the men's quarters while hardly any of them cracked a smile.

The knee-high Kaniz wondered at their imperturbable demeanor and it was much later he could reconcile the difference between the masculine role models from his northern origins to those in the South West who were his mother's relatives; Yoruba men whose courage didn't debar conviviality.

For Alhaji and his kinsmen, actions were far superior to words. By every standard, by keeping him close all weekend, Alhaji was demonstrating without verbalising, how much he loved and had missed his son. He seemed determined to fit the last seventeen years he had lost with Kaniz into one weekend.

Kaniz was glad to be reunited with his father. It was as if a piece of his life had fallen back into place again. In a bid to connect virtually, to feel a bit of the bond they once had and perhaps just catch a glimpse of his father's photos, Kaniz had scoured the internet for references to Alhaji but Ishaya Mamane had almost no online footprint. His son now knew it was deliberate. In Alhaji Mamane's line of business, discretion was key.

On Saturday, Alhaji did not allow Kaniz return to the barracks to change from his fatigues into civilian clothes. He had taken him to his own closet and told him to choose whatever he liked and get dressed. Alhaji had stacks of unworn clothes with some still stored neatly in their shopping bags. The trousers were a few inches too short, but the son improvised and made the best of the borrowed garb.

They had gone together to fetch Isa home from the hospital. Alhaji didn't say much; he was listening intently to Kaniz. Sometimes, he just seemed content that his son was right there with him. At other times, he was asking questions, putting together timelines.

Ishaya Mamane had a sharp native intelligence and Kaniz had learned as a child not to even attempt to lie. It was just easier to keep his stories straight if he stuck to the truth, if not, Ishaya Mamane was a skilled interrogator who would ask the same question in so many different ways that he would trip up anyone who was saying anything else but the truth.

In all, it was a beautiful weekend, the only shock was Isa. Kaniz was especially looking forward to meeting Isa, who though closer to the age of a son, was his only sibling. Growing up, he had been surrounded by cousins from Alhaji's large extended family, but it was like an unending procession, they were always *passing through*. After finishing school or whatever they had come to the Mamanes' household for, they moved on.

After a few painful separations as a young child, he tried not to be too attached to the relatives. Isa was his very own and he was looking forward to meeting the young man who had been a baby when he had last seen him. However, when he saw Isa he had to admit that Isa was definitely a wizard with filters on instagram. He was much leaner than he appeared in his instagram photos and something was off.

Kaniz had assumed Isa just looked like his fair skinned and slim mum, Aminat, but this was different. His first thought was that Isa was a sickler but that wasn't possible. Alhaji was AA. He'd found that out as an eleven-year-old filling medical forms for secondary school.

Just when he had convinced himself that his first impression was wrong, the doctor had passed through for the usual briefing in Isa's private room as he was being discharged and as a matter of fact, had reminded Isa that he was now old enough to take personal responsibility for his health and keep an eye on his sickle cell anemia. Kaniz had cast a glance at their father at this point and Ishaya Mamane hadn't batted an eyelid; Isa's condition was apparently no news to him. Something was wrong and it was obvious that Alhaji knew. No wonder his father had put Aminat away.

Isa himself, though cautious at first, had quickly warmed up to Kaniz.

Kaniz wondered how Alhaji was going to explain his sudden re-emergence to Isa but for now decided to flow with the tide. The fact that he actually flew fighter jets seemed to have Isa enthralled in the interim, and for now, his older brother could do no wrong in Isa's eyes.

By Sunday, he had taken Isa out for lunch and he was rapidly developing a strong fondness for the young man whose physical suffering had taken such a toll on his life. Isa had lost a year in school to illness; at seventeen plus he was just preparing to take his IGCSEs and had missed out a lot on activities especially team sports, relegated to watching and cheering from the sidelines.

He clearly had potential but had to work hard at his academics to catch up with lost school days. As he listened to the lithe young man over lunch on Sunday, Kaniz decided, "I will be there for you Isa, I will protect you from all I suffered."

Before leaving the mansion on Mamane Close on Sunday evening, Kaniz had to sit with Alhaji and get a clear idea of what the week ahead was to be like. He too was striving to make up for what he had inadvertently put his father through so he was doing his best to accommodate his father's wishes. He also knew it would be just a short while before Alhaji got used to the idea that he was back for good and he would relax. So, for now, he tried to work with Alhaji's plans.

When Alhaji had set out the week's plans, Kaniz had declined his father's invitation to return to Mamane Group headquarters on Monday; he had to be at the office during office hours. It wouldn't be in good form to start skipping work hours this early at a new posting. He would have dinner with Alhaji later at the Mamane residence when he was done at the office on Monday. Dinner at the house on Mamane Close was very welcome as it was either that or dinner at the Officers' Mess and Samson's culinary prowess had only gotten better over the years.

Samson had taken it upon himself to get a cook for Kaniz, but for now, he was taking matters into his own hands and ensuring Kaniz was fed in what he believed was an adequate manner. He seemed convinced that Kaniz had not eaten a bite in the seventeen years since he saw him last and was determined to redeem the situation with his erstwhile charge.

Kaniz had agreed when his father asked that they meet at the Mamane Group office on Tuesday. He could pull the time off at lunchtime. He went straight from the base and would again return to the base after lunch, then work as late as was necessary to clear his desk. He was determined even more than ever to continue to perform exemplarily because he had decided his days in the air force were numbered.

For one, his business interests in Colombia and elsewhere were demanding more of his time and he needed to focus. The pay for a group captain was also interesting to say the least. It had been alright when he was always on foreign posting and paid to reflect the expatriate posting but – in-country? No. He was augmenting his income from his other businesses and it made sense to focus fully on them. However, before he left the air force, he intended to leave an exemplary track record.

After getting security clearance on the ground floor, he entered the lift and pressed the button for the 15th floor. The two ladies who had stepped in after him were headed for the 12th floor. He still had his perennial aviators on when they stepped in and he was trying to hurriedly round up a phone call before the mobile signal was lost to the lift shaft. He had scarcely cast a glance in their direction beyond his polite "Good afternoon."

They felt very comfortable speaking freely in Igbo because from his name tag "Ishaya", he was clearly a northerner and when he finally took his aviators off, his features were distinctly northern. Even his accent when he greeted them as they stepped into the lift and he rounded up the phone conversation he was on was decidedly northern.

"Chineze check out this guy," the first lady who stepped in was saying. They must have been returning from their lunch break. "Why so fine? Even with this scar?" referring to the obvious scar on Kaniz's left temple stopping just at his left brow and breaking the brow line in two thirds and a third.

Chineze decided to follow her friend's cue and look at the tall, muscular figure. She cast Kaniz one of those sideways glances ladies try and steal without getting caught.

Kaniz could see her clearly from the mirrored lift doors even as he

continued to type on his phone. Every self-respecting man who had passed through the rites of passage knew how to intercept a woman's furtive glances. It was a cult secret amongst men how bad women were at stealing glances especially when checking out another woman's appearance. Women were just too obvious.

Chineze was impressed by what she saw and turning to her friend she said in Igbo, "The height! See the flat abs, see the broad shoulders and biceps, look at the muscles! Just right! Not like those bouncer types that can't get their suit size!"

Her friend let out a chuckle at this remark. She stole a glance. "See o, not one ounce of fat. Just perfect."

Chineze felt she needed to be accurate, so she conceded there was a flaw. "Apart from this scar o, but it just makes him more attractive." She turned to her friend. "Some guys will cut their hair this low and all kinds of 'formations' will come to light."

Her friend burst out in a low laugh in spite of herself.

Chineze continued her analysis. "An afro is not optional for some men o. They know what is under the afro!" More laughter from her friend.

"See the uniform on him. As if they poured it on him. This is custom-made for him o. This blue though, this isn't the army. Who are those who wear blue?"

Since there was no native word for air force her friend rolled her eyes like "duh" and flapped her arms to denote flight.

"Ah!" Chineze clued in and almost said "air force" out loud if her friend hadn't eyed her seriously and brought her to her senses.

"See his chest. Covered in medals. I wonder what he did to deserve all these medals. No argument. This guy is handsome o! Hmm. Instead of some girls following a fine man like this it's a man with a pot belly older than their father they would be going out with."

Her companion was instantly interested. It was obvious that these two had shared many a tidbit in their time. "Who?" she asked, her eyes lighting up.

Chineze replied, "Hmm, we were just told in HR to get the left corner office on the 14th floor ready for the big boss's girlfriend. She is going to serve here apparently but not as a corper. Can you imagine? She will be reporting directly to the MD of QuantumTech. It's the GM's office we are preparing. No interview, nothing. Do you know anywhere, anywhere in this country where a corper serves as GM?"

Even Kaniz who was eavesdropping, smiled inwardly because it appeared the lady in question, the subject of the gist, was definitely a super-corper. She could not be an ordinary youth corper at all.

The other lady was stunned. "The waiting list for those who want to serve with QuantumTech is almost at 150 right now. We have even rounded up interviews. Eeehh!" She snapped her fingers for effect.

Chineze was on a roll now. "No interview at all. You know the GM position had been taken out of the organogram at that last restructuring last October? Well that's the position she is being given technically. That is if her package is to be what we have been told to make it in the offer, with a Toyota Prado jeep and a driver and... hmm... let me not even discuss the salary. We HR professionals must maintain confidentiality."

At this last remark Kaniz almost gave himself away with a chuckle which he quickly contorted into a grimace. Confidentiality indeed!

Kaniz was not interested in their conversation but he was held hostage in this lift. It was soon at the 12th floor and the colleagues alighted but not before Chineze and her friend had said their *byes*.

"Would you be needing any directions at all?" Chineze said in such an affected British accent that it was a genuine shock to him after the native language she and her friend had both been conversing in just split seconds earlier. As she held unto the lift door, he thought to himself how some ladies miss it sometimes. If she was interested in him she should have spent the last three minutes they had spent in the lift together trying to make conversation with him and not her companion who she still had all the time in the world to talk to later.

"That's so kind of you," he replied. "I know my way."

He raised his left hand in a slight wave to demonstrate that the conversation was over as far as he was concerned and with his right hand, pressed the "door close" button for good measure. The lift doors jerked as they attempted to close again and Chineze wistfully released her hostage.

Her companion contented herself with a furtive backwards glance as the lift doors closed finally and the lift whisked him away to the 15th floor.

"Nwanne!" Chineze said to her friend Chioma as they walked away to their offices, "That was something!"

This was not the first time this had happened to Kaniz. People just assumed he couldn't understand any other language but that which his looks suggested he spoke. They took to speaking in their own native language as if he was invisible. He had attended a federal government college in the South East and had not only picked up the language but had made several friends he was still close to till now. Some of his closest friends were from the South East and they spoke Igbo when they were all together.

When it came to languages, he actually was a polyglot and had a few surprises up his sleeve. Just to make conducting his transactions easier while stationed in Colombia he had also brushed up the Spanish he had first picked up in the US.

Kaniz didn't like gossip but he was cooped up in the lift with the ladies, so he had no choice than to listen to them. If what they said was true – it was a suspicious situation, a real mess. Alhaji wasn't this careless before he left home.

"Kaniz, things are not always what they seem," a voice within him warned. "What business is it of mine?" He shrugged as if shaking the inner voice off.

He stepped out at the 15th floor and walked briskly to the Chairman's suite. The receptionist was all smiles and kept saying "Welcome, sir" as she motioned with her hands, pointing him in the direction of the Chairman's office. His father's secretary was no less friendly. As soon as he stepped into her office, she jumped up smiling, flashing a gold tooth.

"The Chairman said you mustn't be kept waiting for even a minute, sir. Let me take you in."

As they stepped into the office, she sucked in her generous middle-aged belly and announced him in a mellower tone, exchanging the professional smile she had given Kaniz for a warmer one. Alhaji seemed oblivious to these cues as he ushered his son in. "Thank you, Hajiya," he said.

"How's Isa?" Kaniz asked as soon as he settled down.

"Didn't he call you before he went to school?" Ishaya Mamane asked, smiling. He knew the brothers were in touch with each other.

"I was in a meeting; my phone was on silent."

"He is getting rapidly attached to you Kaniz. Rapidly attached."

"I like him too," Kaniz replied.

"Shehu, sir... this sickle cell matter..."

Alhaji looked him straight in the eyes. "You know already he can't possibly be my son. But what was I to do? You were gone, I didn't have any hopes of another child."

Kaniz gave his father a quizzical look prompting further explanation. As much as Alhaji would rather keep silent on the matter, he had regretted so many things he didn't tell Kaniz and he had sworn at the time Kaniz was presumed missing or worse, that if he ever had a second chance with his son, he would do things differently. He would never let anyone come between them again, least of all, a woman. He would trust his son's word, spend time with him and understand him better and there would be no secrets. So he decided to elaborate a bit on his plight.

"Son, you need to understand that philandering women can be very suspicious. They suspect their spouses of what they themselves are up to and my findings revealed that to stop me from taking a second wife," Alhaji paused and inhaled deeply, "to stop me from taking a second wife, Aminat took certain ill-advised and diabolical steps, with repercussions that went far beyond what she herself imagined."

He sighed. "However the solution is here already by God's grace. As for Isa, I have brought up Isa as my son. He has no idea he is anything but my son. Can I count on you to accept him as your brother?"

"Shehu—of course that's done already," Kaniz said with firm assurance.

"He would eventually know because of his condition. I know that's inevitable but it's too much for him to deal with right now."

Kaniz could see that Alhaji cared for Isa, he was genuinely fond of him. "Shehu has changed, he has mellowed," Kaniz thought. "Isa's father, I hope Isa's being with us won't be an issue?" he asked.

"Isa's father is dead," Alhaji said in a flat voice.

Kaniz almost shuddered at Alhaji's tone.

"Hajiya Aminat? Could she cause trouble with the man's relatives?"

Alhaji sighed again. "About two years after Aminat left me, she succumbed to mental disease and the last I heard of her a few years ago, she had passed on."

"What?" That was altogether too tidy. Surely Alhaji couldn't have... no he couldn't. His father was not a murderer.

"Those sad times are behind us now Kaniz. Restoration has come." At those words, he looked at his watch and saw it was already 1:32 p.m. Rola was meant to have been here for 1 p.m. He dialled Khadijat on the intercom.

"Hajiya Khadijat. Have you heard from Miss Bolade yet?"

Rola didn't strike him as someone who would be running late without getting in touch at all. She seemed too polite and disciplined for that.

"She is here," Khadijat voice came from the speakers and there was a hint of something in her voice, something Alhaji couldn't quite place.

"Haba! Haba! Khadijat. I told you this is an extremely important guest and you were to extend to her every courtesy. How could she arrive and you wouldn't tell me?"

"You were with someone important, Chairman," Khadijat replied flatly.

"Escort her in immediately," Alhaji said. "I will deal with your matter later."

The door opened a few seconds later and Kaniz turned his head to the right slightly and looked at Khadijat's face. To a casual observer, it was expressionless, but he could see a barely imperceptible twist of her lips. Before his first posting as defence attaché, Kaniz had been trained by the FBI in interrogation, hostage negotiation and other skills which could be useful in defending the embassy under aggression. He could read micro-expressions and body language and he could tell something was definitely up with Khadijat.

Rola came in behind the secretary. She gave Hajiya Khadijat a pleasant, "Thank you ma'am" and a smile that went unacknowledged as Khadijat walked out of the Chairman's office.

Before she could even greet Alhaji, he had boomed out his greeting to her.

"Good afternoon my dear Rola," he said smiling. "I apologise on behalf of Khadijat. I hope you weren't kept waiting too long? When did you arrive?"

Rola smiled and at her smile, Kaniz, who had turned towards the door to look at the visitor, inhaled sharply. Rola was speaking, he could clearly see her mouth moving but he couldn't follow her words.

Rola replied, "No, sir. I haven't been here too long. I came in just before 1 p.m."

Rola was avoiding getting Khadijat in any further trouble but she still had to let Alhaji know she hadn't arrived late. She had wondered herself why Khadijat had been so cold to her when she arrived. Khadijat had barely acknowledged her presence and had silently motioned with a flick of her right hand at Rola to sit in one of the visitors' chairs by the wall. This was in spite of the warm smile Rola had given her and the copious ma'ams she had spiced her inquiry to her with. In sharp contrast, the receptionist in the 15th floor lobby outside had been exceptionally pleasant to her. It was all very confusing.

Kaniz's eyes were drinking in every facet of Rola's features. Why was she so familiar? He scanned his brain and finally had to conclude that he had never met her. Why then did he feel he had known this complete stranger all his life? The surreal feeling coursing through his being was not a physical attraction, he had enough experience to know his reaction was far from physical. This was something much deeper, more real and infinitely more sublime and irresistible.

The lack of a physical attraction was not because Rola was not physically attractive. She was favoured with more than enough for any full-blooded man to be physically attracted to her, he mused as he gazed at her. Her skin was a dark mocha that glowed as if lit from within. Her high cheekbones gave her almost heart-shaped face its defining shape. Her broad forehead was an indication of obvious intelligence. Her dark brows were like the two outstretched wings of an eagle and her almond eyes as she drew nearer were like caramel pools drawing him in till he felt like he would drown in them.

Still speaking with Alhaji, she turned her head away slightly, gesticulating with her head towards the door behind her and on her right. As Kaniz caught her profile, to him, her profile was reminiscent of a sculpture carved of the finest marble. He decided that her profile with the bridge of her nose rising to a delicate tip was even more beautiful than any other feature she possessed. She was about six feet tall in her heels, her height, counterbalanced by her curves to eliminate any allusions to a gangling damsel.

No, hers was the quintessential definition of "Junoesque". Her waist in this simple black dress with the emerald obi sash. That waist; he felt he could span her waist in both his hands. A simple white gold cross with emeralds nestled at the base of her neck and he could see the cross move with her gentle breath, rising and falling, rising and falling.

As if observing himself remotely, he noticed his own breathing was falling in sync with hers. Suddenly, from nowhere, a still voice within him floated up and said with such finality and calm assurance, *"This is the one you have been waiting so long for."* He shook his head. This was senseless. The mission he had at hand couldn't brook any distraction and even if his circumstances had been different, it was completely presumptuous to be so sure so soon about even exploring a friendship of any sort with this random lady.

"Kaniz," his father was speaking to him and Alhaji's voice thankfully dragged him out of his reverie. "Kaniz, meet Rola. Rola, remember? The lady I was telling you about. The one who saved Isa's life." Kaniz had never in his wildest dreams imagined that Good Samaritans came in such stunning packages. This is the lady who took Isa to the hospital? This elegant maiden knelt by Isa's side in the mud? Her head bowed, performing CPR?

He thought of the head on that graceful neck, bowed, and his mind wandered. That was her own hair on her head? Her hair was full and healthy and a deep black. She wore her hair pulled away from her face. He wondered what it would be like to run his fingers through her hair. At that moment, he was overcome with a longing to just hold her close, her head on his chest as she listened to his heartbeat, his fingers in her hair, running through her hair... He took a deep breath to clear his head and exhaled slowly. What was this? Was this an enchantment or witchcraft?

"Rola, meet my son, Kaniz. Group Captain Kaniz Ishaya of the air force" – Kaniz waited for the inevitable elaboration he had heard Alhaji launch into all weekend – "the youngest group captain in the history of our air force; that is since 1964, the youngest!"

There it was! Alhaji had even done some research and added the date of inception of the air force this time for full effect. Kaniz shook his head silently at his father's introduction but Alhaji was on a roll, his pride in his son was unconcealable.

Rola extended her hand and as Kaniz reached out to shake her hand he felt a jolt of electricity pass through him. Crazy! What type of clichéd reaction was this? He was now genuinely displeased with his traitorous reactions. He was a rational engineer and this rubbish going on right now defied all logic. It was irrational to feel anything akin to electricity when there was no source of alternating or direct current, besides, the weather was humid and not dry so there was no static electricity. What was this hocus pocus then? He couldn't wait to leave and clear his head and yet, he sighed, yet he felt like never leaving her.

He was aware he was acting strange and so he spoke first. "Oh! Thank you, so much Rola," he said soberly, clasping her right hand in his huge hand. Her hand seemed so tiny in his. "Thanks for all you did for Isa. We can't thank you enough."

"Alhaji, sir," Rola turned away from Kaniz to Ishaya Mamane, "I keep saying we couldn't have saved Isa's life. We only assisted him, that is all, sir," she said.

"Oh, sit down! Sit down, both of you," Alhaji said, beaming and waving his hands in the direction of the visitors' chairs set before his huge Brazilian rosewood desk.

When everyone was seated, Alhaji said, "Rola is an enterprising, future-forward electronic engineer. She was part of those who built that security app, DefenceWare, that you might have heard of. It's actually in use in some of the latest hardware we supply. Imagine my surprise when I discovered she actually developed it. What were the chances? I have asked her to come and join us at Mamane Group, QuantumTech to be precise. She runs her own start-up, Synergy, in New York, but she is home for one year and she wants to sort out her youth service so I thought, where else but here at QuantumTech?"

"Quite impressive," Kaniz said. So, this was the girlfriend the gossips had been referring to. Of course she couldn't be treated like any other corper. If she was indeed this accomplished, then QuantumTech was privileged to have her and not the other way around. Deep inside him, he heard that voice again, still and calm, *"I told you things are not always what they seem".* He concurred silently and made up his mind never again to rush to judgment again especially where Rola was concerned.

Rola. Had Alhaji not said the Good Samaritan's name was Morolawe Bolade? Rola must be the short version.

"To me, you will always be Morola," he said in his heart, "I like that better. Mo-ro-la." He spoke the name in his mind drawing out each syllable.

Rola was looking at him with that sweet childlike smile and he gazed at her in return. Then he looked away abruptly as if he was embarrassed to be caught thinking about her; as if she could see his thoughts.

The response to her own smile seemed weird to Rola. Why couldn't he smile? Alhaji's voice interrupted her thoughts.

"And I am really proud to be the father of a decorated hero. Kaniz here has been on missions to many neighbouring and foreign countries, including Darfur and Iraq. He has served as defence attaché, most recently in Colombia and he is now back home with us. He also has a master's in aeronautic engineering."

His military training was what was keeping Kaniz in line now because he frankly wanted to leave and sort his feelings or his brain or whatever it was out.

He contented himself with listening and nodding except he was spoken to. He knew he risked coming off to Rola as rather introverted or worse still, snobbish, but that was the least of his worries right now. Alhaji kept trying to draw him into the conversation but Kaniz kept silent, a nod here and there was enough to tide him over this conversation. He was listening as Alhaji and Rola were discussing Isa. Rola offered to put Isa in touch with her younger brother Olaotan who was taking almost exactly the same courses Isa was taking for his IGCSEs in May/June too.

He could only nod in acquiescence when Alhaji – without consulting him first – offered his services to drop off Isa at the Bolades' on the day agreed by way of "and Kaniz can drop Isa off on that Saturday? Kaniz, if that's alright with you?"

"And what am I to say now, Shehu?" Kaniz thought as he nodded.

"Isa told me you had both agreed he would be at your barracks that weekend." His contempt seeped through at the word "barracks". "This way, you can inject some tutoring into the weekend? It actually works well because I have to be in Abuja till that Saturday evening. I will be back in the evening, but it would be too late to start bringing Isa to your place at that time".

It dawned on Kaniz what was being arranged. It meant he would have to see Morola again in less than two weeks. That was ill-advised. He wanted to gain the mastery over this maelstrom of stimuli first. While his head despaired, something within him was elated at the idea of having an excuse, any excuse at all to see her again soon. He didn't even have the strength to refuse. He just nodded again silently.

He would have a late-night meeting with the team the Friday night before he had to drop Isa but they could hold the meeting in his quarters and he could sort out the drop-off on Saturday afternoon.

"Shehu, I think I should allow Miss Bolade and yourself to sort out QuantumTech matters." Kaniz stood up.

"Ah ah!" Alhaji said, clearly surprised. "We were all going for lunch, Kaniz."

"But you didn't tell me Miss Corper, who has destabilised my equilibrium, would be joining us, did you?" Kaniz thought. No way was he going to have lunch with Morola this afternoon. No way. Spending more time with her right now was out of the question.

He was sure he was rapidly becoming unsociable in Morola's estimation, but it was more important to him to maintain control than to look good in her eyes right now.

"I really have to leave, Shehu. I will come over later, sir." He was moving determinedly, picking up his cell phone and walking to the door.

"And how about Rola?" Alhaji said. It was clear from Alhaji's expression that his son's rude behavior was quite surprising to him.

Kaniz stopped and turned around. "She didn't know I would be here this afternoon, did she?" He had said the words before he reflected on how rude he sounded. "Miss Bolade, it's been a pleasure." He smiled ever so slightly at her and managed to maintain eye contact. It was tough even with his skills to read her expression. She seemed slightly amused, perhaps? Seated gracefully and composed, like a duchess, with her legs crossed at the ankles.

"Vixen," he said to himself. At some subconscious level, he was angry with her for whatever part she played in making him lose his composure. She smiled back with a steady gaze and it was obvious to Kaniz from her calm composure that his ordeal was not mutual. He was in his own private torture chamber alone.

"Same here Group Captain Ishaya," she said. She flashed that smile again and her eyes crinkled at the corners.

He straightened his uniform as he bowed slightly to his father and made for the door. Group Captain Ishaya was totally oblivious to the dashing figure he made to his audience in his navy-blue uniform, as his long legs moved him in his feline stride towards the door and exit.

Kaniz got into his car, a graphite Audi Q7 he had shipped into the country weeks ahead of his arrival in Lagos. He turned up the AC on to full blast and rested his head on the black leather back rest, his aviator sunglasses on, shielding his tortured eyes. Trying to collect his thoughts as he exhaled, his left hand flew to his scar and left brow instinctively.

He muttered his desperation to God. "Save me. What just happened in there? I can't come this far to fail now," he said. "Where were *You* when all that was happening to me in there?" What was that? Was it ten years of celibacy that was now beginning to toy with his mind? Well, if that was so, why hadn't he had the same problem with any other woman before now? Why her? He had certainly met *many* women as beautiful as her, but nothing like this had ever happened.

Perhaps she was fetish. He had heard about the voodoo some women prepared to ensure that they were irresistible. From what he heard, these women could add whatever specially concocted voodoo junk over which the names of their targets had been invoked to their kohl and line their eyes with it or add it to their powder and apply on their faces. So how did she know she was going to see him today? She had never met him or even heard of him and from what he had heard, the voodoo had to target a certain individual. So it was unlikely to be voodoo. She would have needed to customise the voodoo.

It wasn't lust he felt for her. He didn't want anything from her, nothing but her love. At this admission, his heart skipped a beat. He wanted to give to her instead. Give to her: his love, his attentive care, his protection, his possessions. Settled deep within him was a firm conviction that she belonged with him.

It was as if they had always been together and though for the last thirty-six years of his life they had been separated, they were now finally returning to each other. He felt instinctively protective towards her, like he was committed to making sure nothing should ever harm her. He wanted to help her fulfill her dreams. Whatever it took to stand by her, he was fully convinced in his spirit that he was ready to give.

Kaniz was baffled at his thoughts. He actually could countenance such far reaching decisions if he had arrived at those conclusions over a period of several months, but he couldn't understand how he reached such deeply rooted unshaking convictions in a matter of minutes.

He was no stranger to the opposite sex but, he had never had such an experience. He knew what to do. He would fast and pray. When he disciplined himself in that way, whatever was a product of a fevered imagination or the result of some weird hormonal surge would lift and even if it was an enchantment, he would be free. Whatever was left after prayer and fasting would be divine, and he prayed sincerely that this would just be a flash in the pan. He really didn't need the distraction.

"Lord set me free; this is just too strong for me."

He pressed the start button and eased his car out of the Mamane Group car park, lost in his thoughts and totally missing the excited security men who were saluting him vigorously.

Chapter Seven

"The heart is deceitful above all things,
and desperately wicked; who can know it?"

Jeremiah 17:9

Kaniz took a look at his flight log. At 10:00 hours he had a flight to Chad. This would be his second flight on that same route. He had received orders to fly this same trip some days into his new assignment. His mentor, AVM Woriabam, had personally hand-picked him for the assignment. The trip had been to pick up medical and emergency supplies for Internally Displaced People in the country. It was part of the air force's unofficial assistance to the congressional task force for IDP matters. Since commercial airliners didn't fly that route, the air force was stepping in to "assist" the politicians.

His brief stated that the medical supplies were from MedAid. From the labels and tags he had observed on the consignments, they came through a logistics outpost in Colombia. The organisation had a distribution centre in Chad and he supposed they chose that hub because there were so many conflict zones in that axis.

He strapped himself into the seat of the plane he was flying today, as he waited to be cleared for takeoff. Earlier, the engineering personnel had concluded their checks and the plane engine was running.

He expected an uneventful flight this Friday. The last time he had flown, it had taken him under three hours to arrive at the location in Chad. The airstrip where he was picking the consignment was in the desert in a remote and off-grid location, but with his experience, it had been easy enough to find. It crossed his mind though that his boss had chosen him to fly the mission because of the challenges of the location and the relatively short runway, just barely adequate for a plane of this specification. The consignment had been in ten sealed cartons. It had been a seamless operation and by 18:00 hours, he was back in Lagos.

On ground in Lagos, he had landed at the air force base and handed over the plane and its cargo to the personnel on ground. From the information he had gleaned, this flight of mercy had been running seamlessly for a few years, since internal conflict had led to a rise in IDPs all over the country. Kaniz's heart went out to them. He had also tasted what it meant to be uprooted from the comfort of hearth and home. If this flight could in some way alleviate their suffering, it was his honour to be chosen to fly.

At the thought of his rude flight from home almost two decades ago and the emotional reunion with his father, his heart was filled with a sense of overwhelming relief. Without a doubt, the troubled days were over.

But what was he to make of Morola? Was she a blessing or a curse? A gift or a massive distraction? Was she his destiny or was she going to make him miss destiny? He contemplated his internal conflict which was rather in dissonance to the striking clear blue horizon stretching before him endlessly. Days of fasting had not made his struggle better. In fact, he seemed to be getting worse.

He smiled as he thought of how he seemed to consider the "situation" with Morola a virulent malady. Thoughts of her had a way of creeping up on him in the most innocuous way, tiptoeing delicately into his mind. The painting of a child he saw yesterday reminded him of her intelligent brown eyes, the jet-black wings of the raven he saw that morning reminded him of her hair.

He shook his head – he was obsessed. "I have to focus," he thought. He had a flight ahead and this was a powerful machine. Kaniz smiled. This was his zone. He was finally free here, pain didn't follow him into the clouds, into this realm of endless peace. It was on land he had mourned, on land that he had been spurned, it was on land that danger threatened. Here in the air, all he had was joy. Here, he shed off the last vestiges of sorrow, and he found liberty. To hurt him, life had to get him back on the ground but every time he was airborne, he was unrestrained.

What would getting involved with her portend for the business at hand? The thought sneaked into his mind. They had all agreed that emotional entanglements were out of the question. There was a meeting this evening, but it was too early to bring Morola up, he still had to make absolutely sure he was right about her.

With over half of the flying time done, his route plan took him to the border between Nigeria and Chad. Soon, he made the crossing into Chadian and in under an hour, he prepared for landing.

The airstrip was a mere black ribbon between the sand dunes, but the sole runway was surprisingly well engineered as he had discovered on his first flight, and he had landed the plane by applying his skill and dexterity.

He made a decent landing and was soon taxiing along the runway. Finally, coming to a stop near a dusty 4 x 4 jeep, an old Land Rover with a trusty suspension. MedAid was emblazoned on the side of the vehicle. He had seen the branding last time but this time it appeared to be peeling.

If there was a piece of information that was key to a pilot's survival, it was the weather, and Kaniz knew the blazing hot sun was a constant here at 13:00 hours. His aviators served him well with this glaring sun. Pierre, Moussa and Ambani came out of one of the vehicles, two first dressed in jalabiya, complete with the ubiquitous tagiya. They were the same people who had brought and loaded the consignment the last time. Ambani, dressed in T-shirt and jeans, carried a machine gun always and Kaniz understood why the weapon was necessary. This was an area of tribal conflicts, with territories transitioning from warlord to warlord like the constant shifts of the sand dunes that dotted the landscape. Insurgents, armed militia and opportunistic bandits roamed freely and it was foolhardy to move without adequate security.

"Group Captain!" Pierre called out in accented English, a hand raised in salutation.

"Bonjour, Monsieur Pierre," Kaniz said. His French was not as good as his Spanish, but he conversed well enough in it.

The men responded amicably. Just like the other pick-up, there was oddly no documentation to be done. Kaniz simply opened the rear hatch to allow Pierre access to the cargo compartment.

It didn't take long to load most of the consignment. This was a cargo plane and it had been a while Kaniz had flown such a rudimentary machine; fighter jets were more his forte now. Just as the Pierre tried to fit the ninth box in, Ambani's eyes bulged as if they would pop out of his skull. He shouted and gesticulated wildly to the northeast of the airfield. Kaniz looked up and saw the cause of his alarm. Three pickup trucks not only crammed full of men but with some riding on the open flat bed at the back of the truck were driving towards them with clouds of dust billowing from their wheels. They made a truly menacing sight with their veiled faces.

"It's an attack," Moussa yelled in French. He took to his heels immediately and dived into the waiting vehicle. Pierre who had been the designated loader, dropped the last carton on the runway in a panic, rushing back into the 4x4. Ambani and Moussa had AK47s. The 4x4 was already in motion, Moussa was driving, while Pierre and Ambani rolled the car windows down and turned back towards the advancing enemy aimed in their general direction and let loose a hail of bullets. Kaniz, realising he was about to be killed by friendly fire, picked up the last box and threw it through the rear hatch like the others and it landed with a thump.

Kaniz closed the hatch and hurriedly climbed into the pilot's seat, adrenaline pumping in his veins. He started the engine. It looked like there were no guarantees of pleasant and uneventful flights for a combatant.

Kaniz increased his speed and as the plane sped down the runway, he realised that there were more mounted armed men riding towards the plane from the sand dunes. He had to take off before the truckloads of hostiles had him within shooting range.

On his immediate right, at the northeast of the strip, the leading pick-up truck was now clearly visible and standing on it was a man carrying an RPG launcher on his shoulders. Kaniz knew that if he did not get the plane into the air before the man took aim, the armed man would send that grenade flying into his aircraft.

He was going to have to risk a short takeoff on this already short runway because to attempt achieving a textbook takeoff was risking being blown to smithereens. He was not about to go down in enemy territory again, not after Darfur and not on a mission like this with no chance of rescue. Kaniz accelerated facing the hostiles, the gap between them closed till he thought he could see the whites of their eyes, mere slits in their ominous veiled visages. He executed the dangerous short take-off with just a foot or two above the heads of the hostiles, rocket launchers and all. He ascended quickly and when he was some distance away from the range of the rocket launcher and its scope, he made a turn and doubled back.

He flew above the airstrip. Dust billowed from the little airstrip, completely obliterating the engineered track he had just taken off from, but he soon made out the car from MedAid being driven at breakneck speed away from the area. The hostiles who had descended on them were still in close pursuit in their three trucks. Kaniz came from behind the hostiles and let loose the aircraft guns, he flew a sortie over the airstrip, there was no time to lock in sights and be accurate, he just needed to buy time for MedAid to get away.

The pursuers had stopped and he saw the slim dust cloud from the MedAid jeep continue to billow and rise in the distance as Pierre and his compatriots escaped their attackers. It was time to head home. It was a short flight and he was good for fuel but he didn't want to push his luck.

Kaniz let out a deep breath and instinctively carried out a check, the instrument panel okayed every system. It was an uneventful flight back home and when he landed in Lagos, the engineering crew joined him as he taxied the aircraft into the hangar. He disembarked, grateful to be on terra firma. He took a cursory glance at the plane, trying to confirm that he had not sustained a hit.

Kaniz saw that part of the fuselage had sustained some damage. Machine gun fire, no doubt. What interested him right now was a sight that he thought he had seen in a flash but had lodged in his subconscious. He opened the rear hatch to check the cargo.

The carton he had thrown in last was his objective and it was close to the hatch so he did not have to reach further into the cargo compartment. He lifted it and discovered that it had been punctured by a bullet, white powder trickling from it. Kaniz closed the hatch and walked away.

At the hangar, he finished off with the handover to the air force personnel, and he observed that the representatives of the task force who seemed eager to pick up their consignment were already waiting at the entrance of the hangar. He left them to their duties. He needed to file a report on the surprises today had thrown up.

Standing before Air Vice Marshal Ebiere Woriabam, Kaniz could not but reflect on the respect he had for the older officer and gentleman. A veteran air force officer, Woriabam had taken the young Kaniz under his wing in his early days in the force. AVM had been posted to Lagos just six months before Kaniz and had set about pulling the strings to get his mentee to follow. The younger officer was indeed grateful for the many opportunities his senior had given him, for the times AVM had looked out for him; as AVM had moved, he had opened doors for Kaniz too. AVM always replied the younger man's expression of gratitude in the same way always – "You deserve it Ishaya."

Group Captain Ishaya deserved the breaks he was being given. He never let him down. What more proof did he need that he had made the right judgment call with this young man? Kaniz deserved his current rank, which was six years above that of his former classmates in his set. In seriously hierarchical structures as the country's military, you moved with your set except in exceptional cases such as Kaniz's. AVM had gone out on a limb pushing for meritocracy to prevail in Kaniz's case.

The older officer, now in his late fifties, had no reason to date, to regret his support of his ward of fifteen years. Kaniz's loyalty was unquestionable, his gratitude oft expressed. His discretion and sense of judgment was stellar and his actions under intense pressure were impeccable. Today was yet another example of why he believed in his strategic thinking and discretionary judgment.

Woriabam leaned forward in his chair as he considered the younger man, elbows on his desk. "At ease, Group Captain Ishaya," he said in his characteristic brisk manner. "Please sit, sit. Well done, good thinking. We don't know the fall out of the engagement yet, we still lack clear intel on who the hostiles were but we could only have defended our allies and that you did, that you did, indeed."

"Thank you, sir," Kaniz responded. He was relieved his mentor approved. Helping those MedAid personnel get away seemed like the right step especially if they expected continual supplies. Dead men don't ferry supplies.

"Permission to speak, sir?"

"Permission granted."

"Do we have oversight of the chain of custody on these supplies we are shipping for the task force?"

"Kaniz, you are aware how political things have become in the country. Every contract awarded in any of the forces is superintended by the congressional task force on defence affairs in charge who take a percentage of the contract cost as shall we say, appreciation for doing absolutely nothing but getting out of the way."

Kaniz held back from expressing himself as instinct prodded him. A percentage? For doing nothing? Things were much worse than he thought.

"There are things we do for the politicians so they allow us go about our business of defending the country with minimum distraction and this is one of them. This arrangement is far above my pay grade and predated my arrival at this posting. I am following orders just as you are. The task force want us to help them freight supplies, we do so. Period."

They were all seated in Kaniz's living room. Paul had been given the night off as the business at hand demanded utmost secrecy. Kaniz's closest friend since childhood, Funso Ajayi, was one of the allies in this endeavour. They had met at FGC and had become friends from their first year. While Kaniz had departed for the US, Funso had chosen a career in the army. When Kaniz had returned home from his forced flight to the US, Funso had been the one to suggest that his friend join the air force because he had always known of his dream of studying aeronautic engineering. Kaniz had followed his friend's counsel and was forever grateful for the direction. Funso was now a well-loved and rising major in the army, working in army intelligence and directly with the Chief of Army Staff. His cordial relationship with his boss was well known and tacitly provided him some leverage. He had introduced Kaniz to Jude King, a long standing and trusted friend of Funso's and a major in army logistics who he had brought on board in this enterprise. Jude was pleasant and friendly and had a more than healthy opinion of himself and his capabilities.

Kola Toriola, Kaniz's own nominee to the Quartet, was a brilliant technocrat and a genius at strategy with vast experience. He was the only civilian amongst them and the eldest of the group. Kola was right up Kaniz's street. Kaniz knew they needed someone with a more robust outlook to issues to assist the Quartet in navigating the complexities of this business. He posited that while they were learning to fly and shoot, people like Kola were learning how to manouevre in the less structured and dynamic world outside the military. They certainly needed Kola, he brought a totally different perspective to things. Kola had proven his mettle over the years of preparation, even while Kaniz was in Bogota, laying the groundwork.

Since Kaniz knew he had a flight today and a meeting with his AVM directly after, he had proposed his partners meet in his house on the base tonight to eliminate any possibility of him getting stuck in the unpredictable traffic and being late.

In spite of the fact that they were indoors, they subconsciously spoke in low tones. Utmost secrecy had been their watchword since inception and even their personal lives were subsumed for this business.

"Our suppliers in the Muerte cartel are ready. All our specs are available - A Grade. I had concluded all arrangements before I left Bogota. All is ready, the only issue outstanding is getting the cargo out on our end when it arrives," Kaniz said. "Funso, any updates?"

"My guy in customs is set. But he is just waiting for mobilisation. You know how many desks and agencies they have in customs from the ship to the port gates?" Funso said.

"Funso! Customs? Customs? Of all the uniformed cadre in this country? No. We can't trust a customs man on this sensitive transaction, as soon as he discovers what we are moving he will hold us to ransom and become a bottomless pit, no amount of money would suffice for him, soon he would be demanding for a piece of the action. No," Jude said. "We can't trust a customs man."

"I agree with Jude. Also, this can't be handled by ship, Funso. It has to be by air. Sea freight is too long – though I see your point for wanting to go through the ports, the ports are as porous as a basket once you have the cash to settle."

"Kaniz, you are handling procurement," Jude said. "How do we guarantee our specifications are met?"

"Haba Jude. I know these guys. I was in Bogota for the last four years; these are the go-to people. It's all from Colombia via the Muerte," Kaniz said.

"And storage?" asked Kola.

"Jude and Funso have that covered," Kaniz said.

"I see that the gaping hole in the transaction is how to get the goods from Colombia here, cleared and intact. We have suppliers, we have storage. How do the goods actually get here and get cleared?" Kola asked.

Kaniz smiled for the first time that evening. "Leave that to me. In fact Funso, we will not be needing your customs guy."

Funso frowned. "Really, what are the alternatives?"

In a few sentences, Kaniz explained how he was bringing in the goods.

"My man!" Funso exclaimed. So we can now let the cartel know they are good to start shipping."

The meeting was concluded in less than an hour. The less time spent at Kaniz's place the less likely they were to arouse suspicion.

They were careful as they exited, watching their backs and not moving together. Kola drove to another friend's house on the base and spent some time with him simply to ensure the sentries at the base would not log him in as arriving or departing with Jude or Funso.

After the men had left and his house was quiet, Kaniz lay in the living room with a single lamp glowing. Soft instrumental music played. Home meant peace for Kaniz, a haven to retreat to after the battles of the day. A place to reflect, regroup and recuperate.

Since Tuesday afternoon's incident though, home seemed to lack something; it was no longer complete. He suddenly felt his loneliness in spite of the fact that he had always treasured his solitude.

"It is not good for man to be alone."

He banished the thought from his mind. "Not now," he said to himself. "I will deal with that later." He now reflected on the day, pondering on how a stress-free solution had been handed to him by the turn of events today. He had escaped death. The firefight played back in his mind. He revisited the danger lurking around that desert. Why had they no intel on the possibility of bandits attacking? Were they bandits or armed militia? What did it matter? Their bullets killed in exactly the same manner. Next time, he decided, I will conduct my own recce on the area before landing. He reflected again on the instability on the continent, just a result of lack of a critical mass of visionary leadership. The most endowed continent in terms of natural resources and yet the poorest. It just didn't add up, there was a missing factor and his blood boiled at the utter waste of such great potential across almost an entire continent.

His phone rang and jolted him out of his thoughts. The screen flashed and it was just a number showing. It was 23:00 hours, he knew who it would be. This was the call that he had been expecting.

"Hello."

A male voice spoke in Spanish on the other side of the line, Kaniz answered in the same language and then, the phone went dead.

Kaniz smiled. The goods had been shipped. They were in business.

Kaniz went through the flight roster for the week. "Ah. There it was in its usual slot." He was up for the usual flight to Chad in forty-eight hours, there was no time to lose making things ready expeditiously on this end. Kaniz immediately made a call to Jude.

In forty-eight hours, Kaniz was on his way to Chad. This time, he was flying a propeller plane, with a much bigger storage compartment. AVM Woriabam had said that the task force had increased their generosity to the

IDPs and from now on, the medical supplies were to be increased from ten to fifteen cartons. More space was needed.

On his approach to the airstrip, Kaniz conducted his reconnaissance and he ensured the coast was clear.

He positioned the plane for landing and within a short while, he had touched down. The MedAid vehicle was there already, its peeling logo now flapping carelessly in the wind, but no one seemed to care.

Pierre, Moussa and Ambani were glad to see him and immensely grateful for the air cover he had given them as they escaped on his last trip. A lot of francophone salutes followed with Kaniz being kissed on both cheeks by laughing, machinegun-toting men. It was a bit incongruous to say the least – guns and kisses.

Pierre and Ambani loaded the boxes into the plane this time. All the boxes were labeled similarly, out of Bogota, except five of the boxes which had a metallic binding and metal staples. Today was uneventful, a simple pick-up and Kaniz was airborne in no time.

Two hours into his flight time, Kaniz was almost in Lagos. He had it all planned and although he could not see them yet, he knew two of their men were already in the planned positions on his flight path.

This was the real crux of today's flight, so he descended to the point where the rooftops below had come into distant view. Then, he put the plane on autopilot and went to the mid-section of the plane. He had had the men in Chad stack the cartons in his preferred order. Kaniz looked down and under his boots was a trapdoor. He had been involved in missions where he had had to drop food supplies to refugees in Liberia, Congo and Darfur, so he knew the drill, but he had had support during those sorties. This time he needed all his experience because he was alone.

He went back to the cockpit and checked. He was almost there. This had to work. A lot was riding on the success of this mission and losing the goods in the shallow bogs below would be nothing short of disastrous.

Consulting the instrument panel, he saw he was about three minutes to commence the drop. He looked of a cockpit window and he could see the outline of a flat-bottomed boat in the swamp below. He stood over the trapdoor, checked his chronograph and then, opened the aperture. He threw out the first box. A red parachute blossomed like an odd mushroom as the box sailed down to water and landed with a splash. He threw out the second and third, until all five boxes had been offloaded, landing as close to the boat as he could make it. He saw the boat begin to move. That was good. The men were swiftly recovering the boxes which were bobbing on the surface of the swamp.

Moving swiftly, he shut the trapdoor and sat in the cockpit. Increasing the plane's altitude as fast as he safely could, as he resumed his flight path to base.

Once he landed, he followed the usual routine and handed the supplies over.

Kaniz made the call once he was in his car.

"Are all our guests at home?" he said to Jude.

"All five guests arrived safely."

Kaniz ended the call and sighed. All was well. Kaniz was relieved, there were so many uncertainties and variables that to have received those packages was an event worthy of celebration.

Chapter Eight

"A friend loveth at all times and a brother is born for adversity."

Proverbs 17:17

Amaka and Rola were seated on Rola's bed, cross-legged like tailors, as they had been doing from high school. In this bedroom some things just never changed. Amaka had always felt secure here. It was especially a haven these days with all she had been bottling up for the last five years boiling up within her. She was especially glad to have her best friend around with her not just today, but potentially for a whole year.

Amaka was wearing one of Rola's lounge T-shirts, one of her Lagos finds. Her own clothes hung on two hangers from a handle on one of Rola's wardrobe doors. Rola was in another lounge T-shirt. It was so comfortable that once she was done with her work and had showered, that was what she had put on and all she had worn all day, working from home till Amaka had arrived.

Rola suspected Amaka had an agenda, in the deliberate way she had insisted on coming straight to Rola's room, the venue of many a heart-to-heart talk. There was something up and Rola knew it would soon be made clear.

"The country is not our inheritance from our ancestors. It's a legacy we borrow from our children, we need to keep remembering this," Rola was saying. They had started a conversation when Amaka called earlier to say she was coming.

The Jos chapter of the Youth Council had procured a permit to march and protest the latest blatant act of corruption – several judges of the Federal

Court of Appeal had millions of dollars discovered in their houses, right after they had delivered yet another very controversial and unexpected verdict on an election. It seemed most of the last election results were being overturned and determined afresh. Three of the protesters had been shot in Jos – two were dead and the third was still in ICU, with his life hanging in the balance. The police claimed the shooting was an error.

"Honestly," Amaka said. "Unless the constitution is suspended, there's no chance of fixing the systemic issues this country has."

Rola contemplated her friend's statement. "It sounds anti-democratic, but you have a point. Take the bicameral system, I think its just a huge waste of money. Did 'they' not say that twenty-five per cent of our recurrent budget is spent running those two houses? Do we need two houses?"

"How about restructuring, Mo? Resource control, state police? And—"

Rola interrupted. "The issues are too many. We need to weaken the centre, make it completely unattractive. In my humble opinion, only a benevolent dictator can take us to the next level. We need more disciplined leaders who are sincerely concerned with the common wealth. The majority are out for sectional or personal interests. We need a servant leader who is ready to lay down his or her life if need be to get us to our goal."

"A servant leader like my friend who is taking youth service so seriously that she left her thriving business behind in New York to serve her country," Amaka said, shaking her head. "I still can't believe it Mo. Anyway, how far with arrangements?"

The call-up letter to serve in Lagos state was safely in hand, the three-week camp had started but Rola was allowed to be up to a week late and from what she heard about the facilities at the camp, she intended to be as late as was acceptable to the authorities. She would join them next Saturday.

"And will your primary posting be at Mamane Group? Have you decided?"

"Yes," Rola said, nodding with certainty. Tuesday's visit had been a clincher. From what she saw, she would get along with Debola, the MD of QuantumTech who was her direct boss. He had researched her thoroughly before she met him on that Tuesday and "was ready to provide her the most conducive working environment to facilitate her productivity in her time with them."

"He was nice Maccky. In fact, I couldn't help wondering if he had been specifically instructed to be nice to me."

After Kaniz had made his rather abrupt exit, Alhaji had brought in Debola who had taken her through the unit and also shown her her office and introduced her to her assistant, Tracy.

"Your what?"

"My assistant."

"Where does a youth corper have an assistant?"

"In the same place where the youth corper has a corner office with a view and a car and driver," Rola replied.

"A car and driver?" Amaka repeated.

Rola laughed. "Yes Amaka, you heard me right. Although I declined the car – it was another Toyota Prado – I accepted the offer of the driver. A driver is very useful in the traffic in this city, not a luxury at all. I should be able to read now or do something useful with my time while he navigates the traffic."

"Alhaji is just compensating you, Mo. So that's all you did for two hours? Tour your unit?"

"Hmm. The Chairman's secretary kept me waiting for thirty-seven minutes Amaka. I looked at the time. I got there at 12:55 p.m. and apparently, someone was with the Chairman, but she didn't even let him know I was around until he called to ask her at 1:32. I was looking at the time throughout." Rola uncrossed her legs and lay belly down on the bed. Her long legs were up in the air and her head, supported on her elbows, was cupped in both hands. Her cheeks were bunched up and her brow furrowed. She looked childlike and cute with her hair slicked back in a ponytail with a scrunchie.

"I know I won't be working with her, so it doesn't even matter, but I hate toxicity."

"I don't want you to jump to conclusions," Amaka said. "So who was with Alhaji? Perhaps it was a meeting that the Chairman had warned her not to disturb?"

"She was nasty Maccky dear, just nasty. You know I am not petty or sensitive like that. I was nice to her but she was nasty. For no discernible reason." Rola was genuinely disturbed. This was happening too often since she came back.

"Mo, when will you get used to the reaction you get from some women?" Amaka said.

Rola gasped. Mrs B had said almost the same exact words when she told her what Khadijat had done. She had been genuinely worried. She had been so polite to Hajiya Khadijat who on her own part had been inexplicably nasty.

Mrs B said, "She was protecting her turf, Rola."

"From what?" Rola asked.

Mrs B took Rola in front of her full-length mirror. Rola was still dressed in the black outfit with the emerald obi sash. She pointed to her daughter's reflection.

"From this."

"Ehen?" Rola shrugged.

"Can't you see it?"

"See what?"

Mrs B shook her head. "I have done you a great disservice Morolawe," her mum said. "I was trying to do the right thing but I may have failed you."

Rola was genuinely confused.

"What do you see?" Mrs B asked.

"Myself."

"And you look?"

"Okay, I guess."

"You don't look 'okay' Morolawe, you are beautiful, extremely attractive."

Rola's mouth dropped open. Her mum had never, ever, said any such thing to her.

"I didn't affirm you on the basis of your looks, because I could see I had an obviously beautiful daughter but I didn't want to raise her up to rely on her looks to get ahead."

Rola was staring at her mum. "Why?"

"Because your looks can get you *noticed* Morolawe but they can't deliver tangible value." She shook her head. "You have a blind spot to your looks.

If you could see yourself clearly Rola, you would understand why you have issues with some women."

Rola's face fell.

"Don't get me wrong, the majority probably grudgingly *admire* you but *resent* you. You are the girl with everything they wish they had. It's called *envy,* Morolawe. You are intelligent and beautiful and it's difficult to not envy people who have *both* intelligence and beauty. Wealth we can rationalise away. We can say the money was made through funny means or someone helped you and you didn't deserve it. Besides, at a deep level, we know money is not necessarily a determinant of worth so we can let that go. But intelligence and beauty?" She shook her head. "No one is forgiven for having that combination. Intelligence and beauty come from God. It means God Himself directly favoured you with *both* and no one ever admits to envying anyone for being intelligent *and* beautiful. You can admit to envying someone's wealth but admitting to envying their beauty or intelligence is saying, 'God obviously prefers you to me, why did He make you more intelligent and beautiful than I?'"

Rola's eyes were wide with realisation.

"I try so hard... to be polite... to get it right," she said. Her shoulders drooped.

"My poor darling, I should have prepared you for this. To make your case worse, you have made some money early in life."

"But Mum! I never talk about money or assets. No one but Amaka and my family knows how much DefenceWare sold for or—"

Her mum cut in and said gently, "I know! I know! You never boast Morolawe, but they can guess some of these things." She shook her head. "Morolawe, your success can make average people uncomfortable. To them you are the woman with everything. We hate the woman with everything in this society. It's worse here because some women have made landing a man their goal. So to those women, every beautiful woman is their rival and not their sister."

Mrs B pursed her lips. "In New York, it would have been better. Instead of seeing you as competition you would have been seen as an inspiration, the quintessential American dream. Here, you are an indictment on those who don't see how they can ever be like you."

That was the reason for the different reaction she got here, Rola thought.

"It's so bad that even if you were merely a character in a movie or book, most women would respect but *resent* your character. Only the truly confident and beautiful women who see themselves in you would like you. We like people who are like us. Morolawe, but how many people are like you?"

"So am I not relatable, Mrs B? I try..."

"Of course you are relatable sweetheart. It's nothing to do with you." She sighed. "People prefer the underdog because the underdog makes them feel good about *themselves*."

This made sense to Rola. That was why even when she was glaringly right, some people would still be on the side of the other party once they felt they didn't have as much going for them as she did. She was subconsciously being penalised for being blessed.

"There's a solution though," Mrs B said.

Rola ears perked up at her mum's words. There was a solution. Thank God.

"Fail woefully with Synergy and everything else, be daft, wear a mask, lose your figure and lose your lovely head of hair."

Rola stared at her, aghast.

"You can't do that?"

Rola gave her mum a look that said, "clearly not".

"Then, not being liked by those who decide to be intimidated by you – no matter how hard you try to please them – is the price for being so endowed. Live with it," Mrs B said with a tone of finality. "Pay the price."

Rola was quiet for a few seconds as a thought hit her.

"No wonder many women don't make it to leadership," she said. "Many people resent strong, capable, successful women."

"Oh, leadership? That's doable," Mrs B said. "Just don't be attractive or stylish and you *may* make it."

Rola laughed out loud.

"Seriously," Mrs B said. "It's an unconscious but entrenched bias. Cerebral and strong women are not meant to be beautiful or stylish. Beauty and style are for bimbos, dumb blondes."

Rola hadn't quite analysed it but on reflection it was true. Even the media pushed the stereotype. Beautiful women were not meant to be intelligent. Perhaps that was another reason she had never even considered herself beautiful. She was a geek. Beauty wasn't celebrated in her world. In fact, it was downright penalised. She remembered how VCs she was trying to pitch DefenceWare to always found it hard to believe she was the real creator of the app. They just never believed that this stylish, black woman was the brilliant geek. She didn't even know she had compounded issues by being gorgeous to boot.

"Do you see why you would have problems now Morolawe? No one knows that you also have *real* issues you battle daily, that you deal with *real* pain. And they will never know by God's grace!" Mrs B's interjected prayer erupted with fervency.

She continued in a conversational tone. "So to them, you have everything. You have a strong faith in God that gives you this air of confidence and an ethereal glow, you are a gorgeous, young, entrepreneurial nerd who loves her job. You have a distractingly striking figure, long lovely legs and a full head of hair." Mrs B shook her head. "Daughter – people like you should be *banned."*

At her mum's teasing but truthful analysis, Rola laughed so hard that she forgave Khadijat and her ilk. She was genuinely grateful for God's blessings she had been so oblivious to.

"Who was with Alhaji?" Amaka repeated, dragging her back to the present.

"Oh, his son."

"The boy? He didn't go to school?" Amaka raised her right brow.

"No, not Isa, it was Group Captain Ishaya. Kaniz Ishaya."

"Kaniz... I have never heard that name. Kaniz. Nice name. Alhaji's son is in the air force and not running his dad's companies? That's very curious. Rich northerners are usually not that independent at all. In fact, forget, northerners or not, upper class offspring anywhere in Africa don't go working outside *daddy's* conglomerate. Your dad would be that rich and you will turn your back on all that and join the air force? Group captain? How much can his salary be in a month? What would Mamane's son be doing with that type of chicken change? All the rigour? The training? There's something more to this story."

"The guy was a snob though, in fact, that's an understatement. He was rude. He walked out of having lunch with Alhaji and me. He just left us there. His dad was like... shocked!"

Amaka snapped her fingers and nodded knowingly. "Uhun! I said there was something. I want to meet this guy. He walked out on his dad? How?"

"That's their business. I quite like QuantumTech though and the MD is the person I will be reporting to."

"Rewind Mo. Rewind. Forget QuantumTech for a minute. Group captain? How old is he? He must be in his forties, late forties. My Uncle Emeka who was a wing commander was already a relic by the time he was made group captain."

"No o," Rola replied. "He is not forty o. His father said he is the youngest group captain in the history of the air force and actually, he just got back from being defence attaché."

Amaka let out a peal of laughter. "Defence attaché. Girlfriend! The guy is a spy. Ehen," she nodded, "I said something was fishy." She leaned forward smiling conspiratorially. "Don't tell me, he went to school in America, right?"

Rola just loved Amaka, with her drama and all. She could only nod in agreement wondering what theories her friend was now concocting.

She winked at Rola. "Don't worry Mo, you don't get it yet. I am sure he is fine, if he looks like the father you described. He must be..." she formed a circle with the thumb and first finger of her right hand with the other fingers pointed in the air in the universal symbol meaning perfect and smacked her lips.

Rola cast her a sideways glance.

"That's his business Amaka, fine or ugly. Rudeness is such a huge turn-off. Arrogant, spoilt rich boy. He didn't smile once, not even once."

"Rola, you really don't have sufficient evidence to substantiate these allegations and your reaction is excessively out of proportion," she thought. For once, she wished she wasn't so rational and she almost snapped out loud at herself, "Shut up, Rola."

"Mo, that indictment doesn't make sense if he is in the air force. The type of training those people go through... this isn't a typical spoilt rich boy o. Besides, what type of men don't 'turn you off'? Men like Tim? That guy has been hanging in the friend zone for how long? When poor Tega crushed on you for how many years and you made him your BFF, he got frustrated and moved on and now he is getting married to Jolomi. And Steve is still there waiting o. He too is your friend, right? Mo, these guys don't want to be your friend. Wake up."

Rola frowned. She didn't like Amaka's joke at all. These guys were really good friends. Men made the best friends, beef-free, and reliable and they could change a flat tire in fifteen minutes.

"Amaka you should stop pulling my legs on this Tega matter. He is my good friend. That's all. I don't like this joke at all. Jolomi may get to hear it one day and believe it. It's not funny. And I am fine, I am not complaining, marriage is so over-rated, most married people I know are so miserable."

Amaka's mood shifted with those words.

"Marriage is over-rated," she repeated slowly to herself in a low flat voice. "Married people are miserable." Her face crumpled and she buried her face in her hands as silent sobs shook her frame.

Rola was confused. Her eyes widened and her mouth dropped open as she sprang up from her prone position. She grabbed her dear friend's forearms like a confused toddler does when trying to console another toddler, all the while doing their best to pry the hands off their friend's face and uncover their eyes as if once they can actually see their friend's eyes, their friend's distress would cease.

"Amaka..." she said in a low imploring voice. "Amaka now, stop this." She sat by her friend on the bed and put her right arm around her.

"And there's no one to talk to," she muttered. "No one will believe me; I am trapped."

"I am here now Amaka. How can you even say that?"

Amaka snorted. "The pastors say good wives don't talk about their husbands to *anyone*."

Which husband was causing these tears? Femi? The paragon of virtue? Femi and Amaka were poster kids for marriage – at least Femi was, she corrected herself. Femi was the model husband: romantic, attentive, she knew how many times he had been made an example to other husbands in their circle. "I just wish Emeka could be more like Femi," someone would say. "Emeka didn't send me anything on Valentine's Day," and Amaka would smile modestly and even as she sat in a sea of roses, cakes, a teddy bear and the biggest cards available in Lagos. She would say like a wise sage, "Each marriage is unique," or words to that effect. No, Femi was cool. It was her friend, Amaka, who was the unromantic "gangsta", who just seemed to always be so pragmatic. Her head was full of work and money. So, what could Amaka possibly say was happening with Femi? It must be a rumour monger, a hater, a gossip who has been feeding her friend lies.

"I feel so unloved," Amaka said.

It was all Rola could do to keep quiet. Unloved? Unloved by Femi or was there another husband Amaka had in secret? The cake Femi bought Amaka for her last birthday was still fresh in Rola's memory – a confection of vanilla with salted caramel decorated in peach, white and gold by no less than Salt Lagos. "My heart, life with U is bliss," the cake had stated.

"They said a good woman keeps quiet," Amaka said, sobbing out loud. "I have been quiet o but I am now fed up. Femi plays out his "love" in public and deals with me in secret. No one would ever believe what he is really like, so what's the use talking?" she wailed. "Who do I talk to who won't make fun of me? Who do I talk to who won't say, 'ehen so it was all just fake, she is sad like us too.'"

"What is going on?" Rola asked.

"I feel so unloved and rejected, Mo. That day I called you five times, that day, I was crying?"

Rola nodded.

"I wanted to leave him that day. Femi is the stingiest, most miserly human being I have ever seen. He would never contribute to anything that is not his own idea. When I say anything, I mean anything. Gifts for my family? No. Investments? No. My car? Not a dime, not a single farthing." She snorted. "And it's not just me he treats this way. My parents? If he would only treat them well so they wouldn't know what's happening, but no. We have been married almost five years and he is yet to give my parents one loaf of bread." She was crying again. "And yet, any time I see his parents, I ensure I give them something!" Now the tears were pouring as if Amaka's heart would break.

Rola's mouth dropped open. Amaka's parents too were victims of Femi's stinginess?

"What game is Femi playing at? How about the teddy bears and cakes I see on your IG page?" Rola said.

"Platitudes and birthday wishes don't cost much," Amaka responded. "Teddy bears and flowers are cheap compared to a wife's real-life needs. So perhaps he does all the showy cheap stuff so when I tell you the truth on a day like this, you will stare at me in disbelief just as you are doing now."

Rola shook her head but couldn't say a word.

"If I try to insist that he should do more, a lecture about the materialistic Igbo tradition will follow and he always says that he doesn't have the money anyway. So what then should I do? Sell his official car?"

Rola was nonplussed. For Amaka's sake, she now wished she could have spent more time in Lagos in the past few years. No wonder Amaka never liked Femi's public displays of affection! No wonder she always seemed irritated when he tried to touch her in public! It was because she wanted real love and not the shallow "teddy-bear-cake-kisses-and-hugs" love. This was it again, this was Rola's issue. Was there any real love anywhere?

"So why won't I feel unloved? Femi can never just travel or go out and come across something nice and buy for me. I mean never."

Rola's heart broke for her friend and she hugged her tighter. As close as she was to Amaka, Amaka had hidden this well. She recalled how Femi would jump to Amaka's side and open the passenger door. The huge photo of Amaka in his office. Was he sadistic? What mind-bending torture was her friend living with? Like Rola, Amaka was also a generous person. If Femi was really like Amaka was saying, then it would be a real nightmare for Amaka, one of the toughest vices in a husband she could ever have to deal with.

"You never said anything," Rola said.

"Mo, I thought he would change and that I should be patient and cope with this myself. You are there for me for everything in every way – emotionally, financially, when I started my business, the wedding... always. Besides, I didn't want to comfirm your worst fears about marriage. The most unthinkable things that society can ever imagine a woman doing, those are the things he has left me alone to do. No insult my uncles and aunties heap on him because of money can make him feel ashamed, he just holds on to his money and refuses to let go. I have been insulted in the family over obligations he has left unmet and came back home to tell him but," she shrugged, "he just refuses to release the money. So when shame wants to kill me, I will go out, hustle and look for the money and do what he should be doing. Femi has put me in a position that demands that I must always be liquid. I work with clients I would rather not work with because I have no choice. Now I am beginning to resent my work because I am chained to it. How does a man just say 'I don't have' and not care how the needs are met? 'I don't have. I don't have.'"

Rola was perplexed, Amaka was beside herself and she had never seen her like this, so heartbroken, so despondent. Where to start? What to say? Femi? Femi who was all over Amaka. The cool guy who never raised his voice? The one everyone loved? Femi the gentleman? This is why one just could not trust any man. This was the genesis of all those incredible crime stories about women with seemingly perfect husbands who suddenly snapped. Rola sighed. It now seemed men had the uncanny ability to be nice and wicked at the same time and when your husband had the perfect reputation like Femi had and was putting you through emotional and mental abuse, no one would believe you. Rola wondered how many women were suffering silently like Amaka was; emotionally abused women married to "Mr. Perfect".

"Why don't you talk to your in-laws about this matter?" Rola said.

Amaka laughed. "Which one of them? Which one of them should I talk to? Is it the one who said when he wants to save money, eeeeehhh," she clapped her hands, "not that he doesn't have money o, he just wants to save what he has, he said he makes eba and instead of cooking soup to eat the eba with, he eats the eba with toothpaste?"

Rola's eyes widened. "Eewo," she said, her hands flying to her head instinctively. "Toothpaste? Why toothpaste now?"

At Rola's use of the Igbo exclamation, Amaka laughed in spite of herself. "Are you now Igbo, Mo?" Her laughter lifted her mood a bit.

"Why toothpaste? Toothpaste is cheaper than soup *nau* and it has a minty taste so the eba wont be 'unaccompanied'. Femi is even better than them." She let out a loud hiss.

Rola was bewildered. "So they are all like that?"

"Hmm. Or perhaps I should report to his father who when Femi was a child made him retrieve from the trash can the leftover eba from his lunch that he threw away and eat it?" Amaka shook her head. "All o," Amaka said. "I have heard horror stories. They are all like that."

Rola laughed. "It's a lie! It's definitely not true."

Amaka's expression made it crystal clear it was completely true.

Rola relented and said seriously, "It's his background then."

"Don't tell me that! Yes, it's his background but don't I also have a background? If your background is defective in an area, drop it and embrace the truth of the Word in that area. We all move beyond our backgrounds. If clinging to your background is destroying your marriage, then let it go. Is your background your god?"

"I could never have guessed," Rola said sadly, her heart breaking for her friend. "So what then does he do with his money? He has a good job."

"Ask him Mo, because I certainly don't know. But I know he won't get involved in whatever I do for us both. Then he does stuff in his name alone. Perhaps that's what he is saving all his money for, *his own*. He is driving me insane. I don't trust him anymore." She was wailing again. "When I find out what he has bought in his name, it's just so devastating, what about me? Why did I buy land in both our names? Property? Stocks? I too have stopped o, since he saves his own money for investments solely in his own name."

She turned to face Rola. "Oh did I tell you he has a joint account in both our names?"

Rola was now confused, this wasn't the action of a stingy man, a stingy man didn't maintain joint accounts in both names.

"Yes, he has the joint account," Amaka said. "But you can never know his online password, never see his cheque book with your two eyes. I don't even know where the cheque book is stowed." She sighed. "I feel so unloved. I am married to a man who will not share anything of value with me."

Rola's fears were rapidly being confirmed all over again. Amaka was not quite done yet because she had so much pent up within her.

"This stinginess is in big and small matters – even common taxi fare. Do you know how many times we would be in a taxi abroad and he would say, 'Amaka pay now, I am sitting on my wallet.' One day, after paying the taxi fare again and again, I understood finally and I told the driver to park well and I told Femi, 'We will all wait for you. Lift your backside up and I will pull out your wallet for you." She rolled her eyes and hissed. "Rubbish."

Rola smiled at the image this conjured.

"Why did I marry him? I have asked myself again and again. He never gave me anything meaningful while we were courting. All the gifts were from me to him, but I didn't really notice. I thought, here's a good Christian not asking me to fornicate. I didn't know the half of it."

"I didn't know this was what it was that day. I thought you were sad, perhaps because of waiting for the children to come," Rola said.

Amaka laughed. "Have children for Femi?" She shook her head vigorously. "Nah. Something needs to change first. Or else, heat will kill the babies. There is a limit to the electricity bill he can cope with. Go beyond what he has assigned to you and he will switch off the air conditioners and turn on the fans. That day last week, the day I was calling you, the heat made me sick, Mo. I was physically sick and yet, it was still 'I love you' all the way. Hugging and pecking me while we were both covered in sweat, with the ACs still off. Saving electricity," she muttered. "Yet, who does his mum thank when I hand over a gift from both of us, a gift that I bought with my own money? Who does the pastor thank when I hand over our Christmas gift?"

Rola was deeply saddened. What then were all Femi's "I love yous" to Amaka about? Love in word only? She knew it! Men could not be trusted.

Amaka sighed. "It's not even about the money, Mo. If I have the money,

I don't mind spending it on us both. It's that he is selfish. He doesn't share what he has, no matter what I am going through trying to get by. It's the tragedy of being married and feeling so alone. I am a single married woman." Amaka was distraught.

Rola felt her heart sinking and the old fears suffocating her. Just when she had thought perhaps, she had an example in Amaka and Femi that perhaps, just maybe men could be trusted to really love like they professed to, here was the evidence again that marriage was a farce. "The best one can have of a man is a platonic relationship," Rola thought. "Once that 'love' matter enters the equation, all the men want to do is exploit."

This is why she kept guys in the friend zone; they were at their best there. "What is the difference between a man who is my friend and one who claims to 'love me'? Is it not just that the 'I love you guy' is after my *body*? While my friend genuinely cares and is happy to relate to the essence of me. Is my friend's affection not a more authentic love?" she thought. She didn't trust any man alive. Any man, no exceptions. They couldn't keep a simple vow to love "until death do us part", so why even make the promise?

Almost all the fellowships and seminars in church were for women, teaching them to be better wives. Where were those teaching men like Femi what real love means? That love desires the best for the loved one? It was always the woman who had to try harder. She thought of what Mrs B went through for decades, all the tears and agony, first hiding it all from Rola until it was too obvious to hide, and now her dearest Amaka too? Amaka, the singular happy married woman she had thought she knew in a sea of patched up unions on live support.

Rola's memory had been seared forever by what she had told no living being, what she could not have told even her mother. Now, just when she thought there was hope, her friend's perfect marriage was just another tragic illusion. When men were your friends you couldn't ask for better friends but when they became a "lover" the games, the selfishness and deceit started. That is why she had never trusted any man enough to let him be her "lover".

Justifications of faith aside, she could simply never trust a man that much. Celibacy wasn't a struggle for her, it was a safe fortress. Never. "No man would ever make me go through this pain," Rola vowed silently.

The knock on the door interrupted their discussion. Amaka quickly turned her face away from the door as Aunty Wunmi put her head through it. "You have visitors," she said to Rola.

"Who?" Rola replied.

"Isa and *Kanis*."

"Really? He referred to himself simply as Kaniz?" Rola turned to Amaka. "Are we up to seeing them, Amaka?" If Amaka didn't want to let her go, she would stay behind and ask Aunty Wunmi to let them know she was indisposed.

Amaka sniffed and nodded. "I will come down later. Let me freshen up a bit."

Rola started to get up, but first, she gave her friend the longest possible bear hug. "Take your time Maccky, don't rush. I will be done with them soon anyway."

Chapter Nine

"There are many devices in a man's heart; nevertheless the counsel of the Lord, that shall stand."

Proverbs 19:21

Rola made her way downstairs into the living room. She had simply paired her lounge T-shirt with a pair of black Hermes Oasis sandals. If Amaka had been in a good mood, her friend would have insisted that she put on some powder and nude lip shimmer at least. She could hear the guests speaking in the anteroom to her left, Group Captain Ishaya's rich baritone and Isa's voice in conversation. They were speaking Hausa and Kaniz Ishaya was saying something that was making Isa laugh. Rola smiled at the delightful sound. Isa's laughter was infectious.

As for "The Duke", so he could be funny? She snorted. She entered the living room and Mrs B was seated, watching TV. She wasn't looking like she was prepared to leave. *Just as well*. Rola wasn't really looking forward to hosting the snob. Mrs B's presence in the living room was strange though because since Rola was a teenager, after receiving Rola's guests or looking in, Mrs B would normally leave to give Rola some privacy after mouthing a suitable excuse. She would however make sure she made conversation with the guest and feel them out first. It was an informal interview that every one of Rola or Olaotan's guests went through and the ritual had served Mrs B and her scions well. However, as Rola graduated, Mrs B had gently eased out of the ritual for Rola. So why was she now firmly ensconced in the winged back sofa in front of the TV, pretending to watch a documentary on gorillas? *Gorillas? Really?* Rola chuckled.

Aunty Wunmi had been monitoring Rola's descent and as soon as she saw Rola was in the living room, she led the guests into the room. Rola chose a seat away from her mum and settled in. Kaniz came in, followed by Isa and on seeing Mrs B where she sat, he immediately went into a steep stoop, his right hand touching the floor.

"Good evening, ma'am."

Isa nodded in Mrs B's direction and mouthed, "Good evening ma'am." He appeared uncomfortable, probably just shy. The surprise on Mrs B's face as all six feet and five inches of Kaniz Ishaya transformed from a vertical stance to almost horizontal was palpable. She almost sprang off her seat to stop him from stooping.

Amaka had tidied up her face and watched the drama from the open doorway. Even in civvies, Group Captain Ishaya cut a dashing figure. Dark, perhaps a bit too dark in her estimation, crew cut, clean-shaven with the faintest dark fuzz of a moustache above a perfect mouth, keen intelligent eyes, chiselled features, broad forehead. Something about his eyes spoke about integrity and at the same time warmth. She stepped into the room and took a better look as he rose to his full height and she added "tall, perfect build" to her description.

"Ah! What kind of errant scar is this, not even afraid to venture on such a distinguished face?" she thought as she saw the scar. The scar on his left brow and temple was prominent but somehow it didn't succeed in marring Kaniz's features. "God loves this man" Amaka thought. "One more centimetre and his left eye would have gone."

He was dressed in beige chinos and a pale peach shirt with the subtlest hint of a jacquard print. The fabric looked soft but crisp with a muted sheen. Amaka strained to glimpse the logo on the shirt. *Girl you need to wear your glasses in times like this*. What was it? From the fit, it was definitely custom-made. Something from Hong Kong? His shoes were very dark chocolate Margielas. Very subtle. You had to know to know. Just the right balance between casual and formal. How much was a group captain's salary again? She cracked her brain? 350k? About $1000? This is daddy's money at work. She couldn't help it, so she glanced out of the window to look at his car, but it was parked out of view. No problem. That will be sorted later. "I will simply insist that we must see him off," she thought.

"You have both met my mother, haven't you, Group Captain Ishaya and Isa?" she said the "Isa" more like a question since Isa had never really been formally introduced to her. "My good friend Amaka," she said as she turned to Kaniz.

As she gazed at Kaniz, Amaka suddenly felt she should have worn something else, perhaps just made more of an effort. She was happy she had kept her wig on, all twenty-four inches of this coloured straight hair with auburn tips. She subconsciously smoothed down her borrowed T-shirt with both hands and extended her right hand towards Kaniz. His handshake was firm but gentle as he said calmly with one eyebrow raised, "Delighted." He actually sounded as if he meant it. The man would make a good politician. He was just so instantly credible when he spoke.

"Sit. Please take a seat," Mrs B said.

Kaniz moved towards Mrs B's sofa and took a seat with Isa, plumb where his dad had sat when he visited them. Rola had no choice than to join them on her mother's side of the room and Amaka sat on an ottoman on the fringes of the seating arrangement.

Kaniz gave Isa an undecipherable look and Isa stuttered and launched into a speech.

"Thank you very much," he said to Rola. "I was told all you did for me. My dad said I would have died if you hadn't helped me. I am really so grateful." Another quick look from Kaniz and Isa added, "Ma'am."

Rola felt so much compassion for the young man, she almost got up to hug him. "Isa, anyone would have done what we did that day. We just happened to be the ones." Her closeness with Olaotan made her good with younger people. She noticed he was still ill at ease and asked some "what class are you in?" type of questions to break the ice. Isa answered politely and she noticed that Kaniz didn't interrupt him once or even interject with an elaboration.

Isa and Rola soon sorted out what help Isa needed academically. Isa would be introduced to Olaotan's Physics and Further Maths tutors and on the days that there was a clash and the tutors couldn't make the time to teach both young men separately, the tutors would take them together at the time they normally worked with Olaotan.

At that moment Olaotan strolled in.

"Group Captain Ishaya, Isa, my brother Olaotan."

Olaotan stooped in greeting. "Good evening, sir," he said to Kaniz. He straightened and said "Hi" to Isa.

It wasn't possible to miss the fact that Olaotan and Isa were both wearing "Palace" T-shirts.

"Man I queued two hours in SoHo for this T-shirt and that was because I got there early," Olaotan said, pointing to Isa's turquoise T-shirt.

"Mine was resold to me. I paid double," Isa said. Everyone else was quiet as the two boys continued talking and soon, Olaotan and Isa made their way to the adjacent private living room. It was too early in the Bolade family protocol for Isa to be ushered up to the den or living room on the first floor. Amaka heard them mention something about FIFA 19 or some other game.

As Isa got up to leave with Olaotan, Amaka had a good look at him for the first time. Kaniz had completely distracted her from really seeing the younger Isa when she first saw them both. The seventeen-year-old looked more like fifteen. He was lithe, not as tall as Olaotan, frail, cute and from his fair skin and frailty, one could tell Isa had not taken after the father Mo had described.

Mrs B and Kaniz were getting along like a house on fire, moving from one topic to the other like old friends. Mrs B turned to Rola with a frown and very unlike herself, when a visitor was around, spoke in her native Yoruba to Rola in a mildly berating tone.

"Why are you being like this? Won't you offer the guest something?"

"Ah, Aunty Wunmi offered us something but we had just eaten before we came, so we told her not to worry and she was very insistent, ma," Kaniz said in flawless Yoruba before Rola could answer.

Mrs B's mouth fell open. "How?" The question was on the tip of her tongue, but she restrained herself, silently thanking her stars that she hadn't said anything more indiscreet. With that interjection in Yoruba, from then on, Kaniz and Mrs B conducted their conversation in a mixture of Yoruba and English.

Amaka's phone rang. It was Mama C, her mother. When both families had become, close referring to their mothers as "mum" or "mummy" was beginning to cause confusion, so christening Mrs Bolade "Mrs B", Mrs Chidozie "Mama C" sorted the mums out. For the dads, "TK", which had always been Mr Bolade's alias crafted after his name Timothy Kolawole and "Papa C" for Mr Chidozie worked. Thus the problem was solved.

"Mama C," Amaka said, by way of a greeting as she picked up the call.

Amaka felt safe conducting her conversation in the living room. Mrs B and Kaniz were engrossed in their conversation and Rola looked neither here nor there. She lowered her voice a bit so she wouldn't disturb the main conversation. Mama C wanted to know why Amaka had been crying on the phone on their last call.

"Mama C, I really can't talk now," Amaka said switching to Igbo. "I am at my second mummy's house and we have a guest."

Mama C's Igbo wasn't very good. She was a Benin woman but she understood enough to follow Amaka's fluent Igbo.

"Mama C, maybe this time, your daughter has finally met someone who won't be another male friend. All the prospective husbands, your daughter has rechristened friends, Tim, Steve, Tega, I am even tired of counting."

Mama C gave a reply and Amaka paused, listening.

"Mama C! If you see this guy? Tall, handsome, he has a scar but that just makes him finer. He is dark sha but its ok. His dressing is exquisite! Flat stomach, see his biceps," she tried not to look at his arms as she spoke.

She paused again. "Yes, I am married now but am I blind?" She rolled her eyes. "Abeg, abeg, abeg! Mama C, I am appreciating God's work."

Another pause. "Mama C, the only problem is that he is not a Christian. There is something spiritual about this guy but coming from his family, he can't be a Christian."

She listened as her mother went on for over a minute. "No o. Your daughter doesn't like him at all, she says he is snobbish, arrogant and rude, but I can't seem to see all that yet. This man seems humble but he too doesn't smile enough. So he looks like a snob. He just said his late mum was from your daughter's 'side' and from what I see, he is really well brought up. If you see how he prostrated to greet my second mummy, now they are gisting like BFFs. Your daughter is just ignoring them." She paused. "Mama C, this man set o. They will make a dashing couple. I need to order their wedding *aso ebi* now, before the rush starts!" She smiled. "But Mama C, there's trouble o, in fact a major matter."

She paused to listen to Mama C and then continued. "If these two darkies marry and there's a power cut, you will need a torch to find their children!" She laughed again, this time loud enough to draw everyone's attention and they all cast her a glance.

"Mama C. I am being rude. Let me call you later, okay? Talk to you later, bye," she concluded in English. "Mama C said to say hi to you both," she said to Rola and Mrs B.

Kaniz moved slightly forward and sat on the edge of the seat in a gesture everyone understood to mean "I am counting down to my departure." He had taken some water on Mrs B's insistence. Mrs B had motioned to Aunty Wunmi with hand signals Amaka knew meant she should pack some food for their guests.

Isa was torn away from his FIFA 19 and summoned from the private living room with Olaotan in tow. Aunty Wunmi materialised with a package in hand. Mrs B motioned to her to hand the well-presented pack to Kaniz.

"It's guinea fowl but its prepared as halal," Mrs B said to Kaniz as she motioned to Aunty Wunmi to hand it to him. Kaniz smiled almost imperceptibly.

"It's alright ma, all I need to do to sanctify this nice meal is to give thanks for it," he said as he accepted the package with a "thank you Aunty Wunmi", directing a special edition smile to her.

Amaka watched as Mrs B's eyes widened at the coded message Kaniz passed as he accepted the meal. She knew her second mummy well enough to know she wanted to put Kaniz at ease and let him know he could freely eat the food without breaching the dietary restrictions of his faith and they had all assumed he practiced his father's faith.

Amaka's hand flew to her phone to give Mama C the news, then she remembered they still had company. She would have to escape to the anteroom or even upstairs for this call because she needed to jump and shout. As she stood up to leave, Rola pulled on Amaka's hand dragging her back so she could join her to see Kaniz and Isa off. Olaotan didn't need an invitation as he had headed out with Isa already.

The sun was setting and the clear sky glowed orange emblazoned with streaks of indigo, lilac and purple. This was a typical Lagos sunset and if not for the humidity, Rola would be too glad to spend her evenings outside. "This certainly beats New York in February," Rola thought. She breathed in the smells of the garden. Something told her she was at the right place at the right time and she couldn't kick the feeling that an incredible adventure was around the corner. Was she going to start a new business here at home? She would just have to wait to see what was in store.

Kaniz turned to her as they got to his car. The ladies and Kaniz were on the driver's side and Isa was on the passenger side talking to Olaotan.

"Thanks so much once more for all you have done for Isa." He was looking deep into Rola's eyes, with an unguarded gaze. "I apologise for having to leave so abruptly on Tuesday. I hope you will let me redeem myself soon. Lunch? Or dinner?"

Rola was stone-faced. Sometime soon? He had to let that drop without pursuing it. The fleeting micro-expression on her face told him it was a distasteful notion to her.

"May I never be that hungry that I need to eat a meal with you," Rola thought. Out loud though, she said, "It's alright Group Captain Ishaya. Never mind about making amends. No apologies needed." She smiled, but it was clear it was a "no!"

"That was knocked right out of the park," Kaniz thought. His calculations had been off. He was pretty sure that with the audience they had, she would agree to at least lunch so she wouldn't seem unpleasant. She was very pleasant about her refusal though. He knew her smile wasn't legit. She just needed him to leave, and so, she was being polite. His heart fell.

Deep inside him, he knew that he wasn't going to give up. The several days of fasting had only exacerbated the situation and he was now more convinced than ever she belonged with him. "Please make a way," he prayed in his heart. Here she was with her BFF bodyguard, Amaka, along with Isa and Olaotan, a whole squad. What more could he say with this audience listening? How could he get her attention? If only he had handled things better on that Tuesday. He had actually prayed for clarity as to why there had been so much drama going on inside him.

"If I didn't call your attention to her so dramatically," the answer came, *"you wouldn't even notice her. You had shut your heart to love and had decided against marriage. How else could I wake you up?"* It was true, these feelings were so unwelcome that he had prayed fervently for hours daily since that Tuesday. Even today he had just broken his fast before coming to the Bolades'.

While fasting and fighting the deep attraction, he would suddenly be surprised to find himself praying for Morola, for her joy, that she might be all she was born to be. He prayed that she would find the right person for her destiny. He was prepared to let her go if there was someone else who would be better for her than he. He knew his burden. He knew the challenge being with him would pose, but he was rapidly and irrevocably falling in love with her. From her social media footprint, her faith was evident and her bold stance of faith only made him respect her more.

He got into the car as Isa and Olaotan said their goodbyes; they had apparently made their own independent plans to catch up. After he had prayed this much and still met a rebuttal, not a chink in her armour, Kaniz was rethinking his position. He was unfamiliar with this. He had never needed to stretch at all to get a woman, so Morola's stance was a complete aberration he wasn't sure he could accommodate. The answer came unbidden: *"This is not 'getting a woman'. Destiny is at stake here."*

With the business he had at hand, he sincerely couldn't afford the distraction. He just could not. So if she was going to be aloof, it was all for the best. No matter how ardent these feelings were, once they weren't reciprocated, it was only logical that they would die out in time. Even if it took years, one day, he would be free. As he thought about his freedom from Morola's "spell", his heart sank and he spoke to his heart under his breath, "Get in line."

As he maneuvered a three-point turn, positioning his car to exit from the front gate, he stopped. Amaka was several steps behind Rola conversing on her phone. She had dialled her mum as soon as she turned around and started walking back into the house with her friend, stepping back a bit as she slowed down to use her phone. Rola had stepped inside the house and was out of sight.

"*Nwanne*," Kaniz called. Amaka heard the deep baritone and turned around immediately, surprised that he called out in accent-free Igbo. She rallied quickly. Anyway, that's easy. "Almost everyone knows the meaning of *nwanne*," she thought as she walked towards him, rounding up her call with Mama C.

Kaniz stepped out of the car patiently waiting for her. She got to him and waited for him to speak. Her hands flew to her chest and she clutched both hands upon her chest as he began to speak flawless Igbo. Calamity! The man speaks Igbo? But how? He speaks Hausa and he spoke Yoruba indoors just now, and the very fact that he spoke Yoruba was sufficient to convince her that he couldn't possibly understand Igbo too. Who could speak all three major languages? How much had he heard her say to Mama C on the phone?

Kaniz had a sincere expression on his face as he spoke to Amaka. He decided to speak in Igbo because Isa could not be allowed to hear what he was saying, if not, he wouldn't have thought it necessary to reveal that he spoke Igbo.

"My sister, I am sorry I had to call you that way. Thank you for answering me. I wanted to let you know why I am here and that I may be departing for a while this evening, but I am certainly not leaving. I have good intentions towards your younger sister."

Amaka was won over at the first sentence. He had called Mo her sister, her younger sister and not just her friend. He could tell how close their bond was?

At that moment, Rola turned back to talk to Amaka and she didn't see her friend behind her. As she peeped through the windows in the entrance hall, she was partially hidden by the burglar bars and the wisteria in front of the window. What was Kaniz saying to Amaka to make Amaka gaze up at him like that? What was wrong with this guy? Was he now chatting up a married woman? With her friend so vulnerable in her marriage at this time? Rola was getting uncomfortable. "Amaka! Please be careful!" she silently prayed. This was the type of guy who had all the arsenal he needed to prey on vulnerable women. She proceeded to her room, waiting for Amaka to come up.

"I have good intentions," Kaniz said. "Don't think I am being presumptuous but if she will have me, I want to make Morola my bride."

Amaka gulped. Something about his words were just so authentic and said with such conviction.

"You are a married woman, my sister. So I will be open with you. I don't want to take advantage of her in any way. I have made plans already to take care of my wife. I know she is doing very well and I am convinced she will do even better. Whatever heights she aspires to, I am ready to support her. I will be right there by her side. I have been working since I was nineteen and made some timely investments. Even in the force, I have had some good postings. I am planning to focus on my business more and leave the air force soon. Amaka, I am not a spoilt rich kid." He smiled.

Amaka grimaced as she realised where he got that from.

"I know I have made a bad first impression on Morola. I have really prayed about this till I am certain, if not I wouldn't be so bold as to speak with you. Help me, my sister, and you will not regret it because I vow to you today that I will do everything humanly possible to make her happy. I am speaking to you openly because I can tell that you love her genuinely. Don't let her throw me in the dustbin of the friend zone too," he said, smiling. "And let this stay between us please? Promise?"

Amaka could sense the sincerity in Kaniz's voice. His every word, his body language, spoke of his genuine intentions. There was nothing more to say.

"It will. I promise," Amaka said. She had one hand left on her chest so it appeared as if she was taking an oath. "Count on me, Kaniz."

He opened the back-passenger door, reached into the car and gave her a box wrapped in rose-gold gift paper. "Can you help me give this to her?" he said, looking embarrassed. "I was going to give it to her myself but, I saw the look in her eyes and she may have refused it."

"I will make sure she accepts it."

"Amaka," he said gravely, "thank you."

He started to get back into the car and stopped. "Please, may I have your number? You should also have mine." They exchanged numbers and with that done, Kaniz and Isa drove off.

Amaka went straight upstairs to Rola's room. She sat on the edge of the bed while Rola lay down, her head on a pillow, typing something on her phone.

Amaka sighed dramatically to get her attention and Rola looked up.

"Amaka! What was that? You need to be careful with these type of men!" Rola said. "I was watching you both. What was he saying to you? Was he actually toasting a married woman?" She shook her head. "Didn't he see your ring?"

"I know I am in trouble," Amaka said, "but first, this is for you. Kaniz called me back to give it to you. It seemed like you couldn't get away fast enough, you had gone inside."

"Oh, was I that obvious?" That hadn't been her intention at all, she felt she concealed her disdain for the guy well and that she had been mature enough to treat him very politely. She reluctantly took the beautifully wrapped package.

"Open it," Amaka urged her. If she wasn't happy in her relationship, she was determined to enjoy her friend's happiness and she was excited because something told her this Group Captain Ishaya was the real deal. And what if he was a northerner? So what? He spoke everyone's language, besides, his mother had been Yoruba like Mo.

Rola looked at the box, shook it slightly, then she began to take the wrapper off. Her own photo was on the box inside. She tilted it to show Amaka. He must have gotten her photo from the internet. All in about two weeks? Since that Tuesday? In the box was a huge crystal bottle and a small card. It had a huge sorry emoji on it. No words, just the emoji and his name "Kaniz" signed in a cursive swirl.

"I don't want trouble," were the first words that came unbidden to Rola's lips. Something told her if he decided to set his sights on her, this Group Captain guy wasn't going to be as easy to deal with as Tim and he wouldn't give up as easily as Tega. This guy would be trouble. "Lord, I don't want trouble." How did a stranger know all she used was oudh? She could smell the oudh through the box. How did he get the scent so right? When she spoke aloud she masked her misgivings with defiance.

"Men," she said. "When they want to seduce you they will do anything." She hissed and packed the oudh up.

"At least try it on now," Amaka implored.

Rola looked at the oudh in disdain. "Using daddy's money to seduce the corper. What a cliché!"

"Mo, this isn't daddy's money o. This guy is really enterprising."

Rola looked at her quizzically. "Amaka, what's going on?"

Kaniz's words rang in Amaka's ears so she changed the subject deftly. "I have a confession."

"What is it, Amaka?" Rola was now prepared for the worst. What had she been discussing with the guy?

"Mo, Kaniz speaks Igbo o." Amaka lifted both palms up as if in surrender.

"Oh. It's now 'Kaniz'?" Rola eyed her friend. "So he speaks Igbo Amaka and...?"

"I goofed. On that phone call in the living room, I may have said to Mama C that he was a fine guy." A slight itch erupted behind her right ear.

"Yes?" Rola prompted her friend, frowning. That was Amaka's business.

"And that you know... that..." Amaka's right ear was really itching now so she gave in and scratched it. "I hoped you wouldn't consign him to the friend zone."

"Uhn hhn..."

"And that you said he was an arrogant snob and a spoilt rich kid."

Rola smiled smugly. That actually pleased her. The rude aristo.

"And that Mrs B was already quite taken by him."

Rola looked at Amaka as if she had just broken loose from an asylum. "You said what?!"

"Hmm." Amaka sighed as she got up from the bed like a tired old woman. "Let me start going home Mo, it's getting late."

"Which *late* is it getting? This is 6 p.m. Amaka!"

"You know I am married," Amaka said. She needed to leave before the full extent of her gaffe was exposed and Femi was as good an excuse as any.

"For real? You're really are going to pull that ace, Amaka?" She was always so amused at how her strong friends made their husbands their excuse when there was something they really didn't want to do.

Amaka dressed quickly and silently and went to the door, her hand on the doorknob. "I will still be driving you to camp next Saturday, right? Please don't see me off," she said as Rola started getting up.

Rola eyed her as if to say, "Who is seeing you off?"

Rola's phone was ringing. "Answer your call, Mo."

Rola ignored the phone and looked at her. "And what else, Amaka?" she said. "What else did he hear?" If Amaka was escaping, it was because there was something she wanted to avoid.

Amaka's lips curled down at the corners. "I may have suggested that your offspring with Kaniz will be so dark, it wouldn't be possible to see them during a power cut without a torch."

Rola's mouth dropped open as Amaka rapidly made her escape.

Chapter Ten

"...If a man would give all the substance of his house for love it would utterly be contemned."

Songs of Solomon 8:7B

Rola looked at her still ringing phone. It was Tim. She sighed. Tim was beginning to get a bit tiresome these days.

"Hello Tim."

"Hi Mo, it appears you are really busy? So I just wanted to let you know I am coming to Lagos for work and I thought you should know that spending time with you when I am around would be one of my top priorities."

Tim coming to Lagos for work? That was highly improbable. An investment banker living the American dream, she couldn't recall any project or client Tim had ever mentioned to her that could bring him to Lagos. She smiled. Tim was starting to take his sword out of its sheath. *Spending time with you would be one of my top priorities*?

"Cool." She would also be prepared for him. He would have to give up finally.

Kaniz was quiet as he drove away from the Bolades' with Isa.

It wasn't all a complete failure. Mrs B was such good company, such a pleasant woman, and it was a huge comfort to have Amaka in his corner. Even Olaotan was on his side. Never mind that the object of his attention herself was just politely tolerating him – he had her surrounded.

Isa broke into his musings. He was excited to have met Olaotan and he couldn't stop talking about him on the short drive back to Kaniz's place.

"You really got along well, didn't you?" Kaniz turned and smiled at his young charge as they passed through the barracks gates.

"We have a lot in common," Isa said. "I like her," he added.

"Huh?"

"I like SisMo," Isa repeated, "very much. You like her too, KB." He called Kaniz KB for kandan baba – small daddy. "Why did you pay more attention to her mum and her friend then?"

Kaniz shook his head and smiled. They had reached his house and were just easing into the carport.

"Isa, when you want a lady to pay attention to you, don't pay too much attention to her before she flows with you, focus on her friends, let her see how charming you are with others." He winked. "When you do that, it also lets her see what she is missing if she doesn't flow with you. And it also makes her rankle without even knowing she is doing so when you don't make her your exclusive focus."

Isa snapped his fingers. "Got it!" he said, grinning widely. "KB, what's rankle?"

Kaniz laughed. "But you got it?"

"Morola... I couldn't say more to her today because she still can't stand me. But she will love me, God help me, she will," he thought.

He was grateful for the uncanny and inexplicable force with which Morola came into his consciousness. Guys weren't famous for discussing their feelings with each other but from the little he could gather from his friends' relationships, the real issue was crystal clear that she was "the one". That was what his "epiphany" on Morola had done for him, driven his conviction that Morola was definitely "the one" beyond the realms of rational and empirical thought. He had heard such stories and disbelieved but now, it had happened to him.

Alhaji was obviously in need of some rest when Kaniz went to drop Isa off at Mamane Close that evening.

"Shehu you work so hard," Kaniz said. His dad needed a wife in the house and someone besides Samson and the domestic staff to take care of him. It was clear that Khadijat had the office front sorted but Kaniz just didn't know how to broach the subject of a companion with him. They hadn't had that type of relationship before he left home. "Perhaps, if I talk about my own plans, we can work our way to his plans to marry," he thought.

"Shehu, I have been praying more seriously about my wife."

Alhaji looked up at his son in expectation.

"Mata was Yoruba, Alhaji. I think I should follow in your footsteps."

Alhaji smiled and said, "Very interesting that you would mention that, Kaniz. I too am definitely going that way again. It seems we like Yorubas." He smiled broadly.

As far as Kaniz knew, Hajiya Khadijat was Ebira so Kaniz was sincerely wondering what Alhaji was talking about.

"It's a deeply spiritual connection, Kaniz. It was revealed by prophecy. The connection is even before she was born. 'When the one that is gone returns, then that which is lost will be restored,' Sekou Traore said. Since she came into my life, Isa was found and restored, you returned, my largest contract was restored and," he smiled triumphantly, "there's more to come. I was hoping we could have lunch together so you could get to know her better but I am sure you had a good reason for having to leave." Alhaji didn't want to be seen to criticise Kaniz any more for his behavior with Rola. After all, she was just a woman.

Kaniz wasn't sure his mind wasn't playing cruel games with him. Who was Alhaji talking about? Who were they to have lunch with? His Morola or someone else?

"Miss Bolade," Alhaji answered his unspoken question. "I had wanted us all to have lunch together, but there's still time, plenty of time."

Things were going well. The Chief of Defence Staff had just renewed their largest contract and with the intelligence reports on impending civil unrest and revolution, had increased the scope by an unprecedented one hundred million dollars. Rola was indeed a restorer: Isa restored to life, Kaniz restored to his life and now, the defence contract.

What joy would her arrival bring next? Alhaji knew what next in his life – he was expecting to receive Rola's restoring touch but perhaps, that would be when he finally embraced her as his bride. He had even taken to calling her Laraba in his thoughts. Laraba had returned. Finally, he would truly be alive again.

At his father's words, Kaniz was overcome with a sudden urge to throw up. The bile rose in his throat and he felt physically and violently sick. The blood drained from his face at the thought of his Morola with Alhaji. No wonder. It all began to make sense. He felt like laughing aloud at himself. That was it! No wonder she had been so unresponsive to him. What wealth had he, compared to his father? He was no match whatsoever. "I have been a fool!" he said under his breath, "a huge fool."

A huge fool for thinking a young lady these days with her own resources would settle for him. If he had as much as Morola, he definitely couldn't be significantly wealthier than her. So she was like so many others who believed marriage had to enhance their financial status. Though he had prospects, she had no way of knowing. She had chosen the far richer man already. No wonder she barely tolerated him.

As far as she was concerned, he was just another... he didn't even know what to think. No wonder. No wonder the ones Amaka had mentioned on the phone had been rejected. She played in the big league.

The hard ball of pain around his heart was enervating. He breathed in and out slowly, relying on his training to calm himself.

Isa came running in, smiling broadly and holding his phone, oblivious to the drama going on in the room.

"SisMo," he said holding the phone out to Kaniz. "SisMo wants to speak with you."

"She isn't your 'sis' young man. She is preparing to be your stepmother," Kaniz thought.

Kaniz's voice was icy cold when he spoke. "Yes?" he said.

Yes? Rola repeated in her mind. Were they quarrelling? Didn't he just leave her place today after a very pleasant visit? At least he got on with everyone. She wondered at not just the abrupt monosyllable, but at the ice cold almost rude tone. The "yes?" sounded more like "what do you want with me?" What was wrong with this guy? His mood swings were almost giving her whiplash. She didn't bother to introduce herself because she had overheard Isa say "SisMo" as he handed the phone to his older brother. So he knew very well she was the one and the frigid tone was a barb directed specifically at her.

"I just wanted to say thank you for the oudh," Rola said. "It was kind of you. You really shouldn't have bothered."

The sound of her warm voice which remained pleasant in spite of his freezing tone destabilised him. How was he meant to continue to hate someone whose only sin was not reciprocating his unspoken and undeclared affections? In every way, Morola was a dream come true to him. "Except she loves much older men and your dad in particular," he thought.

He steeled himself. Imagining her in Alhaji's arms muddled his brain, disturbing his focus.

"It's alright," he said. "You needn't have worried about calling, it's just a trifle."

"Thanks, sir. *Some of us* just can't help being polite. It's just the way we are. Thanks again, sir," she said and ended the call.

"What have I done again?" Kaniz thought as the phone went dead. "Why must I always be the jerk? The uncouth one? She always comes off as pleasant, polite and cool and I appear crass." He sighed, as he handed Isa's phone back to him.

Isa just stood wondering what all that was about. Perhaps this was another hard to get trick KB was playing? This was a rather nasty one though. He wasn't sure he would copy *this* move from KB's playbook.

Kaniz tried to put the thought of Alhaji and Morola out of his mind. Like a dark pall, it hung over him all night. He tossed and turned in bed as he tried to sleep but his soul was tortured. He had to let every thought of being with Morola go. He surely couldn't put Alhaji through this again? Was history a sadistic master who kept repeating similar pranks? He remembered the needless confusion of almost two decades ago and swore to himself – Alhaji would never have any reason to disbelieve him again. How could he have landed in this snare? The trap of believing his stepmother-to-be was his?

"How did I miss it?" he asked. "After all these years? I have never missed You. Am I deceived? You make no mistakes, so the mistake must be from me." He groaned as the ball of gnawing pain in his chest gripped him like a vice. "I let go, just set me free, take away this consuming devotion I have towards Morola." Even as he said her name, his heart still fluttered. The days of fasting and praying had only increased the intensity of his ardour. The more he prayed, the more his devotion had grown. It had been a surreal time of battling with this deeply spiritual attraction. He knew how to deal with physical attraction. Fasting, prayer and avoiding contact with the object of temptation sorted that out for him. He had done all that but nothing had worked, indeed, he was much "worse" than that fateful Tuesday.

"Take away the devotion I have towards Morola, set me free."

"It's a gift," came the reply.

"What's a gift? This complicated frustration? This pain that aches so much I feel my heart will implode? This hollow emptiness whenever I contemplate a life without her? What's a gift, Lord?"

"The love you have for her is a gift."

Kaniz's night got progressively rougher and he hardly slept. In the daytime, he found enough to distract him. He brought work home, there was the business at hand. He planned his next flight to Chad.

At night he had to attempt to sleep and the silence in his bedroom mocked him, he was left alone with his thoughts. He hadn't gone to Mamane Close after church yesterday, he couldn't stand to see Alhaji, he couldn't stand to trigger off another wave of repugnant thoughts. When his father called at about 8 p.m. wondering why he hadn't been "home" all day, he had mumbled something about work being intense and told him he had to start getting used to his absence.

It was 3 a.m. now. Fatigued but tortured, he prayed for morning so he could escape to the office and be immersed in his duties. Work had always been a panacea for him. Day finally broke and with the morning came clarity. He had decided finally, he would walk away from Morola. Alhaji could have her. Alhaji deserved to be happy after all the pain of the past. Marriage was not in Kaniz's plans before anyway, before Morola had literally swept into his innermost being like a tsunami. His decision to walk away and give up on Morola brought such an unrest within him, such a conflict that he shouted aloud for respite.

He was aware that he was all alone, no one else could hear him as he yelled, "What else do you want from me Lord?" He looked up but could only see the ceiling. "I give up!"

The answer came, still and quiet, just a knowing within him, deeper than the despair and the pain. "*Let me sort it out, hold your peace.*"

Whatever that meant, Kaniz decided to stick with his own decision. Let Alhaji have his desire. His heart was an empty void at the thought of his decision. He moved like an automaton, eyes bloodshot and got ready to go to work.

Kaniz was seated at his desk allowing busyness to work its magic. For the last few hours, he had been free from thoughts of Morola and Alhaji. Work always brought him peace. His phone rang at about 11.00 a.m. and he smiled instinctively as he saw the name, but as quickly as the smile came, he remembered his changed circumstances and the smile morphed into a frown. It was Amaka.

They made small talk for a few minutes while Kaniz wondered why she had called. Finally, she got to her point. "Kaniz, can you drive Mo to camp on Saturday?"

His heart jumped for joy. This was just the opportunity he had wanted, at least two hours alone with Morola, in a car, no audience, nowhere for her to escape to. Then he remembered, he couldn't accept. He shook his head as if physically steeling his resolve. He would have paid for this opportunity just two days ago.

Why hadn't Amaka mentioned Alhaji and Morola's tryst to him though? Or why had she made Morola sound unattached when she spoke with her mother on the phone? Maybe Amaka didn't know. She certainly seemed like a sincere, down to earth person who would level with Kaniz. Perhaps Morola just didn't tell her friend what she had been up to and what her plans were.

What a fickle casanova he would seem once he told her "no". What bothered him the most was that he could not explain to Amaka so he wouldn't jeopardise Alhaji's relationship with Morola. If he told Amaka what informed his stance, she might not find Morola's relationship with Alhaji palatable since Amaka herself was apparently married to someone not that much older than her from what he had gathered of the conversation at the Bolades' on Saturday. His dad was so much older than her friend and if he told Amaka what ailed him, Amaka could try and persuade her friend to end things with Alhaji. What good would that do for him?

He couldn't pick up where his father had left off. It was an abomination, so why bother telling Amaka? She would soon find out in due course.

"Amaka, I can't," he blurted out, his tone was deflated.

There was silence from the other end. Amaka thought he meant he was otherwise engaged on Saturday, but there was something in his defeated tone that told her there was more to the statement. Though they had an understanding about Mo, Amaka was wary about pressing him further.

"Well, if anything else comes up, I will let you know."

"Don't." Perhaps a clean break would be better but the very idea of giving up on Morola and coming to this decision without ever even getting the chance to tell her how he really felt about her was agony for him. A clean break is just what it would have to be. "Don't," he croaked.

"Don't? Don't what?" Amaka asked.

"Don't bother. Just don't, please," he said.

"Is Mo right about this guy?" Amaka thought. As solid-looking as he is, is he really this ambivalent? If he was so capricious, then, maybe he actually didn't deserve her best friend. She decided to let it be.

"Okay, sir," she said, her tone cold.

Kaniz didn't miss the implication of the "sir".

"I can't thank you enough for believing in me and please, trust me when I say my actions this morning will become clearer soon."

"It's okay," she said in a tone that made it abundantly clear that it was definitely not okay and she ended the call.

Alhaji's conversation with Kaniz had set him thinking. It was time he made his intentions known to Rola. He had thought he would speak with her when she started at QuantumTech, when she returned from camp. However, Alhaji recalled the stories he had heard about camp, it sounded like a veritable cauldron of estrogen and testosterone with young adults set free of all scruples and restraints for three weeks, safe in the knowledge that whatever happens in camp stays in camp. She deserved to know what he, Ishaya Mamane, offered and be guided by his offer before young casanovas had their chance. He reached for his phone.

Rola picked up the call after it rang just two times. "That's a good sign," Alhaji thought. She is eager to speak with me. He asked Rola to come over and sign off some vital papers that QuantumTech needed to take back to the youth service secretariat to complete her posting to the firm. In truth, Rola had already been posted to QuantumTech and it was such a done deal that only through a long, drawn-out and convoluted procedure could she be free of the decision she had taken to work at his company.

"Thank you, Alhaji. I will be there, sir," she replied.

Alhaji placed his gold-plated iPhone on his desk. She had been ever so pleasant. Things were moving rather smoothly. The prophecy had already gone ahead to mysteriously make all things work out well. He was on an obstacle free course, his path was clear.

"Thank God." He had to be grateful.

Hajiya Khadijat had been surprisingly civil though tight-lipped and Rola had been ushered in as soon as she arrived. Alhaji also seemed a tad more animated than usual, making small talk. She wanted to sign the papers and be on her way as soon as possible. She had driven to the Mamane Group headquarters herself and the traffic wasn't friendly at all today. The earlier she left before the traffic became worse, the better.

"Alhaji, sir, you asked me to come and sign some papers?"

"Ah! The papers," Alhaji said as if just recollecting. "I think MD QuantumTech is sorting them out, he may have decided to scan your signature from one of the documents you had already signed."

Rola wondered why the MD hadn't just gone that route before. Why had he needed to call her in? She smiled "In that case, sir," she said, reaching for her bag, "let me be on my way, you are at work and you are very busy, sir."

Alhaji cleared his throat. She was aware again of her first impression of his voice on the day they first spoke on the phone – he spoke with the dulcet tones of a veteran broadcaster. Quite attractive, Rola admitted to herself.

"Now that you are here Rola, I actually have something else to discuss with you."

Rola searched his face for clues but got nothing. Must be something to do with work as usual she concluded.

"My dear, do you believe in prophecy?"

"Prophecy?" she blurted.

Alhaji paused, head cocked to the right, hands pressed together in a power triangle, waiting for a reply. How was she to explain that she believed in prophecy only if it didn't negate scriptures?

"It depends, sir."

Alhaji got up and that was the first time Rola noticed the flat rectangular emerald box that he now picked up from his desk. She couldn't help but notice the figure he cut, even as he got up. He was dressed in a powder blue babanriga and he was looking as distinguished as always. The man must have been something to behold when he was younger. "Like his son, Group Captain Ishaya," the thought popped into her head. And she tried her best to shut the errant voice up. A woven cap was poised high on Alhaji's head. Didn't he ever take off his caps?

He came towards her side of the desk. From the box in his hand, he retrieved an exquisite long sautoir in diamonds and rubies. It looked like a Lebanese creation. The diamonds caught the lights in the office and blazed like white ice; they made a breathtaking sight. She could tell that this piece of jewellery was really expensive; easily worth at least a quarter of a million dollars. Was this intended for her? She could put a down payment on an apartment in Chelsea with what it cost.

Alhaji took the necklace out of the box and dropped the box in front of her. She saw that there was more – a pair of stunning ruby and diamond earrings that matched the sautoir. She heard a rustle of fabric and was immediately enveloped by a whiff of sandalwood and frankincense. Alhaji was standing at her back and bending towards her, his huge hands at the nape of her neck as he tried to put the necklace on her neck. As his rough hands brushed the soft skin of her nape, Rola felt revulsion rise up within her.

She turned around so fast she almost got whiplash.

"Sir! What is going on, sir?"

She instantly jumped to her feet. Alhaji had a height advantage and she felt instinctively that to resist him, she was better off standing. Unfortunately for her, as she stood up, she was trapped against Alhaji's slight potbelly, face to face with him. He moved yet closer to her and she felt a wave of revulsion.

"Rola, I am too mature to play the games young men play," his voice was sincere. "I want to make you my wife. My *first* wife, Rola." He paused for effect. This was a singular honour he was bestowing on her and he needed her to understand clearly that the purpose of the gift was to demonstrate to her that jewellery like this would be par for the course for her as his first wife.

"I am not married at all. I will take care of you Rola, you won't lack anything."

Rola always listened rather than rush to speak; she kept silent.

Alhaji took her silence for acquiescence. He knew she was a spiritual person too. Her actions towards Isa alone were ample proof.

"It has been prophesied Rola, you were meant to return to me and you are now here, and this time, nothing will cut your life short."

What? Hang on. "Alhaji, you must be mistaken. I don't know who you think I am, but I don't believe in reincarnation," she paused and stared him straight in the eyes. "Not in the least Alhaji. Besides, you must be older than my dad and I don't see you in that light."

Alhaji wasn't sure that he could hear her clearly. Was she actually turning him down? He frowned and shook his head – that couldn't be. She probably needed to see his gift clearly. He moved to put the necklace into its box and hand it to her.

As he moved, he created the space Rola needed to wriggle away. She took advantage of the escape route and stood well away from him.

Alhaji held out the jewellery box. "This is yours, Laraba. It's yours to keep." His voice was soft now.

"Laraba?" she said. "Laraba? Who is Laraba, Alhaji?" She hastily grabbed her bag from the floor. "Alhaji, I need to decide if I will be working with QuantumTech after camp." She shook her head as if to clear it from the unwelcome proposal. "What has just happened may make things really uncomfortable for us."

"Rola," he said sternly, "this has nothing to do with QuantumTech, you don't ever have to see me if you don't want to while you work here." Suddenly, his voice was soothing. "Calm down."

"Good bye, Alhaji," Rola said as she briskly made for the door and exited swiftly.

Rola couldn't quite recall how she got to her car but she sat in the driver's seat, shaking. The very thought of marrying Alhaji bent her mind. And he had called her Laraba. Who on earth was Laraba? With trembling hands, she riffled through her handbag, it seemed to take her several minutes but after just a few seconds of searching, she finally found her phone, retrieved it and dialled Amaka's number.

Alhaji sank into the nearest chair. It was the very same one Rola had gotten up from minutes before. He could still smell her fragrance trapped in the leather. He dropped the box on his desk.

What had he now done? He had moved without spiritual backing and failed. But it was only temporary, he reassured himself. Now was the time to call in reinforcements. It was time to fly to Dakar. He had to get this right. This was his second chance with Laraba. His chance to make things up to her. She had died in a car accident on her way back from delivering the tender for Mamane Group's first major contract. That contract had turned his fortunes around and she hadn't been around to enjoy the fruit of her labour. Even their only son hadn't been educated with his wealth. Of what use were the riches in the end? Except to attract to him the seductress who had almost sunk his destiny?

"Alhaji, I need to decide if I will be working with Quantum Tech after camp." Trepidation gripped Alhaji as he reflected on her statement, she wouldn't be returning here? How was he to perfect his plan to bring her into his home? What did she mean by that?

"Ah!" He smiled.

The returnee had no idea that it wasn't that simple with the youth service protocol. Once QuantumTech didn't "reject" her, she couldn't get another posting from the youth service corps and the top brass were his people. He would ensure she was never rejected by QuantumTech and never got another posting from the youth service secretariat.

One phone call made right away would sort that out. She was definitely going to be working in QuantumTech. She just didn't know it yet.

Chapter Eleven

"As the lily amongst thorns so is my love amongst the daughters."

Songs of Solomon 2:2

Fridays were not the slow workdays at the base as they were in civil service establishments where most workers made the onset of the weekend an excuse not to do any meaningful work for the day. Fridays were as busy as every other day and Kaniz was in the thick of administrative work; one thing he wouldn't miss when he left the air force was the paperwork.

Amaka, his phone screen announced as he was distracted by the sound of its ringing. He thought he had put it on silent at the meeting with Air Vice Marshall Woriabam earlier in the day. He was missing a few things these days. He had to put this Alhaji and Morola's distraction behind him and focus.

He was pleased that Amaka still called him but he checked himself.

"Hello Amaka." He tried to sound friendly.

"Hi sir," Amaka said. "Can you spare thirty minutes?"

"I am sure we can work something out, Amaka. When do you have in mind?"

"It's noon now. Shall we say 1:30 p.m.?"

"13:30 hours? Today?" That was close. Alhaji had mentioned that Morola had visited him at QuantumTech on Monday, things were definitely progressing quickly between them. There was no point postponing hearing the bad news Amaka had for him. It was now clear that he was right to have made Amaka an ally. At least he made a right judgement call in that regard. A sobering dose of reality may be the shock treatment he needed to rid himself of these errant feelings for his father's lover.

He considered himself a realist; that was one of the traits that had helped him thus far, but admitting his frustrating situation to himself did nothing to make him feel better in this case, his heart just ached the more. Morola was his father's lover. He sank deeper into the dark well at that thought.

He would leave work for an hour or so. Work would still be there when he got back and besides, she had asked for only thirty minutes of his time. To refuse would just be obdurate of him.

"Fine, I'm in. Where?"

"There's a Thai/Asian fusion place on Tolu Adenowo Close near your base. It's called Sattaya. Should I send you a google map link for directions?"

"I will find it," he said.

"See you at 1:30."

Talking about food, he realised that all the fasting had affected his appetite. He had continued his abstinence on Sunday, praying for clarity and liberty from the grip of emotions or whatever he was enthralled in. He hadn't been eating well. Maybe something with holy basil could help.

Amaka came into the restaurant about five minutes after he was seated. He had chosen a corner booth where he hoped they would have some privacy. He just wanted to get it over with, he was a busy man and he had not had time for frivolities like relationships for several years. The mission he had ahead of him didn't allow for such pursuits. With this over today, the unwelcome interruption could actually end and his life could return to autopilot.

"Hi nwanne," he said, trying to put the meeting on a friendly footing.

"Hi Kaniz," she replied.

"That's better," he thought.

A waiter came over and he ordered a soup with holy basil and Amaka ordered a papaya salad for starters.

Amaka looked at Kaniz. He looked drawn, and he had lost weight. Despite how annoying he had been when they last spoke, her heart went out to him.

She touched his hand. "Have you been well?" she asked. "You look pale."

Kaniz was genuinely ashamed that Amaka could see he had been affected, but he was tired of bluffing, tired of being defensive.

"I went from fasting to loss of appetite. I will be fine. Thanks Amaka," he said gravely.

"You know, of course, that Mo saw Alhaji on Monday afternoon?"

He gulped. This was it then. "Yes," he managed to say.

"Did Alhaji tell you what happened?"

"Oh yes, he actually did. He told me Morola was coming to visit." His left index finger stroked his scar and he closed his eyes fleetingly.

"Mo was going to visit Alhaji?" Amaka's look was quizzical. "He didn't say what happened?" She shook her head. "Forget I said that. It's not the type of thing fathers discuss with sons."

Her words were twisting a dagger already lodged deep in his heart. No. A father does not discuss his lover and his romantic trysts with his son. He doesn't. Kaniz let out a sigh of resignation. Amaka needed to stop the games and say what she needed to say. "Morola is pregnant with Alhaji's child." What else could she have to say? He was ready for the worst.

"Alhaji asked Mo over to sign some papers. When she was there, he tried to give her a gift which she refused and then he also proposed to her, if we can call what he did a proposal. Mo flatly refused. She called me after and she was extremely upset Kaniz. She had never ever seen Alhaji in that light before that moment."

Kaniz was finding it difficult to process what Amaka was saying. "She and Alhaji aren't together?" He said half to her and half to himself in a tone of extreme incredulity.

She shook her head. "Certainly not. Kaniz, it's your turn to be open with me. Is that why you said you can't drive Mo to camp tomorrow?" She leaned forward in her seat as she spoke. "You thought Alhaji and Mo were in a relationship?"

Kaniz merely nodded, still too dumbfounded to speak as he processed this turn of events.

"They are not in a relationship?" he asked again, his brow furrowed, trying to get the fact deep into his skull. Morola was not committed to Alhaji?

Amaka shook her head again. "Nah, no way! Alhaji seems to think she is Laraba, who is Laraba?"

Kaniz's head snapped up. He suddenly remembered the mumbo jumbo Alhaji had been saying about "the prophecy". So this wasn't really about loving Morola at all, this was because Alhaji thought Morola would bring him some advantage. What had he said? Kaniz hadn't been listening, he had been too stunned. Something about "restoration".

"Is that what was wrong? Is that why you were giving up?" Amaka asked.

"What else could I do?" He shrugged as he spread his hands, palms up. It would have been an abomination to have considered any other course of action. What upset the imperturbable and stoic Kaniz the most was the way this whole episode had shattered his invincibility, penetrated his armor and turned him at the ripe old age of thirty-six into a lovelorn teenager all in a matter of days. He was too ashamed to share this with anyone. He who had prided himself in his self-control. "Perhaps that is it," he thought. "Perhaps I have been giving myself the credit for remaining steadfast for the last ten years. Maybe I am being forced to confront my human frailty? Maybe I am being humbled? That must be it."

"They are not in a relationship Kaniz and the very thought of such a thing bends her mind. The coast is clear. I am speaking so frankly with you because you have been very open with me and we are not playing games here. You seemed completely convinced when we spoke on Saturday and you are not a boy anymore. At this stage, you should know what you want. I think Mo's resistance to you is partly because you got off on the wrong foot but the rest is not personal," Amaka said. "It's about men in general," she wanted to add, but bit her tongue.

Kaniz was engaged and listening intently. Had a man hurt her badly? What was Morola wary of? What was she running away from?

"So will you take her tomorrow now? I can ensure it's all sorted," she added.

He reached out and touched her right hand. "What time should I be there?"

Kaniz was parked outside the Bolades' by 9 a.m. Amaka had said 9:15 a.m. He had arrived in Lekki at 8:45 a.m. but had gone to a fast food restaurant just to buy water and some snacks that he was sure no one would actually eat, but he had time to kill. Also, he couldn't seem too eager. He popped the bottles of water into the car's cool box and wrapped the scotch eggs and meat pies in the plastic bags. Something told him that wasn't the *Good Housekeeping* way of preserving the food but no one could actually indict Kaniz for being domesticated. He knew the basics and tried hard but that was all, cooking was for women when he was growing up so the little he learnt, he learnt simply to survive when he left home and later on in the force. Army rations at the war front had made him eternally grateful for any barely edible food. If his wife couldn't cook, then their cook would cook. Cooking was not a core competence he required in a wife.

He had to step into the house and ask for Morola. Amaka had assured him all loose ends had been tied. Kaniz considered himself reasonably bold. He had faced tank fire, been shot down from the air, had ejected and parachuted from a burning plane and lost an inch of his height from the resultant spinal compression, but all that seemed to pale in comparison with going in to the Bolades' house and springing this surprise on Morola. He took off his aviators and pressed hard on the bell.

The gateman had called the house to announce his arrival and Aunty Wunmi opened the door.

"Ah. You are welcome, sir. You are welcome, sir," she kept repeating like a broken record, grinning like a Cheshire cat even as she bobbed curtsy after curtsy like a cork in a pond.

She took him through the anteroom straight into the living room and as he noted that he had graduated from the rank and file who were detained till cleared in the anteroom, his courage was bolstered.

Aunty Wunmi must be picking up some signals to make her this pleased to see him. Things may have shifted in a positive direction with Morola. He had noted only a black E Class parked under the carport. He sat and observed the living room. The Bolades' had elegant taste for sure.

Morola appeared in the doorway and he caught his breath. She was more attractive than he remembered. She was definitely ready for camp in her blue bootleg jeans which – he had to admit – counterbalanced the curve of her hips perfectly. She had on espadrilles. He rose to his feet as she entered. Morola was also wearing a crisp white shirt, as Kaniz was. They were "twinning".

The crisp short-sleeved linen shirt with a bishop's collar which he donned today on blue jeans was from Pablo Calatrava of Bogota, who kitted out the few in the know in the diplomatic corp. The quality was unbeatable in fabric, cut and fit. From his shirt pocket hung his trusty aviators. If he wasn't so nervous about his mission this morning, he would have cracked a slight smile.

Rola stopped when she saw him and frowned. What was he doing here? Had his father sent him to her? She quickly looked at his hands, he was carrying nothing. At that moment, her phone chimed. She looked at it – she had a text message from Amaka. She looked back up at him.

"Group Captain, we weren't expecting you today?"

Kaniz ignored the obvious barb. In *this* context, to be told you weren't being expected by a Yoruba person, or even a "proper" English person for that matter, was a way of saying very politely, "what in the name of all that's holy are you doing here?" To make it worse, she still stood, suggesting he stayed upright too. He was not welcome to sit. He had just been dissed by a fine example of the diplomatic Yoruba race.

His mum had tutored him while drawing parallels between the societal nuances of the world's ancient empires, from Britannia to the Oyo Empire. She had explained that because of the sophisticated complexities of running the vast empires and the exposure and the social dexterity needed in dealing with the diverse people who constituted these empires, their cultures had acquired layers of sophistication and diplomacy embedded into their expressions. So, like an English aristocrat would express himself with deft diplomacy, so would a quintessential Yoruba person. He took Morola's "diss" well – like a man on a mission. Like his late mum would say, "Turn it into camwood and rub it on your skin." Kaniz knew the prize would be worth this diss.

"Amaka has spoken to you?" he ventured with perfect equanimity.

"Amaka will be here in ten minutes at the very most," Rola said, looking at her phone instead of her watch for the time. "She offered to drive me to camp. It is at least two hours," she said. "And I hear the traffic can be epic!"

She looked at her phone again. "She just sent me a text message perhaps to tell me exactly when she would be arriving." she said confidently, smiling.

She clicked on the message, no doubt she would get some ammo to dispatch Kaniz summarily with.

"Mo dear, something came up. I can't take you to camp today but I made alternative arrangements. Kaniz should be at your place soon, he very kindly offered to help me out." Several heart and kiss emojis followed the words. Rola had to read the message again because she was sure there was something she had missed. Incredulity was quickly replaced with irritation. She sat down heavily on the ottoman. Kaniz quickly sat down again on his chair too.

Rola quickly keyed in her destination in the Uber app. The app was finding drivers but nothing came up. Kaniz's face was unfathomable as he pretended to read a coffee-table book titled *This is Lagos*. He studied it like he was going to write a dissertation on it. The only way Morola would get an alternative to his taking her to camp today was if God had stopped answering his prayers. That was his first order of business once he knew he was to stage this coup with Amaka. "No Uber, no driver, please," he had prayed.

Rola was flummoxed. Uncle Sam, their chauffeur had taken her mum to a family wedding in Abeokuta. If this wasn't the last day of resumption in camp, she should have been there herself. The other driver, Joe, had taken her dad to Ijebu for a funeral. She thought of calling them, but it would make no sense because by the time they returned, it would be way too late to get to camp.

She would have driven herself though she didn't have the foggiest idea where she was going, but the Prado had been dropped at the garage yesterday evening so it could be serviced since she wasn't around. Wait. Was it not Amaka and Mrs B who had persuaded her to get Uncle Sam to take the Prado in? The G Wagon was gone with her dad, the Range Rover with Mrs B. She couldn't take the E Class on the bad roads; it was too low.

And now, though she had been trying to get one, it appeared there was no Uber available to take her that far. She called Amaka. She would just have to sort herself out and come for her. Amaka's phone was switched off, so she called Femi.

"Hi Rola," Femi said cheerfully. Femi was no help, Amaka had left home fifteen minutes ago. "She said something about the spa and her phones would be off?"

Amaka went to the spa? So that was the "something that came up" in her text? Today was not going as planned at all. "*Many are the plans in a man's heart but the Lord's counsel, that shall stand*," the still quiet voice within her said. "Ah!" She was well and truly stuck with Group Captain Ishaya.

She looked up at him. "Group Captain, sir," she said, bracing herself to eat humble pie. Kaniz looked up, his face was inscrutable.

"Amaka told me you offered to take me to camp because she can't make it?"

Not a word came from Kaniz. He didn't trust himself to speak.

"Thank you very much. Can we start going, sir? I hear the traffic can get really bad and we don't want you returning to town late."

Kaniz stood up fluidly and Rola couldn't but notice that he moved like a panther. "He carries the height well," she mused. Then she caught herself, murmuring under her breath, "Rola how is that your business?"

"What can I help you with?" Group Captain Ishaya asked, interrupting her thoughts. He was standing, ready to take any luggage she had into the car. Not even a smile. What an arrogant man.

This was no doubt going to be the worst trip she had ever gone on, but she needed the ride. She was really stuck.

Rola was trying hard now to remember why she found this Group Captain Ishaya so obnoxious. Oh yes, he walked out on lunch with his dad and herself. Then he was super cold when she had called about the oudh. He was so aloof and formal. She reflected on that. He wasn't aloof with everyone. Was he not laughing with Isa when they visited? And with Mrs B too? She had decided to just try and have a pleasant trip today since it was inevitable that he was driving her to camp, but she was wary of Kaniz. He had been ambivalent in the past, sweet one moment and cold the next. It was a really tiring routine.

He had his aviators on as usual and she wondered if it was to protect his precious eyesight or because he felt he just looked too hot in them.

She was totally surprised though because just fifteen minutes into the trip, it was obvious already that it was going to be a fun trip. He was surprisingly good at making conversation. They had discussed their education within the first five minutes, Kaniz hadn't been asked the "Where did you study?" question in a while. Alhaji had, of course, told them both *what* they had each studied on the day they met but not *where*. It was just as well he knew her focus beforehand because from Morola's discourse and analysis, he would have taken her for a political scientist. Most engineers weren't this diverse in their knowledge.

"So will you consider going into politics?" he asked. "What this country badly needs in governance is a breed of people who have the fear of God, but those who consider themselves religious or spiritual don't want to touch politics with a bargepole. You know, the perennial 'politics is dirty' refrain."

"Sadly, that's why we get ruled by the dregs of the society," Rola said. "And ruled is the right word, because we don't get much governance anyway."

"It's a shame that people of faith avoid politics. Religion that is not relevant to life is not true religion, at least, not the way Christianity defines religion. Religion should be relevant to the welfare of the people. A righteous nation is not one that has churches and mosques on every street; a righteous nation is one that takes care of its people. It shouldn't be that the only way you know you have a mosque or church in the community is the nuisance they create, noise and traffic jams, Fridays and Sundays. It should be the value they bring to the community.

"We need our clergy, pastors and imams to take up the responsibility of teaching their congregations that political engagement is key and," she added, "not in the way some actually impose candidates on their congregations but by teaching them well enough to equip them with the tools to make the right political decisions.

"Like Holy Johnson would do, 'teach them what values to look out for in real leaders – competence, character, capacity, track record, morality.'"

Kaniz gaped. "No. You can't know Holy Johnson! Hardly anyone does and that list of values... that's so accurate."

"Of course, I do know Holy Johnson. Those were the first nationalists when the church was in the forefront of the nationalist struggle in the late 1800s. After he had used his platform as a preacher to disseminate nationalistic ideologies through mainstream methods such as drama, he later even went into politics, the legislative council if I recollect correctly."

"Morola, I am impressed!" He stared at her. Without a doubt, she really had been chosen for him. Looking at her, no one would expect that this tastefully clad, curvaceous, ebony Juno cared a hoot about governance and leadership and even knew about Holy Johnson. Even the internet had scant references to him, so she definitely didn't "ask Google". She had extensive study tucked under her belt.

"You know, when I consider the dissemination of ideas, I wonder why from the church to the UN, to government, those in authority don't seem to realise that the only way to take an idea mainstream and get the people to adopt it is to reach them through mainstream methods. Get to them through their influencers with subtle but consistent messaging. With such a burgeoning movie industry in this country, I can't believe how we waste the opportunity to push out the right narrative about ourselves. The average person who watches our movies really believes we are a nation of money-loving ritualists."

"Morola for president," Kaniz said as he finally took off his sunglasses.

Rola chuckled. "So the aviators aren't glued to his face?" she thought. There was a comfortable silence between them; Kaniz was mulling over Morola's words.

"You call me Morola. Why?"

"You don't like being called Morola?" Kaniz raised his right brow as he inquired, frowning ever so slightly.

"Everyone else calls me Rola or Mo except when the matter is serious and my parents call me my full name, Morolawe."

He smiled fleetingly and looked straight into her eyes. "I am not 'everyone else', Morola," he said softly. Something about the way he said that and his look unsettled her.

"You could go into politics too, you know?" she blurted, deflecting.

"Pardon me Morola, I didn't get that?" Kaniz had been lost in thought... reflecting over the last couple of hours. Rola had aced his "interrogation" and surpassed it. He had used all the arsenal at his disposal to ferret out every single bit of information he needed on her vision, value system, world view, attitudes and now he had a complete psychological profile of Rola under his belt.

He couldn't believe who God had sent his way. If he had been planning to get married and on an active search, she was definitely who he would have sought out for himself. The congruence and alignment with his vision and his needs was startling. She wasn't just beautiful, she was lovely – genuinely sweet and so full of life. Her softly chiming laughter and her smile thrilled him to no end. He knew he was falling deeper in love every moment he spent with her. No wonder their first encounter had been so dramatic.

"Why don't you consider going into politics yourself, sir?"

"I don't think that's the path that would be most efficient for me to influence things," Kaniz said, the look on his face inscrutable.

"And the air force is?" she asked. "Oh sorry," she said at the frankness of her repartee.

"It's alright Morola. I really needed a scholarship to study my dream course and the air force offered me one." His mood shifted at his words.

"There is some sadness there," Rola thought. There was more to the story. It struck her as odd that with his father's wealth, the air force had sponsored his university education.

He sighed. "It's a long drive," he said. "Let's have some music."

As he put his iPod on, Rola steeled herself to be inundated by some barely tolerable music, but she was completely blindsided by his playlist. The sound filtered through the car powered by the Bose speakers and B and O surround sound system and *No One Like You* from P Square came on. "This is so unfair," she thought. She managed not to sing along when the lyrics floated into the car. *Hello, how you doing, my angel, my one and only...*

the only one that I am missing wey dey bring me joy and blessing... but before we walk down the aisle... He glanced at her with a look she couldn't decode. *I just want to let you know, you are the finest... no one be like you... I have been many places, seen many faces, no one be like you... you are my destiny...*

She survived *No One Like You* with her composure intact but the next song threatened to scatter her decorum. It was Kiss Daniel's *Mama* and it was all Rola could do not to jump on her seat when the beat started. How on earth did this Group Captain guy know her favourite music?

"Was it Amaka who told you the songs I like?" she asked.

"No," Kaniz replied. It was just what he liked and he was glad he had made the right choice.

Rola felt stupid for suggesting he had even done research on her. She mentally kicked herself and vowed not to be caught in such a presumption again. Before she could stop herself, the first line, *feel the mama,* seeped through the car and into her cranium. *You know I like you... I won't lie to you...* She was singing and dancing along on her seat. Who cared what he thought about her? He should just get her to camp. She never needed to see him again and she would deal with Amaka mercilessly later.

"Talk to me o mama..." Kaniz and Rola were singing a duet. Hit after hit rocked the SUV and even oldies wafted through the speakers. As the tempo of the playlist calmed down, they fell to talking again about the country, about leadership, about the way forward if this much discussed revolution ever happened. An all-out revolution would not be the way forward, they had both agreed.

"Even the most famous of all revolutions, the French revolution of 1789 lasted for almost a decade characterised by terror and upheaval, it had taken the ascension of an army general, Napoleon Bonaparte, to end it," Rola said and Kaniz nodded.

"I agree. And the key players in the revolution like Maximilien Robespierre ended up being guillotined. Recent revolutions like the Arab Spring haven't delivered on their lofty expectations and the Iraqi revolution only ushered in a reign of totalitarian Ayatollahs. The Russian revolution was also not the success communists thought it to be. Have you heard the story of Stalin's adherent who when he found out about the atrocities Stalin presided over, committed suicide?" Kaniz asked. Rola nodded. "Sad story. It appears revolutions usher in dictators and not a return to vibrant democracy. So, in the end, all revolution seems to achieve is replace a ruling class with another ilk of ruling class whose orbit is the new dictator."

"But do people learn? Revolution was not the way forward, we know this from history, yet the talk of revolution in the country now is deafening. Perhaps if a revolution was inevitable because of the state of the polity, a firm hand or council which guides the helm of affairs during a transition and a quick return to democracy may work."

Kaniz looked at Rola with a look she couldn't define when she said that. He was honestly dumbfounded by the analysis she offered. The armed forces prided themselves on being the smartest and most disciplined cadre, the most qualified to lead the country and this arrogant stance had informed wave after wave of coups in the past and a disdain of civilians, but here was a young civilian lady breaking down the various parameters of peaceful societal change. Their views were so similar it was uncanny. They had read the same books. Within an hour, they were finishing each other's sentences.

Rola began to feel she had known him for decades. She couldn't but notice that he was attentive. As soon as she had settled down and they were on their way, he had asked if the temperature in the car was right. He had offered her water and even had paper straws. That was a nice detail, the straws, with serviettes.

"Group Captain, be honest. You have driven charter limos before, right?"

He laughed, a very pleasant genuine sound and it struck Rola how rarely he laughed.

"I just really care about my passenger," he said as he turned to her with his barely-there enigmatic smile.

It had been a pleasant journey so far. She was enjoying his company, but then, a dark thought flitted across her consciousness – if he was so assiduously caring, why could he be so nasty? Rola suddenly fell silent.

She couldn't forget his obnoxious behavior. Not that easily. If she didn't understand the reason, the rationale behind anything, she just couldn't engage it. She sank back into the plush leather seats which smelt faintly of a male fragrance, leathery and faintly spicy. The new car smell was still perceptible. She turned and looked at the road ahead.

Something about the set of Rola's jaw made it obvious to Kaniz that she was switching off. Kaniz glanced at her. They were nearing an intersection and the traffic was slowing down gradually, the music was low and the playlist was on "Kenny G" instrumentals.

Rola was always partial to the melancholic sound of the saxophone. "This was so unfair," she thought again. Surely she was being hypnotised or how else could this playlist and the atmosphere it created be explained?

The traffic crept slowly, sporadically stopping and moving.

"Morola, are you tired?" Kaniz inquired softly. "We will be there soon. Pele."

His voice was low and gentle. Something about his voice made her turn and look at him and the look in his eyes made her heart skip. Something was up, the mood in the car was pregnant with... with *something* she refused to allow herself define. The air was so charged, it was practically crackling. Rola quickly reverted to studying the road.

"I am fine," she said in a flat tone.

"Look at me, Morola," he said in a tone so caring and sincere that she found it difficult to resist. It wasn't expressed as a command so she turned towards him.

"Is everything okay?" His brow was furrowed, his eyes were probing and the kind concern was unmissable. Rola was hoping this crazy traffic would clear up so they could be on their way and he could concentrate on driving and stop talking to her in that tone. His sonorous baritone draped around her like a warm wrap of the softest cashmere and she felt so very secure. That was something she had never felt with any man, secure. She felt safe. "Not so quick," she thought. She jerked back to her senses. How could she ever feel safe with this ambivalent guy? Who knew when his next mood swing would be?

"Group Captain Ishaya," she began.

"Kaniz," he said, still looking at her in that disconcerting way. "Please call me Kaniz." His voice was strangely husky, he was still staring at her with that strange look and this infernal traffic was not moving at all! Rola tried to shake up the mood, lighten the tension.

"Oh this traffic," she said.

He looked at her and could see the cadence of her breathing had changed. The thought flashed through his mind that he was right in believing he had a chance with Morola. Perhaps, one day, she would feel for him a fraction of what he felt for her right now. The last two hours had flown by like two minutes. He had lost track of time. She was so vastly read, so intelligent. He had never met a woman quite like this before, never.

"Group Captain—"

"Kaniz," he said again. "Morola please, call me Kaniz." His voice was now almost a whisper.

"Alright," she thought. "Kaniz," she said under her breath trying out his name. That was why she didn't want to call him his name. There was something almost alluring about his name. As she said his name, she turned to speak to him and caught him quietly contemplating her. She met his gaze steadily.

"Kaniz," she said.

That was the first time she would say his name and it sounded so very different coming from her. His breath stopped as he looked into her eyes, he felt like drowning in those almond-shaped pools. He exhaled and shook his head again in a desperate bid to clear his mind. His heart beat faster. It was his turn to look away. He dragged his gaze away and stared at the road ahead, focusing on nothing in particular.

Thankfully at that very moment, the traffic moved a few feet and he made a show of driving the short distance, taking the opportunity to gather his thoughts. It was official. He was neck deep in love. Actually, who was he kidding? He was in way over his head.

"Kaniz, I don't understand. Why do you have these mood swings? You are cold one moment, warm the next? What is it?"

What was he to say? "I was suddenly overcome by some alien encounter when I met you and so I was fighting back? I felt this deep attraction I had never felt before and I hate not being in control so I resisted? I had to escape you, escape from your presence to gather my thoughts"? He couldn't say that yet, she wasn't ready for the truth. The traffic stopped completely again and he decided to take the plunge. He had to answer, say something at least.

"Morola, when you called to thank me for the oudh, Alhaji was just telling me about you and him and... Morola, when I heard your voice on the phone..." His left elbow rested on the car door on the driver's side as he massaged his scar as if it still hurt, as if to relieve some discomfort. He didn't know if it was safe for him to proceed, if it was too early to let her know how he really felt. He kept looking ahead. "I couldn't just deal with the thought of you and Alhaji together. I couldn't cope."

He turned and looked straight at her, straight into her eyes. That was it. He had said it. It was off his chest. She could interpret the information any way she liked.

Rola turned her head slightly to the left and looked at him. He seemed oddly unsettled. His carotid artery throbbed and a small vein on his right temple pulsated visibly. She observed the huskiness in his voice, the dilated pupils.

Oh no. This guy was not truly attracted to her was he? No way! "There goes another good friend," she thought. They had had such a blast on this ride. She thought she had made a firm friend for sure. This military guy too? She would have to get away from this one quickly. Her eyes narrowed. Something cautioned her again – this guy couldn't be easily contained; to try to "manage" Kaniz was to attempt to play with an active volcano.

It was as if he read her thoughts, because, at that very moment, he turned to her, looked directly into her eyes and said, "Morola, you can't run away from me." His voice was steady, his face was calm and determined. "It won't work." He shook his head gently for emphasis. "It simply won't work." He repeated with finality, his jawline set. He turned back to face the road ahead.

She was flustered by an alien emotion. She had no reply to his statement, perhaps because no one had ever been this direct or bold with her before.

Morola, you can't run away from me... it won't work. Why was he always so cocksure?

She was destabilised and started to babble. "There's absolutely no relationship between Alhaji and me. He had never even said anything to me to suggest... to suggest any untoward interest. He tried to give me money to say thank you for Isa's case but I didn't take it. My family was there on the day. I had never been alone with him before Monday. I was seeing him for the third time ever that day. In fact, on Monday, when he..." she stuttered and started trembling as she remembered.

Kaniz couldn't help seeing her so distraught, he instinctively leaned towards her and held her close. Then he tenderly placed her head against his shoulder and she didn't stop him. The fresh scent of her hair filled his nostrils and he had to clench his fists to restrain himself from touching her hair.

"It's alright, Morola."

His voice was tender, reassuring, calming and his head was bent slightly so his voice spoke right next to her right ear; she could smell his fragrance, it was an oudh, leathery and spicy, his body chemistry giving it a smell that was uniquely his. He smelled so good. Something deep within her heart stirred.

She needed to break the spell, so she spoke. "Who is Laraba? Alhaji called me Laraba."

Kaniz could feel her soft breath against his chest filtering gently through the fine linen of his shirt as she spoke. His heartbeat quickened at the sensation.

"Laraba... Laraba was my mother," he whispered in his deep baritone and she could *feel* his voice through his chest as well as hear it. It was not an unpleasant sensation. Her head snapped up at his reply and she swiftly put some distance between them. She looked up at him in confusion.

"Alhaji thinks I am your mother?"

She looked up at him, searching his face, her eyes wide. He wasn't finding it easy to concentrate on anything with her face turned upwards to him like that, all he yearned to do was kiss her upturned lips. Her face was so close to his that her breath, fragrant like cloves, caressed his clean-shaven face. This was way more dangerous than he could have anticipated. His voice had gone down an octave by the time he could speak.

"He thinks you are a reincarnation of my mother and the time they had together was the happiest time in his life, so..." His mind was on its own tangent. "Why are we talking about my father?" he felt like shouting out loud. "At a moment like this?"

Rola was oblivious to the effect her closeness had on him, so she pressed further. "And you? You believe that too?" she asked.

He was amused. "I don't believe in reincarnation, and besides, I am not Oedipus."

His meaning was not lost on her – *unlike Oedipus, the object of my devotion is certainly not my mother; I am attracted to you.* She fidgeted under his gaze. Why did he always seem to be the one in charge? He had let her go as soon as she lifted her head up and was now calmly, openly just gazing at her face, his back to the driver's door, in no hurry. His greatest ally was the dastardly Lagos traffic, keeping them both hostage in the comfortable confines of his car.

"You are so beautiful," he muttered, almost reluctantly, as he shook his head slightly. He exhaled and turned to steer the car as the traffic moved and Rola was thankful for the timing. They drove in silence for the final ten minutes of the journey. No words were needed, each was lost in their own world.

"I have moved too fast." Kaniz thought. "I hope all is not lost. I should have slowly gotten close to her and become her friend."

"And let her dump you in the friend zone? No. With her, you make your intentions crystal clear."

It was not planned, but, perhaps, it was just as well the way things had gone. He could tell Morola had a wall of defence around her, around her emotions. She gave off a "don't come too close" vibe while staying pleasantly cool and composed. If Alhaji's faux pas on Monday had not thoroughly rattled her, she would never have allowed him to get so close to her. It was clear that she intended to keep him at a safe distance.

"And I intend that there be no distance whatsoever between us. Morola, I will be as close to you as the air you breathe," he said to himself with firm determination.

Chapter Twelve

"And no marvel, for Satan himself is transformed into an angel of light."

2 Corinthians 11:14

Driving in through the gates of the camp, Kaniz wondered if Morola had thought this through. Would she be able to stay two weeks here? He saluted her resolve. There was no air conditioner in sight and though the campgrounds were relatively clean from what he could see, he shuddered to think of what the bathrooms would be like. He looked at the low bungalows where the hostels were located. Would she be able to sleep in the heat? She had never shared a room even way back in university so how would she cope with strangers here? He felt like whisking her straight back home.

Camp registration formalities were completed expeditiously, sped along by esprit de corp as the camp commandant, an army captain, took the requisite note of the returnee corper's attentive escort. Her one suitcase was now set down in a room she shared with two others, Titi and Chinny.

Rola saw Kaniz off back to the car. Standing by the driver's door, the looks Kaniz was receiving from the ladies as they walked by were amusing to her.

"It looks like you have some admirers here," she quipped. "I really should go now, I am spoiling your market just by their seeing me with you."

He had a serious but wistful expression on his face. "I have been off the market since the moment I met you Morola," he said, matter-of-factly.

He had been observing the guys looking at Morola, some turned around to give that "casual" backward glance guys usually felt they could get away with.

A thought struck him. "You mean you can't see the looks the guys are giving you Morola? Really? I think they want me to disappear completely so the coast can be clear." He stared at her with a questioning frown and she looked back at him, her face blank.

"You really have no idea the effect you have on men, do you?" He looked at her as if she was a science experiment, with curiosity. Her body language told him she was guileless, unpretentious, innocent. "No, you really don't," he said and shook his head. "Amazing," he added.

It couldn't be, could it? Was she really inexperienced at twenty-eight? No. He shook his head. Amaka's voice came back to him. "It's not about you. It's not personal." There was definitely a story here.

She turned. "I graduated seven years ago. These guys probably didn't meet me in uni," she said dismissively. "Besides relationships are certainly not my focus now."

"Life happens," he said quietly. "Many are the plans in a man's heart but the counsel of the Lord, *that* shall stand."

Rola started, surprised to hear the very words that she had heard in her spirit before they set out that morning.

Rola still had a question but she feared now what the answer would be.

"Group Captain," she said. Kaniz shook his head slightly and sighed. He understood what she was doing by calling him "Group Captain". She was restoring the distance between them, compensating for allowing herself cry on his shoulder. "That day we met, why did you do that? Walk out on Alhaji and me that way?"

Kaniz raised his right brow and looked at her straight in the eyes. "Are you really sure you are ready for the answer?"

Something about his voice and his eyes warned her that she wasn't ready. "Thanks, sir. I sincerely appreciate the ride," she said.

"You have no idea what today means to me," he said. Lifting her right hand a bit and bending his own head slightly, he brushed the back of her hand lightly with his lips. She could feel his lips warm on the back of her hand and a strange thrill coursed through her veins. He straightened and with his steady gaze still on her. "Morola, *I* am not going to be consigned to the friend zone," he added in an oddly husky tone. He dropped her hand, turned and got into his car.

Rola's heart skipped. Why did he have to be so direct, so factual with his declarations? Let him go. She was just glad to be rid of him. So why did she feel he shouldn't leave just yet? Why was she feeling so bereft as she watched him drive off?

Alhaji waited till he felt Traore would be free that evening before dialling Senegal. He wasn't going to lose his one chance at building his future after all these years. Traore picked up the call himself and Alhaji dispensed quickly with pleasantries and launched into the real meat of his gist.

"Great One, I found her, she has returned and it is exactly like you said."

"It can't be otherwise than I prophesied," Traore said. He was surprised at how surprised his devotees were at his results. Was he not the great marabout? Is that not why the rich and powerful flocked to him from all over the globe? As for Alhaji, his generosity set him apart. Sekou Traore was particularly fond of him.

"You do not sound well. What ails you?" Traore asked.

"Great One, this matter is not for the phone, I need your help."

"When can you come?" Traore said.

"I have a few meetings to attend to and I can be with you tomorrow afternoon," Alhaji replied.

"It is done then," Traore replied. He was a man of few words.

The matter was settled. On his return from the marabout, the matter would be a done deal. Rola would be his.

Alhaji ended the phone call and dialled Kaniz's number. He was seeing less of and hearing less from Kaniz. In fact, he hadn't seen him since Saturday after he arrived from Abuja and Kaniz had dropped Isa off. It must be work, Alhaji concluded. Isa had seen him a few times it seemed. He had asked that Junaid stop by at Kaniz's place on his way back from lessons at the Bolades'.

"Look at that," Alhaji thought. "She is not even in my house yet and she is taking care of Isa already." Beyond his weird behavior on the day they met, he hadn't even bothered to ask Kaniz what he really thought about Rola. It would be good if the two of them finally got along. It would certainly make his life easier.

Kaniz didn't pick up. Alhaji checked the time. It was 8 p.m. Maybe he was flying. Perhaps even on one of their military exercises. He was a grown man. If he didn't return from Dakar on time tomorrow, he would ask Khadijat to sort Isa out. Thinking of Khadijat reminded him she had to tell the crew they were going to Dakar tomorrow. He reached for his phone to call her.

The house was empty without Rola, she filled the house with light and joy. She had only been around since Christmas and yet, the house was not the same without her. She had been home at the weekend and it only made it worse for Mrs B when she returned. She told Mrs B she had found a solution to the poor living arrangements at camp but she shouldn't bother asking her what since she knew her mother would worry about the solution endlessly. Mrs B was concerned but didn't want to pry. After all, Rola had lived alone for years now.

Since she was a child, her daughter had been so sensitive to her environment. Despite Rola's assurance, Mrs B was almost in distress. Perhaps they should just have *arranged* this youth service matter? Even if they didn't arrange it, she could have been going to the camp every morning but Rola hadn't thought it fair on any of their drivers, driving six hours a day for two weeks. Was their family just too idealistic? Had they made the right decision?

Mrs B looked at the screen as her phone rang. Truecaller revealed it was Kaniz Ishaya. She smiled as she picked up the call.

"Hello? Kaniz? Thanks so much for the beautiful fruit basket you sent on Sunday. It was really lovely."

Kaniz assured her it was nothing at all, he was glad she liked the fruit basket and thanked her for accepting the token. He was just calling to find out how she was doing. He was sure she was missing Rola.

"How thoughtful of you Kaniz; I miss her I must confess." Amaka had mentioned that he had dropped Rola off at camp, so she thanked him, wondering with a mischievous smile how Amaka had dumped Rola on Kaniz. All Amaka had asked of her was to make sure the Prado was unavailable and no driver was available for Rola that Saturday and Mrs B had done her bit. She certainly didn't think it would be bad at all if Kaniz and Rola got on well. He was such a gentleman and there was just something so sincere, so genuine about him.

"I am thinking of passing by and seeing Morola tomorrow," he said casually. "My unit has exercises in the area. Perhaps you would like to send anything across to her?"

"You know, she was home at the weekend so she took what she needed with her. I wouldn't want to bother you."

She was home at the weekend? Kaniz took some time to digest the information. Morola came home for the weekend and she didn't even call or ask after him at all? He sighed. He was strangely wounded by this information.

He had made sure he planned his unit's exercises at the air force base not more than fifteen minutes from the camp. He didn't need to divulge those details to Mrs B though. He had done his best not to call Morola since he dropped her off and it had been twelve long days already. He couldn't hold out any longer; he had to see her.

He had his work cut out for him with his Morola. There would be no easy route to her heart. Why did he have such a tough assignment? Why not one of the many ladies who practically threw themselves at him? He wasn't going to be defeated by Morola though. He was determined not to give up. Besides, he was not doing this alone; he was praying about every step. No matter how small the decision, he sought guidance. On the day he dropped her at camp, he had asked, "Should I play music on the trip?"

"You should."

"Are love songs kosher?"

"She has emotions, Kaniz."

"Amaka! How could you? I was almost hypnotised o."

Rola didn't know how else to explain to her friend how she ended up being in Kaniz's arms and being comforted by him. It had to be the power of music; music was potent. Ah, she had learnt the hard way. Only worship music from now on.

"The guy was playing P Square, Kiss Daniel, even Kenny G, all the way to camp. For real Amaka? You threw me to the lion?"

"Mo love, I was sincerely busy o. If I didn't go to the spa that morning... you don't want your friend to die, do you?"

"Drama queen," Rola said, kissing her teeth.

"The guy has moves though, Mo. I respect him. With all that military vibe, I thought both of you would have prayed all the way to camp and then switched to playing martial music—"

"He has scope o. Maccky, I swear he is dangerous," Rola reluctantly admitted with a sigh.

Amaka was rocking with mirth. Kaniz was so full of surprises and she was liking him more – cool guy, spiritual but sensible and he seemed to understand women a bit. No matter how strong, he knew Mo still had emotions and he was strategically finding his way to her heart.

The camp was on a regimented schedule, the bugle was blown for every activity and just right then, it went for 6 p.m. activities.

"I have to go, Amaka the betrayer. I will deal with you later."

Alhaji settled in the private jet on his way back to Lagos. One hour to land. He looked at the contents of his briefcase, now a few thousand dollars lighter but carrying more precious goods in place of the money he had relieved the suitcase of. Goods that would sort out issues that the money could never have sorted, not with a woman like Rola who had spurned his material gifts. What Traore handed to him looked so innocuous but Alhaji knew that size and spectacle didn't matter in the spiritual space. There was some heavily perfumed soap in a tin – this he was to bathe with every day he planned to see Rola – and a lamp, a rather ordinary earthen lamp with a rope wick. A bottle held the special oil that fuelled the lamp. He was to fill the lamp with the oil and put on the lamp. The Great One assured him that as long as the lamp remained burning, Rola could not possibly have any man but Alhaji on her mind. Even in her dreams she would see Alhaji. It was settled.

"Sometimes, love needs a little help," Traore had said. He had "helped" many people this way.

"What happens when the oil finishes?" Alhaji had asked.

Sekou Traore had laughed. "She will be yours, way before the oil finishes. Don't worry. Get ready to plead with her to wait till you marry her before she moves into your home. You have no idea what you have in your hand now. I have had people travel from abroad and leave all they had behind within twenty-four hours just to answer the call of this lamp once it is lit. The deed is done, get her bride price ready. Just ensure that twice a day, morning and night, you trim the wick and call her full name and her mother's name."

At home, Alhaji placed the lamp on the floor in his closet. He trimmed the wick carefully and poured in the oil. The fragrance wafted upwards caressing his nostrils, it had a strangely attractive and sweet smell. He had taken some matches from a surprised Samson who had offered to help him light whatever he needed lit. Now he was in his closet alone lighting his lamp, the lamp of hope.

"Morolawe Bolade, daughter of Kikelomo," he said three times.

Oh no. He hadn't specifically asked the Great One how many times he was to call the names.

Would three times do the trick? Should it be seven times? He added four more repeats for good measure. It wasn't costing him money to merely say her name and her mother's name. He secured the tin of soap away from prying eyes in his closet, which he usually locked when he was out of the house. He didn't need to know what the ingredients of the soap were but he had heard strange stories about these concocted soaps. Once he got the results he needed, who cared what was in it? He shrugged.

Rola tried to make herself comfortable in the strange bed. She was counting not just the days but the hours till she left the camp. She just couldn't let her mum, TK or Amaka know how she had suffered, if not, Amaka would make a huge deal about her refusing to "settle" the issue some other way. TK would whisk his daughter out and Mrs B would tie herself in knots with worry. She was well and truly on her own on this journey. After two sleepless nights, her car arrived on Monday and she finally devised a way of coping. She checked into a hotel very close to the camp. Every local government seemed to have a Hotel Plaza, it was such a ubiquitous name. It was not the Ritz but it had clean running water, clean bathrooms and air conditioners and that was all she needed.

After a week of fast food, she had brought home-cooked food over the weekend which she put in the fridge in her room and she warmed her meals in the small microwave she bought just for this purpose. Not like she ate much but she needed to be nourished.

She tossed and turned on the crisp and clean sheets. She ensured that she brought all her bed and bath linen from home. Tucked under her own duvet after a full day of rigorous physical exercises, she was thankful that the air conditioner in her room – though humming audibly – was working well. After her first night, she had had to change rooms from 207 with the loud air conditioner which seemed to have aspirations to become a lawn mower. It was all noise and no performance. She had to move to 209 the very next night just to ensure she got a room with an effective air conditioner.

Rola's slumber felt oddly drugged. As if she was being dragged into a deep well. As soon as she fell asleep, she saw herself walking on a powder soft beach of crystal sand. The sun was a radiant orb in a cloudless azure sky and the sound of seagulls filled the air. The water was turquoise and the sound of the ocean waves as they kissed the seashore lulled her as she walked towards her beloved in the distance. There he was ahead of her, but she could just barely make out his form. Her heart yearned for him so badly it was as if it would explode with longing. She moved closer till she was by his side. With a flourish, he turned and swept her into his arms and only then did she get to look at his face for the first time. It was Alhaji Mamane.

Rola woke up and sat bolt upright in bed, her heart palpitating. She was sweating. Alhaji? How? In that dream, all her being had longed for him. Even now, she felt Alhaji's warm embrace from the dream.

A thought floated into her mind. Would it really be so bad to give in to Alhaji's proposal? A wave of unease rose from deep within her. Her eyes felt heavy and she rolled over. Unlike her insomniac self, she fell asleep in minutes. The same dream recurred all over again. She was on the lovely beach and ended up in Alhaji's embrace. She woke up the second time as if rising out of a deep well and was now afraid to fall sleep again. She checked the time - 3 a.m. Too early to get on the roads, too early to get to the camp. The first bugle went off at 5 a.m. She would shower and take some time to meditate and pray and clear her head. Something was definitely afoot.

Alhaji woke up. Age was the best-kept secret. No one had warned him about the frequent bathroom breaks when praying for his long life and prosperity. He now had both long life and prosperity and also frequent trips to the men's room. He yawned as he sat up in bed, still sleepy. Sleep was now a divine gift that he didn't take lightly. He wished he didn't have to wake up fully to do his business because, at his age, falling asleep again might be a challenge.

He looked at the clock on top of his huge TV screen, the fluorescent hands glowed in the dark. It was five minutes to 3 a.m. exactly. Midnight to 3 a.m. was the marabout and his disciples' prime hours of prayer. They were an hour behind Lagos and therefore in the thick of their prayers right now. Alhaji sent up a silent prayer joining theirs. There was no distance in prayer and he was convinced his own little sincere and heartfelt prayer would add some value to theirs. On his way back from the bathroom, he passed through his closet and checked on his lamp. Was it his imagination or was the flame actually burning higher and brighter than it was when he had gone to bed? He looked around and ensured there was nothing flammable around the lamp and then returned to bed.

Rola was napping on the bed in camp as she tried to do during the day instead of rushing back to the Hotel Plaza and back again for the last evening drill. Her roommates had gone to have lunch. If they had been around, resting would be out of the question. They would have had something to say and she knew the topic they preferred. They had seen Kaniz when he had come to drop her off and the way Kaniz and herself were "twinning".

Titi laughed as she said he was looking at her "as if he wanted to swallow you". If that was an accurate depiction, then Rola had quipped that it was a rather "cannibalistic love". They pointed out that his attentiveness towards her lent credence to the fact that they must have an "understanding". It had taken days to convince them they were just friends. At which point, Titi had declared that if this was friendship, then the friendship was quite lopsided.

Many of the guys she met in camp when referring to the moment they first saw her, recalled seeing her "with her fiancé" when he dropped her off. She didn't even bother correcting their impression. Their presumption about Kaniz and herself kept some of them at bay but some were incorrigible and still persisted in spite of the thought of Kaniz and the imposing figure he cut when he dropped Rola off.

Since Rola was insistent that Kaniz was just a friend, Chinny's next order of business was how to hook up with him and she was looking to Rola for tips. Since Rola didn't need him in that way, there was no point for such a fine guy to *waste*.

Rola was finding it difficult to relax. She was tired from waking up so early and yet, thoughts of Alhaji Mamane kept churning in her mind. No, his belly wasn't that bad. She knew guys just in their forties who had bigger potbellies. The guy was distinguished-looking, perhaps even handsome, come to think of it. The tribal marks made him look like a warrior. He stood tall, significantly taller than her dad. What did it matter to her that he was older than TK? The heart knows what it wants. She had dreamt twice, imagine that? Twice in just one night.

"In the mouth of two or three witnesses every word shall be established." What were the odds of having the same dream twice? This must be a divine message to her.

"But," she thought, "we judge every prophecy and vision by what we know of the Word. No encounter, no matter how spectacular, is superior to the written Word."

"The enemy also appears as an angel of light," the words floated into her consciousness.

The way she felt about Alhaji since she had woken up was like she had drank a love potion. She had even called him just to hear his voice but the network was bad and the call didn't connect.

Despite the compelling emotions she felt, something deep within her was uneasy, unsettled. Deeper than the feelings of attraction towards Alhaji, was a deep-seated restlessness with the whole idea of being with Alhaji in a relationship of any sort.

"But, even now I am awake, I can feel his love," she said to no one in particular. Alhaji loved her in that recurring dream, he really loved her. He was sincere and real. No wonder he had proposed without any protocol. She felt sorry for him but was this what real love was like, full of fear? Why was she so terribly afraid? Why didn't she feel any joy or peace?

Her phone rang, jerking her out of the beginnings of light slumber. Kaniz. She hadn't heard from him since he dropped her at camp.

"Hi Group Captain."

Kaniz shook his head sadly at her salutation. He grudgingly respected her for her principles, no matter how hard her principled stance made his life. So that was it then! He was back to "Group Captain". So he had effectively taken one step forward and two steps back. His hand wandered to his left temple. He could put this in perspective, he had been in warfare. It was not enough to take a position from the enemy like a strategic hill or bridge, you had to secure it, or else, the enemy would recover it. Obviously, he hadn't taken nor secured his position in her heart yet. He had thought of her, virtually every waking hour in the last twelve days but he wanted to give her some space so "absence would make the heart grow fonder". It appeared that absence had made her recover fully and set her heart harder against him. "I should have called her, even gone to see her," he thought.

For the last twelve days, it was all he could do not to dial her number when something reminded him of her, when someone said something she would have said, when he saw a book she had read, when he wanted her opinion on something... almost every hour, something came up and he thought of Morola.

Returning to the moment he said, "Hi Morola. How are you doing, Sarauniya?"

He had that gentle tone again. Rola ignored the "Sarauniya" bit; he was just incorrigible. What was that word and what did it even mean? Though she had to admit that the word had a nice ring to it.

"I am fine," she said.

There was no way she was going to let him know how roughing it in the last twelve days had shaken her up.

"Where are you, Morola? What are you doing at the moment?" he asked. "Any activity? A drill perhaps?"

"No, I am just lying down; resting before my platoon meets again. Thanks so much for dropping me off at camp the other day. It was really kind of you. Where are you?" she added, merely reciprocating his question to her. Where else would he be but his office in Ikoyi? She knew that but she had nothing else to say to him and she needed to dispatch him quickly, go back to her meditation and sort out her thoughts.

"Look out of your window." Was that a smile in his voice? *Look out of her window?* She reluctantly raised herself slightly off the bed and rested on her elbows. She dragged herself off the bed and went to the only set of windows in the room, opposite the three beds. Who was that? The tall figure in the camouflage fatigues? With the aviators that never seemed to leave his face? That had to be Kaniz, striding towards her. How could he be here? Like a flash, he had covered the distance between them and he was at the window sill. He took off his aviators and hitched them on the front of his uniform. He gazed at her and with just one look into his eyes, the spectre of Alhaji that had visited her in the dreams at night was completely banished.

"Sarauniya... Morola," he whispered as he bent slightly and took her hands gently in his through the open window. Looking into her eyes with his steady gaze, the look in his eyes was tender.

Chapter Thirteen

"Jealousy is as cruel as the grave, the coals thereof are coals of fire, which hath a most vehement flame."

Song of Solomon 8:6

Kaniz had parked under a tree and they could sit in the car there with the air conditioner on and talk for a while.

"Oh, you have braids on now?" he said.

"With the heat and the constant drills in the sun, this is easier," Rola explained.

How had she been? Was it all the drills that made her so thin or had she been ill? Was she eating at all? He spoke to her as if, as if... she searched for the word... as if he was *responsible* for her.

She almost said, "Who asked your opinion on my weight?" but she wasn't in the mood to fight today. Those dreams had left her in a confused maelstrom of emotions. She was just surprisingly and genuinely happy to see him. She could see two trucks in air force colours parked under another tree, well out of earshot. There were men in fatigues in the trucks.

"Are they with you?" she asked, changing the subject, trying to divert the scrutiny of his gaze.

"Yes," he simply said, explaining no further. "I should make sure you get something to eat," he added, half speaking to himself. He shook his head and smiled. "Do you know I got us some snacks the Saturday we drove down here?" The way he said "we" made her wonder. Was he making them a "couple" now?

"I must have been distracted by something, or," he paused, "someone." He gave her that look again, "Because I forgot them in the car till the smell took the car over two days later."

"Ugh." Rola squeezed her face but she was laughing.

She looked cute when she laughed, but she was losing weight. She had on this ridiculous khaki uniform but then, they were both in uniform. He pointed at her and then at himself and asked in his droll humour, "Are we twinning again?"

Some of Rola's "admirers" passed by Kaniz and Rola on their way back to the hostels after lunch. They could see Rola and her "fiancé", he was dressed in full combat fatigues as Rola sat in his car, talking and smiling.

To the guys who had stubbornly persisted in chasing after Rola, Kaniz was a portrait of power in his uniform. They could also see clearly two truckloads of men all dressed in combat fatigues parked not too far from the couple. The ardent casanovas were ruing their machismo and cursing their bravado. "Of all the girls in this camp, they had chosen to disturb this officer's girl? What type of bad luck was that?" they were thinking. At any rate, to an observer, they all seemed to quicken their pace as they passed by the Audi Q7.

"So, where do we go, Sarauniya?"

He dialled one of his officers on his cell phone and dispatched them. The two trucks peeled away as the men departed.

"Anywhere but the Hotel Plaza," she quipped. "What's Sarauniya?"

"It means queen," he said as his barely-there smile flitted across his lips and his gaze stayed unwavering on her face.

Kaniz was too bold for her, he wasn't playing fair. He couldn't call her "queen" without her permission. He just couldn't! They weren't dating. She wasn't a giggly debutante, so she tried not to fidget under his gaze but she was beginning to lose the will to fight him. Something deep within her always felt she was *home* when she was with him... *he* was home. His serious, sincere gaze was still on her.

"God help me, I have missed you terribly, Morola," he whispered, his gaze still on her face. He breathed out audibly. Starting the car, he looked at her again, "Let's get you something to eat."

Rola didn't protest. It was easier to allow him to take charge. She was beginning to lose the willpower to protest but a dark thought flitted across her subconscious and an old fear rose to the fore. "Not so fast," her rational mind protested and she shook herself mentally from his spell. She decided that her resolve was weakening simply because it had been an emotionally charged period for her. All that "queen" and all the other emotional ramblings were just the art of seduction. It was just his lust driving him.

Once a man got what he wanted, even if he was content to wait till marriage, once he got what he wanted, the infatuation would begin to wane. That was all it was. The huskiness in the man's voice as arousal hormones flooded his system, his heartbeat racing, his pupils dilating in attraction to allow a better view of the object of his desire. She knew better. It was all physical attraction, nothing beautiful, nothing to do with love. Like a bucket of ice-cold water, her thoughts woke her up and dragged her abruptly out of the warm emotional cocoon she had been in. His "spell" was broken.

Kaniz felt the shift even as he sat on his side of the car driving. She had deliberately withdrawn from him again.

Her phone rang. It was Tim. These days, she just tolerated Tim's calls as his obvious desire for more than she had to offer was causing her stress. But was Tim not safer for her than this bold warrior who seemed to have tossed her into his harem without her permission? This call was well timed, it could come in handy.

"Oh Tim. Hi darling," she drawled. She put her phone on mute at the "Hi darling," and blew kisses at Tim.

"So I am wrapping up my discussions with ETN, the private equity firm I was telling you I had a meeting with yesterday. It seems it's a done deal, they are on board."

At this, Rola actually blew him a kiss through the mute phone.

"The temperature was minus six yesterday you know..."

"Aww," she crooned.

The network was bad because they were in motion and in the sticks. Tim was going on and off the line and it was clear as soon as she answered the call that he couldn't hear her side of the conversation, though *she* could hear him so she took advantage of that to perfect her charade, for the audience of one.

"I miss you, Mo. When I visit, we have serious matters to discuss."

The statement jolted Rola but she rallied quickly and continued the farce. "Miss you too darling," Rola replied, glancing first to ensure the "mute" button was definitely on. The SUV picked up speed at almost the same time the line went off. She was oddly relieved. What was Tim about to say?

Kaniz wasn't happy. Something in him churned at the conversation. He had no right to expect her not to have such conversations. He had no hold over her, but that didn't make it less difficult to bear. He wasn't being rational, but right now, he was deeply hurt. In fact, he was wounded. He couldn't bear her speaking in such tones to some other guy, whoever it was. He had come all the way into this bush to see her and she was blowing kisses to some man while he sat by and listened? Really?

He was silent as he pulled into a fairly decent restaurant serving home cooking about thirty minutes from camp. "Home Cooking" – the restaurant signage proudly announced with a stylised cooking pot logo. Ordinarily, he would have noticed the ridiculous obviousness of the branding but his mood was foul. He turned in and got down from the car quietly. He helped her out of the passenger seat without a word. His face was strained, his left eye twitched. His lips were pressed firmly together. He was trying to keep calm. Trying not to say anything he would regret. He was calm, or so he told himself.

He spoke in monosyllables when spoken to while Rola's conviviality remained unabated. Rola ordered some fish and spinach.

Kaniz wasn't hungry, not in the least, but it was polite to eat something so he ordered his late mum's comfort food and as the waiter left, Morola laughed.

"Amala? Really Kaniz? Not tuwo?" It was such an indigenous choice from her tribe that even she wouldn't make that she was genuinely tickled.

He had scarcely said two words to her since they got into the restaurant but all of a sudden, he replied her. "Oh, I get it," he said, nodding with sudden realisation. "Is that it, Morola?" he said, frowning, his voice hard. "Do you have a problem with my being a northerner? Is that my sin? Is that why you dismiss me so lightly, without a thought for what I feel?"

Rola's mouth fell open. She hadn't seen Kaniz like this before, was he angry? No, he was hurt and she wasn't sure if she liked herself at that moment for being the one who hurt him.

"No," she said. "It's not like that..." She sighed, and she thought to herself that she sounded like a bad script from a cheap home video. She really had never cared where anyone came from. Her best friend was not from her area. The Bolades weren't ethnocentric.

"What is it then, Morola? Just tell me what it is. Why are you always shutting the door in my face? Why must you *prove* to me that I don't matter to you?" He tried to protect himself and mask his anguish with his stern tone.

He felt his voice was too strident, she looked perturbed, so he reached across the table for her hands and she took them off the table quickly before he could touch her.

"Morola, tell me what you want me to do. What should I do to prove you can trust me?" His voice was now low, almost pleading but when she looked up at his face it was a study in calm dignity.

"I don't know what you want from me," she said in frustration. "I just don't know what you want Group Captain Ishaya Mamane. What do you want? Why are you here?"

She was genuinely perplexed. Why was he going through all this trouble over her? She looked at him again, with his looks, Kaniz could have any number of ladies, what was he after? He didn't seem like one for flings but how to tell? Like her people said, "Truth is not written on one's forehead." If only he could tell her what he was really after, she would *know for sure* if he was telling the truth.

They were alone in this quiet "joint" and could speak freely. Kaniz sighed.

"You don't know what I want? You really don't know?" He shook his head in disbelief. He looked into her eyes searchingly... No, she wasn't toying with his feelings. Her eyes were open and unguarded and from his training, he could see that all the cues pointed to her sincerity. It appeared she really didn't know his intentions towards her. He reached for her hands which were back on the table once more and this time she didn't snatch them away.

"I want you, Morola, all of you. Nothing held back." He spoke soberly, steadily.

Her heart fluttered. Nothing had prepared her for this man's candour; no man ever spoke to her so directly. None. Something inside her heart moved, the walls around her heart quaked but she rallied.

"But you don't even like me, Kaniz."

It was his turn to gape in amazement. "I don't like you, Morola? I don't like you?" His eyebrows were raised, his eyes wide. Genuinely confused, he repeated her words slowly, incredulously. What was she saying? What he felt for her kept him awake at night. His heart bubbled with joy with the deep assurance he had that she belonged with him in spite of these painful jolts she was giving him.

"Morola, I don't like you." His voice was a deep octave. "I love you, deeply, like I have never loved anyone in my life and I simply want you to love me back, Morola."

He gently took her right hand and placed her palm on his chest. Through the fabric of the fatigues, she could feel his heart thumping, racing fast under her palm.

"This heart, my love, under God, this heart of mine is yours."

She withdrew her hand sharply as if his chest burnt her palm. "But you walked out on me the day we met, you couldn't bear to stay with me another minute. You were rude to your father just to get away from me."

An errant thought flitted through her mind and she gave it voice. "Is this some*thing* between yourself and your father? Are you Mamanes playing some weird game with me?"

Kaniz was about to explode and tell her off at the ludicrousness of her statement then he heard, "*See the situation from her point of view, reassure her.*" Kaniz took a deep breath as if to calm himself down.

"Morola, I left that day because what I felt for you was so strong; I was afraid I would mess up and at that time, it was frankly unwelcome. I was shocked by the suddenness of what I felt for you and I had to be sure it wasn't lust, not just a physical attraction."

He lowered his head and dropped his voice as he looked intently into her eyes. "Morola, I withdrew to maintain my sanity. I escaped on that day to maintain my self-control. I fasted and prayed from that Tuesday till I brought Isa to your house on Saturday, for almost two weeks."

She could hardly believe what she was hearing. So it had all been a defence mechanism?

"The more I prayed, the more devoted to you I became. What I feel for you is pure, when I think I can't possibly love you more, it escalates, sometimes I feel my heart can't possibly contain it..." He suddenly spoke in a stream of Hausa. He was trying to control what he expressed and he said things he didn't want her to hear, things between himself and his Maker.

He fell silent, his chin on his right hand, his right elbow on the table, his long fingers covering his face, with his eyes closed, he seemed to be battling something. Finally, he opened his eyes, dropped his hand from his face and spoke to her calmly, sincerely.

"Morola, just give me a chance to prove myself, let me into your heart. You have locked me out."

The waiter chose that moment to deliver their food and leave them to their meal but Rola's appetite was now completely suspended by the tumult Kaniz's declarations had unleashed in her. Kaniz's appetite seemed to have been restored by the load he had gotten off his chest.

Kaniz didn't know what to do. Morola wasn't eating. He wasn't hungry before now and he had actually brought her here so *she* could eat. This couldn't become an aborted mission. He felt like feeding her himself. Yet he didn't want to offend her; the independent capable woman.

"*Put yourself in her shoes.*"

"I am not a woman! I simply say what I mean and do what I say. She is just so complicated."

"*Put yourself in her shoes.*"

He left what was left of his meal, picked up his chair and sat next to her at the circular three-foot table. He sat on her right and picked up her fork from her plate; he picked a small piece of fish with the fork and raised it to her lips. He was surprised that she parted her lips and received the morsel, but the shock at his tender action almost innervated Rola.

Emboldened that she allowed him get so close he spoke gently.

"Morola, grant me the privilege to stay right here by your side. Allow me, my love," he breathed, and as if inexorably drawn to her, he bent his face towards hers and his lips brushed her alabaster smooth cheek. His free hand caught a stray braid that had fallen in front of her face and he smoothed it away from her face, ever so gently, his tender movements belied his towering frame and sober mien. His gentleness was melting her heart.

Rola struggled with the surge of emotions welling up in her. This wasn't her plan; this was rapidly spiraling out of her control.

They rode in silence back to camp. As he parked and she was about to get down, he leaned forward slightly, his right hand covered her left hand on the car seat. He was looking at her intently.

"Morola, I don't have the strength to stay away from you anymore," he said in a hoarse whisper, shaking his head slightly, as if wondering at himself. The last twelve days had been harder than he could have imagined, it was pointless. He just gazed at her, she averted her eyes, then he spoke again.

"Can I call on you when you return home?"

She nodded gently like a child, in agreement.

"May I come and take you back home from camp tomorrow then?"

She had planned that one of their drivers would come and fetch her and drive her back in the car.

"The car... how will it get back to Lekki?"

"One of my officers will drive it to your house. When should I be here? Is 1 p.m. okay? Or should I be at the Plaza?"

Rola could only nod, it had been a very emotionally tasking day for her.

"Let me get that for you," he said, and went round to open the passenger door. She stepped out and they both stood by the car door. He stood facing her, the sun was setting and the camp was bathed in shades of orange and shades of azure. Even in her uniform, standing right there in front of him, he knew she was his wife. When he had put marriage firmly behind him, the door to more than he had dared hoped for was opened to him. It was time to fulfill his mission.

Kaniz moved closer and held her hand. She didn't move away.

"Morola," he started, then stopped. He looked into her eyes. What was that fleeting emotion? Apprehension? While he was fully committed, it appeared *she* needed more time to trust him. He actually empathised with her. If he hadn't had the encounters he had over the last few weeks, he could never be this convinced of the veracity of his position where she was concerned. She needed time; she needed his assurance. He took a deep breath and swallowed his words.

Rola could see his temples throbbing. What was putting Kaniz under such pressure? He lifted her hand to his lips and gently kissed it.

"I miss you already," he said gently. But what he wanted to say to her was, "Morola, my love. Marry me, if you would have me. Then I vow to do all that is humanly possible to make you happy, God helping me." But he needed to give her more time; it was only fair. He would also put the time to good use. He wasn't accountable to himself alone. He had to tie up some loose ends first, especially with the business at hand.

Rola prayed fervently before attempting to sleep that night. She definitely needed a good night's sleep. She prayed against deception, she prayed that the light would shine and show her the truth. She prayed that His will be made clear. She fell asleep and into the very same dream again! She was on the beach, the waves were choppier this time. She saw the figure ahead, he was wearing white this time, a white caftan. She rushed towards him and as she got to him, Alhaji turned to her with a loving smile.

"Get out you spirit of deception!" she said and the smiling face melted as if a mask was being peeled off. Under the mask was the most grotesque face like a gargoyle's. She wasn't sure what the emotion that oozed out of the face was, but it wasn't love.

The apparition vanished in a flash of black smoke, and right where Alhaji had stood on the seashore, was an unlit earthen lamp. She picked up the lamp and threw it into the ocean with great force. It landed with a huge splash and a boom. It was just a lamp, why the boom?

Rola woke up instantly and she felt suddenly free. What just happened? Alhaji became a gargoyle? A horrific face? Did it mean the truth was revealed? Were his real intentions horrific? Gone was the strange love that had consumed her yesterday. She thanked God for her restored peace, the confusion was gone. She drifted off into a restful sleep.

Alhaji woke up with a start. He had been startled awake by a loud noise. He was wide awake and he sensed a strange presence in the room. He looked round him as he sat upright in his bed. He stepped into his closet and looked around the bespoke dressing area. Nothing seemed out of place. Yet he could feel that malevolent alien presence.

Just as he was about to switch off the closet lights and close the door, he looked back and saw his lamp – the flame was out and the lamp seemed to be drenched with some sort of liquid. He moved closer to the lamp. It was wet, but the closet floor was bone dry. He sank to the floor and sat by the lamp of hope, dumbfounded.

"No," Jude's voice boomed. "You can't."

"Jude, keep it down," Funso said. They were in his aunt's house and the last thing they needed was to have someone overhear them.

"Jude, I understand your point and that is why in utmost respect for this group and my commitment to our cause, I have reverted to the group before taking any irrevocable step. But my mind is made up."

"Getting someone to sleep with is not that complex, we are officers, it's easy. Why do you want to complicate everyone's life, Kaniz?"

They had all agreed before the Quartet was formed to avoid emotional entanglements. No one would talk to a girlfriend or spouse about the business at hand because a partner could be used as leverage against them.

"Did I tell you sex was my problem, Jude? Are you not listening to me? I said I am marrying her. Regardless of the fact that I started this group, if you no longer feel comfortable working with me because I'm no longer adhering to what we agreed, I understand, and this will be my last meeting."

"Easy," Kola interjected. "Kaniz, Jude is right. This wasn't the agreement at all. Any of us could be killed or jailed. It's simply unfair to a spouse. I am the oldest in the group and it's not as if I haven't met a few ladies since we started this business, but we all agreed, and so, in deference to what we all agreed and looking at the danger inherent in our business, I have decided that marriage and children will have to wait. Besides, I think from all indications, we should be able to round up the business this year; so why not wait?"

"Exactly," Jude said.

"If the momentum that is gathering makes it clear that we can round up this business this year, let the man marry," Funso said. "I know Kaniz, no matter how the ladies pressure him, casual stuff is not his style, if he says this is what he wants, I trust his judgement. Kaniz, you have my support."

A pregnant pause followed and finally Kola's voice broke the silence. "And mine," he said, relenting.

Jude wasn't impressed. Rules were rules.

"Thank you," Kaniz said. "Thank you for your confidence in my judgement."

Chapter Fourteen

"Thy Kingdom come. Thy will be done on earth as it is in heaven."

Matthew 6:10

Kaniz was at the Hotel Plaza reception by 12.30 p.m. He didn't think it wise to go up into a hotel room to meet Morola. It could give the wrong impression to a casual observer. He had sat in open view in the reception and waited for the hotel staff he'd asked to bring the keys down to him. He had then given her car to one of his officers to drive straight to the Bolades' place in Lekki.

Even with his best efforts to control it, an unbidden joy seeped into his soul as he saw Morola come down with her suitcase. He really wasn't sure how to greet her. He gave a "side hug", which was safe for now.

"Thanks so much for picking me up, Kaniz," she said, avoiding his direct gaze.

"There's nowhere else in the world I would rather be," he replied, soberly. He was not going to attempt to hide his feelings from her, he loved her, he was not afraid to let her know. She needed to be convinced, perhaps, with that conviction, she would grow to trust him more. "Where are the other things you brought?" he said, taking the suitcase from her.

"I gave the nice chambermaid the microwave. She was ever so kind and she has two kids, she will need it."

Morola reminded Kaniz of his mum. Laraba could have given her heart and both kidneys away. "Morola," he snorted, softening his reaction with the faintest of smiles on his face.

"Hope your clothes are all coming back?" knowing, even as he asked what the answer was. He had noticed the suitcase was a lot lighter than it had been when he brought her to camp. "Actually..." she started and stopped when she saw he was smiling. She smiled at him too and everyone in the reception turned to watch the rather dashing couple as they made their way out of the Hotel Plaza.

Rola wondered if Kaniz was real. He always sat her comfortably in her seat first before turning round to the driver's side to sit. Truth to tell, she felt just a little bit uncomfortable with this, there was nothing wrong with her arms, she could open a car door by herself. She was well able to take care of herself. She was not sure how his chivalry made her feel. Did he really mean all these things he did? Was it a charade? What was he after? What was he really, sincerely after? Never mind whatever he was *saying*. She desperately wanted to relax and just enjoy Kaniz, but everything she had seen so far told her it wouldn't last. Men couldn't be trusted.

Kaniz was impressed that she was punctual and didn't play the games he had seen some women play just to keep guys waiting.

"You look good," he said as they settled into the car for the long ride home.

She couldn't see his eyes. His perennial aviators were on. "So do you," she ventured and got a slight smile in return.

She was wearing a simple yellow dress with flared sleeves. She was extremely comfortable in it. She had on black suede Louis Vuitton sandals with block heels. Her eyes were shielded by her Prada "Jackie O" vibe sunglasses with a tortoiseshell frame. Her braids were in a neat donut at the top of her head exposing her long elegant neck. She didn't know it, but she made an exquisite sight.

She had made up her mind there would be no staring into her eyes today; she was too aware of the psychology and the science of attraction. If two people stared into each other's eyes long enough, they began to feel drawn towards each other. It wasn't "love", it was a trick casanovas understood and used well.

Kaniz was dressed casually as usual. Being in uniform so often, he dressed down whenever he could. He had on a beige linen shirt with short sleeves. The heat and humidity made this fabric and sleeve length a firm favourite of his whenever he was in the tropics.

Rola couldn't miss that his civvies and his uniform were always a perfect fit. His biceps rippled in this short sleeves. No wonder he wore short sleeves so much. "Show off," Rola thought. She rolled her eyes behind her sunglasses. His broad chest dove tailed into a "V" at his waist, his lean hips and his long legs were clad in dark denim.

Wait! She interrupted her thoughts. "Did she just say to herself, 'his lean hips'? Oh no! What was happening to her? "Group Captain, my life was working perfectly before you came along," she wailed in her heart. She analysed her decision. She had reluctantly agreed that Kaniz could pick her up because, frankly, he was just such excellent company. He was so intelligent and had this droll sense of humour she liked. It could be almost a three-hour journey and she just would rather be with him for the ride than with one of their drivers, that was a fact she couldn't deny.

If he would just stop being so intense and making her heart flutter incessantly. "Honestly," she thought, "this guy would make a really good friend." She had also decided to return with him because she was rising to the challenge, determined today to break every hypnotic aura that Kaniz was dispensing. She had to put an end to the advantage he had gained over her because of her isolation in camp and the surreal events of the last few days which had made her vulnerable. She was going back to real life now, to normalcy. She knew how to combat every trick he tried today. She knew just where to start.

"Penny for your thoughts?"

Kaniz had been simply staring at her. He seemed just content to watch her.

"Group Captain, it's a long journey. Let us pray."

"I like that," he said, bowing his head instantly with the slightest of smiles. He clearly expected her to lead the prayer.

Rola didn't trust men, but she trusted God so much. Her faith in Him was so childlike and sincere and it was evident as she prayed. She spoke as if He stood right there by her, in simple words that spoke of a deep intimacy. She committed the journey and all they would say and do on the journey to Him. She asked that He be glorified and pleased with them and all their words and deeds. She knew she needed this prayer to protect her emotions.

"Amen," Kaniz said. "That was beautiful. We really should pray together more often."

He eased the Audi Q7 out of the hotel car park and they were on their way. Morola was quiet and Kaniz decided to allow her time with her thoughts.

"May I play my music?" she asked.

"Please Morola, feel free. Do you need any help with the Bluetooth connection?" he asked.

"No thanks, I'm good." He couldn't know that she was actually familiar with the system since it was similar to the one in the Range Rover Sports she drove in the States.

"I shouldn't ever forget you are an engineer," Kaniz said. She didn't respond. "She's very sober today," he thought. But, he was just getting to know her. No matter how he already felt about her, he still had to "learn" her.

Rola had deliberately chosen to play worship music after what happened last time. She had initially chosen to pray as a buffer but when she ended the prayer, she knew it didn't do the trick. Instead of the prayer becoming a fire wall separating her from him, she now felt so much closer to Kaniz.

It wasn't physical, it was several levels higher and deeper. It was like scales fell off her eyes and she was suddenly seeing him for the first time and she was discovering she had known him *all* her life. How could prayer make matters "worse"?

"God is love" suddenly began to make some sense to her. A deep compassion for Kaniz came over her. He wasn't just "a man", he was her brother, a sincere son of the same Father who seemed to genuinely want to please their Father. He didn't appear to mean her any harm. He had actually been *really* kind to her. His only offence was being a man and professing to love her.

As her playlist started, the melody of Hillsong's "So will I, 100 billion x" filtered from the speakers and filled the car, and thereafter, track after track of intense worship music rolled out. They weren't conversing with each other today, they were both worshipping and at the sight of a strong, dignified Kaniz in sincere worship, in surrender, his love for God so palpable, her heart melted. There was something about it all that was just so inspiring, so endearing... so *powerfully attractive.* In that moment, the barrier she kept up around her heart to keep *all* men out dropped, and Kaniz strode into her heart. "God of Creation, there at the start before the beginning of time..." A deep peace filled the car. Rola couldn't stop her eyes from getting wet and was grateful for the sunglasses she wore which hid her eyes. "If the stars were made to worship so will I..."

In that moment, that seemed suspended somewhere between eternity and time, Rola knew with an unshakeable conviction and finality that was beyond the realm of human influence that the only way she wasn't going to become Kaniz's wife was if she chose to deliberately disobey her Creator. It wasn't a resolution she came to through deep rational analysis. It was a knowing she couldn't shake that floated up from her deep consciousness as if she had buried it there beneath baseless arguments and doubts. With irresistible strength, the conviction arose and took an unshakeable hold of her spirit and soul. She was like one awake after a deep slumber.

The playlist was on repeat and much later the song started again. "If the wind goes where You send it so will I, if creation still obeys You so will I..." She had issues with trust, she had so many questions in her head, but to keep fighting Kaniz was to fight her own self. She now knew that to marry Kaniz was her destiny.

The tears of surrender rolled down her eyes, unbidden, uncontrollable, they escaped the sunglasses and created rivulets down her cheeks. Her well-laid plans to return to New York after the service year were suddenly out of her hands. The tears stung her eyes at this thought. Her independence was being absorbed into an interdependency with Kaniz, and at this realisation, more tears flowed.

The atmosphere in the car was one of intense worship and surrender. Someone infinitely greater than they both was with them in the car. Kaniz eased the car gently into the empty parking space right in front of him.

They were in VI already and Rola didn't even know. He parked and took off his aviators, reached over to her, lifting the sunglasses gently off her face, dabbing her eyes with the tissues from the box he had in the car. He drew her gently towards him as he leaned inwards towards her and held her in his arms.

The tears were still pouring down her cheeks. She wasn't sobbing or wailing, she was just peaceful and surrendered. She was done fighting. She still didn't have all the answers but she knew she was done struggling. She had to trust her Father.

It was as if he could read her thoughts. He spoke gently, almost in a whisper. "It's okay to cry my love and it's not weakness either to surrender. This," his voice came from beside her right ear as he laid her head gently on his shoulder and she didn't resist, "this wasn't my plan too. After several days of praying, fighting it, fasting, I surrendered." He shook his head. "I am not ashamed to let you know I love you Morola." His eyes had the gentle look he seemed to reserve for her only. "I am not afraid you will take me for granted. When you are faced with the will of your Creator, if you are wise, then you surrender."

She had no reply; she was just wetting his lovely linen shirt with tears. Normally, a woman's tears confused him, made him uncomfortable but not these tears. These tears endeared her to him even more, showed him her vulnerability to her Maker. In spite of her struggles, she submitted to Him. He had no trouble reaching her heart. *This* was what Kaniz had desired and prayed for the most in a wife, one who yielded quickly to God's will.

"We are both trusting Him, we will work this out together Morola. Hmm?" he said gently still cradling her head on his shoulder, his cheek against her hair. He looked into her eyes reassuringly. His eyes were sincere and sober. "I have no plan B. I am in love with you already, my Morola." Whispering to himself, he said, "We *will* make this work my love." The words were uttered as a solemn promise.

Chapter Fifteen

"... my son is a young lion that has finished eating his prey. Like a lion he crouches and lies down; like a lioness – who dares rouse him?"

Genesis 49:9

Working at QuantumTech promised to be a good experience for Rola. It would be her first time of working in her country and she was not disappointed by the structure and the work ethic.

She reported directly to Debola Laoye, the Managing Director of QuantumTech, the IT arm of the Mamane Group. Right from the day she met him when she came for a look-see at QuantumTech, he had been very welcoming. Debola was just the kind of boss she needed right now, no stress. One more bit of stress added to Alhaji's issue and it would have been curtains for herself and Mamane.

With the news of Synergy's award-winning app going ahead of her, her reputation amongst the nerds of QuantumTech was no less than rock star status.

Debola personally showed Rola to her office, a spacious left corner office. The entire 13th and 14th floors of Mamane Towers housed QuantumTech. The room had elegant but functional furnishing in beige and black and, behind her desk and by her right, the walls gave way to two huge sheets of glass giving her a breathtaking view of Victoria Island. Lagos looked so stunning from this vantage point above the din of traffic.

Rola's assistant, Tracy, was ready to start work. Debola had introduced them on Rola's first visit to Mamane Group. The introduction to the rest of the QuantumTech team was to be at the management meeting. The immediate order of business was to familiarise Rola with her next project. Incidentally, a major defence contract had just taken off and the Chairman had specifically mentioned he wanted Rola working on them. Debola would normally have bristled at such an intervention but meeting Rola and seeing what she was clearly capable of, he couldn't have wished for a better fit. The Chairman got this right.

Nerds seemed to be the same on the East Coast as in Lagos and she fit right in. By the time Rola arrived home after her first day of work, she was optimistic that the year ahead was going to be time well-spent.

Amaka was deep in thought. Rola couldn't figure out what had come over her friend in the short time they had been speaking. Amaka had gone from animated and smiling to moody and taciturn.

"Amaka you are the one who said I should give you all the gist," she said, "now you look depressed."

Amaka looked up and shrugged. "It's nothing."

Rola was silently glad she hadn't shared what had happened on the journey back home with her friend yet. If she wasn't happy about Kaniz's visit to the camp, how would she take the news if she told her she was convinced Kaniz and herself were meant to be together?

"You don't like the fact that Kaniz and I are getting close?"

"Haba! No, no no please," Amaka protested. "From the first day I saw Kaniz, this is what I wanted for you. Something just told me you both belonged together."

She had to explain to her friend that when she saw someone being treated the way she wanted to be treated she didn't feel envious of the person. She felt enraged at Femi. A deep rage.

She sighed deeply. When she saw a generous husband, a sacrificial soul, a man who really cared beyond the ephemeral "show" of teddy bears and cakes, who really truly cared for his partner, it was like a trigger. Something went off again inside her, no matter how sincerely she felt she had forgiven Femi. Pure rage filled her heart again as the bitterness she felt at his errors came pouring back into her soul afresh, worse than the first time it actually happened. It didn't matter how many times he had pleaded for forgiveness, it was just like a Band-Aid being ripped off a wound, over and over again. It was like she was in a cycle of bitterness these days, reliving the experiences again and the man, when she engaged him, the man kept singing "forgive me" like a track on auto-replay but kept doing the same thing again and again in a different form.

"Rola, it just makes me sad to see what Femi has turned us to with his stubborn selfishness and stinginess. If he was just not selfish, we could be so happy. You know how pleasant he can be when he wants to be."

Rola nodded. She figured her friend's moodiness was brought on by thoughts about her own relationship.

"It's like a spirit, a real spirit comes on him when it comes to money. He says it's his background. It's a neurosis. I googled and I think it's a neurosis. A fear of not having that becomes miserliness that takes hold of them from childhood and... and..." she was stuttering from anger and frustration, "destroys their psyche."

"Amaka, google didn't say all that, I'm sure." Rola chuckled.

Amaka continued her soliloquy. "What if I clung to my background and insisted on spending every Christmas in the village, what would happen? When I can adapt, what makes it impossible for him to let go of a defective background and mindset?"

"They say women adapt better than men. Have you talked to him about it?" Rola said. As she spoke, Rola felt like she was fast becoming an agony aunt; one of those "Dear Aunty" columns in the tabloids.

Amaka looked at her as if she didn't hear her well. "Have I talked to him? What else do I talk about almost every day?"

"Pray," Rola said, "and be guided to a counselor, someone he truly respects."

"TK?" Femi really respected Rola's dad.

"Not TK o," Rola shouted quickly, alarmed.

Amaka smiled ruefully. "Rola, that was your dad's past."

Rola's look needed no decoding.

"Besides, failing in one area of marriage doesn't mean he is useless to counsel someone in another area now that he has learnt his lessons."

"I really don't want to talk about it," Rola said, turning away. "Too many bitter memories."

At that moment, her phone rang and Rola let the phone ring through. It rang again and then she picked it up.

She tried to be cool as she heard, "Morola." It was Kaniz. "My love," he said in a gentle whisper. Her heart melted at his voice.

From his tone, she could hear the sincerity in his voice and she could see that most irresistibly tender look in his eyes when he said the words.

Was it his deep baritone or the sheer sincerity and boldness with which he spoke that melted her? What if he changed? What if whatever seemed to come on all men she had seen also came over him too and he changed? None of them seemed capable of keeping the promises they so sincerely and passionately made. She found herself praying silently. Kaniz would be different. Kaniz would not betray her like her father betrayed her mother.

"Hi Kaniz," she said coolly, her tone belying her churning emotions.

"The Chairman wants to see you." Her boss had poked his head through her office door but barely stepped into her office to inform her himself. Rola wondered why he didn't just use the intercom. He probably thought it was really important.

She went up to the Chairman's office, past the friendly Becky and straight to the medusa of the 15th floor, as she had started to call Khadijat in her mind.

Khadijat seemed to be getting weary of her hostility and she made an effort to be civil but Rola couldn't be bothered now. "Too little, too late," she thought. She was a pleasant person but if anyone was deliberately and obstinately unpleasant, she would give as good as she got.

Alhaji was fully prepared to see Rola. He had bathed head to toe in the special soap that morning and he knew today's encounter couldn't go awry like the last time.

"Ah Rola," Alhaji welcomed Rola in his booming voice. He must really love blue voile, Rola thought. His babanriga today was of yet another blue voile with his perennial woven cap.

As soon as she saw Alhaji, the first thought that struck her was how attractive he was. The strange pull she had felt in the dreams welled up immediately; she felt like a sweet warm blanket was draped over her.

Under her breath, she said, "I refuse this deception!" And as if the attraction was an enchanted shawl that had been draped round her shoulders and had been yanked by an invisible hand at her words, the strange pull lifted and the rose-coloured lens she had been looking at Alhaji through just seconds earlier shattered. She could see him clearly – an older, distinguished-looking gentleman, with a slight paunch.

He motioned for her to sit in one of the visitors' chairs.

She sat on the edge of the chair and looked at him.

"Rola, you may have misunderstood what happened in this office before you went to camp," he said.

She just stared straight at him.

"I am not a young man. I don't start what I don't have every intention of finishing." Alhaji searched her face for clues that he was making progress in his cause and drew a blank. Was the soap this powerful? She was just staring, poor girl. "She must be rendered speechless with love," he thought. The great marabout's powers were so potent, she had no choice in this matter. She was probably completely inundated.

"I am asking you to be my wife, I am not playing games here. You will be my first wife. There's no woman in my house now. No Mrs Ishaya Mamane." He paused as if for effect, but Rola didn't say a word. "Let me tell you what is going on here my dear. When you understand, you will appreciate God's wisdom. It had been prophesied that someone who had left my life was returning and with her, all that had been lost would return."

Rola actually nodded, encouraging him to speak because she actually wanted to hear this story. Besides, with no strange emotions coursing through her, she was in control. She was good. He could speak for as long as he liked. He was paying for her time after all. If he wanted to waste her working day, that was up to him. She smiled sweetly.

Alhaji was so encouraged at Rola's smile. Haba. He had not paid nearly enough to Traore, the results were undeniable.

"And with her return, my losses would be restored," Alhaji concluded.

Rola was still nodding and smiling.

"You came into my life Rola and Isa was found. Kaniz my son, who had been dead to me for seventeen years walked into my house by himself. By himself. All within three days Rola! God is great! I don't need to say too much about the contracts restored. You are working on one of them at the moment."

She had many questions but she could ask Kaniz those questions later. Where had Kaniz been for seventeen years? How had he been dead to Alhaji?

"How was I the one who had left your life, Alhaji?" She just had to ask because that part of the story was just not adding up.

"Hmm, very wise question my dear, very wise." He nodded. Paused. His hands were placed together in a triangle in front of his face, the tip of his index fingers touching the bridge of his nose. Alhaji actually made quite an imposing figure. He could have almost any woman he wanted. Why did he not have a wife at the moment? What was wrong?

"My beloved wife Laraba, Kaniz's late mum" – Rola detected a flicker of pain at that word "late" – "Laraba left us on the 28th of October 1990 and you were born—"

"Sir, I don't get it." She knew she was born exactly a month after his wife's death, but she needed a full explanation because she had determined that this was the last time she was having this conversation.

"Rola, are you so unversed in the spiritual realm?" He looked behind him and glanced at a huge golden frame and for the first time, she saw a photo of a beautiful dark woman. She seemed vaguely familiar. She had Kaniz's eyes and smile, though the shape of her face was closer to Rola's and her high cheek bones were a lot like Rola's. She was curvy too. Rola felt genuine compassion for Alhaji.

"Wow," she said, "she was beautiful."

"No," Alhaji said. "She *is* beautiful," he added, looking directly at Rola. He rose from his seat and Rola got up immediately. She wouldn't be trapped by him again.

She shook her head. "Alhaji, I am not her; I don't believe in reincarnation, sir. It's not true, we all die once and after that, we must all give an account to our Maker, sir."

He laughed. "You know she was a Christian too when we met?" he said. "Oh you didn't know? She was also a Yoruba woman. Laraba is a Hausa name which means Wednesday. My wife was born on Wednesday." Alhaji was still amazed at how Laraba's love for him had made her fight her way back to him, through the grave, through everything, in spite of all the odds. And he loved Rola. He loved her like... he examined his feelings; he loved her like a *daughter* actually. But what did it matter? Love was love. He was blessed to have her.

"Rola, did you ever wonder why you suddenly left the US, returned home and insisted on serving? Have you wondered why you are here in Mamane Group? Do you know Laraba was the one who encouraged me to start Mamane Group? The one who stood by me when I had nothing?"

"Alhaji, I appreciate what you must have gone through." She made to leave, thankful she didn't come upstairs with her bag. She was simply dressed for work in a sleeveless navy-blue shift dress with a row of pearls and simple pearl and gold earrings with nude Louboutin kitten heels on her feet.

"No, don't go yet," he said desperately, panic-stricken. Alhaji was standing by her side now, covering the distance between them in two strides. He grabbed her right shoulder as she turned to leave. The strength of his grip was like a vise. Rola let out a cry of pain.

Alhaji was mortified. He was by no means a violent man; he could never justify striking a woman. "My dear. Sorry." he said, now thoroughly confused, trying to see what he could do to make things better.

Rola would ordinarily be livid, completely incensed but she looked at the much older man who stood crestfallen in front of her, stricken with guilt for the hurt he had caused her inadvertently and she felt true compassion for him. If she had been almost deceived by those dreams, who knows what Alhaji was going through right now? The power of the dream encounters was so real that if she had not been able to break their enchantment, no one could have convinced her they were mere deceptions.

"Alhaji, it's deception, sir. I pray you find the happiness you are looking for but I think if you want me to remain here and actualise this project for QuantumTech, it's better we never ever discuss this again," she said in a tone reflecting her compassion and turned to walk briskly out.

With Rola's departure. Alhaji sat in his chair in deep reflection. He had bathed with Traore's soap not once but thrice for three days before he took the step of inviting Rola. What was happening?

Rola thought she could hear a familiar voice in the open plan office outside her office, but she was, perhaps, just suffering from wishful thinking. Her door was always slightly ajar. It opened widely now as Kaniz stepped in. Rola smiled spontaneously; she couldn't help it. She hadn't been expecting him but it was always fun to be with Kaniz and today wasn't too busy. The project was waiting for client approvals anyway.

He closed the door and walked over to her seat behind the desk. He still didn't know how to greet her whenever they met and what he really felt like doing, he didn't think was appropriate for the stage they were at.

"What stage are we at?" he reflected. He couldn't resist touching her though.

He came around to where she sat and leaned over her for a hug. That done, he walked round the desk and sat in the visitor's chair. His smile flickered for a moment as he settled down and she instantly remembered Laraba's photo. He had a restrained version of his mother's smile and her startling brown eyes.

"I knew you wouldn't go for lunch if I don't take you," he said. "The busy youth corper. Can you spare an hour?" he asked. "There's this new place on Tolu Adenowo Street, at the end?" He was apparently coming from his office, just a short trip across the closest bridge. She knew with Kaniz it wasn't just about lunch or dinner. There was an agenda, a major item to be discussed.

They were always talking about important issues, not about other people or even minor events but about issues that mattered to them both; what they were about – their hopes and dreams and aspirations. It appeared that without physical intimacy and its complications, they were free to engage on a much deeper level, the level of the spirit and soul. What they now knew about each other in a matter of weeks, some couples who had been married for years did not know. Kaniz was so open and she on her part was so frank that their unique personalities in a relationship was a recipe for developing heart intimacy at turbo speed.

She reached out to arrange her papers out of his view; they were all marked "confidential" and she took that responsibility seriously. She didn't believe that sharing other people's secrets was a sign of closeness in a relationship or provided fuel for intimacy.

As she reached out for the file close to him with her right hand, he glimpsed the bruise on her upper arm and shoulder.

"What happened?" he said, frowning as he touched the bruise on her upper arm and she started, not from pain, but from what seemed like a jolt of electricity she felt as his fingers brushed her arm.

Someone's large hand was clearly imprinted on her upper arm and shoulder. She reached for her bag to fetch the scarf she carried in her bag for eventualities.

Kaniz's voice had changed. "I asked what that was Morola. Who hurt your arm?" She looked at him and his eyes were as hard as granite. His lips set together in a firm line. She stopped rummaging in her bag. She had never seen him like this before. She couldn't even try to make a diplomatic play on the story because of the expression in his eyes.

"Alhaji," she blurted. "Alhaji was trying to stop me from leaving, he sincerely didn't mean to harm me, he wasn't even being violent, it just happened." She knew Kaniz wouldn't listen. She heard herself sounding like the classic battered woman, making excuses for her abuser; but this time, she spoke the truth. Alhaji had really meant no harm.

His eyes narrowed. "Alhaji? Today?"

He stood to his feet immediately, all six feet, five inches of him and as if noticing for the first time, it struck Rola that he was in uniform. Something in his eyes told her trouble was imminent. She started to babble. She sprang up and walked to the door and stood with her back to the closed door facing Kaniz. "Listen first," she said.

He stopped and stood expressionless, listening. She explained what had happened. He didn't interrupt her. He didn't say a word. His eyes were dark and grim. When she was done talking, he just motioned quietly with his right hand indicating that she should step aside.

"Morola, I will be back in a short while. Can we leave immediately I get back?" His voice was calm.

"Kaniz!" Alhaji said, grinning widely. "Where have you disappeared to? We haven't seen you since you dropped Isa off weeks ago, or should I say *I* haven't seen you? Isa seems to always be at your place."

Kaniz's eyes were as cold as ice. "Good day, Alhaji," he said, "we really need to speak."

Alhaji couldn't imagine what the matter could be. He motioned to Kaniz to sit. Kaniz took his seat.

"It's about Morola," he started.

"What about her?" Something told Alhaji whatever was to follow couldn't be pleasant. Kaniz probably didn't like Rola and didn't want him to marry her.

"Alhaji, you really will have to stop this issue you have with Morola."

"Aha," Alhaji thought. He had guessed right. Kaniz really just didn't want him with Rola.

"Why don't you like her Kaniz? She is simply an amazing young woman," Alhaji said.

"Alhaji, your attention is causing Morola considerable distress." Alhaji wondered how Kaniz knew and his face betrayed his wonder. "I just came from her office now and I saw the bruise. Morola would really like you to stop immediately and just let her be."

"Kaniz, how dare you? What is your business? How dare you talk to your father this way? This is way beyond you, talking to me about such matters—"

"On the contrary, sir, it is very much my business. I care about Morola deeply and I won't have her abused. I will protect her even against you, sir."

"That's simply impossible!" Alhaji exploded. "What's going on?" His face showed his consternation. "Not again!" Alhaji shouted. He felt he was in a recurring nightmare. "You care about Rola? Abomination."

"Yes, Alhaji. For you to even consider the proposition on your mind would be an abomination. She should be like a daughter to you."

Was there truth in what Aminat had said about Kaniz back then? If not, why was his son interested in the young woman his father wanted? "Kaniz, not if I have anything to do with it. You would take from me my only hope for a normal life? Are you joking?" He shook his head and wagged his finger at Kaniz. "I will deal with you mercilessly. I will cut you off!"

Kaniz got up from his seat, towering over the older man, who remained seated. "Alhaji, honestly this is deception. Rola isn't mother. And remember that years ago before you could even cut me off, I cut myself off?"

"I forbid you ever to see Rola again!"

Kaniz looked at Alhaji quizzically. "Alhaji, let Morola be," he said once more with finality. "Good day, sir," he added.

Alhaji got up from his seat and rose to his full height. "Never let me see you again Kaniz. Never ever show your face to me again, if you know you won't give up your quest for this young lady," he looked at his son with incredulity. "What is it with you? Look at you." He made a sweeping gesture at Kaniz. "You can have any young lady you want, why go after the *only* one who is my solution?"

Kaniz empathised with his father but the older man was clearly in the grip of gross deception. Even if Morola was amenable to marrying Alhaji, (which she wouldn't ever even hear of) and Alhaji married Morola as he was bent on doing, it would still end in disaster, since she wasn't what Alhaji thought she was. There was no point giving up Morola for a lie. He marvelled at the wisdom behind his first dramatic encounter with Morola. If he didn't have the depth of conviction he had about her, this was the moment he would have given up on the idea of their being together.

"Alhaji, I never intended for this to happen, I love her. What I feel for Morola is beyond my understanding and she isn't the cure for your affliction."

At that last word Alhaji's hand instinctively flashed through the air and only Kaniz's razor sharp reflexes as he moved his head back sharply stopped the slap from landing directly on his face. He gave his father a sad, rueful look.

"Goodbye Father," he said, walking out.

Morola didn't know what had transpired between Alhaji and Kaniz but she knew it was major. He was back in her office and stood by the door, he didn't step further into the room, so she stood up at her desk. He seemed tired. Drained but stoic.

"Morola, let me take you home."

"The car," Morola protested.

"The car will be safe in the car park," his voice was calm, measured.

"And tomorrow morning?"

"I will bring you to work tomorrow morning. I want you with me now," he lowered his voice, "please." He was calm, but she perceived it was with some difficulty.

She knew something had happened and began to seriously doubt if she should even consider being with Kaniz. Was it worth coming between a father and his son?

Chapter Sixteen

"...but wisdom is profitable to direct..."

Ecclesiastes 10:10B

"Amaka, I can't shake the feeling that there's something going on. Kaniz is hiding something from me. There are some phone calls he gets when I am with him."

Amaka jumped in before her friend could land. "And he goes out to take the call? Ewo!"

"Amaka you can shout though." Rola rolled her eyes. She had seen the looks the mostly expat crowd in the restaurant they were having lunch in in VI turned and gave Amaka.

"No Amaka, he doesn't go out to take the call. He begins to speak in Spanish. And I understand Spanish a bit, what with living in New York and all. He and these people are always referring to the *mercancias*."

Amaka looked blank.

"That means the merchandise," Rola said. "And there's talk about *dinero*, that's money. And you know, what bothers me is that Kaniz seems to be open about everything except these calls. He drops the phone without any explanation about what they were on about and just continues relating to me as if all is normal." She paused. "Someone who could stay away from his own dad for seventeen years, that kind of person is capable of anything," Rola added under her breath.

"You know I am a fan, Rola, so anything you say about Kaniz," Amaka shrugged, "you need serious proof to get me on board. I mean, solid faith, fine guy, loves you. Like, obviously just loves you, for all to see. Ok, maybe he isn't too loaded but he is clearly comfortable and has prospects and you really don't *need* any man's money so... Mmm," she took a bite from her sole mernuiere, "this is good. Rola don't worry. Give it time. I honestly think you feel this relationship is too good to be true and you are subconsciously trying to sabotage it." She shrugged. "You just can't allow yourself to be happy."

"But it has caused trouble with his father."

"Abeg, abeg, abeg." Amaka's *abegs* always came in threes when she spoke pidgin. "*His father* is the one causing the trouble for everyone."

"I think it's just better if I... if I let Kaniz go."

Amaka's eyes were round with amazement; she seemed ready to release another loud "ewo" with a mouth full of sole. Rola quickly covered her mouth with her palm. "Ssh! Amaka!"

Amaka restrained herself and moved to her herb rice. "Mo darling," she followed the mouthful with a sip from her glass, "I am sure it will all work out. Deep down in me, I am just not worried." She arranged a forkful of rice. "Hmm this is good. Are you not eating baby girl?" She looked at her BFF with concern. "Eat now."

"I am really not hungry," Rola said, playing with her food.

"It's true. I agree that you are not hungry because you wouldn't waste lobster. You don't seem crazy in love with the guy yet, so you can't be on a lovelorn hunger strike over him either." She reached into her friend's plate. "Anyhow, this food shouldn't waste," she scooped some lobster from Rola's plate with her fork. "Mmm, I am telling you, this is mad."

Rola eyed her. Why did Amaka feel constant commentary on the food was necessary? Especially while Rola was talking about matters that were deeply disturbing.

"When did they open this place? It's not up to two months, is it? It seems there's a new restaurant open every week on the Island," Amaka said.

"Amaka, I can't allow myself to fall in love with a guy like that, not at this stage. I am certain we are meant to be together, but I know it won't work anyway if I am too clingy."

Amaka looked up, aghast. "You will lose him by paying him all the attention he wants?"

Rola nodded. "In reality male/female relationships haven't changed that much. No matter how men talk about how they don't mind women chasing them, it's only true for one-night stands and flings. But for the person he wants to spend the rest of his life with?" She shook her head in answer to her own question. "A woman can't chase a man directly, not like a guy chases a woman. A woman chases a man until *he* catches her. It's done subtly."

"A woman chases a man until *he* catches *her*?" Amaka said. "Until *he* catches *her*?"

Rola nodded. "He needs to feel at all times that the chase is *his* idea, that *he* is in control. Anything a person chases in life runs away – especially a guy. Men are still hunters apparently." She shrugged. "My male friends tell me that they need to feel it was *their* choice to get into a relationship, not that they were pressured in any way into it. They need to feel they got what *they* wanted. I am not advocating puerile games but many of us ladies bore men by being just too eager and available."

Amaka had stopped chewing, her fork held aloft. Rola had always been the one with a bevy of serious suitors. Tim was flying in two weeks, all the way from New York and there were so many others in the wings. She had to know something Amaka didn't know or she had to be doing something right. She knew her friend was not a tease or "putting out" so it wasn't a physical issue, it was something deeper.

"So Mo, we women can't even say 'hello' to a guy first now?"

"Haba! Maccky that's not chasing nau. Most serious men can't easily approach a woman they like in a social setting for fear of being rejected. The girl may have to open the conversation in a casual friendly way – ask for information... whatever... first."

"You are confusing me o Mo."

"It's easy, be friendly. Guys are human beings too and the serious ones are tired of being seen as being out for only one thing when they engage a woman."

Amaka gawked. "They say that's what is on every guy's mind o!"

"Maccky haba! That's just not true! You don't have to engage guys on the basis that it must lead to a romantic relationship or assume that's what he too is engaging you for. That's what puts undue pressure on both parties. It's the motive that matters. If you are simply asking a guy for directions do you get tense? Relax! No pressure. You can be friendly, but don't chase him. There's a difference. Amaka, we have digressed. Coming back to Kaniz and I... it's just obvious to any guy that he is not the centre of my universe. I am not desperate."

Amaka could testify to that. "Anyway, you are a fine girl. You can have any man you want."

"Beauty is overrated you know. Looks can draw a man in, perhaps make him notice you but it's your ability to engage him that will keep him attracted to you. Haven't you seen women whose husbands are way finer than them and still the guy is super attracted to them?"

Amaka nodded. She knew a few. "We were always of the impression that those ladies were good in 'other areas'," she coughed suggestively.

Rola laughed. "Perhaps. But if a guy isn't already in love with you, you can't keep him with 'other areas' only. From what I gather, this desperation is putting the guys off, Amaka. How can a girl be asking a guy 'where are we headed?' First, if you are in that position where you don't know where you are headed there's already fire on the mountain. You have already been placed on the back burner. Second, if you get any other answer but the exact answer you want to hear, break it off."

"Ah! Break it off? Where will she get another man? Men are very scarce these days."

"Clinging to him won't make him choose you. He will just keep you in reserve till his princess comes."

"Like Dayo and Priye o."

"Amaka, we should try and understand the guys' perspective too. Desperation puts them under serious pressure, so you ask a guy 'where are we headed?' he feels serious pressure and he will subconsciously react to you for it. He needs a chance to determine by himself where he is going. Don't forget that they can't take a quality decision when we are always available. We are choking them. We need to give them space to decide in our favour."

"So if you now fall in love with Kaniz, what's your plan?" Amaka gesticulated with her fork.

"Don't stab me with your fork, baby girl." Rola laughed and then shook her head. "My point is that you only remain a challenge to a guy when he doesn't have a hundred per cent hold on you. I know Kaniz is 'The One', but its early days yet to start behaving like we are an item. There's no ring on my finger." She smiled and waved both hands as if saying, "See?"

"Like today, he had assumed we were supposed to go out together, but I simply told him I had something else planned."

Amaka just looked at her friend with eyes wide open and her mouth agape.

I've done that quite a few times," she said quietly. "I have a life Amaka, and one person can't replace all my relationships. That would even be putting too much pressure on him too. I still need to relate with my solid girlfriends. Besides, anything you chase, Amaka..."

"Runs away from you," Amaka completed. "Mo, you? How do you know these things?"

"My male friends confide in me, I read, I observe." Rola smiled. "I am a virgin," she said, "not an idiot."

Tim arrived from New York just in time for Tega and Jolomi's wedding so Rola invited him.

Both the bride and groom were Rola's friends. Jolomi was a popular On-Air Personality at LifeFM and her fiancé, Tega, was a lawyer and human rights activist. Whereas Jolomi was excitable and always upbeat, Tega was more reserved and the most animated he got was when he spoke about his work. Tega was in the news often and he was a familiar pundit on many television stations. Rola was happy for Jolomi and Tega because it was pretty obvious that Tega was still really fond of her. Getting married was the inoculation she hoped would make Tega immune to those errant feelings.

Rola's driver, Ibrahim, courtesy Quantumtech, had gone to pick up Tim in her car, while Kaniz and Rola rode to the wedding together. Kaniz had been to the Bolades in good time to pick Rola up. Rola was sure he arrived early to spend time with Mrs B. Mrs B and Kaniz got along so well and it was also a good excuse for him to get to know TK better. Kaniz had insisted that he would drive her to the wedding if she wanted him to come.

Well, she wanted him to attend and he knew that; how else could she use him to scare Tim away? She had wanted to pick Tim and take him to the wedding, but this new development had put paid to that. However, it was worth it having Kaniz attend with her. He turned out looking really debonair in a lovely grey suit with faint pinstripes, a crisp shirt with the faintest of pale pink tinges and a tie in an interesting shade of claret or was it burgundy? Wine, in any case. His outfit accentuated his broad shoulders and slim waist. His legs were like a rugby player's.

"I wonder what he would look like in shorts, he never wears shorts," she caught herself thinking. "Oh my! Kaniz Ishaya you were sent to destroy me, without a doubt you are my nemesis!" her rational mind screamed. She never ever had these types of thoughts about anyone, what was happening to her? He really looked unsettlingly handsome. Her heart skipped a beat and she averted her eyes.

Anyone could see that they made a lovely couple. From the admiring looks Kaniz got and the baleful looks the ladies cast her way, she knew her opinion on Kaniz was shared by so many others. She hoped Tim would also share the popular opinion, contemplate Kaniz and settle happily in his slot in her friend zone. She really hoped he would; she genuinely liked him but as a friend.

Tim's primary aim had not yet been achieved, since Mo just always seemed to have company when she was with him, but she had promised to see him after the wedding and Mo always kept her word. It wasn't a bad trip regardless as he was feeling so at home in this country. Well... that is, once he got used to the noise. People didn't just talk, they yelled. But they meant no harm. He smiled to himself; they were so friendly and hospitable.

Tim was glad Rola had invited him to her friends' wedding, it seemed to him a sure sign that she wanted his company. He was concerned though and had asked how they could accommodate him at the last minute. Rola had merely laughed at his reservations.

Now that he was here, he understood. He was just another "extra" they had prepared for. Everyone had been so friendly, Femi, whose accent had a "British tinge" and his bubbly wife Amaka. Everyone except "Scarface", Mo's friend, whose look had made him feel... he couldn't even put a finger on how Kaniz's expression made him feel. He wasn't unpleasant, he was just aloof. He comported himself with the reserve of aristocracy – dignified but with barely a smile. He conversed but he was far from garrulous. Tim felt like a schoolboy in Kaniz's presence. Amaka and Femi got along with Kaniz very well though. So maybe it was just him who had an issue with Scarface.

Tim looked at the sheer opulence of the wedding reception. Were those "chandeliers" of real roses hanging from the ceiling all over the hall? He counted under his breath. Sixteen suspended bouquets, each about six feet across. Every single table had a flower arrangement of lilies and roses and candelabra and he guessed there were over a hundred and fifty tables of eight to ten people each.

Even the dance floor was branded with the names of the couple. It was clear that there was a colour code; almost everyone but the bride's friends wore gold outfits.

Rola was looking even more beautiful than he had ever seen her look, like a real African queen. Is this what African women were like in their element? She had taken her headtie off just before the reception. She had looked regal in it and he wished she had left it on.

The couple coming in was something he had never seen. Mardi Gras had nothing on it. The couple's female friends were in burgundy and their headties had gold details while the male friends wore a beige shade of agbada close to gold with gold caps. Looking at those men he suddenly felt dowdy in his Ermenegildo Zegna suit.

Then, there was the dancing. He had never seen dancing like that before. The live band outdid itself, and then, the DJ took over.

There were several sections on the menu with different cuisine and each section had starters to dessert. How was he going to survive when he returned to the States without "small chops"? Without a doubt, each bite of the smorgasbord clogged his arteries and shortened his life span but he rationalised that one had to die of something as he took another mouthful of mosa followed by whitebait fried to a crisp. When the "grills" rolled out, he was sure it was a joke, it had to be. Barely an hour after a three-course meal, they were meant to down a whole fish and a side of chips? Or a choice of sides of fried plantains and fried yam? Why? He was shocked to see Femi dispatch his fish to the bone while skillfully detailing the head *after* his mix of smoky jollof rice, plantain and moin moin, and then Singapore noodles and shredded chicken in sweet and sour sauce. A whole goat was roasting on the spit outside the airconditioned tent, yielding cutlets of spiced meat so hot it could incinerate one's innards. He tried a mouthful of the asun and it was torture, but uncannily irresistible. So, he took another mouthful.

"No pain, no gain, Tim," he said to himself. He added asun to dodo, akara and jollof rice to his honour roll of cuisine. The sound of champagne corks popping filled the air. This was like a feast in Asgard. He must have been transported by Dr Who's TARDIS to a parallel universe because this certainly couldn't be "Africa".

He voiced his thoughts and Amaka said to him, "Well, Tim, Mo's people have spread the art of merrymaking throughout the country. The Encyclopedia Britannica described them as a merrymaking tribe off the coast of West Africa, can you imagine?" she said, laughing. "They're the official ministers of enjoyment o, not just scholars and entrepreneurs."

"All work and no play... makes Jack a dull boy I guess," Tim said.

"Africa" was getting more interesting and Rola more alluring. He was glad he made the trip. It seemed you never really knew an "African" completely until you travelled to their home. He reaffirmed his commitment to marry Rola and decided they would visit her country often. He scanned the hall in wonder. This wasn't a wedding between royalty, these were at most, upper middleclass folk. How could just two families afford this royal affair? Meanwhile, he was told that this was a "normal" wedding. There was a smoke machine belching smoke as the couple took their first dance and an array of concert level stage lights changing the mood on a cycle. This was "normal"? What a country.

Kaniz didn't understand why there seemed to be such pressure these days to hold these grand weddings. He was glad Morola shared his opinion.

Tega and Jolomi's parents were probably upper middle class, comfortable perhaps, but not "filthy rich". Yet he had overheard Morola on the phone with Jolomi bemoaning the hall rent – $30,000! That could make a deposit on property somewhere. Even if the parents had wanted to splurge on the wedding, could the couple not have asked for property instead? The flowers were silk flowers but the decorator had charged $10,000. So they were *renting* silk flowers for a few hours for $10,000. He didn't think there was any way this wedding cost less than $100,000 and yet, the couple apparently didn't own one piece of real estate between them and were moving into a rented three bedroom flat far away on the Island after the wedding.

From what he understood, everyone was trying to "trend". After trending for forty-eight hours, something or someone else would take over and what would they return to? Their rented apartment? Or did they plan to move into the rented silk flowers?

Kaniz knew Morola had invited him to this wedding so Tim wouldn't consider his being invited to the wedding a "date". He didn't mind being "used" because he wanted to be there to protect his turf. He was now crystal clear that his Morola and Tim weren't "dating" or "seeing each other" or "talking" or any of the other terms this generation seemed to get themselves twisted in. Tim and Morola were obviously good friends, that much Kaniz could clearly see. She was at ease with Tim and considered him a friend but Tim was obviously very much in love with Morola. It was obvious from the way he looked at her, the way he looked for any excuse to touch her.

Kaniz on his own part had laid his cards on the table with Morola from the onset. These indefinite relationships were a major challenge in his opinion. Tim or whichever party was eager to progress the relationship would be frustrated, and Morola or whichever party was happy to let sleeping dogs lie could just hang in there till they found who they really wanted to be with. As long as there was no definite *marriage proposal* or *defined objective* which demanded a response within *timelines* clearly articulated, the uninterested party could not be held accountable for wasting the interested party's time. In this case, Morola was not wrong to leave Tim in the "friend zone". Till Tim laid his cards on the table, there was no reason to refuse to be his "friend".

Kaniz wished Tim could have arrived and been some nondescript guy but Tim didn't cooperate, he was almost as tall as Kaniz with a well-built body and he wasn't bad looking at all.

"Who am I kidding," Kaniz thought, "the guy is handsome. And his face isn't scarred, like mine." He felt a twinge of sadness at that admission. It was clear from Tim's physique that he and Morola were indeed gym buddies in New York.

Kaniz couldn't blame Morola for being so relaxed with Tim. Tim's own father had not complicated issues by spooking Morola. He could tell that Alhaji's issue hung between Morola and himself like an impassable gulf, he could sense her struggle as she tried to put it aside only to wonder if there was any point in acceding to a defined relationship with Kaniz. It was also obvious that Morola didn't mind walking away from their relationship and she wasn't even eager to define it either. None of those "Let's define this relationship Kaniz" stuff with her. On any known day, she could be out with Steve or Tim or any of her other friends. She saw him when she could see him. He was left to make whatever he wanted out of it.

Kaniz looked at Tim and Morola laughing. Morola always seemed happy with Tim. Her fun-loving side was clearly evident with him. Should he just stop trying and let her go? The very thought was like a knife twisting in his gut. His heart sank. Tim was the simpler choice. Tim was the choice that made business sense. Those who bought Morola's apps were venture capitalists and Tim's clients were venture capitalists. Morola and Tim lived in the same city and Tim had an apartment in the Upper West Side. But he lived in a house that wasn't his. To her he was the twice disinherited son of a billionaire, she knew nothing of his prospects. Everything with Tim was so much less complex. "But she doesn't love Tim," he said to himself. "And has she ever said she loves you too?" The doubt swept through his soul. Kaniz shook his head inwardly. In spite of their definitive and dramatic encounter in the car on the way back from camp, Morola had never once reciprocated his declarations of love.

He willed Tim away in his mind. "Tim Simmons go back home; she is taken." But was Morola really taken? Was his ring on Morola's finger? What claim did he have to Morola?

The couple's first dance was done and the friends were invited to join the couple on the dance floor. Within seconds Kaniz noticed that Tim had dragged Morola on to the dance floor. She wasn't resisting much though, he noted. Tim's Afro-Caribbean genes stood him in good stead on the dance floor and some of the other wedding guests turned just to watch them dance. She looked amazing with the outfit she wore accentuating her curves. Tim was handsome in his pinstriped suit. Kaniz sat and watched. What was his Morola and this Tim playing at? And yet, what right did he have to be upset? What understanding had they reached? Who was he to her? One of the many guys who claimed to love her?

The music started to change to "Lady in Red" by Chris De Burgh. It was the DJ's ode to Rola in her burgundy outfit. Kaniz wasn't going to allow Tim dance to *this* song with Morola while he just sat and watched.

He got up from their table and stepped on the LED dance floor, moving effortlessly through the dancing bodies to Rola and Tim.

"May I borrow my date for our song?" he said to Tim. He couldn't even bring himself to smile politely, extending his hand to Morola he drew her into his arms.

Tim conceded Rola to him and returned to his seat. Rola knew "they" certainly didn't have "a song" but couldn't tell what Kaniz was thinking. From the set of his jaw and the twitching vein on his right temple, she knew he was barely controlling whatever emotion he was dealing with. Yet, his arms around her were gentle. She could never have guessed he could dance so well. His left hand was at the small of her back, and his right hand entwined around hers tenderly as they danced. "I have never seen the dress you're wearing and the highlights in your hair that catch your eyes, I have been blind... Lady in red is dancing with me cheek to cheek..."

As he drew her closer to him and she felt his muscular body against hers, an alien exhilaration took hold of her.

"Sarauniya, I can't share you with anyone," she heard him whisper, "I just can't." He shook his head and continued in his low whisper. "Is this how you would have danced with Tim?" He bent his head towards her as he rested his cheek gently against her hair. Her full jet-black hair was in an up-do for the wedding. Her fragrance wafted up, enveloping him. She was wearing the oudh he had given her. He had not planned on the effect holding her this close was having on him.

"Morola, you won't drive me crazy," he said under his breath in Hausa. He could feel her heart racing and he could tell she was not unaffected by him too but he wanted so much more, not just a physical attraction. He muttered to himself, secure in the fact that she could not hear him above the pounding music, "I love you so so much. If you would just yield a little, just a little, and let me love you, we could be so happy together." He bent lower and muttered in her ear. "Since I am here as nothing more than your scarecrow, just to scare the pests away – we had better make 'us' more convincing, yes?"

His eyes were grave as he said sarcastically, "Your friends are all watching us? Well, let's give them something to look at." He twirled her around and swept her off her feet and leaning over her, he brushed her lips with his and lingered.

Morola's pulse quickened, as her eyes closed. She was suddenly breathless. What was Kaniz doing?

"Morola, I love you so much it hurts, why won't you trust me? Why do you keep resisting me?" His voice betrayed his emotion. "Sarauniya, stop fighting *us,* you *know* we belong together," he said, and she felt his sweet breath on her lips as he spoke.

Chapter Seventeen

"And why wilt thou, my son, be ravished with a strange woman...?"

Proverbs 5:20

They were at Ocean Towers on the Island, with its stunning view of the Atlantic Ocean. The sound of the pounding some floors below was vivid, and it seemed to mirror the churning tension between the handsome couple at the banquette in the corner.

"I am glad you finally made time to see me today, Morola. Tim has left I presume?"

Rola smiled innocently, ignoring his sarcasm. "Yes, he left yesterday."

"Oh."

They made small talk about the view, about work but Kaniz was fed up, he needed clarity and not small talk. He knew what they *both* had encountered in the car on the way back from camp, yet she kept him emotionally at arm's length. She seemed to know who and what he was to her and was running away from the fact.

"If you don't mind my asking, what are your plans after the service year, Morola?" No point making small talk. He remembered his errant thoughts at the wedding, it was better to clarify.

"My business. I work remotely and things are still working out so far, but Synergy is my focus. In fact, I think I should be in New York for a week next month, if it's alright with Debola. You know, my boss."

"New York?" Kaniz asked with a raised eyebrow. Not now. New York meant her being with Tim again too soon. "For how long?"

"I will just take a casual leave so, perhaps a week away from work at most."

"Morola, what about us? Where are we headed?" his tone was grave as he leaned in and looked into her eyes.

"I don't know Kaniz, you tell me." She met his gaze steadily, unflinching.

"You know what I want, Morola. I love you. I have not hidden my intentions."

She looked away.

As she looked away an errant thought crossed Kaniz's mind. Was it his scar? His left hand was on the scar, his eyes pained. Did she find it that repulsive? Could she not bear to look at his scarred face? Tim was flawlessly handsome; he hadn't seen her looking away from *him*.

"Kaniz." Morola had turned back to him, breaking into his thoughts. It was as if she could see into his mind. "Kaniz, this actually gives you a kind of rugged and mysterious attraction." She reached out and touched the scar lightly and a bolt of electricity zipped through his veins. He drew a sharp breath and frowned slightly. It was the first time she had touched him like that. Now her face was earnest, her brows were furrowed.

"Kaniz, that's it. You are surrounded by *mystery*. There are still so many unanswered questions." She looked at him, her gaze unguarded. He could work with being considered *ruggedly* attractive, slight progress. So far, Morola had made him question all he had taken for granted. "Fair enough," he thought, "she can't commit to an unknown entity."

He threw his arms wide open. "Ask anything Morola, anything at all, if it's my story to tell, you can be sure I will tell you, I don't want any secrets between us."

"Why were you away from home for seventeen years?" She shook her head. "Who stays away for seventeen years? What happened?" She was still looking at him intently, searching his face for answers.

Kaniz was seated across the table from her. He sighed. His brow was furrowed. "It's not a beautiful story," he said and he looked away. He knew Morola was a straight arrow; she had lived a very sheltered life. He was afraid that if he told her about his past, she would run away from him completely.

"You will have to trust her at some point."

"Yes, I will but when she is committed. Right now I have no claim to her—"

"And she won't commit any further if she doesn't know you any better. Trust, have faith."

"My father's wife was attracted to me." He let the words fall between them like a death knell.

Rola's brain went into overdrive. What had happened? Had he slept with his father's wife? What craziness was that? Was he some kind of pervert? She moved back physically, subconsciously desiring some distance from him.

"*Patience, Morola, patience.*" She listened to the still voice she had always relied on. "*Hear him out.*"

She gave Kaniz a look that meant, "And? Go on?"

Kaniz was clearly uncomfortable. His elbows were on the table and he wiped his face with both palms as if he was trying to clear invisible cobwebs away from his face. He was thinking to himself, "So tonight I am going to lose you finally. But you are not actually mine now anyway. But how did I get into this mess, how did I let myself fall in love with you so deeply?"

He took a deep breath and sighed loudly. His left hand moved and found the scar on his left temple and he began to bother the scar with his eyes shut.

Rola instantly knew he was deeply agitated. "How bad can the matter be that he can't even speak?" she thought.

"*God is love.*" As if it was just a minute ago, she remembered the encounter she had in Kaniz's car on the way back from camp. She had allowed Alhaji's shenanigans harden her heart against Kaniz; Kaniz who had shown her nothing but love and kindness. Her heart melted as she watched him struggle. His hand on his temple, eyes shut. He may not be her "partner or significant other" but he was certainly her brother and he was proving to be a very good friend and an excellent human being. He just didn't deserve the way she was treating him. He was not TK. He wasn't Alhaji Mamane. He was Kaniz Ishaya and she couldn't make him pay for the sins of his entire gender. She moved closer to him on the banquette, thankful for the dim mood lighting and the ambient music that kept their conversation and actions private. She gently held his hand and drew it off his face.

"Trust me," she said softly, looking at his face. "You need to trust me too Kaniz."

Laraba, Kaniz's mum and Alhaji's first wife had died in a mysterious car accident, talk of sabotage still hung in the air. Alhaji was bereaved and disconsolate. For eleven years, he refused to take a wife. Kaniz remembered not one serious relationship in all the eleven years. Ishaya Mamane wisely protected his motherless child from his relationships even if he had any. Kaniz was away a lot in boarding school anyway and the first long stretch he spent at home as a teenager was after his A levels. He was to enter into university straight away but his dream was to study aeronautic engineering and he was willing to stay back home for a year taking his SAT and preparing to go to the US.

That very year was the year Alhaji married Aminat. At twenty-three, Aminat's age was closer to Kaniz's than her husband's age at forty-six. Kaniz lived in the guest chalet, as did his male cousins his age. The house was full, he was hardly ever alone with Aminat, but it wasn't long till Aminat began to hint to Kaniz that it was the younger Mamane she was interested in. Kaniz couldn't comprehend it and didn't take the hints seriously.

"But she would brush herself against me and it was getting really weird. If I raised an eyebrow she would pretend she was just playing with her 'son' and make me feel guilty for thinking anything inappropriate was intended." He shook his head. "I was only nineteen and she was playing with my mind."

Alhaji travelled a lot, it was the nature of his business, the same business that kept Aminat in the lap of luxury. As far as Alhaji was concerned, Aminat had her friends to keep her company while he was away. All he needed and deserved was her attentiveness when he was around. Aminat's circle of friends were mostly young wives of rich men her age and not only did Aminat cast her eyes on the young Kaniz, her closest friend Bilquis did too.

"That's if we could call them friends in the real sense of the word. The backbiting was vicious. It appears that when women make men, and the attention of men their primary focus, the rivalry is intense."

Bilquis was relentless and to Kaniz, while she wasn't unattractive, at twenty-six, she was ancient. Younger girls had crushes on him and he was absorbed in the Lagos party scene. What use did he have for wax-print-clad-older-women dripping with jewellery? No matter what *he* thought, the idea of being with the innocent Kaniz seemed to be an obsession with the young widow. Aminat's pursuit too was becoming relentless. She would show up in Kaniz's chalet at odd hours and the young man didn't know how to get her off his back.

"It wasn't love or anything deeply emotional. I could tell she had other indiscretions. I think the idea she had in coming after me was that I was a safe choice; if the affair resulted in a pregnancy then the child would look like Alhaji and the DNA would be close enough.

"Whenever Alhaji travelled, her movements became very suspect indeed and I actually saw a fair complexioned man leaving one of the rooms in the guest chalet at about 1 a.m. one day, while Aminat left the same room fifteen minutes later. Foolishly, I let her know I had seen her. I came out and said 'good morning Hajiya'. From that day on I was in trouble."

Kaniz's hand was on his scar again.

"Alhaji was in my chalet when I got back from a party one night at about 2 a.m. holding a bag of weed I had never seen and a pack of condoms. No matter how many times I told him they weren't mine, he wouldn't believe. The only person who believed me was Samson. He had been with us before my mum died and he looked out for me. He knew Aminat had planted the weed and condoms in my chalet. He knew about Aminat's interest in me, he knew about her indiscretions. But how could he tell Alhaji about his young wife without wounding his ego? If Alhaji sacked him and he had to leave, how would he continue to look out for me? So Samson kept quiet."

It was obvious that Alhaji's mind was poisoned from then on. Aminat had Isa a few months later and Alhaji's full attention shifted to his young wife and her son. Kaniz couldn't get anything right with Alhaji anymore, his SAT was excellent and he was set to proceed to the States but Alhaji completely forgot all the promises he had made to his first son. Suddenly, Kaniz was the good for nothing drug dealer and the womaniser. Kaniz was crushed, he had waited a whole year at home getting his SAT and US admission sorted, now it was sorted, his father would not even stand him being in the same room with him anymore. The young Kaniz told his trusted friend Funso as young people would do and they started thinking of an appropriate plan.

"Morola. You know Major Funso Ajayi my friend who I introduced you to?"

"Major Ajayi? Yes. The day we were returning from camp, you had to collect something from him? Right? You said you were in FGC together?"

"Right, that's him!" Kaniz said. He couldn't help but smile at her, Morola had such a razor-sharp mind. "Funso likes you," he added.

"Yay. I passed the 'interview'," Rola almost said sarcastically. Instead she said, "Aww, he seems like a good friend. So what did you both decide you should do?"

"Funso and I came up with a plan only two silly teenagers could have hatched. When we have children, I intend..." he stopped and tapped his head. "When *I* have children, I will do my best to be close to them. It's a shame that teenagers are usually left to take advice from other teenagers who are no wiser than themselves, just because they feel that their own parents would never understand. I can tell you and Olaotan are close to your parents." He looked at her and said wistfully, "that's what I want for," he paused, "for my children and myself."

Funso and Kaniz decided that to get Aminat off his back, Kaniz should accede to Bilquis' advances, after all, he had held out for about a year, the woman was a widow; he would be rendering her a "service", he was a young virgin.

They would ensure Aminat knew so she would stop disturbing Kaniz once it became clear that he had chosen her friend over her. Kaniz gave in to Bilquis and Aminat knew.

"I told her," Kaniz answered Rola's unspoken question. "I told her and left enough breadcrumbs for her to follow. Perhaps it was postpartum depression or sheer wickedness, I had no inkling Aminat could go that far in her revenge. She set me up, I can't even tell you for decency's sake what she planted in my room as evidence to support her claim that I had seduced her. Till today, I am convinced she took the matter to diabolical lengths so Alhaji could believe."

Isa had just been born. Aminat allowed Alhaji to harbour doubts that Isa might be Kaniz's son. To let Aminat go would be to expose himself and his son Kaniz. Alhaji was in a quandary and he lashed out at Kaniz who he felt was his nemesis. The situation became intolerable and Kaniz began to fear for his life at Aminat's hands. Aminat had Alhaji firmly in her grip. Kaniz just decided and left home one day. Not even Funso knew where he was till he was in Atlanta and he called home.

"I think that was when Alhaji began to believe in marabouts. He must have felt if he had had adequate protection, Aminat would not have been able to decimate us with such a great devastation. She came from a background where being fetish was par for the course."

"But seventeen years? And no one saw you?" Rola asked.

"I was in the US for the first few years." He had a faraway look in his eyes as he cast his mind back. "I really suffered at first Morola, but I got lucky. I made some money and bought my first property – a rundown house. I renovated it and flipped it and things started looking up. I thought I would come back home and start a business, so I returned and by this time, Funso was in the National Defence Academy. He explained to me how my dream of becoming an aeronautic engineer could be fulfilled if I joined the air force and I did. The air force sent me back to the US for my degrees."

"Seventeen years?" Rola repeated again with raised brows.

"Most times, I was out of the country – in uni, Colombia on postings, Somalia, at war in Darfur. I got my rapid promotions from distinction on the battlefield. An awful price to pay for promotion." He touched his scar subconsciously. "Terrible price."

"No one knew where you were? No one saw you? For seventeen years?"

"Funso knew, but Funso can be trusted. How did you think I got addicted to aviators? I was out of the country but the very few times I came across any of Alhaji's friends, I was shielded. I recognised Alhaji's friends but in their wildest imaginations, they couldn't imagine – even if I sat opposite them – that Air Force Officer Ishaya was Kaniz Mamane. Not when they had been told Kaniz Mamane was a drug-addled degenerate. You see what you expect to see. Besides, you can't find an intelligence officer who doesn't want to be found. Sarauniya, you really should eat," he said, gesturing at the delectable entrée they had been served. "Our salads can't get any colder, but I don't want Mrs B to think I am starving her only daughter. Eat? Please?"

While she had reached out to him, she had moved closer and now sat at a place setting next to him. Her plate was close, within his reach, so he picked up her fork and lifted some rocket to her mouth. She parted her lips.

"I love it when you let me do that. It shows you trust me a little." He let out a sad sigh.

He seemed sad, Rola thought. Was he thinking he was losing his father, and it was over a woman again?

"Is history being repeated?" she said aloud. "Kaniz, if you and I get any closer, you are going to resent me for coming between you and Alhaji."

He stared at her incredulously. "Don't be ridiculous," he said, a little too loud. "It's his marabouts and superstition coming between us, Morola. Alhaji doesn't even love you. It's not that sublime. He just believes you are his cure."

"His cure?" Rola asked, her eyes wide.

"Just never mind," Kaniz said with a dismissive flick of his head and wrist. "Let's eat."

"Morola, you haven't even seen where I live," Kaniz said, as they got into the car to drive her home. "What if I am one of those ogres in Yoruba fairytales? The ones that borrowed human bodies to marry women?"

Rola laughed. She remembered those stories. Oh my! Stories that warned young women against greed.

"Kaniz! You know that story too? You are just a local Yoruba man with internal tribal marks."

They both laughed at the idea of invisible tribal marks. Perhaps because that story was hardwired into her moral system or she just wanted to reciprocate the trust Kaniz had reposed in her today, Rola agreed. It was not too late, barely 9 p.m. She could visit with him for thirty minutes.

"*O sé yèyé*," he said, shocking her by the ease with which he spoke her language. His Yoruba was far better than hers.

They set out for his house.

"Speaking of my Yoruba roots, you must meet my cousin Rekiya."

"Rekiya is a Hausa name," Rola said.

"Well, my mum's family all migrated to the north. Most of my cousins have Hausa names. I have a Yoruba name though. My mum called me Ademiniyi." A wistful look flitted across his face for a second as he recalled happier times.

"Ademiniyi," Rola said softly. "It's a lovely name, classic and rare. You know the meaning, don't you?"

"My crown... my prince, is honourable," he said quietly.

And I will call you Ademi, she thought. "My crown, my prince." She caught her own thoughts straying and mentally kicked herself.

He deftly switched back to his subject to escape the sad thoughts creeping in. "You will love Rekiya. She loves you already."

Everyone around him loved Morola; some perhaps a bit too much. He was thinking of Alhaji.

"When do I meet her?" Morola asked, and he was dragged back to the present.

"She is coming down from Abuja next month for Air Force Week. It's my last Air Force Week before I leave the air force. I want you to be there. I have made the arrangements... if that's alright with you." He let the news drop.

"Leave the air force?" Rola was extremely surprised. He made such a good officer, as if he was born to it.

He held her hand close to his chest with his right hand as he drove, keeping his left hand on the steering wheel. "We will talk about it later." He pressed her hand to his lips. "Hmm?"

She loved the soft way he always said that "Hmm". It was like a mother's coo.

He let go of her hand to concentrate better on driving, but she didn't know if she wanted him to let go just yet.

They had driven in comfortable silence for a while before Rola broke the silence. She had been reflecting on all he had told her at dinner.

"Kaniz, Aminat did what she did to ensure Alhaji disinherited you," she reflected.

"And she certainly succeeded. I was too young to realise but after a few years away, it dawned on me. Morola, I battled with forgiving Alhaji. The last thing on my mind was reconciliation and coming home. I was done with him forever, or so I thought. It took God's grace to forgive and to be really sure things were safe with him again. When I knew I had finally truly forgiven him and the time was right, I came to see Alhaji, just a few days before you and I met. In fact, I actually had just returned to Lagos from Colombia only two weeks before then."

"Isa is SS, you are AA. Kaniz, you and I have discussed these things. He can't be yours."

Kaniz looked at Rola in bemusement. "Of course he isn't mine, and he isn't Alhaji's either. Alhaji is AA too. But I just like the young man." He looked at Rola, taking his eyes off the road for a few seconds. "Maybe I have no control over who I love," he said wryly, looking straight into her eyes.

Rola wished he was just less confident, less expressive, more like the other men she knew. No one, absolutely no man she knew spoke so openly about their feelings. It was like a contest with the others, as if they were always jousting with her. So much... so much, she searched for the words; so much fear. Kaniz had no fear it seemed. Why?

"Perfect love casts out fear," she heard deep within her soul. Kaniz was an oasis of peace and his love for her had won her over completely, and she loved him. She loved him. The thought struck her like a thunderbolt. But everything seemed so complicated. Was she too actually plagued by fear? She stared in the dimly lit car at his handsome profile as he drove. She stared at the face she now uncannily felt she had always known forever. "I wished for you before you were known to me. Your face was in my mind before I saw you with my eyes," she quoted in her heart.

"Kaniz Ishaya, I love you with all my heart," she whispered to herself in sudden realisation.

"My love, I didn't get that."

Kaniz had been concentrating on the slight traffic. He hadn't heard her clearly, and she had spoken in a quiet whisper.

"I said it's a bit chilly tonight, right?" she deflected.

"Really? Let me warm up the air a bit. I don't want you catching a cold on my watch."

He was smiling tenderly at her as he increased the temperature of the car AC only on her side, and she braced herself, prepared to sweat as a punishment for not owning her declaration.

Chapter Eighteen

"And Jacob served seven years for Rachel; and they seemed unto him but a few days, for the love he had to her."

Genesis 29:20

They entered through an anteroom into Kaniz's living room. Rola had low expectations, so she was pleasantly surprised. The TV and sound system with multiple speakers were prominent on the feature wall. An L-shaped grey fabric sofa, a grey ottoman in the same fabric and a black lounge chair were the only pieces of furniture in the living area. A nest of glass stools was in a corner on a deep pile rug in silver-grey. He had interpreted the medium-sized space in the best possible way: in a Scandinavian minimalist vibe.

A spherical Scandinavian inspired chandelier in white and a chrome cantilever lamp with a white cylindrical shade and marble base stood at the corner of the sofa complemented by a black lounge chair. A phos floor lamp gave more light to the living room and completed the look. Simple horizontal blinds were on the windows no drapes were anywhere in sight. Kaniz reached for the remote control of the B&O system, and Rola wondered what music he would be playing today.

"Clair de La Lune" streamed over the room. Piano classics? Kaniz. Just as you thought you knew him, he sprung another surprise.

"It's not a big place. Let me take you round." His place was pristine, and she felt sorry for the woman who would have to keep up with Group Captain Ishaya's clinical neatness.

Feeling sorry for yourself already? The thought floated into her mind and she jumped with the truth of the statement. She knew at a level deeper than logic and rationale that *she* was the woman. It just didn't seem right to tread on the rug in this immaculate dwelling with dirt from the outdoors, so they sat down on the black lounge chair at the edge of the seating arrangement. She took off her shoes. "You have no dining furniture yet," Rola said.

"Actually, I thought you could help me choose," he said sheepishly. "We could go shopping when you make the time for me? Hmm, *busy* Morola?"

"You have a rug there already though," she said, pointing to the flat-woven cream and grey rug in an ethnic pattern.

"I had the rug for years," he replied. "I shipped the things I wanted from my apartment when I was leaving Bogota, gave the rest away and leased out the apartment." She followed behind him when he got up.

"I made this a den – a study and a gym," he said at the first door. She saw a desk and both walls filled with books. There were free weights on the rubber mat and a treadmill tucked in the right-hand corner. He took her to the next bedroom. "Officially, Isa sleeps here when he is here. In reality, he ends up in my bedroom."

Rola paused a bit. He was taking her to his bedroom? Did Kaniz have an agenda? Did he sense she was now in love with him and wanted to take advantage of the lowering of her guard? She looked at Kaniz's broad muscular shoulders as he walked ahead of her. He was so much stronger than her, and she would be blamed for coming to his place at night if tonight went south.

Kaniz sensed her sudden apprehension. He had been holding her hand and felt it stiffen.

"But Morola, don't you trust me that I would never take advantage of you?" He seemed slightly exasperated. "Come," he said gently, and she followed him.

"My bedroom." He opened the door, and it was a crisp bedroom with a dark grey padded bedhead, beige wall to wall carpeting and neat rows of shoes on a rack. Nothing was out of place.

She commended him on his neatness.

"Years of keeping your bunk neat for inspection. It's not a habit you can get out of."

They returned to the living room.

"Please sit," he said as he gestured to the sofa. "What can I offer you?" He reached for the intercom and dialled. His cook materialised, and Rola heaved a sigh of relief. She had been worried for nothing; they weren't even alone in the apartment.

She asked for some water at room temperature and sat on the sofa while Kaniz sat on the rug by her side. Paul, his cook, reappeared with the water in a tall glass on a tray. Rola thanked him as he placed the glass on an ebony coaster on the glass stool next to the sofa by her side, and he faded away into the kitchen.

Kaniz was looking up at her. "Morola, I am leaving the air force this year," he said out of the blue. It was time he let her know he had plans. "I need to focus more on my business interests. I now need to plan to take care of my family. I told you I started out with property? I have some condos in Miami that I let out on South Beach and some properties in London and other places. They have turned out to be good investments. I have two portfolio managers who take care of things generally. I wasn't thinking about a family before to be honest but now," he exhaled, "*now* things have changed. I thought *you* should know." He was staring at her again.

He reached beside the sofa on the floor and picked up a slim black velvet box on the rug. He opened it, got up and went behind her. His hands were gentle at her nape as she felt him clasp a necklace on her neck. It was a simple rose gold chain with a pendant in the shape of a heart. The outline was of white diamonds and in the centre was a stunning ruby.

"My Morola, never forget, my heart is yours." His slight smile was wistful as if he stated a fact he knew he had no control over.

She looked down at the heart nestled in her bosom and gasped. It was beautiful.

"I can't keep this." She started to fiddle with the clasp lying on her neck as he handed her another box.

"The earrings," he said. She didn't touch the box.

He gently took her hands off her neck and reached down to slip the earrings into her handbag.

"Please don't do that. No pressure please, it's yours." He had felt like showering her with expensive gifts, but he wasn't sure how she would interpret his gifts. The fact that she hadn't accepted his father's gifts was informative, so he had restricted himself to giving her tokens of his affection but finally, when he couldn't resist any more, he went ahead and ordered this for her and hoped she wouldn't think he wanted to buy her affection. He sat down, this time on the sofa right next to her.

She just stared at him blankly.

"I know it's asking for a whole lot for us to be together. You had your plans neatly sorted out before we met but if you allow me, my love for you can make this work, Morola. *We* can make this work. I vow to make it work. Just allow me." He took her left hand and placed her palm on his face. She could feel the beginning of a stubble on his clean-shaven face as her hands seemed to tingle. He was just staring in her eyes.

"Give *us* a chance," he whispered in his dulcet voice. "Just give *me* a chance. Let me love you, Morola."

She sighed and covered her face with her free hand.

"Sarauniya," he whispered as he took her hand off her face gently. "Look at me." She turned her head slightly in his direction.

"Do you love me?" he asked softly, and her heart skipped at those words.

She was silent. He was staring intently into her eyes. "Your eyes tell me you love me, Sarauniya. They tell me you are mine. Tell me then... *say* it, Morola."

She hurriedly shut her eyes and turned her face away. "I am so scared." Everything was so intense. She was trembling inwardly all of a sudden.

"Of who? Of me? I would never hurt you my love, never."

"I have been so hurt."

"Whoever hurt you, please don't make me pay for his sins."

"He betrayed my trust," she whispered.

"You can trust *me*. I have never lied to you; I have never been like... like this with anyone." He placed her hand over his heart. "You can trust *me*."

She could feel the steady throb of his heart. He was not ashamed to let her know what he felt for her. His eyes were so full of love. Looking at him, she felt her heart would explode.

"Marry me, Morola. Do me the honour of being my wife. I vow to love you, to cherish you and protect you as long as I live, God helping me."

She wondered at how his vulnerability never detracted from his calm dignity in any way. He remained his sober, dignified self. She was stunned into silence at his sudden proposal.

It was obvious he didn't know what to make of her silence. "I love you, Morola," he said. "Am I moving too fast for you?"

She could feel the throbbing rhythm of his pulse from his jaw as he held her hand to his face. He let go of her hand, reached into the pocket of his trousers and brought out a black velvet box.

"This has been in my pocket since the day I visited you in camp." He opened the velvet box. As he did, the solitaire baguette cut diamond caught the light, and the reflection bounced off the walls and ceiling.

"I don't know what to say." She knew she loved him back. She loved Kaniz deeply, but she was afraid. There were too many doubts. It was just easier to say no, or say nothing. "I can't... I don't know what to say."

"Tell me what you feel then." He spoke quietly, holding both her hands in his as he gazed into her eyes.

"Fear," her response came in a low tone. She looked away.

"Mrs B, Kaniz has invited you to the Air Force Week," Rola said as she sat on the bed by her mum who was reading the news on her laptop, wearing one of the comfortable caftans she liked lounging in at home.

Taking one of the IVs from her daughter, she adjusted her glasses and read it. "Oh, he got us special booths. Fancy." She raised her brows. "He has done well. Will he be flying?"

"I believe so."

A frown crossed Mrs B's face. "You don't *know*?"

"Kaniz and I haven't really spoken in almost a month, mum, and I don't want to ask Isa." Isa was so fond of Rola. He was fast becoming a fixture in their house, visiting or studying with Olaotan.

"He doesn't call me and I am not going to call him."

"What happened?" A deeper frown creased her face.

"He proposed and..."

"And what?"

"I didn't quite accept."

Mrs B's face was contemplative. "Well, its alright to take some time to consider his proposal. From what I know of Kaniz, Rola, his faith isn't the issue?"

Rola shook her head. "Ah no, Mum. He is an inspiration."

"Is it the Alhaji matter?"

"It's a big challenge, Mum, but there's more." She shook her head. "There's just so much; Alhaji, the rift between Kaniz and him, my business in New York..." her voice trailed.

Mrs B saw her daughter was conflicted. Her protective instincts kicked in, and she reflexively moved closer. She placed her hands on Rola's shoulders and nodded knowingly. "You are right, but something tells me Alhaji's issue will be sorted with time, sweetheart. We have both discussed how to handle Synergy. I think we both know the reason why, darling, but did you tell him?"

Rola shook her head.

"He isn't even talking to me – at least not the way he used to." Kaniz seemed to have changed, withdrawn way back into his shell. "I have hurt him too much this time." Tears sprung to her eyes at the thought of hurting Kaniz.

"Morolawe, you love Kaniz." It was a statement of fact and not a question.

"What is love, Mum? Real love."

"Tell me what you feel for him."

Rola's eyes were wet. "When I am with him, I forget about time. He makes me feel so alive, so loved, so desirable."

"No, that's not love, Rola." Mrs B smiled. "That's how *he* makes *you* feel. That means the minute he stops doing those things that make you feel good about yourself, you will stop loving him. Many people feel they are in love because the other person makes them feel good. That's self-centred; it's all about them. That doesn't last. Tell me, what do you feel *for Kaniz*? Men prize respect much higher than what we women call love. In fact, some don't understand what we mean by love. They want to be respected. So let's start from there. Do you respect Kaniz?"

"I respect him so much, mum, so much. He is so disciplined. He keeps his word, he is so calm, and his faith inspires and challenges me. The first day I saw him worshipping was the day I think I began to love him. I look up to him. I am happy to let him take charge. Who am I kidding? I actually admire him, Mum!

"I don't want anything to ever hurt him, Mrs B. I don't want anything to stop him from becoming who he was meant to be, and all he was meant to be. I believe in him, I believe in his future. I want to help him achieve his goals. I want that honour of working alongside him and if I am not the best person to stand by him, then I would, I would..." she stuttered, "I would let him go." Rola felt she was rambling, but she had to talk to someone she trusted.

"He is a handsome man, Rola. It's easy to be attracted to a man who looks like him. What if something happened to him? What if something marred his features? What if he couldn't walk?"

"Would he still be Kaniz? Would his soul still be intact? I wouldn't ever love him less because of such things."

"It could be a mental illness that adjusts the very nature of the man you know now."

"But I have met, and I know the real him, Mum. I will fight with him to get the real Kaniz back."

"When he is hurt, how do you feel?"

"I want to cradle him in my arms and smooth his furrowed brows." There were tears in her eyes now when she thought of how she herself had hurt him. "He seems to have so much pain he carries, so much anguish." She looked at Mrs B. "It's never far from the surface. I want to make the pain go away, to give him joy instead. Mum, I want to be the one who takes care of Kaniz."

"And if he hurts you?"

"It would have to be a sincere mistake. I know the way he is with me, mum. I have tested him too many times, but he has remained so kind." She shook her head. "He would never knowingly hurt me and so I would have no choice than to forgive him."

"Morola, call Kaniz. Tell him whatever the issue is."

She cradled her daughter close to her bosom and wiped her daughter's tears with the tissues by her bedside. "You have my *full* support, darling."

Rola dialled Kaniz's number, and it rang through. That was not unusual. Kaniz could be extremely busy or even flying, but he would always call back in the past. Now, she couldn't predict his reaction.

She was startled as her phone rang almost as soon as she dropped the call.

"Hello Morola." Kaniz's voice was ice cold.

"Hi Kaniz. Thanks for the invites."

"You got them? The office must have sent them. They have had our guest list for over a month now." It was a statement and not a question.

"We hope to be there."

"We?"

"Mrs B and Olaotan too."

"Isa will be coming with Olaotan actually." So he was still speaking to her brother? How like Kaniz.

"Kaniz, will Rekiya still be around?"

"She should be around." His voice stayed cold.

"I was wondering if you could make some time next week after the air show at the weekend?"

"Time for what exactly?" His voice was hard.

She swallowed. "Time for us to see," she said meekly.

"I will let you know," he said curtly, in a tone that obviously meant "no way". His tone hurt.

He fell silent. It was like, "Is that all? Are you done?" She had no choice but to end the call.

Kaniz was alone at home. He gasped as he dropped his phone. He was in pain. His heart actually ached.

"Morola! It's been four weeks, and I miss you more each day. When will I be free of you?"

"*When you die*," the answer came.

"Why is this happening to me? Have I not known enough pain for one lifetime? I didn't ask for this!" he shouted at no one in particular as anguish filled his heart. "I have been hurt enough. I refuse to be hurt anymore. I just refuse." He shook his head.

He wondered where the lie that men didn't feel emotional pain came from. He shook his head. "A man's pain is the worst. We don't love easily but when we do, we feel more deeply, hurt more and heal slower. There's no one to bear our burdens with us because we find it so difficult to talk about what we are going through. It just isn't easy to be a man," he pondered.

He couldn't call Funso to tell him the budding relationship was definitely over between Morola and himself, but Morola could call Amaka if she had been in his shoes and after a good cry, they would both have gone to the spa or whatever it was women did to toss men on the garbage heap of oblivion. He had no one, he just grappled with his pain alone.

He had never really loved any woman before. He had flings in his twenties but nothing serious. He was a strikingly handsome man who seemed reserved till he got comfortable and let down his guard, and his reserved, dignified mien seemed to attract the ladies like a magnet. They made it easy; too easy. A full-blooded man would find it difficult to resist and in the earlier days, he didn't bother to try too hard to resist. However, at twenty-six, when he had made up his mind to do things right, there had been no looking back. Then he met Morola, and he struggled with his intense feelings and fasted and prayed fervently, until he attained clarity.

"This is the one you have always wanted, this is the one you ***need****. Don't be afraid to love her because you can't fail. True love never fails. Don't fear, perfect love casts out fear, no games, no tricks, love does not lie, be bold. Love her as I love you."*

But his love had failed. Yet he hadn't taken for granted that he knew all there was to know about how God had loved him. He had delved into study and saw with fresh eyes – perseverance, sacrifice, openness, bold declarations. How could anyone say, *"Greater love has no man than this than to give his life for those He loves"* and yet, those He loved still didn't give a hoot? Unrequited but unrelenting and unconditional love, one Man loving the fickle and giving His all *before* getting an appropriate response? And this was the way men were to love their wives? No wonder so many marriages had issues! It took revelation and great grace to love like this.

When he rose that Saturday to visit Rola's house for the first time, he looked up to heaven. "I promise *You* I will love her like no one has *ever* loved her," he had vowed.

It had been surprisingly easy. The avalanche of emotions which had swept over him the first day was a gift; all he did was to stop fighting it and be carried along by it. He was completely intoxicated with love. In that regard, loving Morola had been the *easiest* thing he had ever done. Yet on the other hand, when he considered the resistance he faced, it was the most *difficult* thing he had ever done. He never did anything by half measures, he went all out with Morola. In desperation, sometimes he relied on his bag of tricks and did what a typical man would do – he withdrew. He gave her space to miss him, to test her. But after he had felt the pain of his rejected proposal, he had withdrawn. What else was left to be done? He had obeyed in this matter of destiny like he had never obeyed before yet it hadn't been enough; he had obviously failed. He had other business going on, and he had lost his father again. He was tired.

Alhaji sat in his office wondering what the essence of his life was. He had not heard directly from Kaniz in over two months. This was going beyond what he had thought. A threat was all he had intended. He felt that by now whatever novelty Rola presented to Kaniz would be over and his ardour would have cooled.

"Blood is thicker than water, young man," he said to no one in particular.

What was going on? He had lit the lamp and kept it burning and the oil was now finished, but he had no results to show for tending the lamp.

To be honest, Alhaji was beginning to wonder why he had to fight for Rola. He was definitely fond of her, even felt protective of her, but she felt like a daughter to him. To be frank, he wasn't particularly attracted to her, but the sage had spoken and the prophecy had been given.

"Who are we mortals before the divine will? But of what use would my life be if I lose my only son a second time?" he thought. "I think I should reconsider my stance. Who do I want to leave all this to? Isa? Even if I do, Isa would need guidance, and who better than Kaniz to guide him?"

"Alhaji?" Khadijat was on the intercom. He must have forgotten she was on the line. "The flight to Dakar this weekend. What time did you want the departure?"

"Forget it," Alhaji said. He wasn't pursuing the matter any further. Nothing on earth was worth losing Kaniz again. Nothing was worth the horror of the last seventeen years.

Chapter Nineteen

"The last enemy that shall be destroyed is death."
1 Corinthians 15:26

Rola let Isa and Olaotan lead their party of three into the huge arena, the venue for the air show at the air force base. She had thought they would be joined by Rekiya, but Kaniz's cousin's flight from Abuja had been delayed for four hours, then cancelled. She had finally booked another flight but would be arriving after the show had started. Rola got all this information from Isa because Kaniz was still incommunicado. There was no chance of meeting Rekiya and no point to it anymore. Kaniz wasn't interested in speaking to her.

As they drove through the gates, it was clear why the base had to be in the suburbs in Ikeja. It was huge, but no one could get a sense of its vastness from the gates outside. Her invite had included preferred parking tags. The parking space was so close to the field. She never ceased to wonder at Kaniz's sensitivity to her. When he couldn't ask her what she wanted, she got the sense that he actually put himself in her shoes and walked through what *he* would want, then went ahead and did just that for her. She had worn rose-gold Zanotti flat sandals in preparation for a hike. She wore a burnt orange bell-sleeved faux wrap dress with a full skirt and a nude sun hat. She carried her dark nude Chanel classic 2.55 and her Chloé reflective rose gold aviators – for extra protection – completed her look.

The colours worked splendidly. Her mum had taken one look at her as she was leaving and said, "You are hoping to see Kaniz after his flight, right?" She smiled as she gave her daughter a warm hug and a thumbs up.

Rola hadn't been able to smile. She wasn't so sure what to expect from Kaniz anymore. She just hugged her mum back tightly and quietly.

The atmosphere was one of martial gaiety, if such a thing existed, and she was glad she came, if only because it was probably all that "bloody civilians" could glimpse into the air force world, especially in peace time. She looked forward to an afternoon of flying at its best.

Rola suddenly remembered how she was fascinated with flying from her first flight she could recall as a toddler. She didn't know women could be pilots – the idea of female pilots still seemed to be slow in catching on if this afternoon was an indicator, with the sheer number of men in uniform around her – so she had planned to be an air hostess and keep flying. "Be careful what you wish for," she thought. "Now you have fallen in love with a pilot on your one-year sabbatical. You had your life neatly planned out in New York, and you have upended your entire life."

She quieted her doubts and looked round. Outside war movies Rola had never seen so many uniforms or so many officers in full dress uniform. If not for the uniforms everywhere and the orderliness in the midst of the melee, one would have mistaken this for a carnival of sorts. There were the usual snacks, drinks and fast food vendors. Rola overrode Mrs B's strict "no street food" upbringing and looked the other way as Olaotan bought some ice cream and some chicken and chips of unknown provenance.

The street food smelt good and she succumbed. "Sorry Mrs B," she muttered under her breath. She had to have some of the whitebait and the crispy shrimps. They came in neat Styrofoam packs with dainty toothpicks. She remembered seeing this same fare sold in newspapers from square glass displays when she passed by Isale Eko with her mum as a kid. Now they had upgraded to Styrofoam packs, serviettes and toothpicks; next stop, they would add cleansing wipes!

They took their seats in what were obviously the best seats in the long bleachers. She read the name tags on the seats next to hers. From the left they read: Mrs Woriabam, AVM Woriabam, then her seat and to her right, Isa Mamane, Olaotan Bolade. Kaniz had her seated next to his boss. Could it be that he had wanted his boss to meet her? Her heart sank. That was before he stopped talking to her, when he still cared.

The row of bleachers faced a runway beyond which were huge open fields all the way into the horizon. AVM Woriabam and his wife were sitting to her left. Woriabam seemed to know her already as he gave her a pleasant smile, his eyes also shielded by aviators. "If airmen stopped wearing aviators," Rola thought, "Rayban would go into liquidation." Out loud she said, "Good afternoon, sir. Good afternoon, ma'am," sliding forward in her seat to kneel slightly.

"Ah, Morola right?" AVM said.

He soon began to fill her in on the day's program and what to expect. Twenty-five aircraft would be on display that day – helicopters, fighter jets, C -130, heavy airlift, medium and light airlift aircraft. He also gave her a brief of what to expect this afternoon – formation flying, with helicopters and fixed wing planes.

The grand finale was the fighter jet Kaniz was flying in an aerobatic display. The L39s were Soviet jets and the incarnation to be flown was released in 2014. The F16 was what Kaniz was going to be flying.

It was obvious Woriabam was proud of his mentee. Group Captain Ishaya was their star pilot. Not just a great combatant and distinguished diplomat but very brilliant and intelligent, a natural leader.

"You have to be careful in dealing with Ishaya," he whispered conspiratorially. "He has an undue advantage. Did you know he received training with the FBI on interrogation techniques and hostage negotiation? Also, what was the name of this man, the one with the special study on micro-expressions?"

"Paul Ekman," Rola supplied.

"Affirmative. He studied his work too."

Gosh, she was in trouble. No wonder he had said, "Your eyes tell me you love me, Sarauniya." He saw her dilated pupils and goodness knows what else, and he knew what the physiological signs meant. No wonder he seemed more sensitive than Tim, Steve, Dave, whoever. He really *was* more sensitive. Women were the ones who were naturally better at reading micro-emotions, but this man was *trained* to do it. He was better than she was even with her natural advantage.

She was jolted back to the present by the announcer, loud on the PA system. The national anthem was about to be taken and the show was about to begin. The air was crackling with the excitement.

First were the rather tame helicopters flying a display of the national flag. She looked over at Isa and the poor lad seemed slightly sleepy. It was all rather humdrum. But from the moment the first jet took off, things started looking up. The names of the pilots were announced, and they saluted and got into their jets. While the displays were good, the names were a blur. She was waiting for one name and one name only.

“Flying the F16 in aerobatic displays, Group Captain Kaniz Ishaya of...” Rola didn’t hear the rest of the announcement. Kaniz strode out in an olive grey... was that a jumpsuit? The force had so many uniforms, she couldn’t keep up.

Perhaps she was biased, but no pilot had looked as distinguished as Kaniz today. Maybe it was the height. Or it was the retro 80s disco-looking jumpsuit. Even from here, she could see his broad shoulders, the broad chest and his sheer height – the garrison cap he had on only added to his height and his long legs were ramrod straight as he stood and saluted. This was what an officer was supposed to look like, she thought. While the other pilots looked like they were wearing infants’ onesies – one had the waist of his jumpsuit almost at his chest – Kaniz cut the figure of a fighter pilot. He walked briskly and climbed into the cockpit of his jet.

He took off in a low roar, and two clouds of white smoke streaming from the triangular F16 jet’s engines while under the dorsal tail glowed an orange orb of “fire”. The trails followed him as he rose in an almost vertical climb, gaining altitude rapidly. As he came back into view, he was flying upside down. Rola was on the edge of her seat. Then he flipped and was upright again. Another fly by and he seemed to be vertical, but he deftly executed two flips about the Y-axis. It was amazing. How did one man gain such mastery over tons of steel while flying at that speed? Defying gravity to create such precision?

The crowd gasped. The jet was in a steep vertical climb till it was almost out of sight. All the heads Rola could see were raised, all eyes following the jet. It reappeared as if plunging down from the sky. Streams of white bellowing from the machine. Someone let out a small scream and just then, the jet righted to a collective sigh of relief and "oohs". Rola knew there was no issue because Woriabam was calm as the jet was dropping from the sky.

The announcer was speaking but largely being ignored. "He executes the last roll, bringing to a close the air force show."

AVM Woriabam and the other senior officers were on their feet saluting, and the crowd was applauding. The F16 came out of the manouevre and flew away into the distance, no doubt to turn around and land where he had taken off.

Suddenly, Rola saw a blinding flash of light and heard a deafening bang. She looked at Woriabam, as he raised his aviators in shock and the horror on his face turned her heart to ice. Another explosion followed seconds later with a smaller flash of light. A projectile came hurtling out of the plane high into the air. The plane was dropping like a meteor, spinning wildly and as they all watched in horror, what was left of the F16 hit the ground in the distant horizon. Another flash of light rose from the point of impact with a distant bang. Rola's heart stopped beating completely for a second, and her world stopped. What on earth just happened to Kaniz?

No one could survive the crash they had all just seen. Deep despair swallowed her soul as a deathly dark hand held her heart in an unbreakable clutch and began to squeeze the life and vitality out of her. She suddenly saw clearly what life without Kaniz was, and it was empty, hollow, dark.

BOOK TWO

Chapter Twenty

"Mine eye is consumed in grief..."

Psalm 31:9

The parachute fell away from him as he hit the ground with a thud. The pain of the impact was not Kaniz's issue right now, neither was the excruciating pain in his back. His eyes were on fire. He felt hands grab him as he tried to stand up.

"I am Wing Commander Gwom of the Air Force Medical Corp, sir. We are here to evacuate you to the air force hospital, sir," a professional-sounding voice said. He was immediately placed on a stretcher by three pairs of firm hands.

"Wing Commander, water," Kaniz shouted. "Water!" He was in pain; he felt like jagged boulders were being dragged across his eyes. He tried to keep calm, but all he saw was white light; no colours, no forms.

The first step Wing Commander Gwom took was to test the PH level of his eyes.

"Group Captain, it appears some level of acid has gotten in your eyes. We will have to get to the opthamology unit immediately."

He had nothing but water for Kaniz's eyes in the ambulance. They were prepared for spinal injuries, burns, fractures but not this. He wasn't an opthamologist. He was an ER doctor.

"Can you see my fingers?" He was waving his fingers, Kaniz could feel the breeze but not see anything.

"Morola, my brother's heartbeat, how I wish we had met in better circumstances."

Rola liked Rekiya immediately. The curvy dark woman reminded her of Kaniz's mother in the photo. She could easily pass for his sister. She gave Rola a warm hug and explained that she had been with him for the few hours since the explosion.

Junaid had taken Isa home immediately, and Isa had been offline since the explosion happened, Alhaji too. First she had gone to the air force hospital and was told Kaniz had been moved, but no one could tell her where. Rola had finally got through to Isa after two hours and found out where Kaniz was.

Alhaji had been contacted, as Kaniz had him down as his next of kin, something he'd done after the reconciliation. On arriving at the air force hospital, Alhaji had immediately decided to move his son to St Paul's. He was contemplating airlifting Kaniz out of the country, but he had to have an evaluation done before the medical evacuation company agreed to airlift him. They were waiting for the ophthalmologist and other consultants to arrive.

"Kaniz wouldn't let anyone call you, not even when we located his phone in his parked car and saw your many calls. He can be very determined," Rekiya said. "The doctors say his condition is more mental than physical. He has compressed vertebrae from the ejection, but the fact that he can't see is a terrible situation to handle."

Rola's heart sank. Kaniz couldn't see? Waves of pure sadness washed over her soul. She didn't want to begin to cry right there and then in front of Rekiya who she had just met, but it was too late. The tears of deep and dark distress just started running down her face. She felt a hard knot of pain in her chest. Not Kaniz! It just couldn't be true! There had to be something the doctors had overlooked.

"Kaniz." She didn't realise she had spoken out loud till she felt Rekiya's hand patting her back. At least he was alive and after the explosion, she had not dared to even hope. They would get through it together somehow. She didn't know what the future held, but she would stay by his side. Her place was by his side.

"I can't replace his eyes – nothing can make up for such a loss, but God help me, whatever I can do to bring him joy, I will do. You won't be alone Kaniz, you will never be alone, Kaniz," she muttered.

"You know how Kaniz has had issues with the dark since he was a child," Rekiya said as if she expected Rola to know. "With this loss of vision, I am afraid. I really don't know what he would do to himself. The dark is the one thing he can't cope with."

"He seems to have lost a lot of weight," Rola muttered.

"That was before today apparently, Alhaji was shocked to see him too. Even now the doctors are concerned. He is refusing food so he has been put on IV fluids. Go in to see him, Rola," she said quietly. "Let me go and get myself a coffee in the lobby, it's been a rough day."

Rola stepped into the private hospital room.

"Kaniz," Rola whispered and put her hand over his. His eyes were covered in bandages and two IV lines fed fluids into his body, but he was conscious. "Oh, Kaniz." She was just so relieved to see him finally. She wanted to hold on to him but with the wires and lines, she didn't even know where to touch him.

Kaniz's heart broke at the sound of Morola's voice. Who had let her in? Who let her see him in this state?

"Who let you in?" His voice was steady and cold. "Where is Rekiya?"

"She stepped out for a minute so we could be alone, Kaniz." She touched his right forearm and he flinched. Did her touch repel him? Was revulsion what he felt for her now? She had heard that when strong love flipped it became an equally virulent hatred. Was that what Kaniz now felt? A hatred as strong as his love had been?

She wasn't going to give up though. She wasn't going to let anything stop her from what she had come here to say and do.

"Kaniz," she said softly, "how are you feeling?"

"I'm fine." His answer was curt.

He wasn't making this easy for her at all, but she just had to forge on. "Kaniz, I love you. Forgive me for whatever hurt I may have caused you. It wasn't intentional... it has nothing to do with you. Please hear me out. I saw the explosion and, in that instant, when I feared the worst, it was like my world had ended, and I knew I didn't ever want to live without you. If you will still have me, Kaniz, I would be honoured to marry you."

Was Morola mocking him? Kaniz wondered. Didn't she know the meaning of the bandages on his eyes? Why now? Why was she saying this now when it was too late?

"Morola," he said, "I don't want your pity. *Kaniz Ishaya the blind pilot.* You wouldn't take me whole, but you want me to believe you now want me broken? Blind?"

"The day you proposed, everything in me wanted to say yes, but I was afraid. I was paralysed with fear that if I commit to you, I would end up being hurt like every other woman I know."

She took his hand, and he didn't have the emotional strength to resist. Her touch gave him a strange feeling, an alloy of comfort and pain. She tenderly placed his hand on her face, cradling it. He could feel the wetness on his Morola's face, but he couldn't do anything. It was too late now. He felt deflated, defeated. He felt he was losing his sanity with the deepest grief. Everyone expected him to be glad he had survived, that he was alive, but was this life? Death was better. Death was what he craved.

"My fear is entrenched Kaniz. I have tried to rationalise it, persuade myself, convince myself, but it lies deep within my consciousness. I can't budge it. I have never told anyone, not even Mrs B, what the issue really is. but I decided I must tell you today.

"TK was my hero, Kaniz. My father was everything to me as a little girl. He could do no wrong in my eyes, and he took me with him everywhere he could. When I was six, he took me on a trip. I don't know where he told Mrs B we were going, but we travelled out of Lagos. He took me to his mistress' house. Why would you take your six-year-old daughter from her mother to a mistress' house? Till today, I haven't asked what he was thinking." Her tears were running freely and drenching his hand, but he still didn't withdraw it.

"I still remember the place like it was yesterday: a two-bedroom flat. I remember what she gave me to drink – it was an orange drink in its bottle. I remember what she was wearing and her hairstyle. My father and his mistress put me in her bedroom overnight, but I got lonely. I wanted to see my father. I started looking for him and cried myself to sleep. I woke up early the next morning still crying for my father, and I finally strayed into a room and there he was, lying in bed with his mistress. They had thrown a coverlet on, but I could see their shoulders were bare, and I knew something was wrong. I knew something was wrong. She wasn't my mother, and they were in the same bed. I found it difficult to comprehend. As I got older and I understood what I saw better..." She shook her head.

Why now? Why was she telling him now? Why was she adding her pain to his despair?

"What had TK told my mum? My hero must have lied. And that was only the beginning of his many lies. I learnt from my father, my hero, the very person who should have taught me otherwise, that all men are liars. Imagine the conflict in me when we are told 'adults can't lie'. Yet my own father was a liar. Lying to my mother to have an affair with another woman.

"It's not you that I don't trust Kaniz, it's men. And it's not your fault, Kaniz."

Kaniz felt like dragging the IV lines out of the way and holding her close, comforting her, reassuring her that *his* love for her would never fade, holding on to her and never letting her go, but what had he to offer her now? He didn't have a clue what the future held. He couldn't plunge Morola into uncertainty. She had a bright future, and he had no future now. It would be unfair of him to take Morola's offer. He was no longer the same Kaniz she had met and fallen in love with. He was now a shell of his former self.

"I trust you, Kaniz, I was wrong to compare you with other men. I trust you. I really want to trust you," she kept whispering.

Kaniz sighed. Every fibre of his being longed for Morola, but not this way. He no longer had anything to offer her. If he couldn't see, how could he fly? How could he make a living? What could they do together? How would he dance with his Morola as she glowed, full of life and her love for music? How would he do all the things she loved to do with her?

She would be stuck with him out of pity and soon, the love she had for him would become resentment. No! He wouldn't be able to take that. He wouldn't be able to cope with Morola resenting him.

"My love, my heartbeat. If only I had known this earlier," he thought. But what would have changed? He sighed. She would have agreed to marry him and right now would have been saddled with a liability, a blind fiancé. Bound to him by guilt and not love. It was better this way. It was simply providential that she had rejected his hand.

His heart and soul yearned for her, to comfort her and let her comfort him as they stood together against this darkness. For this moment, he was grateful for the bandages. His eyes were wet with tears that stung his eyes, but the bandages soaked up the tears. He willed himself to be strong.

"Thank you for sharing. I empathise with you, Morola. I am sorry to hear you were hurt so badly. I would really appreciate if you could leave now. I actually need to rest." He withdrew his hand from her grip abruptly. "Goodbye, Morola."

Morola gasped at his words, and he almost recanted. She was motionless for a while, then he heard her as she moved. He could smell her fragrance, feel her soft hands on his face as she gently cupped and brushed his forehead with her lips, and at that moment, he knew it was pity she felt for him. She had let down her guard; it was because he was now weak. She would have never done that if he wasn't lying here unable to see.

Morola was the type of person who would tend wounded animals. She was a compassionate soul and that was all he was now in her eyes: something wounded and in need of care. He steeled himself to resist her, resist her touch. She paused, and he could hear her struggling with her tears, but what choice did he have? He had to let her go. His heart filled with agony and with finality, he turned his back to the direction of the sound of her voice.

"Goodbye, Kaniz," she whispered, and she was gone.

Chapter Twenty-One

"I am forgotten like a dead man out of mind: I am like a broken vessel."

Psalm 31:12

Kaniz heard the door close as Morola left the room. He waited a few minutes, breathing heavily, steadily, trying to calm down.

When he knew she must have left the floor and certainly be in the lift on the way out of the hospital, he doubled up in a foetal position as sobs racked his being.

"My heartbeat," he groaned, in a low voice. He spoke in Yoruba, secure in the knowledge that no one could understand. "My love, I held nothing back from you, nothing." The pain threatened to tear his heart apart. "But now I know I have to let you go. I was trying to live without you. I have fasted, I have prayed. Oh how I have prayed, but the more I pray the more I love you. What is it about you? Who *are* you? Why is your spell so strong?

"I had let you go. Now when I can never have you, you now offer your hand to me? What type of cruel fate is this? What is my sin that's so unforgivable? Or am I paying for the sins of my forefathers? Why do my own sufferings never end? Why do I have no respite? My mother left when I needed her most, my only parent rejected me. Joe was blown to pieces before my very eyes. And just when I thought You were now smiling on me, when You sent her to me and I loved her so completely, when I loved her without restraint, the way *You love me*, You stood by and watched her reject me. You stood by and watched me suffer and because that wasn't enough anguish, because that wasn't enough pain, I must now live in darkness."

At the thought of his blindness, his words gave way to a yell born of unalloyed agony. He was gasping now as the words came out of him in a staccato cadence, from a place of deep anguish and confusion. "Why, why, why is my mere existence such agony?" His voice was barely louder than a whisper. The thought of existing in darkness tortured him, drained his soul of all vitality.

"If I was even to suffer in darkness and she was by my side, if I could hear her voice, feel her touch, perhaps... perhaps I could survive it, survive the gloom."

Kaniz began to pray. "Kill me. Let me die, just let me die. Not darkness. Not this perpetual night. Let me die. Be merciful, oh Lord, and end my life."

His heart monitor began to beep loudly as his heart rate shot up. He heard a flurry of activity and the sound of people entering the room. He felt their hands as they began to tend to him. An injection sank into a vein in his left forearm, and he began to descend into a deep dark well but not before he heard one of the nurses say, "Miss, what happened to him? What happened?"

Alhaji couldn't thank the medical lead of the evaluation team enough. He knew too many people who had suffered because of doctors' misdiagnoses in this country to settle for any doctor's diagnosis without a second and third opinion if need be. Dr Abe had just assured him that Kaniz had burnt his corneas but not irreparably. His eyes would heal in a matter of days and though Alhaji could take him for a complete physical later if he chose, Kaniz would benefit more from being allowed to rest for about a week instead of being put on a medevac plane and flying again right now.

Rekiya could now understand why Kaniz loved Rola so much. Kaniz had forbad anyone to as much as even mention Rola's name but for the four days Kaniz was in the hospital, Rola was there. She only went home to shower on the first day. She stayed in the waiting area or right outside Kaniz's private ward in the Intensive Care Unit. Whenever Kaniz was asleep, Rekiya let her in while she took that time to rest. Kaniz had sunk into a deep and dark depression. Even after Dr Abe and his team had overturned the dire prognosis the St Paul's doctor had given on Kaniz's sight; he was still in extremely dismal spirits.

As long as the bandages were still on, it appeared he just couldn't cope with darkness. The doctor explained to them several times that there was nothing much physically wrong with Kaniz. The bandages would come off, and his corneas which had been bruised by the chemical fumes from the explosion when he ejected from the aircraft would have healed. His flight goggles had protected his eyes from the worst of the explosion.

He had been in pain from the vertebral compression he had suffered from the ejection and the bruised ribs from his landing, but he was in remarkable physical condition. The spinal compression and damaged vertebrae would heal in three to four months though he was now half an inch shorter. He could even fly soon but not in an aircraft with an ejection seat.

Kaniz allowed Mrs B visit him, and she came daily at 4 p.m., the official visiting time. Olaotan and Isa were inseparable, and Olaotan visited with Isa. Anyone but Rola was welcome. They kept it a secret from him that she was just outside the door or down the hallway. She was the one who kept them all in good spirits.

"Sis, you rest. I will take over," she would say. "What should I get for you? This hospital's latte is horrible! Let me get to Coffee Affair. Stevia and cream for you, right? With hazelnut syrup and a pain au chocolat?" She had mastered Rekiya's preferences from day one. Kaniz was sedated a lot in the four days his eyes were resting and healing because he just could not cope with the dark. His eyes were healing, but his mind was suffering. He suffered debilitating panic attacks and his heart would race. This was why he was in the ICU: not for his injuries but to monitor his heart rate.

Rekiya could rest when Rola was "on duty". Alhaji had warned the nurses not to bother Rola, so she slept on the guest couch in Kaniz's room at night while Rekiya rested on the bed in another private ward. If the Mamanes were ready to pay for a private ward for a healthy relative, who was to stop them? The first night Alhaji had passed by the ICU and seen

Rola on the uncomfortable couch watching over his only son, he had almost cursed himself.

Where could he start to make amends? How does one roll back seventeen years and more of insensitivity? He couldn't blame Aminat's enchantments or the marabout. If he wanted to make this right, he had to take personal responsibility for his failures. He suddenly remembered he had to let the MD of QuantumTech know Rola may be too tired to work days after pulling these all-nighters at the hospital. He reached for his phone and called Khadijat. She should sort that out.

Kaniz was always flitting in and out of consciousness. In his subconscious, he was twenty-six years old again and back in that hellish wooden box in Darfur, buried under the ground, hostage of the rebel faction leader Musa Bandir.

His rebel faction had taken over a few hours before Kaniz flew in a joint peacekeeping mission. The Allied Forces had absolutely no intel on Bandir, yet he was a dark horse. He was so under the radar that he had never even been profiled.

Joe had been Kaniz's close friend and co-pilot. The joint mission had gone terribly awry when Bandir's men had shot them down. They ejected safely and were hiding out in a shelled outbuilding that used to be a family dwelling. Food was nonexistent, and the water in their emergency kit was running low.

A young boy had discovered them. Kaniz and Joe's only surety of safety was to shoot to kill. In this territory, there were no children. No one was innocent. Innocence had been destroyed by the ravages of war; anyone could be an informer. Kaniz had killed before but not a child, and he wasn't about to cross that line. Neither himself nor Joe could fire point-blank at an unarmed child. He didn't look older than eight or nine. They couldn't possibly keep him hostage with them as they hid, so they had let him go immediately and began to move their position.

It soon became apparent that they had been discovered. Sniper fire pinned them down in the building for almost two hours and when the

IED came sailing through what had been a window into the room they were holed up in, Joe, who was closer to the window, threw himself on the device, saving Kaniz from the worst of the blast. In his dreams and waking moments, he still saw the light reflected on Joe's face as the IED exploded, burning an eternal memory on his retina like a macabre daguerreotype.

The rebels had moved in to pick up their bodies, and finding the badly injured Kaniz alive, took him captive. They were divided as to what to do with him. Should he be a means of sending a strong message to the Allied Forces that they meant business by decapitating him on video? Or was he more financially valuable as a hostage to the rising rebel leader who needed funds to buy arms and to consolidate his break-away faction?

They decided they could kill him any time, after extracting some value from him. To show the Allied Forces that he wasn't to be trifled with, Bandir ordered that Kaniz be put in a wooden box and buried. He sent a message to the Joint Forces, letting them know he had their soldier and time was running out for him.

Kaniz had suffered in the blast. The shrapnel had cut through his left temple, and he could feel the dried blood on his face, but his torso had absorbed most of the shrapnel. He couldn't examine the extent of his injuries or lift a muscle in the cramped wooden box. His body wracked with agonising pain, and the heat in the airless wooden box, covered with its burden of earth, was oppressive. There was no way out.

It was obvious that Joe had escaped a far worse fate by dying instantly. Kaniz now faced a terrifying and insanely agonising death. He couldn't breathe; the air was thick with dust. Every breath he took was hot and more dust than oxygen.

If the lack of oxygen didn't kill him soon, the bleeding would. The heat and the dark were rapidly driving him to the brink of insanity. Musa Bandir had unknowingly tapped into Kaniz's Achilles heel. Kaniz had been claustrophobic since Farooq, Rekiya's younger brother, had locked him in a closet when he was four years old.

They were playing hide and seek, and the six-year-old Farooq locked him in and couldn't find the key. He had screamed for what seemed like hours till he was hysterical. Rekiya had been the one to get adults to rescue him.

He yelled with all his being, but it was futile. He knew no one could hear, but his fear took over. He could feel the dust coating his tongue as he coughed and spluttered, the rough planks above him adding abrasions to the exposed parts of his skin. His whole body was cooking with the heat. The sweat ran into the abrasions, the blood out of the deep lacerations. He had to shut his eyes lest the grit blind him. His eyes streamed with tears.

He yelled again with all his might.

Calm down so you can conserve oxygen.

That was the first time he heard that still voice. It was a rational thought, so he obeyed.

I will get you out of here.

How? He had no hope. If he had been an American soldier, his hopes would have been dim at best; but at least he would have had a tracker on. But he didn't know how deep under the ground he was, and the tracker would most likely not have worked. How would they have picked up the signal? How do you rescue someone from a man you didn't even know existed till the moment he had contacted you to inform you he held your soldier hostage?

Even in the horror of that wooden box, he couldn't get his friend off his mind. "Why did Joe do that? Why did he die to save my life?"

Joe was the best friend anyone could ask for. He was from Jos, a regular church boy who had endured endless teasing from his platoon about his faith and had been talking to Kaniz about his loving heavenly Father since they met in boot camp months ago. Joe talked about God as if he knew Him personally, trusted Him implicitly.

Kaniz liked Joe but not his message. He didn't join the force to hear about God. He joined partly to escape Him. Where was God when almost all his mother's extended family were killed in pogroms in the north because they were Christians? Where was He when Mata, who trusted Him so much, who still secretly kept her faith and served Him in spite of her in-laws, died? Where was He when his mother was wrapped in a white cloth and her only son couldn't see her mutilated face because of the devastation in the accident? he couldn't look at her one more time to say goodbye? Where was God when his own father, the only parent he had left, turned on him?

Where was He when the boy whose life they spared had gotten Joe killed and gotten him into this hellhole? Joe was so good, so generous and kind, always ready to lend a shoulder to the "orphaned" Kaniz, yet Joe was dead and did Joe's God help? Did He lift a finger to help Joe? Kaniz didn't trust this type of God. Kaniz had watched his friend without a moment's hesitation throw himself on that IED.

I love you more than Joe loved you.

The voice kept speaking to him. About the love Joe never stopped talking about. As the voice spoke to him, he began to understand. It wasn't that there wouldn't be suffering or darkness but in it all, he would never be alone. He had vowed there and then that if he made it out of that grave alive, he would live solely and completely for The One who got him out. He may not have all the answers, but he would obey The One who did. An incredible presence filled the wooden box at that moment and even in the terrible darkness and debilitating heat, he was now at peace.

The ECOMOG soldiers who saved him later said they had been guided by a young girl who said she saw when the soldier had been taken into the building. The wooden box which was his prison and should have been his last abode, was one foot under the earth but would have been impossible to spot if the little girl had not shown them. Why did battle hardened ECOMOG soldiers trust a little girl? No one could give any answer beyond there was just something about her you didn't argue with. They tried to find her afterwards, but no one seemed to have ever seen a girl who even remotely fit their description around.

The wounds in Kaniz's torso should have killed him, but each piece of shrapnel that tore into him missed his vital organs by mere millimeters. He should have bled out in minutes, but he had lasted several hours. It was inexplicable.

That was why when he met Morola, he had obeyed the still voice he had first heard that day in the grave. It was why he didn't play any games, why he loved her with a pure love. True love wasn't about the physical, it was about sacrifice, giving. When it mattered, Joe had been there and without hesitation, he had put his friend first. Kaniz knew what it meant that "no greater love can a man have than to give his life for his friends". That was the kind of love he had for Morola.

"Morola," Kaniz groaned in his stupor. He had, in essence, laid down everything for her, had been completely vulnerable to her. He was deliberately expressive and had revealed his deepest emotions to her without fear. It was exceedingly difficult for him at first, but he had done it.

"You told me 'love has to be spoken too, a woman needs to hear, you have to fearlessly express your love' and I did. Still it failed. You said to me 'A woman is a multiplier, son, she multiplies what you sow in her. Sow love into Morola's heart and what she will give you back is love.' I sowed unadulterated love but still..."

Is there not a gestation between seed time and harvest? Is patience not required of every farmer? Patience. The words dropped in his heart and calmed him.

"Morola," he groaned again.

It was as if by saying her name, he had conjured her. He knew he had to be dreaming again because he could smell her fragrance, and he imagined he could hear her familiar voice praying very quietly for him.

"Morola."

He had thought loving her the way he had been commanded to would make him look foolish, would make him her slave, but it had only set him free. How beautiful it had been to love her fearlessly and confidently. How liberating it had been to love unconditionally. Painful sometimes, but always beautiful.

Trust me once more.

"But she rejected me," he said aloud.

How many years did I reach out to you before you loved me back, before you responded? Have you loved her that long yet?

"She was my heartbeat. I loved her. I still love her... so much."

"I love you back, Kaniz, with all my heart. Please don't ever tell me to leave you again," he heard Morola say. It sounded so real. It had to be the sedative messing with his mind. The dream was so real he could feel her lips brush his cheeks.

"You need a shave, pilot," she whispered and gave her delightful little laugh.

It was his fevered imagination, a hallucination. The darkness was bending his mind; it was driving him crazy. Where was the peace he had felt since that day in the dark grave? Why was he so tormented now?

"Give me my peace back," he pleaded.

Surrender to My peace, stop struggling.

He surrendered, and he fell asleep again, enveloped by peace.

That was the problem with hospitals, Rola thought, sniffing through her tears which kept welling up despite her efforts to swallow them. There just was no privacy in hospitals. She had to hide out in this shower room to finally be all alone for a few minutes. She knew she came across to many as a "strong woman", but being a "strong woman" didn't mean she didn't feel pain. It just meant her pain was not for public display.

She wished Mrs B was here now; she needed her wise confidante. The grief she felt threatened to overwhelm her. Her childhood issues had subjected her to so much analysis and introspection from a tender age that inspite of African societal pressures, she had long understood quite clearly that the 11th commandment was not "thou shalt marry". If she ever decided to marry, she was going to marry for the right reasons and marry the right man for the path she had chosen in life. She had determined she would never be dependent on a man for her joy or her provision. She had focused on her purpose and was making a success of her life and with faith in Him, God had blessed her efforts.

Now Kaniz had come along, and his love for her was so unrelenting and overwhelming that he had almost convinced her "they" could work in spite of the almost insurmountable odds against their being together. He seemed determined to make marriage with her work. But could it? He seemed determined to support her vision but in the long run, with their circumstances being what they were, would he? Even if their circumstances were different, she had her own inner conflicts that paralysed her with fear.

Another spasm of sobs rocked her, and she gasped aloud as she realised with finality that her lifelong issues had finally cost her her chance of finding love with Kaniz just as she knew they would.

She reflected over the last few months. Because of the encounter in the car on the way back from camp, she had decided to obey and started battling bravely with the several levels of conflict raging within her. How was she to leave the promising business partnership she had going on for her in New York for a life here with Kaniz? Perhaps she could run Synergy remotely from Lagos and travel often. She had seen that a woman who was not financially empowered was at the mercy of her husband. She had seen how some silently disrespected their wives for her *continuous* dependency. A woman didn't have to have millions; she just had to demonstrably have enough to have an alternative if she found the treatment she received unacceptable.

She had seen too many women stay helpless as their husbands dealt with them emotionally and physically because they didn't have the financial capacity to have any other option. She shook her head. "Too many women are suffering," she murmured. She was not going to let her business suffer for any reason; that was a clear priority.

Kaniz had promised to support her, but what if he didn't understand the true cost of "supporting her" as he had vowed to? She would have left her independent thriving life to settle, in a male-dominated society where everyone blamed the wife for any issue whatsoever in the marriage. Yet she didn't believe in divorce. For Rola, if one chose to marry, then marriage was for life.

Kaniz had chosen her over his father *for now* but the reality remained that blood was thicker than water. Experience dictated that it was impossible that he wouldn't make up with his father even if it took decades. One day he would resent her for coming in between his father and himself and she would be the loser. Perhaps he would even long for his lost inheritance and resent her for her own independent wealth. When he tired of her like "they" all seemed to tire of those they had sworn to love, what would she then fall back on? Where would she pick up the pieces of her life and her decimated business from? Yet, she struggled with the knowledge that Kaniz was the will of God for her life.

It was a choice she had to make in faith. It was a difficult choice to justify rationally. Why not Tim? Tim was a good enough Christian and was perfect for her in almost every way. Why hadn't God chosen Tim for her? Then came the F16 crash, and everything suddenly came into sharp focus. The incredible pain in her heart when she thought Kaniz had perished in the crash, the indescribable agonising pain. Her life felt empty, dark. Nothing else seemed to matter apart from the fact that she could no longer be with him; be by his side for life. She also couldn't imagine life without Kaniz in that instant. All she could see ahead was a barren bleakness if he wasn't in her life.

The relief when she got to St Paul's that evening and saw he was alive was indescribable, but what type of life was he condemned to? The trauma of the hours when they all thought he had lost his sight. The hollow ball of pain in her chest that threatened to choke her at the thought of Kaniz being blind. The feeling as if the breath had been knocked out of her completely. The sheer agony of reliving the trauma she felt as a six-year-old, dragging up pain too deep to articulate as she spoke to Kaniz and then, then even after baring her most protected feelings till she was raw, Kaniz still coldly told her to leave.

Though she saw clearly that he loved her in spite of his cold words, he had resolved to let her go. He knew what he wanted – if he could love her as much as he clearly did and still be ready to be without her, it was a rational and firm decision. It was a final decision. It was settled. It was done.

Rola was tired; tired of being the strong woman Mrs B raised. She was emotionally worn out. She plunked down the toilet seat and its cover, sat on it with a huge sigh and put her head down, her hands covering her face as she sobbed as if her heart would break. How did she get herself into this mess? Why did she drive down Jaja Road that day? Why did she help Isa? At the thought of Isa, a smile flashed briefly through her sobs. Her dear Isa. At least Isa was alive, and Kaniz would see. Her gratitude to God knew no bounds when she was told he would see, though she still waited with bated breath till the day the bandages were to come off, praying without ceasing.

She would be here while Kaniz needed her, but this was it. It was over. When she left St Paul's, the Kaniz chapter was closed finally. At her decision, the pain swept her soul, but she was resolved. She said goodbye to Kaniz in her heart.

"Kaniz," she sobbed in the silence of the bathroom. Her voice echoing in the hard, tiled space. "If only things had been different. If only our circumstances had been different..."

Pain filled her heart at the finality of her decision as the racking sobs shook her body.

Stepping into the room she shared with Rola to pick up the book she had meant to read while seated with Kaniz, Rekiya heard muffled sounds from the bathroom. She moved closer and they were sobs coming from behind the locked door.

"Rola?" She knocked on the door. "Rola?" she said louder. There was no reply, but the sobs continued unabated. "Open the door, Rola!" Rekiya said more loudly, desperately, as she now rattled the door handle vigorously. She heard the sink tap run for less than a minute, then a pause and feet moving towards the bathroom door.

"Sis?" Rola said calmly, as she stood in the open bathroom doorway. Her eyes were dry but red and swollen. "I got your lunch. Have you eaten, sis?" She pointed to the table by the bed with Rekiya's packed lunch on it. "Is there anything you want me to do?" she said, putting on a brave face. She spoke through her blocked nose, even as she sniffled, cleaning her nose with the tissue in her right hand.

As she looked at Rola struggling bravely, Rekiya's heart melted for the beautiful younger lady she had come to love already, who had tried to be so brave and keep her new "sis" in good spirits in spite of her own grief. She instinctively leaned in and hugged Rola tight.

As Rekiya held her, Rola's tears started running silently again as her shoulders shook with agonising racking sobs. The pain was overwhelming. She felt the pain would break her heart in pieces.

Chapter Twenty-Two

"It is of the Lord's mercies that we are not consumed...
they are new every morning: great is thy faithfulness."

Lamentations 3:22,23

Alhaji sat in his office, his brow furrowed as he reflected on how his obsession with restoration had almost caused him the loss of everything he held dear. He had sworn on his life that he wouldn't let anything or anyone get between Kaniz and himself again and had almost failed the very first time he had been tempted.

He couldn't believe that Kaniz could forgive him, but he had. It was difficult for Alhaji, but they were finally able to speak about "the incident". Aminat had wrought much evil to the Mamane men. Rumour had it that it was a concoction she had been given by one of her many marabouts that led to her insanity and subsequent death.

Alhaji sighed. The last few days had been hectic. Khadijat had been a rock, and he hadn't thanked her properly. She had held the fort at the Mamane Group so that he could be by Kaniz's side as much as possible. She had arranged for the evacuation with lightning speed and taken charge of Isa in a way he had never anticipated.

He dialled her number on the intercom. "Hajiya Khadijat, come."

She came into his office and stood in front of him.

"Hajiya Khadijat, I just wanted to thank you for your support over the last one week. It was very traumatic, but we thank God. My son is alive, and he can see."

He held an envelope towards her. "This is a small thank you."

"No, thank you, Alhaji."

"No?"

Khadijat was a single mother and for the fifteen years she had been with him, she had never refused money. It probably wasn't enough.

"Oh! Sorry!" he said and pulling open the top drawer of his desk, he added more notes.

"Take, Hajiya."

"No."

Alhaji was confused. "What do you want Hajiya Khadijat?" he asked. He had a meeting in the conference room in five minutes, so he rose up and picked up a file emblazoned with "Mamane Group".

"Nothing, Alhaji."

"Nothing? Are you sure?"

She seemed to consider for a few seconds and then shrugged imperceptibly. "If you insist though, there is something I want."

Ishaya Mamane was relieved. "Do say, Khadijat. If it is something I can do then consider it done."

"You promise, Alhaji?"

Alhaji smiled to himself. The woman probably wanted her company car changed or something for her daughter. What really did she think was so difficult, so expensive, that she took him through all this drama?

"A hug is what I want, Alhaji Mamane," she said quietly.

"Are you okay?" were the words that came to his lips, but he bit his tongue. All these years, Khadijat had served faithfully and never asked for anything. Whatever he gave her had always been enough, and she just turned down $5000 for a hug? Well, she could have her hug. She was a single woman and he was a widower, so no law was being broken. Besides, he was very fond of Khadijat, so the thought of hugging her was not an unpleasant prospect at all.

"Come then, Khadijat," he said and stepped out from behind his desk. A quick hug, and he would be off to his meeting.

Khadijat stepped towards Alhaji. It appeared they had both consulted different dictionaries for the meaning of "hug". Khadijat's head just reached his chest in her low shoes. She put her arms round his waist and pulled him close. "Thank you, Alhaji, for all you do for me and Fatima."

Khadijat's fragrance bathed Alhaji's nostrils. Her wax print smelt of sandalwood, and it was not an unpleasant fragrance at all. Her slightly chubby frame fit his snugly. Alhaji was not expecting such a robust embrace, and he reasoned that so as not to be seen as standoffish, he should reciprocate. It was like a switch turned on. Under his babanriga, he could feel a stirring, something he had not felt since Aminat had left him.

Khadijat began to step back, taking her hand off Alhaji's waist, but Alhaji held her loosely.

"Khadijat," he said gently, "there's no rush."

He drew her closer again, catching a hint of a smile on her face.

Alhaji smiled too. He would have to ask HR for another executive secretary. Khadijat's role was about to change.

Alhaji would not let Kaniz out of Mamane Close for a week after he was discharged. Rekiya had decided to spend a few more days in Lagos. Between her, Alhaji and Samson, he was getting a lot of care.

Kaniz was half-listening as Rekiya caught him up on what he had missed when he was at the hospital. They were seated on the pool terrace, side by side. There was a lull in the conversation, and Kaniz looked at his cousin.

"Rekiya, I don't know what I would have done without you."

"Kaniz, it was not just me. Everyone was supportive. Alhaji was beside himself with worry – look how he got Dr Abe in. Mrs B was there every day. Isa and Olaotan, Major Funso too. Even AVM Woriabam kept visiting. You are loved, Kaniz."

Kaniz winced as he thought of how he had forever lost the one person whose love he desired the most. "When the doctor took off the bandages, and I could eventually see everyone, Rekiya, I knew God loved me particularly. I just knew. I have gone through a lot, but God loves me specially."

"You know He sends people to show us His love too?" Rekiya said.

Kaniz smiled slightly. "I know. Thank you, Rekiya."

Rekiya cleared her throat. "I couldn't have made it without Rola, Kaniz."

Kaniz looked at her, puzzled. "Morola?" He snorted, his face twisted to mask the pain he felt at the mere mention of her name.

"She came on the first day and I told her to leave and, and…" He paused to take a deep breath, his brow furrowed. "And she never came again."

He attempted to cover his face with his hands in his characteristic reflex action when he was in emotional turmoil, as if by wiping his face clean of the conflict, he would also wipe his soul of the churning and this time, he tipped his glasses over. He smiled ruefully. "These will take getting used to."

"It's only for three months, Kay," Rekiya said, using her pet name for him as a child.

She leaned towards him and looked him in the eyes so he would pay attention. "Rola never left your side except when you were awake and even then, she was in the waiting room. Or in my room. On the first day, she went home to shower and when we got the other room afterwards, she moved in there with me. She only left the evening your bandages came off and we were told you were coming home the next morning."

"She was with me?" He was dumbfounded.

"Always."

So it had not been a dream or the sedative playing tricks on him. Morola had actually been in the room with him, talking to him.

Later that evening, Alhaji called Kaniz to his bedroom wing.

"Kaniz, I need you to see my will." The document was open in front of him.

"Alhaji, why now?"

"Anyone with a wife *should* have a will, anyone with children *must* have a will. In brief, I am leaving everything to you; you are my only son. I have left the block of flats in VI to Isa, the one on Waziri Avenue. I know you will take care of Isa and your siblings. Sponsor Isa's education to any level he desires in any institution of his choice. We will have to choose when to let him know his circumstances, but the records are here in my safe, in a letter I have written to him."

"Isa is my brother and my son, Shehu. Put your heart at rest, father. Anything a father does for a son, I will do for Isa by God's grace," Kaniz replied. "But siblings? Siblings? Where are they, Shehu? What are you hinting at? It's always better that we know each other now when you are alive. I can't be wasting time on DNA tests *fa*!" Kaniz smiled, wagging his finger in mock warning.

"Kaniz! Kaniz!" Shehu laughed. "Things are happening! So just in case siblings arise, you know..."

Kaniz shook his head at his father's mischievous smile and the twinkle in his eye.

"Wait, Shehu, things should be done decently and in order."

"I solemnly assure you, Kaniz, nothing untoward will happen. I assure you. Relax son," Alhaji said. "Kaniz, I think I need to ask your forgiveness again." He rose. Kaniz quickly stood up too because he wasn't sure what his father was up to with the look in his eyes.

"Our tradition will not allow me to prostrate to you, Kaniz, but if I do, it's not too much. Laraba would be grieved to see the way I have treated the greatest gift she gave me." He hung his head in shame. "Kaniz, think about it. It was when you came back into my life that all was restored. It was not Rola, Kaniz. It was you. You came to Mamane Group the day Isa was found. You showed up here at Mamane Close soon after, and the contract followed. Now..." Shehu couldn't help but smile. It felt so liberating to know he was completely alive again. It restored an element of his confidence he couldn't describe. "Now everything else has followed. Kaniz, it was not Rola that was 'the lost' that returned. You were the lost one that returned and in your wake, you brought restoration."

Kaniz couldn't care less about any prophecy. He was happy as long as Shehu had found closure.

"So, Shehu, am I right to assume that you have no objection to my marrying Morola?"

"Objection? Objection? If you want to marry her in a synagogue, walahi, I will be there with you on the front row, Kaniz."

"Now, Shehu, *that* is a tad dramatic," Kaniz thought.

"Kaniz, allow me to handle everything. Forgive me, but my people have done a little of their findings on you." He raised his palms to stop Kaniz from speaking. "It's a bad habit, but it's just what they do. We are a defence and security outfit, Kaniz. Anyone pops up in my life after seventeen years, they don't ask me, they just check." His palms were still up. "Son, I know you are comfortable. Why you live in that barracks..." He shook his head as if to say, "I can't imagine."

"Let me throw you a wedding that will shut Lagos down. That's all I ask."

Kaniz was instinctively going to say "no", but he said, "It's not my choice, Alhaji. Besides, I don't even know for sure where I stand with Morola anymore."

Alhaji laughed. "*Me*, I know where *you* stand. We all know where you stand with her. The entire St Paul's hospital knows where you stand. You are standing here wasting time, son. Doesn't that your car have GPS? In case you don't know the way to her house anymore."

Olaotan was the best ally a man could have. In spite of Rekiya and Alhaji's words of assurance, Kaniz hadn't gotten even one phone call from Morola since he was discharged, and it was almost a week. He didn't want to risk calling her; too much had happened. He thought it was just better to find out when she was home and meet her there.

Olaotan had just sent him the signal that Morola was home. What would he say? Kaniz thought as he drove to her house. Had he not said to her, "leave me", after she told him what she probably had never told any other living soul?

He drove in silence to the Bolades' house. He was oblivious to the beauty of the creek at twilight; the streetlights reflecting off the waters of the lagoon and peeping through the palm trees that lined the lagoon banks. He ignored the speedboats still flying on the water, and the occasional yacht still navigating back to its private jetty. His thoughts were on his mission, and he knew he had no way of playing this right.

"I surrender. Help me."

As long as you are surrendered, I have you covered.

Aunty Wunmi had to restrain herself from hugging Kaniz. "Uncle *Kanis*! When I saw the explosion on the news, ah!" she exclaimed, her hands on her generous bosom. "I said, no! My enemies will not laugh at me o! My enemies, die by fire! Look at you today!" She stepped back and looked at him. "I like this glasses o, and this traditional fit you well well."

Kaniz was wearing one of Alhaji's caftans. Alhaji had practically held him hostage in Mamane Close since he was discharged.

"Aunty Wunmi, it was your prayers o," he said in Yoruba. "It was your prayers God answered."

Aunty Wunmi broke into a dance.

"Is my wife in?"

"She is!" Aunty Wunmi said. "In fact, you are Akinmorin, the warrior whose path is divinely ordained. She just stepped in not up to twenty minutes ago. Come, let me take you upstairs."

"*Upstairs*? Are you sure?"

"Am I sure, Uncle *Kanis*?" She pointed a finger at her bosom. "Is this not my house?" she said, with the confidence of one who had paid her dues.

She sat Kaniz in the family living room. Olaotan was out of his room the instant he heard Kaniz's voice.

"My man," he said, greeting Kaniz with a fist bump.

"Olaotan, you delivered."

"Count on me, KB. Ah, KB, these glasses fit you, with the cap and beard, everything. New identity?"

"The beard goes off before Monday." Kaniz stroked his temporary fuzz.

"Ooh, the handsome bearded villain," Olaotan pulled a mock supervillain face.

"Get out, Olaotan!" Kaniz said and laughed. Morola entered into the family living room, and Olaotan got out quickly. He knew when three was a crowd.

"Aunty Wunmi, you didn't say..." Rola's voice trailed off as she saw that Aunty Wunmi too had left.

She turned to Kaniz. "I didn't know it was you. I would have dressed" – she gestured with her hands at her knee length jeans shorts, black T-shirt and black Chanel flipflops – "more appropriately."

He stood. "It's great. You look good as always. Besides, you are at home."

"Well, denim shorts, you know," she said, pointing down at the offending article of clothing.

"Morola, thank you," he said simply.

"Whatever for?" she asked, gesturing to the sofa. "Please, sit."

They both sat on the same L-shaped sofa. She sat on the ottoman area.

"I was told you didn't leave the hospital when I was there. You stayed by my side."

She shrugged, her face expressionless.

"Morola, forgive me." His tone was contrite.

"There's nothing to forgive. Perhaps you were right, Kaniz. Perhaps I really shouldn't complicate your life with my phobia."

"Ah!" Kaniz thought. "What is this again? Complicate my life, Morola. Please, complicate my life forever. I need your type of complications." Out loud, he said coolly, "Why do you say that?"

"Kaniz." She shook her head.

"No secrets anymore, Morola, please."

"How is Alhaji?" she asked. He had been remarkably kind at the hospital and seemed to have taken to referring to her as "my daughter".

"He sends his profound apologies. Morola, he really is extremely sorry. He is really embarrassed that he was so misguided. I don't think it's something we should ever mention again. Can I ask this of you?"

She found Alhaji's apology believable. His attitude throughout her stay at St Paul's had been impeccable. She nodded. She would rather not remember the elderly man's gaffes.

"And," he said with a mischievous twinkle in his eye, "apparently, Alhaji is sorted."

"Kaniz. What's going on in Colombia with merchandise and all?" She dropped the question like a bombshell.

Kaniz was in shock. How did she know? Where to start? What to say?

It wasn't his secret to divulge and at the same time, it wasn't fair to ask her hand in marriage and not clear up such a matter.

"I understand a bit of Spanish," she said by way of explanation.

"Morola, I wish you could just trust me on that."

She kept staring at him.

"If I tell you, it could gravely endanger your life and that of your family. You are familiar with the world of security and defence. It's work, and it's classified information; highest level of security clearance. It could put so many lives in danger." His hand was at his temple as he spoke, and his eyes were closed. "If I tell you, Morola, you will really have to marry me then," he added.

She chuckled. "It's a burn after reading matter, right?"

"It's that serious *fa*!" They both laughed. She always laughed when he threw in his mother's very indigenous dialectical twangs.

He was suddenly sober again.

"In the hospital, you said you loved me, Morola. Is that still true? Do your feelings for me remain unchanged?"

She nodded.

"Morola, use your words," he said. He moved closer to her, and she was strangely flustered.

"What did you say in the hospital, Morola?"

"I..." she stuttered. "I think I said a lot of things."

"Your feelings for me, Morola, what did you say?"

"I said... I said that I love you, Kaniz."

"Do you still love me, Morola?"

He moved closer to her and held her face in his hands, gently tipping her face towards him. She was quiet.

"Do you?" He looked into her eyes.

She was strangely silent, silent for way too long.

"Oh!" Realisation dawned on him. "You were just pitying a wounded man then, Morola, weren't you?" He snorted. "Now I can see. What do you have to say to me?"

She tried to look away. Something about his gaze always made her heart flutter.

"I said, I said... Oh Kaniz! You know very well what I said!"

"I am here now, and I want to hear you tell me." His voice was getting huskier. "Morola, was it pity then? Was that it? Now I can see, now I am strong again, things have changed?" he asked.

His eyes darkened with pain. "It was, it was really pity." His head dropped in disappointment, and he dropped his hands from her face and withdrew, moving out of her personal space. "It wasn't real." He shook his head, a sardonic smile on his lips. "You like mending the broken," he said, his left hand rubbing his scar. He got up and off the sofa and turned to walk away.

"No!"

Rola stood up quickly and placed a hand on his shoulder.

"I love you, Kaniz, and if you still want us to get married, then I accept your proposal. It would be an honour to be your wife."

Kaniz turned towards her slowly, as if he wasn't sure he was hearing clearly.

"What did you just say?" His brow was furrowed.

"I love you, Kaniz. If your proposal still stands, I accept. I will marry you," she said.

He drew her into his arms and held her close, letting out a deep sigh of relief.

"In the hospital, I thought I was dreaming. I thought it was a dream." He buried his face in her hair. "My love, you understand there's no way out of this if we get married. I believe death is the only exit." He smiled playfully at his own words, but he was serious.

He let go of her for a moment so he could look at her face. "Morola, is that what you are saying to me? You promise you won't ever leave me?" His eyes were sober and sincere. He looked at her, and her eyes were full of worry.

"Kaniz, what if you also change like all men do? Their love always seems to wane. How long before your heart strays too?" Her voice broke.

"Morola, I have faith in God. I love you so much that I should be afraid you would hurt me too, but I choose to trust God that you won't. Have you ever prayed about your husband?" he asked.

She nodded and said quietly, "Ever since I was six, I have been praying."

"Do you think I am the answer God sent you, Sarauniya?" He smiled soberly, still looking in her eyes. "Am I your husband?"

She nodded and whispered, "Yes."

"Then trust God first, Morola. Then trust me."

He held her close again. Her head was on his shoulder, his cheek resting against her hair. He held her hand in his. "I vow to love you with all that I am and all that I have. I vow to cherish you. I vow to support you, to protect you as long as we both shall live. God helping me, nothing but death will separate us, Morola. Now promise you won't ever leave me." His voice was husky. "Vow to me now, Morola."

She could feel his heart beneath her cheek even as she felt his voice. Something told her he told the truth. She felt a profound peace.

"I won't ever leave you, Kaniz," she whispered. She chose to trust God.

He kissed her on the forehead. "My love," he whispered and placed her hand on his heart. "It's yours," he whispered, "from the day I met you." He paused. "I have your ring," he said in a low octave laden with emotion. He brought the ring out of his pocket and slipped it on the right finger. It fit perfectly. He lifted her left hand to his lips. "Thank you for accepting my ring, Morola."

"Kaniz?" Morola said as she saw Kaniz off to his car.

"Hmm?"

"Why did you tell me to leave? In the hospital. Why?"

"I thought you would be happier with Tim or with any of your suitors. I was no longer the man you met. If I had been visually impaired when we met, it would have been different but... that wasn't what you bargained for."

"It was really cruel though."

"I only want you to be happy, Morola. Forgive me." He pulled her close. "Please."

"If you tell me to leave you again, Kaniz Ishaya, I will." Her eyes and tone told Kaniz she was serious.

"Sarauniya, never! Am I crazy? Never," he laughed. Then he paused and asked, "So, when can I see your dad?"

She was surprised. "What for?"

"To ask for his daughter's hand?"

She wasn't angry with TK, but the strength of the repressed memories she dragged out so recently had left her emotionally raw and not favourably disposed to her dad. "You will talk to him about what happened?" he said, not expecting an answer. "At least give him a chance to make amends. The way Olaotan talks about your father, he seems like a changed man."

"Oh, I'm *sure* he is," Rola said. But what's done is done. And I am in love with you and still struggling with the baggage, Rola thought to herself.

Kaniz sensed her reticence and drew her into his arms, laying his forehead gently on hers.

"Sarauniya, if I could forgive Alhaji, not once but twice, you can forgive TK... you will forgive TK, my love," he said. "Regardless of what he did to you. But let me act right. Let me do the right thing, Morola."

She nodded. "I will set it up."

"Tomorrow?

She nodded.

He let her go but held onto her hand. "So, when are we getting married? I am ready tomorrow if you are." He smiled faintly. What exactly were they waiting for?

A cloud moved across her face at his words.

"Morola, no more secrets." His heart sank. Was she going to withdraw again?

"Kaniz, it's not you that I don't trust. I am just not ready for... It's just that since I was a child, the... I am just not ready for..." She stopped and took a deep breath. "I have always believed that men only want one thing from women, and they would lie and do whatever, even get married, so they can get it."

"Hmm," he nodded, "you are saying that you think I would rush you to the altar so I could make love to you?"

Why was Kaniz so direct? Hadn't he heard of tact, of euphemisms?

He moved closer again and tipped her chin up gently with the tips of his fingers. His voice was husky when he spoke. "I have longed to do this for months. Since the very first day I met you," he said as he bent his head towards hers. His eyes were closed as he gently, tenderly brushed her lips with his and lingered in a deep kiss.

Morola's being was ablaze with new emotions. She closed her eyes instinctively, perhaps to manage the sensory overload. She had been kissed before, but never like this. Something deep within her being yearned, at that moment, to be as close as possible to Kaniz, to be one with him. Her legs felt like giving way and her heart was racing wildly. Their breath mingled, and he slowly lifted his head and looked into her eyes. She felt oddly breathless and was relieved to see that she wasn't the only one affected. His breathing wasn't steady either; his eyes were like dark pools.

"Morola, I love you, and I can't deny the fact that I desire you, more than you can understand for now." His voice had gone an octave lower. She looked away, but he gently turned her face back to him.

"It's not evil, Morola." He exhaled, shaking his head. "What I feel for you is a gift. Open your eyes. Look at me." She had shut her eyes against the intensity in his.

"I kissed you simply because I wanted you to glimpse just a tiny bit of what I feel for you. You have no idea." He sighed. If only she knew what he really felt. "But I promise you that when we are married, until you invite me to do so, I won't make love to you. Not until you want me as much as I want you. I will wait as long as that takes. I have waited ten years already. I can wait for as long as you want."

He gazed at her, and his eyes were smouldering. "Can you trust the love I have for you now?"

Chapter Twenty-Three

"His left hand is under my head, and his right hand doth embrace me."

Song of Solomon 2:6

"It takes one to know one," they say, and TK could tell this was not the kind of man he had been. He really hadn't known what to expect when Rola had said her friend, Kaniz, wanted a few minutes of his time. One look at Kaniz, and TK could guess why he was there.

Kaniz swooped down on the floor and said, "Good evening, sir," in Yoruba.

TK was aghast. The man's towering height made the greeting all the more dramatic. "Get up! Get up! Please, don't do that."

The younger man was so sober and dignified, and he had such an aura around him that TK wondered what type of journey he had been through in life to make him so grave at thirty-six. It was usually deep suffering that produced this type of equanimity and maturity in a man this young. Mamane's son? This man was meant to be an arrogant brat. TK decided he had to find out what the story was.

He was impressed when Kaniz confirmed what he was indeed there for.

"Sir, I would like to humbly request your kind permission to marry your daughter."

He didn't know young men still honoured their prospective fathers-in-law this much. He knew who his father was, but TK still took Kaniz through the mill of asking about his family. They did the whole lineage interview and moved to his resume. Next up was a character profiling, his strategic plans coming right after.

Kaniz wondered if TK too had attended FBI interrogation training; he was a natural. He could ask the same question a dozen ways, smiling even while he was setting you up.

"How long had have you known my daughter?"

"Over four months, sir."

"Just four months? Is that enough time to make such a lifetime decision?"

"It depends on the level of engagement and interaction in the four months, sir. Some couples don't know what we know of each other in four years and if it is alright with you sir, could we get married in another five or six months?"

"Are you sleeping with my daughter?"

Kaniz almost fell off his chair at the question. Just when he had been lulled into a sense of security. TK was almost as good as a professional interrogator.

"No, sir."

"No?" Did he find her unattractive or did he have any "problems"? These things started from about age thirty sometimes, he thought, smiling to put Kaniz at ease. Kaniz was already thirty-six, nothing to be ashamed of. He had remedies to prescribe.

"No, sir. It's by choice. I have been celibate for a while. The understanding I have about sex is deeper, sir, and doesn't allow for such a celebration of love and intimacy outside the marriage covenant."

TK's face was blank; no help there for Kaniz. He would have to elaborate.

"Sir, it would be wrong, and it would be a farce. Besides, if we had been intimate, we wouldn't know each other this well yet. Real intimacy takes time to develop, and sex in courtship always gets in the way of real intimacy, sir."

That "sir". Always that "sir", TK noted. Perhaps the military background.

What were his plans for his daughter? What were his plans to take care of her? Did he know his daughter was an entrepreneur? Was he planning to conscript her to the kitchen and bedroom? Did he know she was very independent-minded? Did he have any idea how intelligent she was? Did he insist on having his stew cooked fresh daily?

"Sir, my late mother was a strong Yoruba woman. She regaled me with stories of Madam Tinubu and Funmilayo Ransome Kuti. She didn't leave out how the Rev. Ransome Kuti supported his wife. I am happy Morola is strong woman, sir."

At the words "my late mother", TK could not but notice the sadness that fleeted across Kaniz's face. It did not stop him from bombarding Kaniz with every question he felt he needed an answer to, and Kaniz answered sincerely and honestly.

TK found himself wishing his friends had been like Kaniz when he was younger. Perhaps he wouldn't have caused his loved ones such heartache. Now he hoped Kaniz and himself could be friends.

"Group Captain Ishaya."

"Kaniz, sir," he interjected. "Please, sir, Kaniz."

"Kaniz, Rola and I were really close when she was younger. I think growing up, she became less of a daddy's girl, but she is so precious to me." He looked into Kaniz's eyes. "So, man to man, let's level with each other. You are a very attractive man. Women throw themselves at men like you. I am not saying don't be a man, just don't hurt her. She is precious to me. Be wise."

Kaniz understood his drift: stray as we both know you must, but keep my daughter happy, don't rub it in her face and be discreet.

"Being a real man is being man enough to keep one's word, sir. I am vowing primarily to God and not just Morola, sir. Let's leave the risk of disease out, it's a covenant your daughter and I are entering into. I am not ready to deal with the spiritual consequences of breaking a covenant. It destroys a man, sir. Destroys the work of his hands, derails his destiny and all for what? How many minutes of a stolen thrill? It's not worth it, sir."

TK was impressed. It was a trick question, and Kaniz had aced it completely. The sincerity and conviction with which Kaniz spoke was like a gavel striking TK's heart. Why hadn't anyone explained it to him this way when he was younger? Why had his vicar never spelt it out this way? Why did he learn only after he had almost destroyed everything good in his life?

"Just one more thing, Kaniz. I am married today only because God rescued me and I have a wife with the patience of Job, which is not necessarily a good thing. When I had almost destroyed my marriage with my own hands, I submitted to marriage counselling, and that was my saving grace. I will only support Rola and yourself in this if you commit to marriage counselling before the wedding."

"Sir, we signed up this morning."

"How long?"

"Eight weeks, sir."

"That sounds about right. By the way, who is taking you?"

"Pastor Tunde Edozien."

TK gasped. "Who recommended him? Mrs B, right?" He smiled. "Excellent choice. Always use a counsellor referred by a much older couple with testimonials. There are too many perfunctory, compulsory marriage counselling classes these days. When you meet true counsellors, you know it's a calling, Kaniz, not a mere prerequisite to get out of the way before marriage." He stretched his right hand towards Kaniz as he got up from his seat, and he immediately rose up too. "I am happy she chose you." They shook hands. "You have my blessings, Kaniz. Take care of my only daughter."

He stooped before TK. "Thank you, sir. God helping me, sir, you will never regret trusting me with your precious one."

"And I will always be here for you both." He motioned for him to rise up. "Get up, please, Kaniz. You keep doing this, ehn?"

TK was pleased as punch, though he was doing his best to hide his joy. What a godfearing, sober, polite, dutiful, wise and intelligent young man. Much wiser than his years. Knowing now how he had had to fend for himself, TK thought, "When suffering is handed over to God, this is the product." Some get twisted and bitter, and others turned out like Kaniz.

Kaniz stood up straight. "One more thing, sir. Alhaji would like me to get an appointment from you, sir. We need to come for a *formal* first visit."

These people weren't joking. What was the rush?

"Ahn ahn, Kaniz! Easy now! I will let you know when later."

Amaka was so happy for her friend. She sighed.

"I knew it sha. I said it. From day one, I said there's something about this man. Mo, but Kaniz loves you sha." She couldn't stop slipping into pidgin. There were just some expressions "the Queen's" couldn't quite nail.

Rola looked at her friend quizzically. "What prompted that declaration?"

"He was going to let you go because he felt he would be a liability to you as much as he loved you, Mo. Aww. What some doctors in this country will cause with their misdiagnoses." Amaka shook her head.

"I guess they are trying their best with the tools they have," Rola said.

"So why not say, 'I should have an orthoradioscope, MRI or whatever diagnostic tool I need, but since I don't have one, as far as I can see, I can't say for certain". Why speak with such authority without the full facts? They will just be talking gbam-gbam like sangomas or ifa priests. Is medicine not analysing a set of facts and comparing the information supplied by the patient and subsequent investigations to another existing and continuously evolving body of knowledge?"

"Amaka, did you cram that from somewhere?" Rola looked at her in wonder.

"Stop it o, Mo. I have two degrees. I may not have studied engineering, but I was told by my professors that I have an analytical mind."

"What you mean in English, Maccky, is that they get information from the patient, carry out the investigations, interpret the results and compare that information and the findings to a body of knowledge on a list of maladies that could possibly be afflicting the patient."

"That is exactly what I said, Mo. So why behave as if its spirits are downloading the information to them as the patient sits in awe before the great *doctor*."

"Maccky, did you date a doctor who dumped you?" Rola teased her friend. "This beef is plenty." She chuckled.

"See the trauma that doctor caused Kaniz and yourself. Can't he be humble enough to say, 'I don't know for sure, but there is a possibility'? That's how most doctors I know in England speak. Here, they just say it gbam!" She looked round, taking in the huge bouquet of red roses that just arrived from Kaniz. "See what the nincompoop would have robbed you of, Mo. We need to begin to sue doctors more in this country."

"So I would have sued for 'misdiagnosis leading to loss of love' right?" Amaka laughed.

"It looks like Femi has passed the virus to Kaniz o. We can't move in this room because of cards," Rola said.

"This one even plays music self." Amaka lifted up a huge card with a cute teddy bear carrying a bouquet of flowers. "Talking of Femi, Mo, thank you. You know when you spoke to me the last time, I knew I just couldn't continue that way with Femi. I went back home that day and spoke with him, and we came to see TK."

Rola looked surprised. "When?"

"Are you ever at home these days? Do you live here anymore? We are letting out your room any minute from now."

Amaka was exaggerating of course. Rola was deliberate about spending time with Kaniz.

"Mo, TK was so helpful. Your dad is wise o and like you said, to 'get someone Femi respects'. It was very key. Femi respects TK. Hmm..."

Her cue worked. Rola took the bait.

"So, what happened?"

"Femi had his own point, you know." She shook her head. "It appears, from our discussions with TK, that it's partly culture shock."

Rola was giving her friend her full attention.

"Femi says he is still recovering from the wedding."

Rola was confused. "Recovering?"

"He spent millions, a huge chunk of his savings. You know the things he had to do, bride price, foot the entire wedding bill, buy outfits for various aunties and uncles. Apparently, that doesn't happen in your tradition. According to him, my uncles too can load one with pressure." She gave an embarrassed smile. "Uncle Nnamdi called him aside at my grandmother's funeral and washed him down from head to toe."

Rola was staring at her friend, unable to say a word. Why would Amaka's uncle feel he could berate her husband? she thought.

"Uncle told Femi that he brought three trucks full of food and drinks for his own in-law's funeral, so what was the useless cow Femi bought for? That was when I think Femi finally flipped. He told TK, 'if I don't guard myself well, these people will never be satisfied, and I don't know what Uncle Nnamdi does for money, but I know how I work for my money, and I can't keep up.' So he just stopped trying. He actually said if not for how much he loved me, he wouldn't have gone along with even the few demands he agreed to for our wedding."

"He will have to meet you halfway though, Amaka," Rola interjected. "You both have to decide what works for your own family, forgetting the uncles and all."

"We agreed we would face the family as a united front, and he is changing actually, Mo. He doesn't want me to revert to TK with bad feedback. I can't say he has completely changed, no," she shook her head. "But I can see attempts. At least, now he knows his background is crazy too. So if I correct him," she rolled her eyes, "at least he knows I am not mad."

"I am so glad, Maccky. Acknowledging that he too has a problem is the first step towards a solution."

"That is a good first step that took almost five whole years my sister, terribly tough years. And you know what? I have decided to focus on the good. At least, his behavior is not disgracing me in public. What if he was showering me with all sorts of expensive gifts and everyone was feeling sorry for me in public because they know his girlfriends?" she asked, spreading her hands. They both knew women like that, whose husbands were so generous with their wives that they even generously gave their wives STDs.

"He has done well, Mo. He has chosen an Achilles heel that keeps my dignity intact. Let me focus on the good. I am adapting, and I am now displaying my cards and teddy bears with joy." She smiled.

Rola nodded. "That's my Maccky. You are adapting, and that's key! *Both* of you will have to change." Amaka was getting it right. It wasn't heaven on earth yet, but her friend was creating a space for her peace within it all. No one was divorcing anyone over resolvable issues. Rola was relieved. She was learning from Kaniz's complete commitment to loving her. Kaniz was demonstrating to her that a relationship, marriage took two people completely and totally committed to giving their *all*. Kaniz! She hadn't heard from him since 2 p.m. Four whole hours! What could the matter be?

As if on cue her phone rang.

"Morola," he said. "My love," he whispered contemplatively and her heart did rapid flip-flops at his voice.

"Oh, hi, Kaniz." she said airily.

"Morola, just to let you know, I had this meeting with AVM that finished later than I expected. I am on my way to Lekki already."

"Okay. I'm here."

"Thank God for this fast. At least I can see you every evening this week. Perhaps we should just keep fasting indefinitely. You are just across the bridge and still, I am not seeing enough of you. How about we go out for dinner tomorrow after we are done praying?"

"Kaniz... that won't be doable. It's this DefenceWare update that has me locked down. When I finish at QuantumTech, I attend to Synergy. Every night."

"You are working too hard if you don't have time for your husband," he mumbled.

"I am not aware that I am married yet," she quipped.

"Hmmm." He seemed to be reflecting as he paused. "The lady doth protest too much. You are shocked at the intensity of your feelings for me and you are fighting back."

How did he know? Oh! It was because her response had been too animated. She quickly regained her usual equanimity.

"Kaniz, I enjoy your company but you know how much I have on my plate, juggling two jobs."

"Morola... I love you so much it should be illegal," he said softly.

She exhaled silently as her heart beat faster but she replied calmly, "I wish your coding was not as bad as my flying, then you would be able to help me." She chuckled.

"Don't hit yourself over the head because you are falling in love with me too. Sarauniya, it's the way it should be," he said.

Rola was having difficulty breathing. She needed to collect her thoughts. "Kaniz. . . see you later," she said steadily.

"You can love me, Morola. Your heart is safe with me. Trust my love for you... trust me," he whispered and dropped the call.

Phone call over, Rola reflected. Kaniz was becoming a part of her every waking hour. They saw each other virtually every day, yet he said he wasn't seeing enough of her. Kaniz... with his bold expressions and his kindness, his strength and vulnerability... he could turn any woman's head. It wasn't easy keeping her head straight. She smiled to herself and shook her head. He was irresistible. She was totally in love with him and was just struggling to keep her composure and stay in control of her feelings. She sighed.

Rola had let herself in with the key Kaniz had given her. She didn't know what to think. No sooner was his ring on her finger than the spare keys were also in her hands.

"These are just keys to a house, Morola. You know you already have the keys to everything that's mine," he had said as he handed the keys over.

The installers had just left, and she hoped Kaniz would like this dining set. She gave him little gifts, but she wanted him to know how much she appreciated his thoughtful kindness at every level. She felt immersed in his love. She had to reciprocate, but it was tough knowing what to get him. At thirty-six, he had pretty much sorted out his preferences. He had a perfumer for years who mixed his custom scents in Abu Dhabi. His shirts were bespoke, from Colombia. Anyway, this was what he obviously needed, so a dining set it was: an unusual rectangular eight-seater clear glass table and contemporary dark grey buffalo hide chairs, very butch.

She would just wait till he came to see if he liked it.

"Mo-ro-la!" He caressed each syllable of her name. It was Kaniz coming in from the office. She looked at her watch, 6:30 p.m. exactly. The way he called her was unique to him. He swooped her into his arms and squeezed her tight. Rola was wondering when he would stop staring at her and look behind them, but he didn't look.

"Was it just the office you went to looking this fab?" he teased. "Or do you have a date?" An impish smile flitted briefly across his face.

"You don't look bad at all in your uniform too."

"Is that the best you can do? I don't look *bad*, really?" he said, winking and striking a pose.

"You look handsome, Kaniz darling." She couldn't look at him.

"Why are you still so shy?" he said, flashing a smile at her. He turned to leave the room. "Let me take this uniform off. Come, keep me company, tell me what you did today."

He was holding her right hand and leading her to the bedroom when he turned back for a second. In his peripheral vision, he noticed something was different. A quizzical look was followed by a look of surprise on his face, and he turned back again "No..." he said.

"Oh no. Does he hate it?" she thought. The buffalo hide was a bit much truly. Gosh! She had goofed.

"No, Morola, you didn't."

"I am so sorry. You don't like it... I just thought I should..." She covered her face; she had messed up. She shouldn't have tried to surprise him. She shouldn't have assumed she knew what he would like. She should have shown him a brochure and allowed him to choose.

He twirled her around. "It's absolutely great! It's even way too sophisticated for this place, but it would be ideal when we leave here next month."

He took her into his arms. "Morola, thank you." He bent his head till his forehead touched hers. "Thank you," he whispered. "This must have cost you a fortune." He kissed her forehead.

Something about the sweetness of her breath and her closeness as he held her close drew him in, and he leaned in a bit more, just a little bit more. She reached forward slightly as if drawn by invisible cords. Their lips brushed, and suddenly they were kissing. Rola felt her feelings start racing from exactly the point they had hit a pause the last time they kissed. Something deep within her yearned to be closer to Kaniz, to explore a bit more of him, so she reached up and with the tip of her fingers touched his low-cropped hair, and then the nape of his neck. She heard him gasp, and he kissed her even more ardently and held her even closer to him. She felt his breath change rhythm, become deeper. She was getting giddy, but slowly, as if in a dream, he lifted his head up.

"This," he said, "this is not a good idea." He looked around as if attempting to orient himself. "Paul is not around? Morola, we shouldn't be alone."

He rubbed his eyes with his fingers. "I need to take a shower. Let me get out of my uniform."

Neither of them stepped out of the embrace. They still stood, gazing at each other.

As if supplied with a sudden superhuman strength, Kaniz stepped back.

"Erm, I think you should just stay here for now, Morola," he said, pointing at the living room and the sofa.

Rola sat down dutifully, feeling conscripted to the "naughty corner".

He was back in less than twenty minutes dressed in a pale blue cotton short-sleeved shirt, blue denims and loafers. He sat by her side on the sofa, clasped his hands as he sighed.

"Morola, September is still two months away. We shouldn't be here together anymore. What do you think?"

"Kaniz, but I like it here. We have our privacy. We can talk. It's quiet."

"Please don't misunderstand me. I love it when you are here, but that," he paused, "*that* can't happen again." He exhaled deeply.

"Cold showers have their limitations." He smiled wryly.

"We just have to make sure we don't go too far," she said.

"I assure you, Sarauniya, if we are alone here, wherever 'too far' is, we will eventually get there."

"If we pray as soon as we see we are both there, that should sort things out." Rola believed in the power of prayer.

Kaniz bowed his head. "Let's pray then."

They prayed, being very open about the fact that they needed wisdom to handle the raging physical attraction. It was a deep heartfelt prayer. When they were done praying, they both lifted their bowed heads.

"Be honest, did that help? "

He shook his head. "Uhn uhn."

"I just think it added another dimension to our situation." She laughed. "It added a layer of spiritual attraction to what we were already battling."

She grabbed his hand. "You are right. Get up, let's get out of here." She needed to clear her system off potent feelings threatening to envelop her and make mincemeat of her principles. She needed to get out of here, to stop being alone here with Kaniz. She jumped off the sofa and pulled his hand. Since he wasn't quite up yet, and she was much lighter then he, she fell backwards towards him and right into his lap. He caught her gently, chuckling.

"It's your fault, Morola. You are literally falling into my lap now, aren't you?"

He had bent his head to speak to her, and his right hand had caught her and broken her fall. His left hand went around her waist, her head on his right arm as she looked up at him laughing. The laughter abated as they looked deep into each other's eyes like they were searching for their reflections. She was breathing rapidly. "Ademi," she whispered.

He groaned and drew in a ragged breath. His voice was deep when he spoke. "You are intoxicating my love. Insanely..." His breath fanned her face. She didn't know who moved or if they both did, but their lips found each other. Her left hand found his head again, and her right hand wound around his waist. Rola knew Kaniz meant to keep his promise to God when he groaned and took her hands off his head and his waist as quickly as he could. He got up, set her gently on the sofa and walked towards the door.

"I am driving you home in the Prado, and I will take an Uber back," he turned and said. "We can't take the Audi while we park the Prado here. It will give the impression that you spent the night here."

Rola met him standing by the locked driver's door of the Prado, waiting for her to lock up the house, join him and hand over her car keys.

"Forgive me, Morola," he said. "*I* should have known better." He exhaled as they both got seated in the car and he started the car.

Chapter Twenty-Four

"And Isaac brought her into his mother Sarah's tent... and she became his wife and he loved her: and Isaac was comforted after his mother's death."

Genesis 24:67

TK sighed, adjusting the newspaper in his hands. Another student rampage on yet another university campus had made the headlines. The protests against the killing of the Jos 3 was still alive. A ticking time bomb – the paper analysed – because this campus protest was the fifth of its kind since the fatal police shootings.

TK was not surprised about these developments. He remembered the days of the Ali-must-go riot in the late 70s, when student unions of all tertiary institutions in the country affiliated to the National Union had boycotted classes over, as some may term it, minimal increase in feeding fees. The army, in TK's opinion, had killed a fly with a sledgehammer, and many students had been cut down in their prime, felled by army bullets.

The *National Inquest* empathised with the students for their courage in standing up for their rights.

He remembered his own days in the university. The country "worked" back then. Undergraduates were treated with some respect. In some regions, education was truly free. Where fees were charged, they were minimal, and most students were entitled to a bursary from their state government.

Nostalgia welled up. Back then, many undergraduates were headhunted before graduation with offers of pay high enough to sustain a reasonable lifestyle. These things would seem to be mere fantasy in the ears of the youth now. Where did go wrong?

He reached for *The Daily Telescope* from the pile of other newspapers on stools beside him. Same headlines, but this time his attention was caught by something different. "Ah, a new Chief of Air Staff has been appointed," he said aloud. He read the story. AVM Ebiere Woriabam had a squeaky-clean record. Amazing. Just the type of personnel with the rectitude to lead the air force into the future.

His mind wandered back to the former story.

TK flipped to the editorial page. The title, "The Audacity that Births Revolution", made him scan the page quickly. He picked up the *National Mail* and checked the editorial. "Revolution! Why Revolution is Imminent." He went through all the editorials of all the papers. Five out of seven were about revolution.

What was the NSA doing? The editors were reflecting and regurgitating the streets. Were the intelligence services asleep? This was basically a rallying call.

TK was a follower of global events, and he knew the narrative was the same as it was all over the world. From the UK to the US to Venezuela, there was a massive distrust of politicians and big business. It was universal, but it looked like the nation's leaders were not reading the signs.

His attention was drawn to an interview with the chief of defence staff, and he turned to that page. He wanted to be sure that nothing would ever take the country back to the days when martial music on the radio and TV meant yet another set of "boys in uniform" were in charge. Though he was tempted to admit that there was some progress then because a huge chunk of the country's infrastructure to date had been built by those "boys".

Was it because the government was nimbler because they were fewer? They certainly weren't saints. They weren't as disciplined as they claimed either, going by the vast resources some had squirrelled away in Swiss banks. "At least someone is thinking right," he thought as he read the interview. The CDS, Lieutenant General Emmanuel Ekanem, when asked what he thought of the suggestions made by pundits that the military should actually take over because of the violence around the country was forthright, saying, "Governance of the country is not our job description. We are to defend the sovereignty of our country. We are not interested in governance."

TK wanted to clap. That was textbook correct!

Aunty Wunmi stepped in and broke into his thoughts. He had a visitor.

"Let him in at once," he said.

Kaniz was two steps behind her; informing TK had been just a formality. She knew who was welcome in this house and Uncle *Kanis* didn't need any clearance.

As soon as he saw TK, Kaniz prostrated. TK chuckled when Kaniz greeted him in Yoruba. It had the classic flawlessness of an authentic accent, tinged with the dialect he had learnt at the bosom of his late mother. It was so delightfully refreshing, so unaffected coming from such an urbane gentleman, as humorously incongruous as a Windsor speaking Geordie.

"Oh no! You must stop this," he said, motioning him to rise. Despite his protests, Kaniz's insistence on prostrating every time just put the younger man in a better light in his eyes. "Welcome, son." There was no word for "son-in-law" or "daughter-in-law" in Yoruba. To acknowledge his serious intentions towards Rola, Kaniz was TK's "son". Centuries of empire had developed the Yoruba language into a sophisticated vehicle of nuance.

"Daddy, Uncle *Kanis* brought basket of fruit. It's in kitchen." TK nodded his acknowledgement. "And *upcake*," she added.

"Ah." TK beamed. Kaniz had hit the right spot with the cupcake.

Kaniz smiled conspiratorially. "I thought since Mrs B travelled, we could have some cupcakes before she is back to watch our diet. But officially, sir, let the records show that I brought fruits."

"Kaniz. You will live long. No one will monitor the food that passes through your mouth." He dialled John's extension in the kitchen. "Serve the red velvet first," he said. "And bring some Darjeeling tea."

Poor John made the mistake of asking if he was to bring milk and sugar with the tea. "C'mon my friend, is madam at home? You know how to serve me!" He could tolerate lemon and honey but only with the incentive of Mrs B's watchful eyes on him.

"Rola said you were home early today, and I was passing by. I thought I should stop to say hello."

"Yes, I just needed a little rest. We are not getting younger you know. Hey, let John get you a drink."

At that very moment, Aunty Wunmi appeared, balancing a crystal carafe of cold water and a glass with lemon slices on a tray. Kaniz gave her his "Aunty Wunmi smile".

"I know you like cold water, Uncle *Kanis*, so I already bring it with lemon," she said smiling back at Kaniz. She gave TK a sideways glance. "John should serve who? When I, Wunmi, am alive and well?" she thought.

"Aunty Wumsy," Kaniz said in Yoruba, "what will I do without you?" Aunty Wunmi was almost pirouetting at his attention. This Uncle *Kanis*, sha. And when he was going, he would still find something for her, John and even Baba Gateman. Some people would come here, speak English and they couldn't greet somebody. But Uncle *Kanis*? This one? If Rola messed up, she would marry him for her!

She smiled coyly at Kaniz. "If you need *hanything...*" she said and rubbed her hands together. She insisted on speaking English rather than conversing in the language she was fluent in.

"Aunty Wumsy!" Kaniz hailed her and smiled again. Aunty Wunmi's heart did flip-flops, and she floated on a cloud out of the living room. Any day Kaniz visited, her day was made.

Kaniz deliberately made an effort to make Aunty Wunmi happy. She genuinely cared for Morola, and it was obvious. She had devoted eighteen years of her life to taking care of the woman he loved.

"Kaniz, a new chief of air staff? Are congratulations in order?

"Yes, sir. Thank you, sir. I am privileged to be his mentee. He has been like a father to me in the force."

"Ah, hearty congratulations are in order then. That would mean good things ahead for you in the air force?"

"Sir, I am leaving the air force at the end of the year at the latest."

"You are?"

As they discussed news, he made a mental note to remember that Morola was extremely discreet. She hadn't shared the news of his departure from the air force with her parents. And it wasn't even a secret.

"Kaniz, but what do we make of all this," TK pointed to the heap of newspapers. "All this deterioration and revolution?"

"You mean, sir?" Kaniz knew better than to answer such a leading question. TK would just have to say what he really meant to say.

TK opened a page in one of the newspapers and turned it towards Kaniz. "So, you agree with this?"

Kaniz saw his superior's photograph and read the headline. Immediately, he knew that this was a Catch-22 situation. If this was what the highest serving officer in the military said, who was he to say otherwise? "I believe the general means exactly what he said, sir. That the police can handle the troubles in the country at this time. And the military's role is to defend the sovereignty of the nation and those in governance and not to unseat them."

TK smiled sardonically. "Have the police successfully done that so far? Kaniz, let us discuss this on a personal level. When I was your age, we had military dictators in this country, and I am not sure we weren't better off. By my calculations, there were fewer people stealing at any rate."

Kaniz smiled. He had tasted TK's interrogation before.

"Sir, the military by its very design is not structured to handle the leadership of a country. It's strictly hierarchical, so it doesn't allow for the upward diffusion of ideas. It's not participatory nor inclusive in its decision making. The CDS is right, sir. The barracks is the place for the military.

"I know that these are your boss' words, but do you truly think that things are under control in this country?"

"Sir, the office of the NSA is in charge and should be monitoring events, and they would take the next course of action when needed."

"And these calls for revolution?"

"Revolution always sounds romantic but always descends into anarchy except a strong dictator steps in. Invariably, the constitution would have to be suspended. In the cases when it's a benevolent dictator, there is progress. But what if it isn't? Revolution always ends up in needless deaths and waste."

"So don't you agree that we need to be sure there are plans in place to stop this cry of revolution from being actualised?"

"Or to nip it in the bud, sir. Yes, such plans need to be in place."

"Ignoring the situation is certainly not the answer," TK said. "So are such plans in place, Kaniz?"

Kaniz laughed. "I am not in the NSA's office, sir. That is not within my purview."

"Dad, good evening," Rola said as she walked in the room. She leaned down and hugged him.

"Kaniz," she said dreamily as she looked at him and smiled. The atmosphere around them both shifted.

"Morola," he replied. "You look lovely." His voice was soft. He stretched his right hand, palm up, in her direction with a tender smile. She took his hand and sat next to him on the love seat. She did look lovely in her smart, casual Friday navy-blue blazer, crisp white shirt, tan belt and very dark denims, with her tan Tod drivers on her feet.

"You are not too tired? Ibrahim drove you?" He still held onto her hand. TK could see Kaniz's attentiveness was genuine; his tone softened when he spoke to Rola and his eyes softened when he looked at her. Within a few seconds, he had found an excuse to touch her.

"See, there's a strand of hair on your face," he said gently. He flicked the strand of hair away, but his hand lingered.

"Are you removing a strand of hair on her face young man or are you styling her hair?" TK almost asked. Touching his daughter like that right there in front of him. It was not one-sided though. The way Rola turned up her head to look at Kaniz; the body language was clear. The way she said his name, the way he answered. They weren't communicating verbally. Some ESP was involved. TK could not but notice the crackling chemistry between the two. They were undeniably attracted to each other, but it was above and beyond the physical. He could see the magical tension between two celibates.

Rola's shyness around Kaniz led credence to Kaniz's assertion that their relationship was not physical yet. They were meant for each other without a doubt. TK suddenly felt superfluous. They seemed to have forgotten completely that he was there. He watched Kaniz gaze lovingly at his daughter and kiss her forehead as she lowered her head and eyes and smiled shyly.

He sighed. He regretted the actions of his past. He could have obviated so much needless pain not even just for his dear family but for himself.

Kaniz had insisted the first thing they did was to pray as soon as they got to their room at the beach resort. For two returnees, the idea of a honeymoon abroad wasn't exactly exciting. They both agreed the hassle of travelling immediately was enough to take the "honey" out of the honeymoon. Planning the wedding and moving houses two weeks to the wedding was tiring but when Rola had said all she wanted to do on their honeymoon was sleep, Kaniz had quipped mischievously, "I am sure we should be able to squeeze in other activities."

They had driven to the resort right after the wedding reception. The sound of the waves was audible from their chalet. They both loved water, so this was just the right place for them.

Rola was struggling to manage on her own, so Kaniz stepped in and helped her with her zip.

"Beige really suits you," he said. His voice was husky. "How do you pee in this?" He laughed, looking at her going-away dress. "Ah, that's why you need a maid of honour. You didn't need this darling." He tossed her superfluous corset aside. "Your waist is like..." He put his hands around her waist and planted a kiss on her bare shoulder. He kissed the nape of her neck and at the feel of his lips against the soft skin of her nape, she trembled slightly.

Rola quickly wrapped herself in her bathrobe, slipping off her dress at the same time, with nothing but her back exposed to her groom at any point; a trick executed expertly by every female veteran of boarding school life. With her bathrobe securely around her, she hopped into the bathroom, closing the door behind her. She wanted to lock the door, but it wouldn't make any sense. They were married. She couldn't lock him out. "He won't come in, right?" she thought. "I closed the door. That means I want to be here alone, right?" She really didn't know how doors and such things worked in marriage. She stepped into the shower cubicle when she was done at the sink.

Kaniz stepped into the bathroom and Rola wondered what he was doing. Then she heard his electric toothbrush. He had said he'd shower after her, so why didn't he just wait? Or should she have let him go first?

The translucent glass of the shower cubicle hid her from his view as she showered but now she was done, and she could still hear Kaniz's toothbrush whirring away!

"Oh no." The bath towels were on the chrome racks on the top of the bathtub outside the shower cubicle. She considered showering much longer, but it was a ridiculously long shower already.

Kaniz had mentally counted the towels – four – and her bathrobe still hung on its hook. He was going to be brushing his teeth or twiddling his thumbs or whatever it was he chose to do until Morola came out of that shower tonight.

"Wow. You take your hygiene *re-al-ly* seriously, Morola. You take it to a whole different level, that's wonderful!"

At that remark, Rola knew there was no point staying on and pretending to shower.

"Pass me the towel please, Kaniz?"

"It's right here, Sarauniya. Come and get it."

"I don't... I said... oh Kanizzzzzz." How could she say, "I don't want to come out naked"?

"Kanizzzzz now. Pass it, please. I will drip water all over the floor."

"The bathmat is right there by the shower door, darling. You are good."

"Oh!" she sighed.

"Okay! Okay! I have stepped out. I am out." He chuckled, and she heard the door close. She knew the coast was now clear and stepped boldly out of the shower cubicle. Kaniz was standing right there, right in front of her with his back to the closed bathroom door.

He gasped in wonder as he looked at her. "Morola, you are truly beautiful," he said quietly. He made no move to touch her; he just gazed at his bride in admiration.

Morola was already lying in bed when Kaniz stepped into the bedroom in his birthday suit, and she quickly averted her eyes. Where was her iPad when she needed it the most?

She was under the duvet, so it could cover the sheer nightie and lingerie Amaka packed for her. She couldn't believe Amaka had switched the contents of her suitcase. She had packed two sets of pyjamas – boxers and halter-neck tops. Now see what Amaka had switched her PJs with. It had to be Amaka because only she knew where Rola had stuffed away this ridiculous lingerie she was now forced to wear which Amaka had gifted her at her bridal shower. It was barely even a handkerchief.

And now Kaniz was *harassing* her with his nudity? She couldn't look. She needed to read her devotional. It was 2 a.m. already; no need to wait till daylight. She was going to study now and maybe perhaps even pray a bit.

"Morola."

"Hmm?" She didn't look up.

"I am looking for my PJs."

"Hmm," she replied.

"Where are they?"

"I didn't pack them, Kaniz. I didn't know when you packed. When I dropped by with Amaka, you told me you had already packed and that you wouldn't be needing clothes on our honeymoon." She shook her head. "You have jokes, Kaniz. *I wouldn't be needing clothes.* When could I even have packed it? How many times have I been in the new house? And I always visit with someone so...?"

He snatched her iPad playfully. "Study me instead," he whispered in her ear, turning her head to him gently. She glanced at him and looked away quickly. Something disassembled within her system with that glance, and she had issues breathing.

"Erm, may I have my iPad, please?" she mumbled and grabbed it back.

"Should I sleep on the sofa in the living room?" he asked, standing by the bed. He had now "dressed" for bed in his cotton pyjama bottoms. His voice was low and soft.

"Why is he asking?" she thought. Of course he was welcome in their bed. She wanted to be with him. She welcomed intimacy, but sex was a different matter. As she had said to him, "If making love is really about love and love is about giving, about making the loved one happy, why then did it come across as if making love was primarily about men satisfying their desires?" Or why was it an index for rating the man's worth in marriage? A whole system had been set up around the paradigm. Give the men sex, and get favours in return. No, she didn't want any of that. If the purpose was really to "make love", then it couldn't be one party satiating their desire at the other's expense. It had to be mutual. She thought Kaniz understood her. She knew he did. Why else would he have said, "I will wait till you want me as I want you?"

"No. I wouldn't dream of it. Please stay," she said.

"Are you sure?"

"Kaniz."

He heard the sincerity in her voice and slid into bed beside her, sitting up with his back supported by some pillows he had placed against the headboard.

"Where are your pyjamas?" she said.

"I am wearing them." He looked at her with genuine bemusement, palms outstretched with sincerity.

"They have no top?"

"I don't even think these come with a top," he said and smiled. "You don't like them? The lounge pants are long though. Are they not decent enough?" He asked, pulling at the black and white plaid PJ bottoms. "And I thought my bride would like them," he said in mock disappointment. "I usually sleep in a pair of fresh boxers, Morola. This is all for you."

He was finding this so amusing. She wasn't. What on earth had she gotten herself into? Mrs B certainly, certainly had not explained this stuff well enough, and no one thought they should explain at all in teenage church. As for Amaka, she would have over-explained, so Rola had avoided her "mentoring".

Kaniz looked at her preparing for serious "devotion". "I will leave you to pray for me, my love. It looks like you are in for a long session. We will pray together when I wake up. I am so tired." He yawned.

"Kaniz."

"Hmm?"

A pillow hit him on the torso.

"That's for what you did in the bathroom."

"Ah! This is domestic violence on my wedding night," he said, chuckling. "I learnt from you. And this is for what you did in the hospital when the bandages were on my eyes." He kissed her on the forehead.

"So you knew I didn't step out?"

"I figured it out later."

"Guy! That your Yoruba. You speak Yoruba like a Yoruba newscaster. It was deep!"

"Ah! It's all good. So if this air force thing isn't selling, I can be an interpreter for a Yoruba tele-evangelist."

They both laughed.

Kaniz had left his bedside lamp on, and she could see his broad uncovered chest moving slightly as he breathed. Rola couldn't sleep and Kaniz wasn't making things any easier by being so fine. She looked at him. He was a specimen. He took care of himself; he was not labouring in vain in the gym. It was a good thing she enjoyed working out too.

She set aside her iPad on which she was studying her bible. Somehow, she couldn't really concentrate on the book of Leviticus right now. Kaniz was fast asleep. He had said he was tired, so he should sleep deeply then. She brushed her fingers on his broad chest and then moved her fingers down to the grisly scar on his torso. He stirred and mumbled something, and she quickly withdrew her fingers. He turned on his right side suddenly as his eyes flew open and quick as a flash, he grabbed her wrist, a wild look in his eyes. Recognition dawned and he let go. He breathed in and exhaled.

"Kaniz, you almost hurt me," Rola said.

He rubbed his face with his palms. "I am sorry, it's…" he sighed. "It's just my reflexes." Thank God I didn't grab her throat, he thought. Thank God. How would I explain that to her?

"Sleep," he whispered, pulling her close to him.

"Your chest is cold," she muttered as she lay her head on his chest.

"Warm it up for me?" he mumbled with a slight smile as he kissed her hair.

"Let him kiss me with the kisses of his mouth, for thy love is better than wine." Rola read the words aloud with a mock "yuck" expression on her face. "Kaniz, what type of scripture is this?"

He responded with a gentle tap on her nose, recalling how her profile almost did him in the day he first met her and now she was his, just as he had been told on that day, *This is the one you have waited so long for*, even when he hadn't been aware he was waiting for anyone at all. She was just a gift to him.

"All scripture is inspired by God and meant for instruction in righteousness. This is a very righteous instruction I intend to obey to the letter," he said smiling. "The physical expression of love in marriage is God's idea, Sarauniya," he added more soberly. He could sense his beloved's deep-seated prejudices from her childhood trauma, and he was committed to patiently help her overcome them.

It was their first morning as a married couple, and Kaniz had given her the reference to read aloud.

"It's there in the scripture. Song of Solomon chapter one verse two."

"I know, but can't you choose a scripture from Leviticus or Obadiah or something?"

"You focus on your focus Morola. This is the relevant word for the hour," he said with mock seriousness.

She laughed in spite of herself.

"Okay. I like this part, a garden inclosed is my sister, my spouse; a spring shut up, a fountain sealed," she read with a straight face. If he wanted to read this interesting book, she would show him there were a few verses that wouldn't help his cause.

"This is a serious calamity," Kaniz thought, smiling to himself. "A garden *inclosed*? On our honeymoon?" He replied, "I have come into my garden, my sister my spouse. I have gathered my honeycomb with my honey, I have drunk my wine with my milk." He paused. "That's a weird combo." He shook his head. "Not together, the wine and milk I am sure, but," he snuggled closer to her, "you get the drift? Unusual mixology notwithstanding." His expression changed; his eyes were more intense now. "Morola, remember the first man and woman? Remember the man was not deceived? Eve was the one who was deceived. Why then did the man too take the fruit?"

Rola didn't want to say what her sharp mind was telling her right now. What was Kaniz suggesting? That the man willingly stood by his wife? Knowing the dire implications? Could any man love like that?

He waited for her reply then spoke when she offered none. "He knew his wife had transited to another type of existence and because when God Himself gives you your wife, you love her unto death, he followed Eve into death rather than be separated from her. God gave you to me, Morola," he said, with sincerity and love glowing in his eyes. "God gave you to me and I love you. God help me, I love you, Sarauniya." His voice was an octave deeper. "Set me as a seal upon your heart, Morola, for love is as strong as death."

Rola found deep comfort in his words. His breath was sweet as he spoke, his lips were right next to hers. The iPad slipped unnoticed from her fingers as her pulse quickened.

"And I love you too, Kaniz," was the whispered reply she could muster through her breathlessness. Did Kaniz have any idea the effect his words had on her? As witty as she normally was, his words always left her speechless.

"My love for you is as strong as death, Morola. Never forget," he whispered as he cradled her face in his hands. He kissed her with such passion that she gasped with the force of emotions his touch unleashed within her.

"This was tangible energy," Rola thought. Why would anyone toy with such a powerful force outside marriage? Perhaps they felt nothing close to what she felt for her Kaniz.

"Welcome to our life together, my heartbeat. Thank you for waiting for me, " he said, his voice soft and low, his lips against hers.

Rola now knew why the honeymoon came right after the wedding: the couple needed to rest. They had insisted on a small wedding and given their parents a clear brief. But the Bolades and the Mamanes had totally thrown it down.

Thursday was the traditional ceremony and Rola had told her mother they had two hours for everything or she would leave the venue. The families quickly conducted the traditional rites, but they still had to change outfits thrice. First was the traditional Yoruba outfit, with Kaniz looking resplendent in his agbada. The spokesperson on the groom's side made a fuss over the fact that his late mother was Yoruba, and Alhaji brought in dancers from Oyo, his mother's hometown.

The dancers were a surprising hit, looking regal in their sanyan aso oke. They carried the bride price on their heads in the carved calabashes Oyo is famous for. Their procession was followed by more dancers carrying the brass bowls of his father's homestead.

Amaka couldn't get over Rola's bride price: thirty cents for a lady with two degrees and a successful business?

"What's with this twenty cents bride price and your dad returning it?" she asked Rola.

"Well, he isn't selling me, so he doesn't need money. He needs the groom's family to take care of me. If he sells me, then they own me and can treat me whichever way they choose."

"Where are the fabrics for the aunties?" Ibim, her friend from Bonny asked.

"We don't do that," Rola said.

"Not even for your mum and dad?"

"Nope. In our culture that would look like, if I didn't get married, would they have no clothes to wear?"

"So what's in all these calabashes and brass bowls?"

"Yams, fruits... oh, and a trousseau of some fabrics and head ties for me."

"Chei! Is that all the in-laws are doing? No wonder Femi said he is still recovering from our wedding o," Amaka said.

Rola smiled. She always found traditional weddings boring, but hers was unlike any one she had attended before. Di, Bev and all the others who flew in from New York were having so much fun and taking tons of photos.

Di had seen weddings from Rola's country on social media with the bride's gifts coming in expensive customised designer brand suitcases but none with these brass bowls and ornately carved calabashes. This was taking pride in heritage another notch, and she loved it. Then there was the nanny goat Kaniz's family had brought. The goat was clad in a gold dress and seemed to know she was a celebrity with the way she trotted into the venue on her leash. She could very well trot because according to the culture, she could never become table meat and had to be left to live out her life in peace and breed, free from the terror of Sallah and Christmas forever. The celebrity nanny goat went on Di's social media feed immediately.

As Kaniz came in with his large entourage, the tent turned white and mint with the men's aso ebi of white agbadas and mint caps. Kaniz had a lot of cousins. Laraba's siblings had taken the injunction to "be fruitful and multiply" to heart. The cousins were not alone. The advantage of the sheer number of people the large-hearted Laraba and generous Alhaji Mamane had nurtured in their household was that, on a day like this, every one of their erstwhile wards was a son. The traditional troupe burst into a praise song of Laraba's lineage.

His mother's family must have emptied a bullion van over Kaniz. Their sister's only son was getting married. This was the son they thought had perished after their own sister had died in such a ghastly manner, and they had thought that there was nothing left to remember their beloved sister who took care of all of them after tragedies wiped out the rest of the family. Not only was her son alive, he was doing well. Not only was he doing well, he was getting married to such a wonderful girl from such a good family. This was their turn to show gratitude to their late sister. Their joy was now full.

Aunty Esther, Rekiya's mum, sat by Alhaji, representing her sister as Kaniz's mum. When the *oriki* started, she was so moved, she wanted to start wailing at the fact that her late sister was not there to see her only son get married, but her other sisters gave her a very stern warning – this was not a day for mourning. She hastily wiped her eyes and joined the dancing.

The couple then changed into outfits from Alhaji's clan. Prayers followed, and then a sumptuous reception party for which Mrs B's committee of friends insisted that the couple had to change yet again! Food and drinks were a recurrent decimal from the minute the first guest stepped into the venue.

Friday was spent recuperating from Thursday's event in theory, but in reality, entertainment continued at both houses. Breakfast for the out-of-towners was sent to all the hotels they were staying in. Some guests chose to come to the house instead, and Mrs B arranged for a live band, which played from noon in their garden as friends streamed in all day and lunch and dinner were served. Rola didn't bother to keep up with the number of catering outfits. Di and Bev had never seen anything like it.

Rola rode to her wedding with TK and Amaka, her maid of honour. It was Amaka's turn to play the role Rola had played admirably for her almost five years earlier. As the Rolls Royce Phantom pulled up at the tent, she saw the silver Bentley Bentayga Alhaji had tried to give to Kaniz as part of his wedding present parked in front of the tent, empty.

"Kai. Mo, you should see Kaniz. Aww. No one said its bad luck to see the groom dressed before the wedding," Amaka said as she tried to give Rola the phone from the front passenger seat. Someone inside the tent was sending her photos of Kaniz and his best man, Funso. Rola was deep in thought. This was not a joke anymore. What irrevocable step was she about to take? Did she know what she was doing? TK's presence in the car only made matters worse. He had been fickle with her mum in marriage but she recalled how Mrs B spoke about TK's love for her during their courtship. Yet, he changed. He wasn't the only one whose legendary love didn't seem to be able to cope with the institution called marriage. Rola's heart sank at the thought that in spite of today's celebration and vows, one day, Kaniz could betray her. Her heart raced wildly as panic swept her soul.

*"Trust Me. I am not asking you to put your trust in **Kaniz**. I am not asking you to put your trust in a **man**. Trust **Me** to keep **you both**. Would I lead you astray? Have I ever led you astray?"*

The voice brought her peace and suddenly, she knew with an unshakeable conviction that everything was going to be alright. She hummed the song she had chosen for the recessional hymn. "Through the Love of Christ Our Saviour, all will be well..."

"Mo, you are exiting the ceremony before entering sef," Amaka quipped.

"I am not alone. I am going into this with the Spirit of God," Rola said under her breath. She turned to her dad and motioned to the tent with her right hand. Uncle Sam was at her door in a flash as she took a step out of the car in her bejeweled white satin shoes and took the hand of her proud father.

The interior of the tent was resplendent – fresh flowers, ivory roses with gold highlights, gold candelabra, ivory and gold candles and gold accessories filled it. The tent was in a lovely garden by the lagoon.

Mrs B had conceded on the numbers and agreed to a tiny wedding of five hundred people, then she took the elegance into the stratosphere. She had arranged to have mobile scent diffusers spraying fragrance into the air intermittently. The guests were seated on glass chairs at glass tables. It was understated elegance all round.

They chose to get married in the evening; there was no point making it an all-day affair, as it would have become if they started in the morning. To stick to the five hundred guests was a battle royale. Olaotan and Isa alone wanted to have forty guests, and no one had even planned for more than the two of them. After negotiations that would be the envy of the Camp David Peace Accords, they got eight invites – four each – with the instruction to invite only their closest friends. They made up for it by being the most handsome teenagers at the wedding, looking absolutely dapper in their ivory shirts and gold ties.

Alhaji on his part was about to start World War III if he wasn't allowed to contribute to the wedding. He had been penniless when he married Laraba, so he had no choice than to comply with the culture of the bride's family footing the wedding bill and truthfully, it hadn't even been much of an event. But he wasn't going to let it happen the second time, not to his son. Alhaji impressed the Bolades. Some would leverage on the culture for a free pass but not him.

Rola had warned that she didn't want any ice sculpture or such over-the-top extravagances, but Morolawe was the Bolades' pride and joy, and this was how worthy daughters were celebrated; daughters who had done things well. Kaniz was equally the Mamanes' and the extended family's crown jewel, Aunty Laraba's only son. Officially, the wedding was out of the couple's hands.

After a very beautiful ceremony with the best choral renditions, at which their vows were taken, the reception followed at the same venue. When Rola came back in for the reception and saw a chocolate sculpture in the middle of a chocolate fountain, she rolled her eyes. A chocolate sculpture in the tropics? No wonder the air conditioning was top notch throughout.

"You said no ice sculptures, and we didn't get one. But you certainly didn't say anything about chocolate fountains," Mrs B defended herself later, with a look of pure innocence.

During their first dance as a couple, Kaniz kept wondering how they got here. This was purely God's faithfulness. Could this be his Morola he held in his arms? He looked in her beautiful eyes. Was this really his Morola loving him back? How long ago was it that he had screamed in agony, "Be merciful oh God and end this life"? And this was what God did instead of ending his life? He looked at his Morola. She looked stunning in her wedding dress. Morola was right; there had been no need to add a wedding dress to the shopping list she had taken abroad. No one could make a bespoke wedding dress like the designers in the country.

His pulse quickened as he gazed at her, and he whispered in her ear, "Mrs Morola Ishaya."

"Group Captain Kaniz Ishaya," she whispered back.

"Who is holding you? Loving you now, Sarauniya?"

"My Amir, my husband."

His hold on her tightened as joy at the truth of her words filled his heart. "Morola, I love you more than you could ever love me," he said. "Shush. It's alright," he said as she attempted to protest. "As long as I have all your heart? It's mine? Sarauniya? Under God, your heart is mine?"

"It's yours, Kaniz," she said.

He sighed with contentment and his heartbeat quickened again as he looked into her beautiful almond eyes. "Morola, you vowed. You vowed today again that you will never leave me?"

She nodded. "Kaniz, I will never leave you. God helping me, I am with you forever."

"This is beyond my dreams, my love," he whispered in wonder as he planted a gentle kiss on her forehead.

Your season of rejoicing has only just begun. The words floated up in his spirit.

Kaniz had not expected Jude to dance at all, but he surprised him by never leaving the dance floor with his pretty date. He was exuberant in his participation. Kaniz noticed that with all the crowd from all over, especially the sizeable delegation from New York, Tim was missing. Kaniz understood. If anyone else had married his Morola, he couldn't have brought himself to attend the wedding. What he felt for her was just too strong.

The fireworks at the end of the reception went on for over ten minutes. Rola was in awe. It was truly beautiful. The Bolades and the Mamanes had "killed it".

She was glad her parents had stuck to tradition and not let her go away from the reception. Amaka and the rest of Rola's entourage returned to the Bolades' house where she changed into her going-away outfit. Kaniz's party had arrived with drums and fanfare. They were admitted with the due protocol, and the sendoff blessings for the couple commenced expeditiously. Kaniz and Rola had knelt in front of the Bolades with the closest members of the bride's family on one side and the closest members of the groom's family (apart from his father figures who were at Mamane Close waiting to receive them) on the other side of the room.

Mrs B prayed for the couple but not before she verbalised her deepest thoughts. "Morolawe, you are a child equal to ten children! When you were the only one for years, some said, 'is it just this one girl you are going to have?' I told them, 'she is more than ten sons to me.' And indeed, you are. You are an *olú omo*, a child who is chief amongst children. You have made your parents proud; you have made your family proud. Dare I say, you have made even your country proud. You will make your husband proud. You haven't given us one day of concern. You haven't followed the follies of this age. You have kept yourself pure. Then it was time to choose a husband, and you let God choose for you. You have chosen well. You have done things right. You have excelled in all ways. You are considerate, you are kind, you are generous, you are loving. You bring us joy; you fill everywhere you enter with laughter. You will also fill the Mamanes' household with joy and laughter. We taught you and brought you up, but you taught yourself all over again. Why would we not celebrate you like a worthy daughter? If we do ten times more than we did to celebrate you at this wedding, you are more than worth it, Morolawe!

"You are my son not my son-in-law," she said to Kaniz, still speaking Yoruba as she embraced him. No other language could suffice for moments as deep as this. As she began to pray and bless Rola and Kaniz, her joy knew no bounds.

TK moved closer to his kneeling daughter as he rounded up his prayers for Kaniz and Rola. He stooped, embraced Rola and whispered in her ear, in a grave tone too low for Kaniz who knelt by her side to hear, "Forgive me, Morolawe, I know I failed you."

Rola looked up in her father's remorseful face and saw his tears. She gasped in surprise, and tears fell freely from her eyes. That instant, from deep within her, she forgave TK. She felt a weight lift off her shoulders like a macabre bird she never knew had been perched there took to its wings and flew off.

The drama between father and daughter didn't go unnoticed. Kaniz allowed them their moment as TK embraced his daughter, even as his own arms ached to hold his bride himself and comfort her.

"Daddy's special daughter!" Her father's sister, Aunty Laide chimed. "See how father and daughter are crying."

"It's alright, Baba Rola!" another aunt said. "Rola, you too stop crying now so your dad can stop." Everyone had a comment to offer, while others just went "Eeehhh" and wiped their own tears. They all assumed Rola and TK were overwhelmed by the moment.

"Baba Rola, you too stop now. You are a man!" the men said.

Rola reached up and returned her dad's hug as he broke down and cried in earnest.

Amaka was thankful for the healing between father and daughter, but she had other worries even as father and daughter mended the rift of decades. The maid of honour took off from the main living room to fetch Quincy, the make-up artist who was on call. "The way we are going now, Mo is going to need a major touch up before we can start going to Mamane Close!" Looking back as she stepped out on her mission, she saw TK cradling Rola and wiping her face with his handkerchief. "Oh! TK had better not rub those false lashes off o!" Amaka complained, muttering under her breath.

The wedding ceremonies had been a carnival, the crescendo of months of visiting and meeting relatives on both sides. So, she and Kaniz got the rest they deserved while on their honeymoon. But more importantly, they talked.

From the very day they started talking on the way to camp, they never seemed to run out of things to discuss. Kaniz's interesting "bible studies" were changing Rola's paradigms. She hadn't known what baggage had developed from her deep hurt. Now, the Word was healing her. If this was what life with Kaniz was going to be like, then Rola felt really blessed. She had been wary of what life with a man would be like, but Kaniz was stress-free. He had his way of doing things which she was adapting to, but the way Kaniz loved her and showed it, it was not too much of a sacrifice.

Rola couldn't believe that he was keeping his word – that he would never go beyond her comfort zone and no matter how increasingly difficult it seemed to be becoming for him, when he sensed her reservations, he would hold back. She would sometimes catch him contemplating her with an inscrutable look in his eyes. He was definitely attracted to her, but her body wasn't his main focus. Her issues were melting slowly as they were confronted by his actions.

Now if only she could say *she* wasn't focusing on his body, but that would be a lie. She lay awake while he slept in one of those his ridiculous no-top pyjamas and stared at him; stared even at the scars on his torso. She snuggled close to him and lay on his broad chest when they were in bed, while her imagination went haywire and embarrassed her thoroughly. Thank God Kaniz couldn't read minds.

She made a note to buy him pyjama tops as soon as they got home, perhaps a kimono top to start, what with his habit of stepping out of the shower and into the room unclad. It was nothing short of unfair. He knew the figure he cut and was deliberately scrambling her mind.

Chapter Twenty-Five

"Therefore will not we fear, though the earth be removed, and though the mountains be carried into the midst of the sea."

Psalm 46:2

They arrived from honeymoon late on Sunday night, and Amaka landed in their house the very next morning. Monday or not, she had to see her friend. She timed her arrival for after Kaniz went to work.

"Mo, this place is so lovely," she said, looking up at the high ceilings. "You know the last time I was here the decor wasn't all done yet. Alhaji did well giving you guys this house."

"I know, right? And he got AD Consulting to design it. It is a great wedding gift."

"Does AD actually still design residences, with their global client base?" Amaka asked.

"For a few discerning clients apparently," Rola replied.

Rola had seen the papers and marvelled at Alhaji's thoughtfulness. "Mr Kaniz Ishaya and Mrs Morolawe Ishaya" was what the deed read.

The grounds were lovely. Rola thought the swimming pool was a bit of an overkill, but it came with the house. There were four bedrooms on the first floor, a gym, a guest room and a huge study on the ground floor. The study was fully equipped, which meant she could work remotely with New York.

"We need to get to work fast to fill these bedrooms," Kaniz had said as they came in the night before. "Hmm? What do you think, my love?"

"I should get tenants?" she asked, deliberately misunderstanding him.

Kaniz chuckled.

She liked the way he always said that "Hmm?" It was ever so comforting, like a mother's tone to her baby.

Amaka and Rola were seated in the family living room upstairs while Paul tinkered around in the kitchen fixing breakfast for Amaka.

"Mo, tell me, now you are like me..." Amaka winked and pointed a finger at her own chest. "How do you feel? My negligee worked its magic right?"

"Come and carry your useless handkerchief, Amaka. What was that?" Morola said. "And where did you put my PJs?"

"I threw them away," she said with a nonchalant flick of her wrist.

"What?! Sis, are you okay? You threw away both sets? Those PJs are super comfy o."

"Please. You can do comfy when you become a grandma. Oya tell me..."

"There's nothing to say."

"That what?" Amaka moved closer to her friend on the grey sofa they had brought from the old house.

"Nothing happened."

"Ewo! Mo has killed me. I am dead! Nothing happened? Zero? Zilch? Ewo! There's a problem! Fine man like that! You can't just tell these days o. My godchildren o! Mo has robbed me of my godchildren! When you were courting, didn't you kiss and at least move closer?" She clapped her hands and clasped them together suggestively. "And check that everything was okay before you married him? You this Morolawe, must I tell you everything?" Both her hands were on her head, and she was hopping from one foot to the other.

"Mrs B must hear this, at least this is good, better now than later, perfect timing. This one is an annulment o, straight away." She paused "The house! The house, Mo. Your name is on it? Right? He will move out. He will have to be the one to move out! Waka shege! Mo, no one said you should sleep with him. But do you expect Mrs B to tell you that you needed to 'test' that all systems were functioning? Must we tell you everything? You are twenty-eight now. You are not a baby any more!" She continued without waiting for a response. "Morolawe has killed us all! After that amazingly beautiful wedding. With fireworks sef! What will we say to people now? Hian!" she exclaimed. "Okay, so you will go back to New York first—"

"Shut up, Amaka."

"Yes... I know—"

"I said shut up, Amaka."

"I should do what?"

"Nothing is wrong with Kaniz," Rola said flatly.

"Nothing is wrong with...?" Amaka processed the thought, and it didn't add up. "So what happened then?"

"*I* wasn't ready."

"It came again?" Amaka stomped her foot on the ground petulantly. "The second time this month? It must have been the excitement of the wedding. It happens." Amaka gave a sigh of relief. No wonder. It was just bad luck. Bad timing. A thought suddenly occurred to her and she straightened. "But you were there a whole week, a week." She was counting on her fingers now. "Seven days plus one. You still had time regardless now." She grabbed her bag and car keys off the grey rug. "Let's go."

"To where?"

"What do you mean to where? Put on your shoes. We are going to the doctor now."

"Why?"

"If it came the second time and lasted more than a week, then we need to see to it. You just got married. We can't be having such issues suddenly. Our enemies must not have an upper hand."

Rola dissolved into laughter, and she tugged Amaka's trousers. "Sit down, Amaka, stop all this drama. Everything is fine. *It* didn't come. I just told you now that I was not ready yet, and nothing is wrong with Kaniz." She smiled knowingly. "In fact, nothing *at all* is wrong with my husband, and I didn't need to *test* before we got married." She faced her friend squarely. "Amaka, 'testing' is just downright going way too far. The mandatory doctor's report during marriage counselling can take care of that. I will just pretend you never said that. I am just not ready yet, and he is prepared to wait for me." She looked away with a defensive expression on her face.

Amaka's jaw dropped, her eyes wide. "You said whaaattt?"

TK was on the phone with Mrs B who had travelled to drop Olaotan off in boarding school two days after the wedding and graciously accepted to settle Isa in also.

"TK, I was sad, extremely sad. For a young boy, what Isa said was profound." She had been telling TK how Isa seemed to have been unusually quiet and depressed two days after they all got to England. She thought he was missing home and had probed gently as she tried to cheer him up. She had guessed wrong; he wasn't missing home.

"It's the wedding," he finally said as she sat with him filling his school commencement forms. In her experience, the best way to get a man to talk about his feelings was not to confront him but to come alongside him. Gently join him in an activity if possible and without drawing attention to what you were doing, just ask the questions, then let them drop, and don't push. That's how she got to be so close to Olaotan. Now Isa and herself were catching up with the paperwork, or at least Isa was, as she was pretending to help. Olaotan was out to see his friend in Hampstead and they were alone in the flat. Her mind raced with worry for her daughter and her new husband. What could Rola's young brother-in-law have against the wedding?

"Hmm, the wedding," she repeated. She knew that by simply mirroring his words, Isa would feel understood and encouraged to open up further.

"Yes, the wedding. It was so beautiful."

"Yes. It was lovely."

"It was. KB just loves SisMo so much, you know. And she loves him too."

"How do you know?"

Isa almost blushed. "I just know. I see the way he looks at her. I see them together. Everybody knows. And I know that no one will ever love me like that," he said with grim finality.

"Why would you think that? Of course, when it's time, you too will get married to someone who loves you like SisMo loves KB."

"I am a sickler, Mrs B, and in my own case, it *shows*. No one will take that risk."

She was stumped for a reply and struggled to find an appropriate response.

"Sickle cell anaemia can be managed effectively now, from what I hear."

She had no first-hand experience since her husband and herself were AA and of course, so were their two offspring. She didn't want to give the young man a blasé answer, not when he had been so open with her about his pain.

"Every time I have a crisis, all bets are off. Even through my own terrible physical pain, I can see everyone around me in emotional pain too. My father, Uncle Samson," he said. "KB hasn't seen me sick. I haven't been sick since he returned. If this was not an African disease, by now there would be a cure or at least something to make this condition more bearable. That is why I am going to be a doctor. I want to find a cure. If I live long enough."

"You will live, Isa." She now understood better what a burden such a young boy was carrying. Even at the tender age of seventeen, Isa lived constantly with thoughts of his own mortality.

"TK, you know what struck me about the young man's analysis? He said, 'If this was not an African disease, they would have found a cure.' Across Africa, is there any country you know of, with all Africa's mineral wealth, that is putting money into research into issues like sickle cell anaemia affecting such a huge sector of our populace? You know, because we are not affected directly, we don't really think of the ramifications. Even a small boy like Isa feels he is condemned to live without 'love'. Do we care about our people on this continent at all, TK? Why do we suffer so needlessly while our leaders are enriching themselves?"

TK's brain snapped to attention. "My dear, speaking about governance, you may want to stay back another week please."

"Why? I need to get back to work."

"Let's see how events unfold, my dear. The rumblings are getting louder. The Youth Council has mobilised the university students again on these election results, and they are to start their protests all over the country and worse still, Alhaji Gidado is agitating that all the election results overturned by the judiciary should be reverted to the status quo ante. You know, if that happens, it means that the president the VP, the senate president are wrongfully elected and—"

"And because he is the highest-ranking elected official in the opposition, he is the de facto president? The guy is learning from Venezuela," she shouted.

"He seems to have made some inroads with the youth and labour organisations. Every university has warned its student union not to attempt the protest but since the Youth Council is not affiliated to the student union, we have to see who the young people will obey in the next few days. Although from what I hear, they have more respect for Comrade Idowu Adams than their student unions."

"Idowu Adams?"

"The president of the National Youth Council," TK said. "So my dear, just one week. Let's watch and see."

"And Morolawe is in Lagos in the midst of all these?" Her heart raced for her daughter. She had just spoken to her, and their conversation was about joyful matters – the wedding, the honeymoon, the new house, how attentive Kaniz was, how happy she was she decided to come home from New York – and now this?

"TK, talk to Kaniz. Let us know what their plans are. It's just youth service. Rola can take some time off and join me here."

"I have spoken to Morolawe and she says wherever Kaniz is, is where she will be. Kaniz says he has tried to persuade her too to take a little time off. It seems it was about to cause their first quarrel. She asked him, 'Would the whole country run away then?' He said to me, 'Sir, you have trusted me with your daughter. Since she chooses to stay back with me, I am assuring you again that I will protect her with my life, and no harm will come to her.'" TK shook his head. "He said 'sir' o, Mrs B! 'Sir, I am assuring you...' The way Kaniz talks, it's like he is not from this generation. We... she made the right decision, Kike. Morolawe couldn't have chosen better."

"Hmm," Mrs B agreed.

"So Kaniz respects her stand and has left her alone o. Kike, you know your daughter. She is like you."

"That stubbornness is from you, TK."

"My daughter is not stubborn. She is principled."

They both laughed through their niggling worry.

Lagos on a Tuesday morning. Traffic everywhere. Traffic moved in those ambivalent fits and starts that all motorists hate. It was just after 7 a.m. and as usual, everyone was on the road at once; school buses, staff buses, private cars, motorcycles and three wheelers. This was the problem with Lagos: everyone got on the road. The ferries and waterways were not optimised. The metro promised to arrive at some point in the future, but not today, so for now the whole city had to get on the road to get to their destinations.

A bus park by the right of this dual carriageway added to the noise, with passengers, drivers, local government officials and touts alike going about their businesses at a high decibel.

More people walked briskly by the side of the road and illegally on the median in between, crossing the road on foot right under the pedestrian footbridge.

Tripping merrily and chatting along the pedestrian sidewalk, were a boy and a girl. The boy's brown shorts bulged with assorted erasers and pencils sticking out, and the girl's brown pinafore was ironed perfectly. Someone really cared for these two. The immaculate white socks, pristine uniforms and the little girl's neat cornrows attested to attentive care.

A convoy was rapidly approaching with the attendant squealing patrol vehicles and police officers. A "big man" was out early today. The "big man" himself was in the third vehicle, a black Mercedes E Class sandwiched by the escort cars, which were Toyota Hilux vans, each with a row of flashing lights front and centre. Traffic parted in waves to allow the speeding convoy through.

Someone had taught this young man to be a gentleman as he walked on the outer edge of the pedestrian walkway, allowing his sister to stay protected away from traffic. The convoy was coming down the road at breakneck speed.

Suddenly, the driver of the leading patrol car swerved to the right to avoid a pothole. There was a loud screech as the driver applied the brakes, and the car came careening down the road towards the children. There was no way the boy could have escaped it, not at the speed the car was travelling. The car hit him and lifted him clear off the pavement, sending him hurtling into the air. He landed with a sickening splash, face down, in the fetid waters of the stagnant gutter. He lay still. Perfectly still.

Confusion reigned for a few seconds. The driver of the car carrying the "big man" swerved to avoid hitting the tail of the patrol car, and the sound of screeching brakes filled the air. The other cars following the culprit escort car applied their brakes, one skidding against the median and the other almost hitting yet another pedestrian.

As it was when there was any type of traffic disruption, cars were backed up for about a kilometre within three minutes. As the convoy peeled off, the picture became clear. It was as if time stood still for a moment; all eyes were transfixed at the spot the boy had fell in. Oncoming cars on that lane stopped.

The girl stood still for not more than a second, confused and horrified.

"Taiwo!" she screamed and, without any hesitation, jumped into the gutter.

"Nooooooo!" a woman shouted, but the little girl had landed in the liquid sludge with a splash.

The gutter was connected to a system of canals that drained into the sea, and the bottom was several feet deep. The local government council had pulled the bodies of people who perished in the waters out over time. It should have been covered as that was the design, but to generate the funds to "settle" those who gave him the contract, the road contractor had left out the covers. The "settled" officials weren't about to let a little detail like leaving out covers cause a problem between good friends, so they approved the road and shook hands over the cash that changed hands. In fact, the contractor had gone on to execute four more roads all with uncovered gutters after this one. Business was good for all but the populace.

No one could jump into the gutter to save both children. The girl couldn't swim and even if she could, the viscous sludge in the gutter made anything but slow agonising drowning impossible. It was like quicksand.

"Get a ladder!" a male voice was shouting.

"Throw her a rope," another was screaming.

A petty trader whipped off her wax print wrapper and tried to twist it into a lifeline for the little girl, but it wasn't long enough. In less than four minutes, both children were motionless. Dead.

The entire bus park now seemed to be gathered around the gutter. Someone screamed, "I know them o! They are twins. What will their mother do? Two at once!"

"Taiwo and Kehinde? Mama Ibeji's only children?" someone asked.

The women in the crowd raised their voices in anguish. The sound of crying and sobbing rent the air. No woman could fathom it. Kehinde's neat cornrows were now visible above the viscous sludge of the gutter. These were children someone invested love and care on. Gone.

The men's deep voices were not missing in the cacophony. They could relate to Mama and Baba Ibeji's loss. Two children? An incalculable loss. Where was this family to start all over again? And why? What a waste. Animated discussions and explosions of anger filled the air. The traffic was now backed up as far as the eye could see. The road was blocked completely by the crowd. This was not a tragedy that could be waived aside as people went about their business as usual.

"They steal our money, make us live like beggars and now they want to kill our children?" asked an elderly driver.

"No electricity, no medicine for hospital," another man added.

"We no fit chop, no fit buy medicine, school fees, nothing. They come they kill our pikin?" a hawker asked.

"Dem they kill our pikin o," another said.

A chant started. "Dem they kill our pikin. Dem they kill our pikin."

"Enough is enough," shouted one tout. "Why he no wait? Why he no carry the child go hospital?"

"Enough is enough," shouted another.

Soon the air resounded with shouts of "Enough is enough!" as the crowd with one mind marched to the governor's office. Perhaps because it was nearby or perhaps because it was the seat of constituted authority, no one knew for sure, but it just felt right to proceed in that direction.

Okada drivers picked up passengers bound for the governor's office for free. The buses in the motor park abandoned their routes as people piled into the buses now bound for the governor's office.

The motley crowd slowly snaked through the streets, chanting. Cars and motorbikes blaring their horns with one aim in mind: someone had to listen to them today for a change.

As the protesters marched, they became a magnet for the disenchanted. Most didn't know about the deaths of the two children and some didn't even know why they were marching, but they were fed up. "Enough is Enough" was a defining rally cry.

As the mob marched into the governor's office complex, the sound of police sirens filled the air. The police had not received timely intel and the protesters had breached the perimeter of the secretariat before they could rally. They panicked. There was no game plan except to stop the mob. One police car came from the left and two from the right, parking in formation to block the approaching mob.

The inspector on duty grabbed his megaphone and commanded the mob to stop. His rhetoric only inflamed the mob further and no one complied. Suddenly, someone threw a rock at the police formation and the rock hit a sergeant full in the face. He dropped like a stone. His angered colleagues fired into the crowd, and the unarmed crowd responded with a hail of stones and anything they could find. A man in the crowd dropped dead and someone screamed. Panic set in, and the mob tried to turn and flee, but their exit was blocked by the protesters pressing in from behind. Oblivious to the happenings at the front, they kept pushing forward. In the ensuing stampede, some protesters were trampled, while others suffocated. It was utter pandemonium.

Social media was ablaze as the story got out. Local news outlets: radio stations, online news sites and TV stations, pounced on the story and over the next few hours, the incident took on a life of its own.

The two children still lay motionless at the bottom of the gutter.

As the story spread and the videos went viral, “Enough is enough” became the rallying cry that attracted the disenchanted and the disaffected. It became a refuge for all the dissatisfied of every ilk. Civil rights groups swelled the ranks as did thugs and in some cities, miscreants and looters. This was all some had been waiting for. Various agitators joined the vanguard as protests erupted across the country. It was like casting a match into dry tinder.

The focus was not on determining who the “big man” was. The issue was just the sheer inequity of the landscape; the corruption and oppression from those who had been handed the public trust, which had created such resentment that was now boiling over.

The labour union, taking advantage of the uproar, announced that strike actions were to commence in forty-eight hours if the legal decisions around the elections were not overturned.

Within the space of a few days, the country-wide protests descended into anarchy and armed robbery incidents escalated all over the key metropolises. The police were obviously stretched thin. TK had to call his wife to tune in when he saw a TV reporter interviewing a policeman. The policeman made it clear that most of the robbers were carrying Kalashnikovs, but the force had inferior weapons. The urgent action was to find out how these guns were coming into the country.

“I am being owed six months’ salary. How could I be expected to face a Kalashnikov with a rifle? If I die who would take care of my family?” the policeman said. “Please, the government should find out where the guns are coming from.”

TK was shocked at how vocal he was. He didn’t seem afraid of losing his job. The psyche of the nation was shifting.

The day after the protest, he had watched members of The Youth Council on “Face the Nation”, a popular talk show which always flirted with controversy. The recent uprisings were the focus.

The consensus was that the Jos Youth Council protest and ensuing deaths of three young people was ground zero. New developments on the Jos 3 were examined first. Aggie Jalingo, a young nineteen-year-old freshman had lost her life during the ill-fated protest. Her mother was the first to be interviewed. She was grave, articulate and well spoken.

"My daughter's soul must rest in peace. We are not going to give up till we ensure our children did not die in vain. They died protesting the overturning of the will of the people by the courts of law and still, no investigation has been opened into these judicial thefts of the mandate the people gave their leaders."

Mrs Jalingo then added that they were working with the youth, civil society and other stakeholders; and wholeheartedly supported these new "activities" all over the nation. TK later learned she was picked up by "security forces" for questioning the next day.

Comrade Idowu Adams was up. From what TK had heard about him, this was a real leader, one with a moral capital. Not one elected by the students through the student union govenment, he had been leading a student organisation with a focus on leadership and good governance. By sheer force of their leadership skills and moral aptitude, his Youth Council network had distinguished itself from the pack and had been the one network the youth gravitated to in times of crisis. It was the followership's fundamental human right to listen to whoever they wanted, and they chose Comrade Idowu and his Youth Council. The added dimension was that the Youth Council had a strong presence in private commercial fee-paying universities where the student union government was virtually nonexistent. The private universities outnumbered the federal and state universities, so anyone could do the math.

Comrade Idowu had the share of mind, the numbers and the benefit of being mentored by a network of more urbane civil rights leaders.

"Comrade Idowu is the man to watch," TK thought.

The speaker of the national assembly Alhaji Dr Gidado came on TV on the fourth day of the protests to warn that if the mandate of the people stolen by the courts was not restored, the situation would not return to normalcy. Sitting by him were notorious agitators from the eight regions of the country. Notable were Capital, who had narrowly missed being convicted of treasonable felony earlier in the year; and Fyneboy, whose appellation was in sharp dissonance to his features, a secessionist and agitator whose errant ramblings set TK's teeth on edge.

TK could see what Gidado was up to, gathering the disaffected and garnering support by making promises that were beyond his power to keep even as president. Gidado was creating a worse mess all in a bid to grab power. If these motley crowd of agitators whose demands were incongruent managed to cause enough havoc to usher Gidado into power, how would he deliver on the promises he was making to them now? TK remembered when a speech half as virulent as Gidado's would have got the speaker convicted for treasonable felony. He switched the channel to escape Fyneboy's bombastic verbiage. His rhetoric never deviated from bitter ramblings.

The News Channel, the country's most reliable news outlet, was airing a feature. Three of the country's most respected pressure groups – the National Labour Union, which was the umbrella body for all blue collar workers including the oil and gas workers and power supply workers; the Congress of Professionals which a critical mass of professional bodies were a part of; and the Coalition of Civil Societies – were now working together. The Coalition for Progress was the name for their network. Their stated objective? To get the nation's leaders elected in the troubled polls to step aside, make way for a transition council and pave the way for fresh and credible elections to be held as soon as possible. The situation had become intolerable.

TK laughed. "Impossible," he said aloud. No one ever stepped aside in this nation. Ministers and other government appointees would fail at delivering on their portfolio and still stay the term while making copious excuses for their failure. Taking personal responsibility for a failure occurring under your watch was an alien notion to these leaders. Their objective seemed to be to hang in there till they were kicked out.

"Effective tomorrow, our members are proceeding on a nationwide strike until the leaders heed our call. Only fresh elections can solve this impasse," the labour leader said.

"This is it," TK said to himself. It could very well work if the leaders of the Coalition for Progress were incorruptible. In the past, similar impasses had been resolved by greasing the appropriate palms. This time, that could be tough, as all eyes were on these leaders of the coalition, and the people had had enough.

TK picked up his phone and dialled Kaniz's number.

"Hello, Kaniz," he said as soon as Kaniz picked up.

"Hello sir."

"Are you watching?"

"Watching? Sir?"

"The strike action! The total shutdown from tomorrow?"

"Yes sir. We are watching, sir. Morola is here too."

Kaniz was watching on several levels. Funso had hinted before it became common knowledge that this strike action was imminent. The Ishaya's diesel dump was filled to the brim. He had also made provision for fuel and had hinted that Rola stock the freezer. They were fully ready for a long siege.

"Kaniz, your thigh muscles are as hard as tree trunks," Rola muttered as she arranged the throw pillows on his lap and laid her head on the pillows. They had just finished dinner and retired to the family living room, on the L-shaped sofa which had become their favourite spot. Kaniz chuckled at her remark and returned his attention to his conversation with TK.

"Are you good for diesel and fuel, sir?'

"Reasonably so," TK replied.

"I can make arrangements to get you some if you need, sir, if you are running low."

"I am good for about a week," TK said.

"Ask him if he is okay with the arrangements for food. I dropped some stuff off earlier. Did John serve him the prawns tonight?" Rola said.

Kaniz glanced at his wife and wondered how many households she was running, before he relayed the message to TK.

"Oh, that's where the huge fresh prawns came from? No wonder. Thank your wife for me, Kaniz. She doesn't want me to miss Mrs B at all. I am good, and I am so grateful," TK replied. He ended the call soon after.

He was genuinely impressed by their concern for him. He had been calling to ensure *they* would be alright and were prepared for the next few days, but he should have known Kaniz would have matters in hand. He had to call Mrs B. She had to stay away two more weeks at the least. He reached for his phone.

The Youth Council kept the streets busy with protests even after the strike actions began.

"Where was Comrade Idowu getting the funding to sustain this momentum?" TK wondered. The sheer scale of the protests, the coordination, the logistics; money was being spent. Where did it come from? Why were there fresh protests springing up even as the government was meeting with and settling all "stakeholders"? There had been protests in the past and when dollars changed hands, the storm usually calmed rapidly.

When your wife is away and the biggest strike in the history of your nation is on, what do you do? You make sure there is diesel to power your generator till the madness is over, make sure all your air conditioners are working at full capacity, pour yourself a long drink and watch the news as you comment aloud to yourself while calling your wife to vent when a particularly imbecilic statement has been made and your rant needs an audience. This was TK's only option. So long as the strike ended before the diesel in his underground tank was expended, this was going to be treated like a much-needed break.

Following the days of unprecedented chaos, the national assembly had begun impeachment proceedings against the president. Under the cover of darkness, Ghana Must Go bags full of dollars were being dropped off like Christmas hampers at senators' residencies. The right people had to be settled. It was a merry season for a cadre of politicians even as the nation suffered seismic upheavals of unparalleled proportions.

His foot soldiers were in the field spreading the cash, while the president addressed the nation in a broadcast. TK, watching The News Channel, thought the president seemed visibly shaken, and his normally challenged diction was now rendered abysmal. Never mind the armed robberies and the gross insecurity in the streets, the president's main concern was this impeachment threat. He declared a country-wide state of emergency while appealing for calm, stating that the chief of defence staff had been authorised to mobilise the army. The army was now to enforce peace in the streets. The police simply had not been effective to handle the crisis. Some were suddenly missing their rifles. Rumours of arms being hired out to the nightly marauders had been going on for decades but now intensified even as the armed robberies escalated. The state of insecurity was intense.

With the advent of the army, dawn to dusk curfews were put in place nationwide. People were seated at home from the strikes, so this was necessary. The pattern of the violence shifted from protests to targeted and isolated attacks. Some people obviously had a vested interest in this instability and were funding it. The students, the thugs, the labour unions all engaged in civil unrest, and this pattern suggested one mind was behind it all.

Chapter Twenty-Six

"He teaches my hand to make war,
so that my arms can bend a bow of bronze."
Psalm 18:34

Kaniz looked up at Rola's face as he lay his head on the throw pillows on her lap. He had found that this was the most comfortable position ever. Or was it just rather very comforting? It was an arrangement that suited them both.

The first time he had found himself in this position and the "revelation" had hit him, he had sighed in sheer bliss and said to her, "I could get married just for this," snuggling closer to her flat belly.

Barely an hour before, he had received a phone call from Kola alerting him that *Operation Shield* was warm. He was struggling with how to let her know he was leaving now, wouldn't be coming home tomorrow night and wasn't even sure when exactly he would be back. He couldn't give her an explanation, not with the classified nature of his mission. It was days like this that had made the Quartet mandate that there be "no emotional entanglements". Yet he had derailed and fallen hopelessly in love.

"Morola," he began.

"Hmm?"

She had been trying to keep up with the reports on the unprecedented happenings on her online news feed. She lowered her iPad and bent her head to give him her full attention.

"Who can stay with you at home for about two days?" he asked, speaking half to himself. "I wish Olaotan and Isa were still around, and

Mrs B is still not back." Another thought occurred to him. "Would you like me to take you to the house in Lekki? At least Aunty Wunmi is there with your dad."

"Kaniz darling, this is my home now. This is where I should stay. I am married to you. What are you trying to say?"

"I need to leave tonight, and I am not comfortable with your being here alone overnight with the state of affairs. I am not certain when I will be back. You will have two officers on guard at all times. Paul will also be around in his quarters, but the thought of leaving you alone here at a time like this... Let me take you to Lekki."

"Amir, you mean you want me to return to my father and declare that my husband could not protect me?"

At the mention of TK, an errant thought crossed her mind. Rola trusted Kaniz. It had to be work. He was too committed to God for it to be anything sinister, right? But two *nights*? It was partly her fault. Her issues had stopped her from getting "her act" together on time and now he was... She sighed, said nothing and just looked at him.

Her thoughts must have reflected on her face for a split second because Kaniz said, "Morola, it's work." He spoke reassuringly and kissed her exposed midriff in her short T-shirt and infamous denim shorts which was her stay-at-home-outfit for the strike today.

"My love, it's work. I just can't tell you what it is exactly, but we should be able to bring this madness to an end in twenty-four to forty-eight hours. Just keep praying for me like you always do."

He reflected on the times he would wake up in the middle of the night even on their honeymoon to hear Morola praying for him, with her head on his chest, and would wonder to himself how long she had been at her intercession for him. He would feel safe as he recalled the verse, *See, I do a new thing, a woman shall encompass a man*. But now she looked concerned.

"My love, I promise you nothing will happen to me. I am coming back to you."

Deep within him, he knew he would return. No matter what they faced on this particular mission, he would return to her. *"Your season of rejoicing has only just begun."* That's what he heard within him on their wedding day.

"Then I will be right here, at home, waiting for you." She cradled his head closer, kissing his forehead. "God be with you, Kaniz."

Contemplating her calm resolve, Kaniz knew he needn't have worried. He should have known she was that strong.

As Kaniz prepared to leave, Rola was shocked to see the caliber of guns she had obliviously been living with. Kaniz's study had compartments she had never known existed let alone seen, which divulged sophisticated weaponry now laid on the desk as he got ready to leave. She just stared. These were not toys. He had placed what looked like a drone in his rucksack. She couldn't help but ask what that was, wondering what software powered it.

"It's a Switchblade," he replied. "It carries small warheads." He smiled, trying to lighten the mood. "Morola, I will be back. Let's sort this out quickly so we can really spend more time together. Hmm?"

She didn't reply, looking away from the instruments of death on the desk. She never liked to dwell on the fact that Kaniz had killed several times before and would still kill if need be. She embraced him and held on to him as tightly as she could, her head on his shoulder, and he held her close. His strong arms around her made her feel so safe. He kissed the top of her head gently.

"Come back to me, Kaniz. If anything happens to you, I..." She sighed. It was unthinkable.

"I will be back, my love. I promise," he said softly. Even in the face of imminent danger, it was difficult to articulate how validating it was to be shown so openly by his strong and independent wife how much she needed him.

Kaniz had left Morola at home since 20:00 hours the night before. The Quartet had been busy since that time. Kola was with the NSA in the office, pushing for clearance to act on the information the Office of the NSA had, to share the plans the Quartet had developed over the last twenty-four months for just this eventuality. The NSA General Dylap Chukum had to speak with the Chief of Army Staff as this wasn't something he could approve alone. The army was in charge of this state of emergency. Funso had that angle covered. General Olakunle had grown to trust the young and brilliant Major Ajayi and couldn't fault the plans laid before him at 20:15 hours. This *Operation Shield* was well thought out and well prepared for.

The NSA called him at 21:05 hours, and General Olakunle was ready and briefed. He green-lighted *Operation Shield* as part of the armed forces' critical engagements in the state of emergency. The Chief of Air Staff had to sign off on it, and that was Kaniz's responsibility. AVM Woriabam had Kaniz right in front of him in his living room when the NSA placed the COAS on a conference call. He signed off on the special squad made up of six air force officers.

The plan seemed solid. The young men had procured superior weaponry, and he couldn't but marvel when Kaniz told him how he had taken advantage of the flights from Chad to bring in weapons from the Muerte, who trafficked weapons for various South American factions. The "IDP relief" shipments had been more cocaine than medical supplies, and Kaniz saw an opportunity in the fact that the shipments were emanating from Bogota through the drug channels. He got the kings of the drug routes, the Muerte, to ship his list of weapons and equipment with the drugs. The Muerte could get anything out of Bogota, anything at all. Once it was available in Colombia, they would get it out.

He picked up his cargo of weapons along with the task force's shipment of "relief items" from MedAid and dropped off his cargo in the swamps for his men to retrieve as he flew into Lagos from Chad. He never arrived in the air force hangar with his cargo. Woriabam was in awe of his young mentee's thinking. He didn't know maybe to praise or punish Kaniz. After *Operation Shield,* he would decide. Woriabam and Olakunle were on board. The NSA could now proceed to the CDS and place before him a fait accompli. *Operation Shield* was now hot.

In field operations, there was no substitute for good intel, as bad intel could make the strong look weak. Funso and his team had sifted through the noise, analysing the intel from various sources for close to twenty-four hours. After two earlier false starts tonight, they were finally moving in not just with adequate intel but with superior weapons and equipment. Victory would ultimately always be decided by the X factor of divine intervention, but Kaniz knew that it was advantageous to go in with superior weaponry. When he was planning, he had to project what the hostiles would have access to, what their strategy would be and what weaponry he would need to gain the advantage. This was a country where arms like Kalashnikovs and pump-action guns seemed to seep in undetected, so raw firepower was not what would decide the mastery. He needed precision.

They were going in with night vision goggles and thermal imaging scopes. He had simply brought these in with his personal belongings from Bogota. Today, the element of surprise would be what would deliver the superiority. So, lethal miniature air munitions or LMAMS like the Switchblade, silencers, the bulletproof helmets with the built-in communications systems with which they could all connect through mics and earpieces, pistols with internal laser guide rods, the Kevlar vests, all which he had brought in with his air shipment "drop" were the real ticket for *Operation Shield*. The equipment they had was best in class.

Though it still a bit heavy, he never knew a bulletproof vest could be this light. The standard-issue ones available to the force felt like lumps of lead, and he wasn't ready to stake his life on their efficacy. From the intel they had, they were going against the four insurrectionists and about twenty of their bodyguards. He only had five men he could trust implicitly whom he had served with in Darfur and Liberia. Besides, to keep communication tight without confusion, they couldn't be too many with the system they were adopting. But six against twenty-four on their own terrain? They would just have to make it work.

For various reasons, the key players behind this sustained upheaval had never met at one venue. Tonight, however, after waiting for days for them to take this step, the Quartet had the information that the insurrectionists – Capital, Baba, Fyneboy, Mayor and some of their foot soldiers and, who had taken advantage of the instability to wreak havoc – were meeting. If they could capture the four leaders alive, then the anarchy would be well and truly over.

The intel indicated that they were meeting in a block of flats at Mushin. The entire block belonged to Capital, and it was just one of the many he owned and could be found in on any particular night. Trying to find Capital was like playing Russian roulette. Last night and this morning had been near escapes for the team. They had drawn unreliable information that could have led them into situations were victory was impossible but tonight, they were reasonably sure that the intel was right and they had his location. Now they needed to bring them all in alive. They were more valuable alive than dead and could divulge valuable information on the entire structure behind the chaos.

It was 00:45 hours as they entered the neighbourhood. Mushin was not exempt from the nationwide curfew, and soldiers had mounted checkpoints on all the major roads, but the men they were after didn't drive down roads. They knew all the alleyways and ferreting them out was like trying to dig a mole out of its hole. Regardless or perhaps even because of the curfew, loud music still streamed out of some houses in the neighbourhood and from some others. The sound of rather animated conversations could be heard. Habitual nightcrawlers were suffering from cabin fever, but there was no curfew against sound, so they were blasting their music and shouting in their houses. Kaniz was grateful for the noise. As the soldiers at the checkpoint saluted the officers in the two trucks, they silently slid into the street.

Capital's block of flats was one of several buildings without power, and the noise from the building generators was an added advantage for the surprise guests Capital was about to receive. Kaniz wondered at the resilience of the people. Despite the curfew and crisis, they still found ways to get fuel for their generators.

Kaniz had brought five of his men with him: Tade, Paul, Powede, David and Mohammed, squadron leaders and wing commanders who had special forces training. They parked about 200 metres down the street and disembarked. Fanning out, they slipped towards the building, keeping to the shadows.

Under the cover of darkness, avoiding the security lights on the building, Tade and Mohammed slipped away to the rear of the building. They proceeded with caution, taking care to stay in the shadows. Halfway around, they stopped. With their night vision goggles, they could pick up two patrol guards from afar. They crept closer, moving in stealth on their elbows, flat on their bellies, and got into position. They stayed still till both men had paced past each other and had their backs to each other, then both of them sprung on the first goon in the dim light.

They covered his mouth and nose as he tried to make warning noises to his mate. Tade put pressure on his carotid artery till the man (as brawny as he was) dropped to the ground. His mate was soon similarly dispatched. With the guards at the rear bound and gagged and secured in the empty gutter behind the block of flats, the unit moved to the front.

Kaniz studied the situation. Three men, three shots, but they had to be simultaneous shots. Kaniz's men crept into position, targets locked in sight, and waited for his signal. He spoke into his mic, and three helmets simultaneously came alive with the sound. Three guns fired in unison as Wing Commanders Powede, Paul and David let loose their shots, the silencers on their pistols muffling the sound. The three guards in front dropped to the ground.

They entered the building carefully. Tade went ahead to scout, and Kaniz went next. Under the staircase, enjoying a late-night smoke with a Kalashnikov slung on his shoulder, a burly guard in a short-sleeved T-shirt was sitting under what Kaniz saw was the electricity panel.

They had to take him out quietly or lose the advantage of surprise as they moved to the first floor. Tade drew out his pistol and in a second, the laser guide's red light was on the target. The smoker was six metres away from Tade's position; just the situation where precision weapons had value.

One silenced shot, and the smoker dropped to the ground, the sound of his heavy body muffled by the Apala music from the next building.

"Thank you KWAM1," Kaniz muttered. Following Kaniz's instructions, Tade took position by the electricity panel, ready to cut the power and also on the watch for any incoming hostiles. The other five men moved quietly up the dimly lit stairway to the first floor. At the top of the stairs, they paused. Kaniz took out a small mirror from his right trouser pocket, reached slightly beyond the wall and positioned it to reflect the huge space on his right. He looked at the reflection, effectively looking around the staircase's enclosing wall without being seen. The hall had been gutted out of what may have been a living room and bedrooms. A wall with two doors at the end of the hall was what was left of the flat. The wall at the end ran almost three-quarter the length of the room and shielded the men behind it from view. The opening at the end of the wall was about three metres wide, reaching all the way from the floor to the ceiling, which was just what Kaniz needed: an opening.

Through the gap in the wall, they could clearly see some men's shadows, and they could hear male voices. From the sound a meeting was going on somewhere beyond the wall. They couldn't tell how many men were there, however, from the shadows, they could see through the gap there were two men seated at the end of a table, and three standing with machine guns.

The insurrectionists didn't trust each other, with the number of bodyguards at their meeting, Kaniz reflected. He reached into his rucksack, took out the Switchblade and sent up the tiny LMAMS. It soared noiselessly to the ceiling, and he guided it along the length of the gutted flat and through the gap into the meeting space.

He looked at the console in his hand, counting quickly while he had visuals – nineteen men in the room. No sooner had the first of the men seen the drone than the warhead deployed with a loud bang. Some men went down, leaving nine still standing, one of whom was about to shoot at the Switchblade. Turning it ninety degrees to the right, he deployed the warhead again. Three men were already making their way out to the left of the drone. The six standing to the right, still in the range of the warhead, dropped down. The three men escaped through a door at the left and into the inner recesses of the building.

Kaniz and his men ran into the meeting space, proceeding with caution. Fyneboy and Mayor were down with bloodied faces, unconscious but alive. The payload of the LMAMS was not enough to be lethal to the men. A bodyguard reached for his gun as Kaniz caught a glimpse of him in his peripheral vision. "Stop! Don't try that," he shouted, but it was too late. A shot rang out, and he was silenced by Paul. Seeing the efficiency with which their colleague was dispatched, the three others who were still conscious put their hands up in surrender. Kaniz took out his comms equipment and called for backup, they had to secure the sixteen men in the large meeting room and the two guards in the gutter at the rear of the building. He moved on in pursuit of the three who had escaped, leaving Powede and Mohammed to stand guard till backup arrived. Fyneboy and Mayor were accounted for, so that left Capital, Baba and a third man.

Kaniz, Paul and David proceeded through the door the three men had previously escaped through. They entered into what seemed like a passageway with a solitary dim ceiling light and three doors leading off it. One door was directly ahead at the end of the passage, and two were on their right. One seemed to lead to what looked like the shower room next to the meeting room that was apparently a bedroom before the floor was gutted. Kaniz's thermal imaging scope picked up the warm body behind the shower room door.

Kaniz dropped to the floor as a spray of bullets came from inside the shower. He spoke to Paul, who reached into his rucksack and got out a smoke mask. Kaniz put his on and tossed a smoke grenade into the shower. He heard the person coughing and went in with Paul. Baba was secured with the others as Powede and David still stood guard. The backup was now five minutes away, but Kaniz was worried. Where were Capital and the third man?

Kaniz heard steps come up behind him, and he whirled around, pistol at the ready, but it was only David returning from dropping off the cuffed Baba in the meeting room. Kaniz looked at his G-Shock, the luminous digits glowed in the dim light. It was 01:15 hours. He motioned to Paul to watch his back as he proceeded with caution to the door ahead. Someone was moving behind the door in there. There he was moving to the wall in the room on Kaniz's left. The figure raised his arm to the wall on his own right and suddenly, the light went off in the passage. Paul pushed

Kaniz to the ground mere split seconds before a shot rang out. The bullet hit the wall on Kaniz's right and exploded with a blast. Exploding bullets! The person he suspected was Capital was shooting with armour-piercing exploding bullets. Kaniz could never have survived it if the bullet had hit any part of his body. This was more dangerous than they had anticipated. They had no idea that he had access to such a level of arsenal. Kaniz lay flat on the ground.

"Tade, lights," he shouted into the mic. In five seconds, the entire building was plunged into darkness and with that, Capital lost the sight advantage. However, he couldn't afford to be cocky. This was Capital's building and he knew the terrain. Kaniz could now see Capital's burly figure in the dark through the flimsy flush door with the thermal scope. According to the intel, Capital was left-handed. He took careful aim at what should be Capital's left arm. In the thermal scope, his arms glowed yellow, his body was a deep orange and his torso was red. Kaniz took aim and shot. The bullet went flying through the door, but Capital moved at that moment, and the bullet hit Capital's thigh. A deep groan came from behind the door.

Kaniz shot another bullet in quick succession, and it hit flesh yet again.

"I surrender," Capital shouted. "I surrender." His best guess was that the shooter had the advantage of voodoo far superior to his own. He didn't know how Kaniz was seeing through a closed door in the dark, however, he wasn't going to wait to be shot at one more time to find out.

"Open the door and come out slowly," Kaniz said.

Captain came out dragging his left leg and Paul secured him. David stepped forward and went into the room. "Clear," he shouted. Kaniz was not convinced. He had thought there was someone with Capital. Stepping into the room, his instinct told him something was off. He fired his gun into the right wall and heard a loud scream. The wall moved to the right. It was a false wall made of plaster, and hidden in the narrow cavity was Comrade Idowu Adams of the Youth Council. *He* was the third man. Kaniz looked at his watch. The operation had taken no more than forty-five minutes.

Chapter Twenty-Seven

"…for the Lord hath created a new thing in His earth,
A woman shall compass a man."
Jeremiah 31:22

The violence was beginning to subside in many parts of the city though the Island was quiet as usual. Not many thought it wise to move around, so the streets were still deserted. Rola knew that though Kaniz wasn't physically present, he would ensure she wasn't in any danger. So being home alone with Paul and the two military men on guard didn't bother her. The internet worked, so she could do her work with Synergy – there was always so much to do.

It was the second night, and there was still no sign of Kaniz; just a call she had missed from him six hours ago while she was in the shower. She couldn't sleep, not since he left, not a wink. Her head ached, and her eyes were red from fatigue. She was now too tired to work, and concentrating was hard.

She was praying, but something was wrong. It was 1:10 a.m. and she was restless. She went to the laundry basket and took out the uniform Kaniz had taken off the night before he left. Just like Kaniz, it was still clean and smelt faintly of him and of his oudh – spicy and leathery.

She took his uniform with her and lay in their bed on his side. She could smell his hair on the pillow, and she lay her head where he had laid his. He felt closer now as she prayed for him again, more fervently now, cradling the uniform. She refused to regret marrying a combatant. He had only a few months left in the force and even for the few months he had left, she had prayed about that aspect of his life. She knew he would be safe. Suddenly a wave of peace washed over her. Hours of sleep deprivation took over, and she really didn't know when she fell asleep.

Kaniz came in as quietly as he could. The main gate opened electronically, so there was no need for blaring horns and gatemen. It had been a truly successful mission despite the inexplicable near-miss when the exploding bullet had almost hit him at about 1.15 a.m. Paul who had pushed him to the floor couldn't explain why he thought he had heard a bullet which had not even been shot yet. With Capital, Fyneboy and the others incommunicado, their followers were truly rudderless. Apparently, none of them had thought of empowering a successor. The tide had turned, and the revolution was well and truly squashed. The army was now fully in charge. Hopefully, now, normalcy could return.

He entered his study, took off his Kevlar vest, threw it on the desk and stored all his weapons carefully in their compartments. He had only his combat T-shirt and his camouflage pants on as he entered his closet and undressed. He was quickly done with his shower and back in the bedroom. He could see Morola lying on the bed in the dim light of the bedside lamp which she left on as he usually requested, but she had left it on even when he wasn't there. She had adhered to his wishes even in his absence. He wondered at how quickly and graciously she was adapting to his ways. It was always a blessing to come home at the end of a day of jousting and wrangling and find peace, to know that his wife was strong but wasn't deploying her strength *against* him but *for* him.

Quietly, he moved closer to Morola's supine form on their bed. She was breathing softly and by the lamp light, he could see that she had bags under her eyes. He wondered how long she had been awake for. He smiled as he thought of how she looked like a baby when she slept, and that's how he saw her after all said and done; the intelligence, the competence, the strength, being the boss at Synergy, she was still *his* baby.

During their honeymoon when the struggle was much worse and he was still getting used to delivering on his promise to her, unbeknownst to her, he was kept awake by his raging feelings while he watched her sleep. He knew her every sleeping expression from his reluctant vigils. The fleeting smiles, the faint worried frowns as if she was solving equations in her sleep and the peaceful mien she had now.

What was that she was holding on to? He looked closer. Her head was on one of his fatigues. She was cradling his uniform in her arms while she slept, placing his uniform against her smooth cheek. Kaniz had no doubt that his wife loved him. She showed it in various ways – the way she respected him, the fact that she adapted to his ways, accepted his quirks without trying to change him and believed in him and openly admired him. That singular fact – that he was privileged to have the sincere admiration of his truly deserving wife, someone who in her own right was worthy of his respect – was such a wind beneath his wings.

It was difficult to articulate, but his Morola made him feel he could take on the whole world and win. The fact that she honoured him publicly. Even on rare occasions when he knew that he had actually goofed, he was safe in the fact that he wouldn't hear anything about his gaffe till they were safely within the haven of their home, then she would give him the feedback he deserved. He smiled to himself as he reflected on the way she touched him, any excuse or no excuse at all would do; her attentiveness to him and even if everything else could lie, her eyes couldn't hide her love. All he had to do was look in her eyes to see the way she felt about him. Why had he felt he didn't need to get married? In these couple of weeks, he had experienced another beautiful facet of life, a phase he would strongly recommend to anyone he loved – if they could be blessed with a wife like his.

If only she was ready to let him show her there were dimensions to his devotion to her she was yet to experience. He was keeping his word, but days like this were tough. All he wanted to do right now was slip into their bed with her and... He sighed. All in good time. He knew she was still conflicted. He sensed her inner struggle as he embraced and kissed her, and he empathised with her. He smiled at the image before him. His strong independent wife clutching his uniform like a comfort blanket, her nose buried deep in his clothes. He changed quietly into his infamous topless pyjamas, slipped into bed and snuggled close to her. As his skin touched hers, she stirred and muttered in her sleep. He didn't want her to wake up now. She was still very shy about her strong feelings for him, and he guessed she would be too guarded to want him to see her this vulnerable; so openly and unabashedly loving him, missing him. If she woke up now, he couldn't trust himself not to... He sighed again. It would be really tough for him to keep his word. It was better she stayed asleep for now.

Indeed, women were multipliers. He had shown Morola love as she understood it, even when it flew in the face of what every fibre of his being desired. He was winning her abiding trust and now, every day she showed him that she loved him back. She was still on a journey, but she was allowing him to lead her, immerse her deeper and irrevocably in love with him daily. He was truly reaping what he had sown. He gazed at her as she cocooned herself in his fragrance and at that moment, he crossed over to another dimension of love for his bride he never even knew existed.

TK's trusty newspapers could no longer be delivered. No one was moving. Most of the newspapers had online versions and released the news from reporters working from remote locations, but TK was old school. He liked to feel the newsprint in his hands as he read and turned actual pages. The online version was not the same; swiping and tapping was not the same as turning the pages. When he explained this to Rola who stuck to her iPad for the news, she had rolled her eyes and told him he and his newspaper habit were responsible for climate change.

The total strike was in its second day and the crisis was now on the sixth day. The television stations were transmitting to those who had the power to watch. Most people were now just depending on candlelight and going to bed early. Only the well to do were still powering their generators at night, but even they applied some caution as they maintained strict dusk to dawn schedules. TK was watching his favourite news channel which had just delivered unprecedented and shocking news. The president was stepping down to make way for a transition council which was to conduct fresh and credible elections within six months.

While TK was still dialling Mrs B, the news analysis came on. He paused to watch. This was why he liked this channel; they gave the news behind the news. The three pundits on the panel weighed in their opinions. They all called in as none of them could make it to the station. The president had been caught between certain impeachment, which would mean losing all his benefits as a past president, or stepping down and keeping his dignity (and of course the benefits of being a past president). In fact, he could even run for the presidency again in the fresh elections. Impeachment would be the beginning of a loss of power for the ruling party and gradually, it would usher Gidado and his opposition party in.

One pundit posited that indeed running again in the fresh elections was the president and the ruling party's game plan since this tenure was on a tenuous mandate fraught with so much controversy. The deal had not been so easy to broker. This was the result of pressure from the Coalition for Progress, which had made it clear to the senate and the national assembly that the country would simply grind to a halt if they didn't take this six-month sabbatical. All they had to do was look around – total anarchy was around the corner. Their greed blocked their reasoning at first, and they hung on to the tattered vestiges of their power, but matters were rapidly snatched from their hands by incalculable events.

It was suddenly getting dangerous to go out with any of their official four to five cars. They couldn't step out of their houses. People were hurling stones at their cars in public now. The same people who had begged for money just weeks ago were smashing their windscreens everywhere they went. Thirteen senators had already lost their cars to angry mobs, and there was the talk of imminent mob attacks on their homes. There were just too many of them for the police to protect all round the clock and already, there was infighting amongst who managed to coral more police muscle than others. A lot of their hired muscle had defected. They defected for a very simple reason – they got a taste of their own medicine.

The first happened in Mushin. Mansur, a hired thug, had returned to his street at the close of his workday at 1:30 a.m. to find his wives and children outside their bungalow, seated on the bare dirt surrounded by dozens of his neighbours holding a vigil his family with machetes and clubs. He thought of spraying bullets on the crowd of over one hundred people, and he was promptly told by the elderly man closest to him to "try it".

"Please, do. It's one bullet for one person. By the time you kill two of us, the third person will kill you too."

These people were fed up and desperate. They had done their thinking: the people who oppress us oppress us with our cooperation. We know the instruments of oppression and they live right amongst us. If we cut off the supply, we cut off the means of oppression. The populace was finally doing the math and realising they were enabling their own oppression. Mansur's neighbours were clear: you protect those who destroy us, and we are here to destroy what is dear to you.

The power of social media was apparent as within an hour, the news had gone viral and dozens of political foot soldiers got home to find their wives and children similarly besieged. In one isolated and sad incident, the thug's entire family was wiped out and this sent a chill down the spine of every political thug. The people hadn't gone after the warlords; they had gone after the foot soldiers, the low-hanging fruit.

The political personnel had a dilemma on their hands. Most of the voodoo they depended on for safety had been on them and not on their family. Where were they to start afresh if they lost their families? The politicians couldn't give refuge to the households of all their hired muscle.

At the rate which the lawmakers were fleeing the country, it would soon become impossible to run the two houses anyway. The Coalition for Progress could see the rapid shift in the demeanour of the senate president and the speaker of the house. What use was stolen wealth when you couldn't use it to buy anyone? When the people have declared that they were no longer merchandise because enough was enough? The key players had reasoned that it could only be business as usual when they returned after six months. Their "structures" were deep and firmly in place.

The bill to usher in the transition council was proposed and, with extraordinary dispatch, heard and passed in emergency sessions of the two houses within hours. There was no way the senate was going to leave governors in charge of the states – or as they saw it, the wealth in the states. The resulting imbalance at the end of six months would destroy their structures. The bill affected all elected officials, even the houses of assembly. Fresh elections for everyone. If the senators were going, everyone was going.

Day six had dawned with her husband gone again just before the break of dawn.

"This is getting crazy," Rola thought. She knew for sure that he had come home. She had woken up for a few moments and had seen him lying in bed by her side. She had sighed contentedly and snuggled up to him, and she recollected that he had put his arm around her and drawn her closer. She had relaxed, content in the knowledge that he was back safely. He could rest, and they would talk in the morning. So where was he now? It was time to find out what had transpired, but where was Kaniz? His text message to her stated that he had been summoned by AVM Woriabam. That was all. No more.

Woriabam was extremely impressed by Kaniz and his team's decisive triumph with *Operation Shield*. These were the days when he was proud to be the effective head of the force. What a victory! With the army in charge of the state of emergency, it was heartwarming that the victory had ultimately been delivered by his boys. The tide had turned because of Kaniz's exemplary, skilled and courageous intervention. How could he reward this young man who never seemed to ask for anything? He was waiting for Kaniz and hoped the young man knew the offer he was about to make was one he had no way of refusing.

At the meeting of the Joint Chiefs, with the NSA in attendance, he had tendered his idea to General Adewale, Lieutenant General Ekanem, the Chief of Army Staff and the Chief of Naval Staff. The NSA and General Olakunle, the COAS, were not just on board but enthusiastic. They had also been intimated with the existence of the Quartet less than forty-eight hours ago when they were needed to greenlight *Operation Shield*, but when the NSA shared the strategy document his DG, Kola, had developed for this exact scenario, the Joint Chiefs had no doubt what they had to do.

The CDS, Lieutenant General Ekanem had raised a point about the Quartets' junior ranks – two were majors and one was the equivalent of a colonel as a group captain in the air force – but the others had pointed out that there were enough of the seniors on the NTC to get the buy-in of the General Officers commanding the garrisons, and the Joint Chiefs were on the NTC. General Adewale was the most respected general in the army. Politics and his disapproval of the excesses of the politicians in this administration were why he was passed over for CDS in the first place. The others didn't express it, but the CDS' political appointment was one of the interventions by politicians the armed forces resented. If anyone should have kept quiet on that table, it was him. Things were now being made right by the appointment of General Adewale. He had tremendous moral and social capital, and under his leadership of the NTC, stability was sure.

Already, the international community was hailing the Coalition for Progress on brokering peace and ending the crisis. The whole world had been watching to see where matters were headed. Any issue in the country would destabilise the entire region. They tiptoed around her; she couldn't be dictated to like some banana republic, and her leaders had been known to ask the international community to mind their own business in the past. This was no ordinary country. It had to succeed.

Kaniz exited the lift on the 10th floor of the Defence HQ. They were to meet at Room 1022. He found the room and as he knocked on the door, he noticed the door sign read, "Chief of Staff/CDS". Why was AVM meeting him here? He entered and was received politely. He could see, through the door to the adjacent conference room whenever anyone stepped in or out carrying a file or running errands, that there was a meeting going on and most attendees seemed to be uniformed men. In a matter of minutes, Funso stepped out.

"Congratulations on Operation Shield, my brother. They decided to let you rest a bit before calling you in. We have been here since the conclusion of the operation but... I am preempting issues. Come in now," he said, leading the way. Why was Funso here? This wasn't his office. But the COAS's office was below on the 8th floor, so perhaps he had a good reason to be there.

As he was ushered in, Kaniz looked round the room. All but four were military men, and his friend Kola was one of the four civilians. He could see General Adewale, a veteran officer and gentleman well respected by all within and outside the army; the chief of defence staff, Lieutenant General Emmanuel Ekanem; the chief of army staff, General Olakunle; Funso's boss; the chief of air staff, Air Vice Marshall Woriabam; the chief of naval staff, Commodore Paul Kwande and the three Joint Chiefs. Even the national security adviser and Kola's boss, General Dylap Chukum were in the room.

General Adewale spoke first as Kaniz saluted. "At ease. Sit down." He motioned to the empty chair beside him and Kaniz sat. The older man had the look of someone who had seen so much that nothing surprised nor perturbed him any more. He exuded a calm confidence. He was dignified and sat ramrod straight in his chair, and his eyes shone with intelligence and a quiet wisdom. He was a gentleman and an officer, and Kaniz respected him immediately.

"Group Captain Ishaya, congratulations on Operation Shield."

"Thank you, sir."

"The Joint Chiefs have studied your strategy document, and the decision has been made to bring the Quartet on board the NTC."

Kaniz let that sink. He wasn't required to speak.

"Looking at your resume, your diplomatic postings, the trainings you have received, your war experience and your recent handling of Operation Shield, the decision has also been taken to make you my chief of staff."

"I won't be having any other deputy, Group Captain Ishaya, so that effectively makes you my deputy." General Adewale felt he had to speak because Kaniz didn't respond. His face was inscrutable but certainly not happy.

Kaniz's mind was racing. What would he tell Morola? This wasn't the plan. He was hoping to turn in his resignation now. He had discharged his duty and delivered on the private mission he had divinely received over two years ago. All he had planned to do was to be there to stabilise the polity when the crisis no one ever believed was going to happen actually happened. He had done that, and all he wanted now was to focus on his business interests and move on with Morola to the next phase of life.

He was considering setting up his US operations in New York where Morola was already based. What on earth was this now? AVM Woriabam glared at him, and Kola looked at him with grave warning in his eyes. If Kaniz turned down this offer, none of the Quartet had a chance to get on the NTC. Kaniz was the poster child for the Quartet.

He looked at Funso for support, but he knew that look in Funso's eyes right now meant "Come on my friend! Don't mess up. Accept immediately."

"Thank you, sir," he said, trying to build up to say. "Thank you, sir, for the confidence reposed in me, however I would have to respectfully decline."

General Adewale's large bony hands grabbed his before the words "Thank you" were out of Kaniz's mouth.

"Congratulations, Group Captain Ishaya."

AVM was beaming. He looked as if he would burst with pride. The CDS's face was implacable, but everyone else seemed to be really pleased at the turn of affairs. They settled down, the congratulations subsiding as Kaniz's mind was devising how to get out of this trap. The head of the mint NTC indicated that it was time to examine the strategy document in detail, and Kola took the floor as they settled down to crafting the way ahead.

"Kaniz is returning with some news and you must support him. Don't be afraid." The words had come unbidden to her during the day.

Rola was now getting concerned. She never liked calling Kaniz if he already said where he would be, but he had left before dawn and it was now 6 p.m. He had been away for two nights, come back for a few hours and had now gone for a day.

What had she signed up for? Would she be able to cope?

"Grace." Just that one word.

She would cope. Whatever news he returned with, she would cope.

Chapter Twenty-Eight

"His mouth is most sweet: yea he is altogether lovely.
This is my beloved, and this is my friend..."
Song of Solomon 5:16

Rola sank on to the seat in the bay window. Kaniz had just broken the news to her about being made chief of staff. He had to tell her immediately. He couldn't wait for a more appropriate time as in twenty minutes, it would be on the 7 p.m. news. She averted her gaze and kept staring out through the window. A casual observer would have thought she was staring at the pristine blue waters of the swimming pool below lit by the pool night lights. She couldn't see anything; her eyes were filled with tears.

"So you are not resigning from the air force any more, at least not right now?" she said flatly, her voice thick with disappointment.

"Morola, I was put on the spot. This wasn't my plan either." His voice called for her understanding.

"Does this mean more days like the last two days? More days like today?" Their lives wouldn't be normal. She would hardly see him.

He shook his head. "It should never be that bad, but I really don't know, Sarauniya."

"No." She shook her head. "No, don't call me that. You do a thing like this and still call me Sara—" she cut off mid-sentence, shook her head and got up hurriedly, tears spilling down her cheeks.

"I have hurt you," Kaniz said, his eyes sad. "My love, I have hurt you."

He caught her in his arms as she started walking off to the bedroom.

She just wanted to get away from him. See what he had done? They had been back from their honeymoon barely a week. This was what happened when you let someone into your heart and let him matter to you so much you want him with you always.

"I had no choice, my love. I am not taking you for granted; don't regret loving me." He held onto her tightly even as she squirmed.

"Let me go, Kaniz. Leave me alone!" she said, but he just held on to her and kissed her forehead.

"Don't walk away from me, Morola. Please don't." He spoke softly.

"Kaniz, leave meeeee!" Her voice was strident as she struggled in his arms.

"I will make it up to you, I vow. God help me, I will make every moment we are together count." His face was buried in her hair. "I wasn't given any choice, I am sorry. Just give me the next six months, and then we have our whole lifetime together."

"Let me go, Kaniz," she said, still squirming.

Kaniz was sure it would be the most stupid thing he could do to obey her right now no matter how serious she sounded.

"I am sorry," he whispered.

"Kaniz is returning with some news and you must support him. Don't be afraid." She remembered and relaxed, dissolving into tears. "Kaniz, I missed you so much and now... now you will be gone so often. These are such unstable times. What if something happened to you? How would I..."

She couldn't bear to even think about it. She started crying, her tears falling silently. She lay her head gently on his shoulder, and he cradled her head tenderly.

He spoke, and his breath tickled her head. "I was counting the hours till I got back to you, Sarauniya. Do you still have no idea how I feel about you?" Kaniz said softly, and she felt his heartbeat quicken. "Forgive me, Morola, I know this wasn't our plan."

"I will support you, Kaniz, with all my heart. God will grant me grace. I will support you," she said, softly but resolutely. As she said the words, she started crying again. This was going to be really hard. He kissed her eyes. Her tears tasted salty. His lips brushed against the tip of her nose. He kissed her lips.

"Thank you, Morola. Thank you. I have missed you so badly," he said softly in his deep baritone as his grip on her tightened. "I am obsessed..." He shook his head incredulously. "I must be obsessed." At his words, she felt the last of her resistance fade, and she melted into his arms. She would support him fully.

Funso and Kaniz had been the ones who made the representation to the NTC for Major Jude King's inclusion. They had been the Quartet after all and not a trio. It was a hard sell because the senior men couldn't see what Jude was bringing to the table. He was a part of the old Quartet, so? Funso and Kaniz leaned on everyone privately and publicly. Kaniz suspected Jude was aware of the reluctance with which he was brought in because the NTC had been sworn in a full week before Jude was brought on board. He thanked Funso and Kaniz sincerely and took his place.

Kaniz had managed to leave HQ at 5 p.m. sharp. A meeting with the South East Council of Chiefs had been cancelled at the last minute, and he was eager to spend some extra time with Morola. Funso tagged along. His bachelor radar sensing a free home-cooked dinner, he decided to come along and visit "his wife" Rola.

They strode confidently through the doors to meet an empty house. Not an empty house, as Rola pointed out to him later, Paul was around. They were still living at the new house on Toju Teniola Close. Security had been heightened all around the area and some houses in the area had been rented to house security apparatus, human resources, hardware and software. Their neighbours were very understanding and actually considered the heightened security on the close an advantage, if not, things would have become really difficult with their decision not to move to an official residence.

"Morola," he was speaking to her on the phone, "where are you? I am at home. Where are you?"

"I am in VI, just rounding up with the estate agent."

"Which estate agent?"

"Synergy office? Synergy Lagos?"

"You didn't..." Kaniz was suddenly aware of Funso's presence. He walked away from the living room so he could speak freely. "You didn't tell me anything about Synergy Lagos office, Morola," he said in a low rasp.

"You are so busy, Kaniz. Perhaps you forgot?" Her response was calm.

Rola knew she hadn't explained in detail to Kaniz, but she didn't say she had told him either.

"What do you need an office for, Morola? You have the study. It's fully equipped. We have everything you need."

"Oh, Kaniz, but we have staff now. Apart from Tracy and I, four others are starting this Monday."

Kaniz was exasperated. He knew nothing about these details, but they could talk about that later.

"Funso and I are waiting for you here. You didn't tell me you were going out."

"Amir, you didn't tell me you were coming home with Funso. But I think I sent you a text message saying I had meetings in VI this afternoon. Look at your phone. I will be with you shortly. I will call Paul as soon as I drop this call now. Tell 'my husband' I am on my way."

Rola had arrived soon after that phone call and met Kaniz and Funso in the living room. Paul had already served refreshments to her specifications, and they were dealing with that while waiting for dinner. She didn't heed their pleas to change from her work clothes first before seeing to their comfort. She simply slipped off her wine Miu Miu heels and sat with the men in the living room still dressed in the wine shift dress she went out in. She took off her pearl necklace with great drama to show she was tired.

"Oooh," she exhaled loudly as she dropped the heavy pearls on the glass stool by her husband. She was preparing the grounds for the discussion she knew would come when Funso left. She spent a nice time bantering with Funso and Kaniz. She empathised with them. These men hardly had times like this evening when they relaxed without their phones ringing. Today's relaxed time was because she had put out her hand and asked them both to drop their phones with her before they could eat dinner. Kaniz dutifully gave up his three phones and sat at the head of the table, Funso dropped two in her palm, and she had smiled knowingly.

"One more," she said and he reached into his top pocket, dragged out another and dropped the third phone in her palm.

"One more," she said again.

"Haba! That's all, 'my wife', trust me," Funso said, but she wasn't buying that. Her palm stayed stretched out till he sheepishly reached into his uniform's trouser pocket, brought out a fourth phone and gave it up very reluctantly.

"Are we done?" she said.

Kaniz intervened on his friend's behalf. "Ahn ahn, Morola. You are a bully." They all laughed. Funso was cleared for dinner, and he sat down meekly. Morola sat on Kaniz's left.

They really had fun on evenings like this. She shook her head. It didn't happen often enough.

After Funso left, she was still tidying up with the New York office in her study downstairs, so Kaniz had come in looking for her. She motioned to him that she would soon be done and within a minute rounded up.

"Bye, Di. We will sort it out tomorrow."

"Morola. Synergy Lagos? Really? And I didn't know? What if I didn't get home early today?"

"I told you, Kaniz," she said. "I did."

"Yes, you mentioned that you would like to start Synergy in Lagos."

"I mentioned that VI would be a good location and that we would be mirroring our US operations here."

"Yes."

"I mentioned that the tech hubs coming up in Lagos are a fantastic resource pool."

"Yes?"

"And that it made logical sense to have Lagos operations because of the cost of human resources here in Lagos versus New York."

He nodded.

"So, what didn't I tell you, Ademi?" She smiled.

He wanted to articulate it, but he didn't know how to say, "You didn't need me. You got it all done independent of me. Paid for the lease, bought equipment, furnished the office, and you didn't need me. You didn't have any problems that you needed me to solve. I am feeling proud of you but a bit redundant too." There was no point quarrelling over this. It didn't sound logical.

"Well done, Morola. I am proud of you," he said instead. "What can I do to help?"

"You have way too much on your plate. I couldn't even imagine adding one more issue, just one more issue to all you handle already." She smiled up at him. "Your just being here for me is enough."

He drew her closer and whispered in her ear, "I know that you don't *need* what I give you, my love, but just let me be a part of your life. Let me be your *husband*. That's what I signed up for." His face was sober, sincere. "Letting me stand by you doesn't make you weak and I need to... I need to feel I am relevant to you, Morola."

He thought to himself, "If I can't make love to you yet, let me at least take care of you."

The next morning, he was called away to HQ before she woke up, but she found by her bedside an envelope with "Sarauniya" written on it and inside, a little note Kaniz had written in his American School cursive.

> My Sarauniya,
>
> So proud of you on Synergy Lagos. This is to help defray some of the expenses.
>
> Your Amir.
>
> PS. Take a look at your WhatsApp messages.

She took a look at her WhatsApp messages, and there was a screenshot of a transfer of $100,000 to her bank account. Her jaw dropped.

"Mo, word on the street is that Kaniz is the bona fide head of the NTC."

"Hmm."

"From the way he thinks and our informal discussions in this house suddenly become policies, I can't say I disagree at all. See the airport privatisation we were discussing barely two weeks ago and today already we have the tenders in the newspaper for airport management firms."

"The leadership dynamic is more complex than one person leading,

Amaka. Thankfully, General Adewale does not seem to have a problem with the public perception. Kaniz and Kola are carrying a lot of the burden of strategy. Meanwhile, General's role can't be played by anyone else. The respect of the entire Armed Forces which he has is what keeps the stability. I wish we had more leaders like him."

Amaka had to agree with Rola. More leaders who didn't care who got the credit for success were needed.

"So where is Kaniz on a Saturday morning?"

"If it's not one thing, it's another, so I don't even bother any more. Today, though, it's the protest against the civil service appraisal exams. The head of service is being briefed, and Kaniz wanted to be there." She shrugged. "Though we have actually just started, I can cope. Six months will pass soon."

"And I am here for you," Amaka said "Seriously." She picked up her phone. "Ah!" she screamed.

"What happened?" Rola said.

They were seated in the family room on the first floor in the huge bay window from where they could see the swimming pool below.

"This man has finally disgraced me o." She was reading a text message on her phone with one hand over her mouth.

"What now?"

Amaka was livid and embarrassed in turn. "Uncle Nnamdi sent me a text message. Remember Papa C's eldest sister, Aunty Chioma, passed on?"

Rola nodded. Amaka had mentioned it even as she moaned at the expenses the funeral was going to drop on herself and Femi.

"He asked Femi for our contribution, and Femi told him his demand was preposterous. Preposterous o! That will be Femi's new name in our family now." She clasped both her hands on her head. "See this my husband? We had agreed that we would discuss these things and always present a united front."

"Perhaps the way Uncle Nnamdi asked him ticked him off or he is not sure you won't bend to your family's demands, so he decided to nip it in the bud."

"Still. Preposterous? My father's younger brother is making preposterous demands? What could he have demanded that is unheard of?

I would have quietly sorted out whatever he asked for on behalf of Femi and I, but now he has exposed himself."

"Amaka! You are jumping to conclusions. You need to hear Femi's side. Although preposterous is big grammar for this uncle to be fair." Rola couldn't help smiling mischievously as she imagined Femi with what Kaniz described as his "Afro-British" accent telling Uncle Nnamdi he was being preposterous. Her mind drifted to Kaniz. Kaniz, with his unexpected, droll sense of humour. Kaniz had wondered where Femi, who studied in the country, and all those with the same "Afro-British" accent got the it from. Perhaps they had all understudied the same BBC newscaster, he suggested. She chuckled to herself again. Amaka's puzzled look at her as she smiled jerked her back to the present.

"Uncle Nnamdi is too extra. I think he wanted you to marry from your area to be honest," she said to her friend. Amaka nodded. "So I am not with uncle Nnamdi on this, but Femi and yourself also need to be on the same page. You talk to Femi about these things?"

"Constantly o," Amaka said, her frustration apparent in her voice.

"Okay, don't talk anymore."

"I should keep quiet?"

"Yes. Most men hear silence better than constant nagging. That nagging without any decisive action following it is just a constant reassurance to him that you are still there talking but going nowhere. He has just tuned you out. Withdraw. Use just monosyllables, but no moodiness. No extra, just display perfect equanimity."

"Let me check that in the dictionary," Amaka said. "Spell it. E–Q-U–A-N- what?

"Stop it," Rola said, laughing. "Be calm, but stonewall the living day lights out of Femi till he is the one begging you to tell him what the problem is. *Then* speak."

Rola was quiet for a while. In Amaka's experience, these silences always led to some profound pronouncements and paradigm-shifting observations.

"Amaka, look at it this way. Marriage is for fulfilling destiny. There's no point being married to the sweetest guy in the universe if your life doesn't make any impact."

Amaka nodded her agreement.

"Everything has a purpose. I think Femi is the way he is and was still chosen for you for a purpose."

Amaka looked at her friend as if she had a screw loose.

"Femi's lapses are the very incentives that push you to try harder and as you hustle, you are fulfilling potential, and Femi never even stops you from all your hustle."

"Ah. He knows I have to make money. How do I pay my bills, *our* bills otherwise?"

"Amaka, can I be truthful with you?"

"Mmhmm."

"Amaka, some other guys won't be able to meet those obligations and still won't let you handle matters, so you will both lack or he would let you pay and then beat you up on top of all you do."

Amaka couldn't argue with that. She knew some examples of such marriages.

"Besides, work is not just about money. You are working to make an impact, develop your potential and enlarge your circle of influence. When Mama C needed approval from the ministry of education for her school, who assisted?"

"The minister of education himself, Peter Abam," Amaka answered.

"Didn't you meet him when you were consulting for his ministry?"

Amaka nodded silently. Where was Mo going with this?

"Throughout the project, did Femi stop you from going for even one meeting?"

Amaka shook her head. "No o."

"Peter Abam is a powerful and good-looking man, Amaka. Not many men will let their wives work with him closely like you did."

"Hmm."

"But Femi didn't stop you. So do you see my point? See your influence and impact expanding with Femi's silent support?"

"Hmm."

"So do you want to be the woman whose husband does everything for her or Femi's independent wife?"

"Can I be both?" Amaka said.

"We all want to be both o." Rola laughed. "We want to work *when* we want to, because we *want* to. We don't want to feel we *have* to work or else the job becomes a terrible burden and we resent it. So we want a guy who allows us *to* choose if, when and how we want to work."

"Those men are not many. But *you* got one of those few men, Mo," Amaka said wistfully. She was still pensive. "I see your point about Femi. I married someone who doesn't seem to really care about becoming irrelevant in my life once I don't depend on him, and so he allows me to be totally independent. His attitude has now given me the freedom to grow. If I had to choose between being arm candy with everything done for me and the path I am on today, I will still choose Femi, but it has its challenges. It's really stressful not having the support I need." Amaka sighed.

Purpose and impact was what mattered at the end of the day, but Amaka felt she was paying too huge a price for this growth because with Femi's increasing irrelevance was an increasing loss of respect for him. Femi thought he was smart; he was saving his money and was getting too comfortable with her doing the things he could be doing. And he was fast becoming immaterial to her existence.

"If Peter Abam or another client calls me now, the chances are that I will jump to action," Amaka thought. "But Femi? I will get round to doing what he wants when I can."

With this loss of respect for Femi came a loss of attraction. She had tried on her own and prayed to stem the tide, but she seemed helpless to stop it. Femi had his money safely in his pocket but was just not attractive to her anymore.

Chapter Twenty-Nine

"Let him kiss me with the kisses of his mouth:
for thy love is better than wine."
Song of Solomon 1:2

Kaniz was getting home tired and late since the National Transition Council was now formally constituted and he had taken his new role as chief of staff. Rola was glad she was equally busy, so she just didn't sit around missing him. She looked at him with compassion as he came in at 10.45 p.m.

"Amir, you are worn out. See, you have two strands of gray hair on your temple that weren't there before. Do you want to lie down for a moment and let me massage your back?"

Kaniz wished he could tell her what she could do that was infinitely better than any back massage, but he had promised her and he was keeping his promise. But if she gave him a back massage...

"No, thanks." He shook his head. "Let me just take a shower and I will be better. I still have work to see to tonight."

"But you haven't even eaten."

"I ate, my dear, I did. At 5 p.m., after the economic council meeting ended."

"You started economic council at 8 a.m. and ended at 5 p.m.? Nothing productive would have happened after 1 p.m."

Kaniz paused as he was taking off his shoes and socks by the bedside and thought about it.

"You are right, you know. Prof began to ramble a bit at about 1.10 p.m. Hmm, sharp! You should join us on the NTC actually."

"I am already on the NTC, Kaniz. You discuss with me and you listen to me." She smiled. It was a fact.

"Let me help you with that. Sit, Amir. Just relax."

She helped him take his shoes off and his socks, noting to herself that as always, his socks were fresh. She placed each foot in her soft hands and rubbed his feet.

"You sat too long and now your feet are swollen." It was a loving admonition. With great effort, he dragged his eyes away from her bent head and her raven black hair. Then, as if he couldn't help it, his eyes strayed back to her head and he ran his fingers through her hair. Her hair felt clean and silky.

"I like the fact that I can run my fingers through your hair," he said dreamily. "Please don't put any of that stuff in your hair just yet. Please?"

"That stuff? A weave?" She laughed. "I am running a bath for you." She got up and went into the bathroom.

"Thank you," he called after her, sincerely grateful for the care.

"No, my love, leave the lights on please."

Morola was about to switch the lights off. She had persuaded Kaniz to take a short nap and then get some work done later.

"You are fatigued, Amir. You would rest better with the lights off."

"No!"

The retort was sharp and very unlike Kaniz. Something told her Synergy New York and the work she had planned tonight would have to wait. Because of the time difference, she was getting almost two full job schedules squeezed in daily. Synergy Lagos was fully up and running now. She turned back into the room and slid into bed with him.

"No secrets, Kaniz."

"No secrets, my love." He sighed.

"You don't like dark rooms?"

He never switched off his bedside lamp, always asking her to leave it on. Rekiya had alluded to issues with the dark in the hospital and from the first night of their honeymoon, though she personally preferred to sleep in the dark, she had adapted to his preference to sleep with a light on.

Kaniz sighed again. Would she think he was weak? Would she still respect him? Her admiration meant so much to him, inspired him more than he could articulate.

"No secrets." He had promised. He had to trust her now.

He gently took her left hand and placed it on his torso, and she felt the mass of gnarled and angry flesh that was the scar tissue on his right side. She had seen it before, but she hadn't asked questions.

"The dark." He shuddered. "I hate the dark."

He told her about Joe, the wooden box and the grave. As he spoke, Rola watched his face. It was if he was reliving the horror, especially when he spoke about the dark and the heat in the box. She wanted to stop him at some point, tell him it was enough, but he seemed determined that there would really be no secrets between them.

"Joe's face as the light from the IED blast illuminated it," Kaniz's voice seemed to come from far away. "There was no fear, Morola. It was just peaceful, calm resolve." His palms were rubbing his face. Had he being trying to wipe the image off his mind all these years?

"All that was left of my friend were twisted name tags and bits of flesh. A hand here, his foot still in the boot in a corner of the room." His eyes went dark at the memory. "I was evacuated. I was in hospital when the funeral was conducted, Morola. Yet another closed, empty coffin." His voice broke. "Just like my mother, another closed coffin." His voice trailed away as if he had journeyed far away even though his body was there with her.

She tried hard not to cry, but her eyes were wet. He tenderly kissed away her tears and took her hand.

"It seemed like everyone who loved me left me, Sarauniya, but it's alright now. I have you now, Morola, and you vowed that you wouldn't leave me," he said gently. But she noticed that his grip tightened subconsciously.

She now understood what trauma he had been going through when those bandages had been on his eyes and why he had grabbed her wrist in vice when she startled him awake and why he asked for her vow not to leave him. He was traumatised by vivid memories. She didn't want to say PTSD. She was aware of all the connotations and since he didn't say that was what it was, she wouldn't.

After the abduction by Musa Bandir, he saw himself as a dead man walking – a man who had been to the grave and back, therefore the life he had now was not his; it was on loan for a purpose. It was not the length of the life but the fulfillment of purpose that counted, so he followed his Commander implicitly. She now understood why he seemed to love her with such abandon, such boldness, such devotion. To him, life was ephemeral and fleeting, so while he was alive, he was going to love this one woman who had been given to him with everything within him. So he lived each day like it was his last: with purpose, with intention, with intensity, without procrastination. Those who had not been through what he had been through were under the illusion that they had control over their lives, but he was too certain now that life was a candle in the wind, and what mattered solely to him was the opinion of The One to whom the winds were obedient. Kaniz made each day count.

She looked at his face as he slept. Kaniz had suffered so terribly that even when asleep, even now when he should be resting, he had a slight frown. Why had Funso and the others added extra burdens to his baggage? Why had someone else not been made chief of staff? By now he should have been focused on his own business but instead, he was saddled with this thankless job. Her heart broke for his pain. What could she do to help? How could she reach his pain and heal it? How could she make things easier for him? As she thought of the suffering her husband had endured, her tears started welling up again.

She wrapped her arms around him and placed her head on his chest. She had found out during their honeymoon that he fell asleep faster when her head was on his chest and if she moved before he was fully asleep, he would moan and mumble half asleep, "Morola." And she knew that meant, "Please come back and lay your head here."

For someone so strong to be so vulnerable was always a paradoxical wonder to her and she had to admit, the combination of strength and vulnerability was an irresistible attraction to a strong woman as herself. It had crept upon her quietly and seeped into her heart silently, but she now caught her breath as the force of the love she felt for Kaniz hit her.

Kaniz got out of their bed gently so as not to wake his wife up. She looked so beautiful as she slept. Today was just not one of those days when he had the willpower to resist her touch. The back massage would have rapidly escalated to a frustrating end for him. By the time he was done with a full day at the HQ, decoding the endless agendas and politics around him and his new assignment, by the time he watched out for the dangers and the dangerous, all he wanted to do was come home and relax in Morola's arms; completely relax in a safe place.

If only. He sighed as he looked at her alluring form on their bed. When she was ready, *she* would ask him. But she had to understand that when he made love to her, he was loving her, communicating a dimension of his love to her and not merely using her for his own pleasure. He sighed again. He still respected her stance as opposed to those who succumbed while seeing their role as providing such "services" to their lover or husband in return for "favours". She was not reducing the physical expression of their love to a mere transaction. Until she saw it as a mutual expression of love, it would be a farce for him too. When they consummated their love, he didn't want it to be a charade.

"Help me, please. *You* speak to her please and show her the truth."

It dawned on him that that was the first time he had asked for divine intervention on the issue. Strange. He prayed about everything, or so he thought. He pulled the black silk kimono Morola had given him after their honeymoon over his lounge pants, put on his bedroom slippers and went to the adjoining study.

Rola woke up, and Kaniz was gone. Her first reaction was exasperation. Did he want to kill himself with exhaustion? No matter how well he did and how hard he worked, there would still be work left to be done. If he collapsed from exhaustion would she not be the one to suffer? Everyone else would continue their lives after one minute of silence. She would be the only one left with incalculable loss.

"You can help him with this stress."

What could she do? She would certainly make sure she got it done right away. Whatever medication it was, she would get the HQ physician to get it immediately.

"What does wine do?"

"Wine relaxes and de-stresses and just makes you feel happy," she said to herself. Kaniz didn't drink though. He liked being in full control of his faculties.

"Better is your love than wine…"

"Yes, such a beautiful verse," Rola thought.

"What does it mean?"

"Love intoxicates like wine, I guess."

"Could love be more relaxing than wine?"

"I don't see how love would practically, physically de-stress Kaniz. How?"

"How?"

Oh! She had been so dense. So there was a way she could have added value to Kaniz's life all along. There was actually more she had to offer to the man who loved her so much. She knew what she had to do.

She got off their bed and went to the bathroom.

Rola was almost by his side in her bare feet before Kaniz noticed her. "Must you work right now?" She pouted.

"Yes, love, not unless you have something more interesting to keep me busy." He smiled wryly.

She kissed the nape of his neck. "I have some ideas. . ."

"Not tonight, my love. Please, don't."

"Am I bothering you?"

The fragrance of her sweet breath and the perfume she had on mingled to toy with his mind. She was always so clean, so fresh. He turned his head to look at her. She was wearing a sheer white negligee and her figure underneath was really disturbing his focus.

"Bothering me?" He smiled ruefully. "You can never be a bother. I am just not..." He sighed. "Tonight, I just may not find it that easy to stop if I come too close to you, my love. Pardon me." He looked away from his bride in the "illegal" negligee and back to the pile of files on his desk.

She sat on the carpeted floor by his side, placed her head gently in his lap and looked up at him.

"Who said anything about stopping?" she said softly.

"What did you say?"

"Did I say I wanted you to stop?" she whispered.

"Are you saying what I think you are saying?"

"Make love to your wife, my Amir," she said. She was looking up at him, and there was a longing in her eyes he had never seen before. He needed no further invitation.

He groaned as he bent his head to hers. "I thought you would never ask."

He kissed her tentatively at first, still unable to fully believe that she meant what she said, but the way she melted in his arms told him something was different about this time.

He lifted her clear off her feet, walked the few steps through the connecting door to their bedroom and dropped her gently on their bed. His voice was husky, and his eyes were smouldering. He lay beside her, supported by his elbows as his sweet breath caressed her face.

"You are so so beautiful," he muttered as he looked into her eyes. "Am I dreaming? Are you really mine?"

"I am yours, my Amir and you are my dream come true," she breathed.

She heard his low moan as he bent his head to kiss her with unfettered passion. Suddenly he paused, his lips were still on hers. "My love, this is when you stop me if you want me to… If you want me to stop. I can't... I just can't..." He was shaking his head.

She reached up and kissed him with deep yearning as she put her finger to his lips. "Shush! My Amir."

Her head was on his chest and she felt a faint perspiration against her cheek. She raised her head and saw a dewy perspiration also on his brow.

"But the air conditioner is on, Amir. Are you alright? You don't have a fever, do you?" She kissed his brow. His forehead was cool. He wasn't warm. His face glowed with a smile of satiation. Rola hadn't seen this look on her husband's face before.

"Don't you perspire when you run long distances or when you have walked for miles?"

She nodded and he smiled. His innocent wife knew so much about so many things but this.

"Well, you have just taken me all the way to heaven and back. Shouldn't I perspire a little bit?" he said, still smiling. She was too shy to meet his gaze, so she buried her face in his chest.

He was incredulous. "Even now you are shy, my love? Even now when we are one in *every* way?" He leaned on his elbow and looked into her eyes as she lay by his side gazing up at him. He shook his head and sighed.

"What is wrong?" she said aloud, concerned even as she thought to herself, "I am a novice. If I didn't please him, will he tell me? What should I have done differently?"

"You are just so beautiful," he groaned, bending his head to brush her lips with his again. "Don't ever leave me, Morola," he whispered.

It was dawn. Rola looked at Kaniz still sleeping. His face was truly peaceful now, relaxed. He no longer had that fleeting frown.

"Love is truly better than wine. Who would have thought it?"

As she moved, her eyes caught something on the cream bed linen. She had read about it. She thought she should get up quickly to clean the sheets as she couldn't leave that there. As she moved, Kaniz stirred and drew her back, closer to him.

"Amir," she whispered into his ears and told him what she wanted to do. She was too shy to speak the words out loud. He looked down and saw the object of her attention which she hurriedly covered with her left hand. He covered her hand with his own hand and took her right hand in his. He spoke gently. "Thank you for doing things God's way."

She hid her face in a pillow, and he gently lifted the pillow from her eyes.

"We are in a covenant, my love. I didn't know then what I know now. Forgive me. If I had known and kept myself then it would have been just the way it was designed to be. I may have failed in the past, years before I met you but no more. The Lord do this to me and more if I defile what He has called holy and if anything but death separates us. Aww, don't cry, my love," he said as he kissed the tears springing up unbidden to her eyes.

"If anything but death separates us," he had said. This was another reason why he was determined to love her so audaciously and without restraint; it was already apparent to him that his new job had put him in the cross hairs of extremely dangerous and powerful people. The security reports were not for the faint-hearted. He was hopeful but God forbid, if anything happened to him, he was determined to squeeze a lifetime of love into the time he had with her. Morola would never forget him. He was resolute. No man had ever been with her the way he had and in this time he had with her, he would ensure that no man who came after him would ever be able to replace him in her heart.

He kissed away her tears and looked into her eyes. "I can't believe you are truly mine," he whispered and drew her closer still. He gently rolled her on top of him with an elfin grin. "I don't think I am rushing to HQ this morning. If we are changing these sheets, let's put them to good use first and do our bit for the environment, hmm? What do you think?" There was a mischievous twinkle in his eyes.

"I think, that without controversy, you a true environmental activist." They both laughed.

The expression in his eyes changed as his eyes took on that smouldering look. "Tell me, my Sarauniya. Whose arms are around you? Who is loving you *now*?" His voice was husky.

"My Amir, my husband, my lover," she said softly, too shy to look at him, her emotions overwhelmed by the new experience.

He let out a low groan as his lips touched hers once more. Kaniz had stopped trying to make sense of his feelings for his wife. He was just going to enjoy her. It felt like he had waited a lifetime to be with her like this. Had they only been married for just over a month?

"Amir, we need to talk."

Kaniz's heart stopped. If only she knew how he hated to hear that phrase. In his mind it meant "You are in trouble." If a lady told her girlfriend, "We need to talk," they would both be bursting with excitement waiting for the talk. Not most men though. The phrase always filled them with trepidation.

"Sarauniya, I have said when you have something to say just say it. Don't say 'We need to talk'."

"Oh, sorry." She chuckled. "It's not even such a big deal. I have been thinking, Kaniz. There's a purpose to everything under the sun. With you in the NTC as chief of staff, I really want to do something about a matter that has worried me since I was a teenager."

His look said, "What is it?"

She continued, "It's this passion I have always had for incarcerated women."

Kaniz didn't want to hurt Rola, but General Adewale and the NTC had already decided there was no First Lady or anything similar in this dispensation; they weren't elected officials and the whole time frame for the transition to elections was six months.

"What is it, my love? I thought I told you we had all agreed there's no pet project shenanigans now?" He was uncomfortable.

"Who said anything about being a 'wife of this or that', Amir? If you weren't in this position right now, it was something I was going to do. It was just complicated with my being in New York and all. I want to do what I can now that we have the ears of the people that matter, and we have the influence to make an impact."

"Morola, you know what people will begin to think if you have a pet project."

"Ademi." She lay her head on his shoulder. They were both in his study on the large teal armchair by the window overlooking the garden. When he was in that chair, it seemed like they both ended up in it together. She was half seated, half draped across him like a comfortable human blanket, and he really didn't want this peaceful moment disturbed by some difficult argument.

"Amir, I am not looking for publicity. I am looking for impact. I don't need the press to follow me around. I just need to make a difference. A life without impact is a wasted life, Kaniz."

He sighed. This was what he deeply believed in. It wasn't the length of the life but the impact of the life that mattered. He couldn't very well tell her not to do what he believed in.

"Your young life has had tremendous impact. Synergy is helping thousands."

She wasn't buying that line at all from the look on her face.

"I can't complain about what I allow, Kaniz. Once I don't do my bit about this matter, I lose the right to complain about it."

"So what exactly do you want to do?"

"First, for the women in prison incarcerated with their children, I want to push for a policy that would mandate that the children be taken into foster care. Even if some mothers may be guilty, the children didn't commit any offence. Also, those who can't afford legal services, especially those awaiting trial, I know I can arrange pro bono services for them with the platform I have now. The prisoners are being treated really badly, and it's beyond appalling. When I visited the prisons for the first time twelve years ago, the soap that was meant for the prisoners was being sold. The prisoners were riddled with scabies! The prison authorities were colluding with contractors to make money off the prisoners' food and starving the prisoners. That's why the recidivism is so bad. That's why the society has so many criminals. The prisons are actually breeding criminals, Kaniz! It's unfair to lock someone up and then starve them and abuse them this badly."

From her tone, Kaniz saw she was really passionate about this cause. He looked at her with a curious smile. "When did this prisons virus catch you so badly?"

"Amir! I had told you I visited the prisons with Mrs B as a sixteen-year-old, and the horrors I saw have never left me." She poked him in the chest. "Have you forgotten?"

Kaniz remembered. It was from their very first conversation on the way to the youth service camp, and she had said, "I once heard on Voice of Change, 'It is better to light a candle than to curse the darkness.' It struck me then that I must do something about it soon, Group Captain Ishaya, or else I can't continue to complain." At that time, she had no idea how to proceed because of the unpredictability of her plans, but now she was in the country for sure, and she was wasting no time in taking action. That day had been emotionally loaded for him. It was no wonder he forgot a detail such as that. He smiled as he reminisced.

"Kaniz, why do you think we met at this time and got married just before the crisis? Let me do something meaningful with this platform."

Chapter Thirty

"He brought me to the banqueting house,
and his banner over me was love."
Song of Solomon 2:4

Kaniz had been uneasy at dinner. Dessert was done. He had ordered coffee and she had ordered peppermint tea. They tried to go out when they could manage it though it was tough making the time. Kaniz always declined any suggestion that they take any part of the service gratis. He just refused to exploit the position he had as chief of staff especially now that the lore of the Quartet was becoming public knowledge and the facts on *Operation Shield* were seeping out gradually. He was fast becoming a folk hero. Add to this the fact that Kaniz deliberately maintained a low profile: no blaring sirens and a simple escort of a pilot car and another behind. They had declined to move from their own private residence on Toju Teniola Close, and they used their own private cars.

This was such a great contrast to what people were familiar with in their leaders that the compliments on Kaniz and Rola were all over social media. The morning shows, the late night shows were all agog. "This Is the Type of Leader We Need", the headlines were blasting. But Rola and Kaniz weren't fooled. The people were fickle. They couldn't be the determinant of a leader's actions. The same people who sang Kaniz's praises today could very easily turn on him the next day.

Morola could tell something was up. She looked around and his aide-de-camp, Abubakar Saleh, was well out of earshot.

"Amir, you are quiet."

"Hmm."

"Hmm?" She gave him a quizzical look. Why did men find it so difficult to start talking?

"You look worried."

"Really?"

"Ademi, talk to me."

"Something is up, Sarauniya. I can't shake the feeling."

"We will pray when we get home then," she said.

"What about right now?" Kaniz said. "What stops us from praying right now?" He bowed his head immediately. "Pray, let's pray together." He reached for her hands across the table.

They drove home in silence with Abubakar by the side of the driver, Bamidele, in front. Since they both still drove their private cars, they had chosen to drive in Kaniz's Audi Q7. Raliat was Rola's minder from the air force. She was on her first security posting. Bright, loyal, grateful for the opportunity and super eager to please. She was in the car behind them with the rest of the security detail of three other male personnel. A pilot car with four personnel in it went ahead.

"My love, do you resent me for getting you into all this stress?" He looked around with a gesture that took in the escort cars in front, at the back and Abubakar seated in front; always there with them, his presence making their candid discussions in the car a thing of the past. "This wasn't what you signed up for," he said.

She sighed. "I committed to you and if this is your path," she shrugged, "I will pay the price with you."

"It could become more dangerous. Funso is in charge of security as you know, and the intel we are receiving..." he shook his head. "I don't want to bother you."

She pointed at Abubakar surreptitiously. She didn't trust Abubakar that much, and she couldn't put her finger on why not. "At the lab," she said, smiling. She had taken to calling their bedroom "the lab" because of the chemistry between them and all the experiments going on in there these days.

He smiled, becoming slightly more relaxed. The thought of the "experiments" cheered him a bit. "When we get into the lab then, Great Alchemist." He kissed her forehead.

He held on to her right hand and placed their intertwined hands on the car's armrest as they drove the twenty minutes from Grant Gourmet to their home.

They arrived home, and Bamidele drove the Audi right under the porte cochere. Bamidele jumped down immediately he put the car in park with the engine still running. He opened Rola's passenger door while Abubakar got Kaniz's door. Rola smiled. It seemed to be becoming an undeclared contest between Bamidele and Abubakar these days; who could get their own liege's door open first. Abubakar and Bamidele then walked them the short distance of about four metres to the door as was their custom.

Bamidele, bringing up the rear, would usually turn back once the front door was opened by the night security detail and return to the car to switch off its engine and park it properly, then he would stay at the ready in case he was needed. Tonight, the night security detail was Squadron Leader Tamuno. He gave Kaniz a sharp salute, and Rola could not miss the respect for Kaniz in his eyes and his pride at this assignment. As Tamuno welcomed them in at the front door, Rola could see Kaniz take his pistol out of its holster right at the doorstep. That was unlike Kaniz. He still probably felt the unease he had mentioned at dinner earlier. She was sure it was nothing though. Perhaps the pressure of his position? She had heard of some threats, but Kaniz didn't discuss them with her so they surely couldn't be that serious, could they?

Chief of staff apparently was a high-pressure role – so much work mostly outside the job description and yet without the recognition. They stepped in with Rola going in first as usual, and Kaniz right behind her with his Glock in his hand. Rola and Kaniz were both coming from their offices, so Abubakar came in behind Rola, bringing with him the usual burden of memos and papers for Kaniz.

Abubakar handed over the stack of memos and files to Tamuno who proceeded upstairs to the converted study with the papers. Tamuno was designated to go upstairs first by security protocol because it was his duty to have conducted a security sweep and ensured the first floor was secure before Kaniz and Rola went up. The front door was left slightly ajar, waiting for Raliat who was disembarking as swiftly as she could from the car behind. Raliat was not going to be outdone in her service by the men. In spite of Rola's protests, she would look for something to carry for Rola too and if she could not find anything to carry, she would simply also escort the Ishayas and their entourage into the anteroom and then hand over to the night security detail on duty, giving him any brief she had.

Rola held on to her handbag no matter how Raliat insisted it was part of her job to carry Rola's handbag.

"Raliat, you carry a gun, don't you?" she had once said.

"Yes, madam."

"The gun is for my protection?"

"Yes, madam."

"If you carry a handbag, how can you reach for the gun on time if we are under attack? Handle your gun well and leave my handbag to me," she said with her winning smile. Raliat just loved her.

Rola could not forget how disgusted she had been when she accompanied her mother to the High Court years ago and had seen so many female judges with their handbags being carried by police orderlies. It was a truly ridiculous sight. Every time she saw a woman who could not carry her own handbag, she sincerely wondered, who forced her to carry a handbag at all when someone else was going to end up holding it? Whose outfit was the lady's handbag to coordinate with? Her own or her designated mule's?

They didn't linger in the anteroom tonight. The anteroom was a clean minimalist space with high ceilings. Between the front door and the high teak doors of the powder room behind them were the two tawny high-winged visitors chairs with a clear glass table in-between. On the glass table sat a tall crystal vase with a bouquet of cream roses, and a beige deep pile rug lay directly under the crystal chandelier in the centre of the room.

Three paintings hung on the walls. One between the two chairs behind them, the second on the wall on the right, next to the door to the study, and the third on the wall opposite. The fourth wall had two openings. One was the rectangular archway that led from the stairway to the first floor and the other was the soaring double glass door which led to the main living room.

Kaniz was uneasy. Tamuno was on the first floor dropping the memos in his study, and Rola was safe with Abubakar in the anteroom. He still couldn't shake the feeling that something was off. Kaniz moved into the main living room through the high double-glass doors still holding his pistol.

He thought he heard a banged door and a muffled scream and turned his head backwards towards the sound with his Glock at the ready.

The sound was from the anteroom. He glanced back into the anteroom to see Morola being held by Abubakar with a gun to her head. Abubakar had her two arms pinned behind her back in a vice-like grip, and his right hand held his service pistol to Morola's right temple. Though Abubakar had his Kevlar vest on his torso and was well protected, he held Morola right in front of him, using her body as a shield. Only his head and his right shoulder holding the gun were exposed.

"Abubakar?" Kaniz took in the scene before him.

"Drop your pistol, Group Captain Ishaya," Abubakar said ominously as Kaniz turned into the anteroom, his pistol aimed. "Or I will blast her head off."

Rola felt his saliva hit her face as he spat the words out.

Abubakar meant to blast both Kaniz and Rola's heads off actually but right now, he had only one chance for a shot. If he shot Mrs Ishaya in the head first, he was sure he would be dead by Group Captain Ishaya's hand in a second, and Mrs Ishaya was not his mission. Group Captain Ishaya was his target but tonight, for some strange reason, Ishaya had deviated from his usual pattern and had drawn his pistol from its holster before they even stepped into the house then wandered off into the living room as soon as Tamuno proceeded upstairs, giving Abubakar no time to carry out his plan. The plan was to shoot Kaniz as soon as Tamuno went up so Tamuno couldn't counteract his surprise attack on Group Captain Ishaya. But Kaniz himself had gone into the living room as Tamuno was going up. Now, Tamuno would be back in less than three minutes. Abubakar had to act fast. He was just improvising now, winging it.

"Drop your gun, slowly," he said as Kaniz's aim at his head stayed steady. Kaniz was carrying a reliable Glock with an internal laser guide rod system, one of those they had imported. Its green laser sight was clearly on Abubakar's forehead though the target was oblivious to it. Kaniz began to lower the gun as if to drop it on the ground but as the laser sight landed on Abubakar's right shoulder, he shot.

Abubakar saw the sight on him a split second too late. His scapula was shattered by Kaniz's shot in the very same instant he saw the laser. Raliat, who had lost thirty seconds to the heavy security front door Abubakar had kicked shut, was opening the door in that same instant and coming up behind Rola and Abubakar.

At the very nanosecond the shot rang out, Rola ducked to the left and dropped to the floor while at the same time pushing Abubakar away with her body weight to her right. Abubakar and Rola sprawled in opposite directions, and Kaniz was on top of Abubakar in a flash, kicking Abubakar's army-issue pistol aside with his right foot. Raliat rushed to her madam and helped her up. Blood splatter from Abubakar's shoulder was all over Rola's face and hair.

Instinctively, the woman in Raliat swiftly wiped the blood off Rola's face with her hand first, merely smearing her face further with her assailant's blood. She turned and trained her pistol back on Abubakar's prone form lying on the anteroom floor. Tamuno heard the retort of the Glock and began to dash down the stairs. He had been gone less than three minutes. Group Captain Ishaya was standing over Abubakar's prostate figure.

"Who sent you?" Kaniz asked calmly.

Abubakar stared back at him and kept mute.

Without a second's hesitation, Kaniz shot him in the right leg and Rola gasped. The sound of the pistol was horrifying. The sickening sound as the metal passed through the flesh and hit his tibia was nauseating. Blood spurted and splattered on the pants of Kaniz's uniform.

"Who sent you?" he asked again.

Abubakar screamed in anguish and doubled over in agony as dark blood from his shoulder and right leg oozed in a crimson pool on to the floor and began to flow towards the rug.

"Stop!" Rola screamed, her eyes pleading with her husband as she saw the alien look in his eyes.

"He touched you, Morola." Kaniz's voice was calm but smouldering with unfathomable outrage. His eyes never left Abubakar. Tamuno was right by his side, watching and wondering who on the security detail to trust. Should he train his gun on Raliat too? What was going on? Oga's ADC attacked? Who could he trust now?

"He touched you," Kaniz said. "Who sent you, Abubakar?"

His pistol went off again as the bullet went through Abubakar's left foot. More blood, more splatter landing on Kaniz.

An ear-piercing scream of agony from Abubakar and then, "Kill me."

Kaniz understood immediately what was going on. "That's exactly what I will not do. You *will* talk."

The rest of the security detail was now in the anteroom. There were seven of them including Bamidele, who had rushed out of the car. Some had stepped into the pool of blood, but no one cared as their focus was on securing the chief of staff.

"Arrest him," Kaniz said to Tamuno, who rushed to do his bidding assisted by Bamidele. Kaniz took out his phone and started dialling Funso. Funso was in charge of security, and they had just had a massive breach.

"Squadron Leader Oladele," he spoke to Raliat, "take Mrs Ishaya to the living room upstairs."

As she was being led away, Rola looked at Kaniz. He was so calm. He had shot a man three times and had only spared his life because he needed to have him interrogated, yet at no time had he even raised his voice. What type of man had she married? What else was he capable of?

Chapter Thirty-One

"I am my beloved's, and his desire is towards me."

Song of Solomon 7:10

Rola had taken a shower and when she saw Abubakar's blood run from her hair and face in scarlet streams onto the shower floor, colouring the white mosaic floor red, she had to stop the gag reflex as her dinner threatened to come back up. The metallic smell of blood clung to her. Abubakar's blood was in her hair, smeared on her face, her neck, streaming down her body.

Revulsion filled her very being. Her assailant, someone who hated her enough to want to kill her, had marked her with his blood. She kept washing and washing, but it was like the blood wouldn't come off. Rola hated blood. Her only consolation was that Kaniz didn't kill Abubakar, but would it have been such a bad thing if he had? After all, he wanted to kill Kaniz and herself. Apart from the fact that Kaniz needed to keep him alive to garner intelligence, should Abubakar have been allowed to live? She was so conflicted. Nothing had tested her faith and ethics so much as this journey with Kaniz and his role as a leader. She could no longer be legalistic in her faith. Her faith had to be relevant and commensurate to the daily challenges they now faced.

Funso had arrived at their house within ten minutes of Kaniz's phone call. He lived just four minutes away. The Quartet all intentionally lived within five minutes of the Ishayas. The night security shift had been changed immediately and fresh officers brought from HQ. Only Raliat remained of the night's original security detail. Everyone else had been taken in for questioning and checks. Funso asked to see Rola, but Kaniz thought it was better she should be allowed to rest. Kaniz was done with Funso downstairs and proceeded upstairs immediately. Raliat was stationed outside Rola's door, standing outside in the family living room. She saluted Group Captain Ishaya as soon as she saw him come up.

"At ease," Kaniz said. "Proceed to HQ for debriefing and hand over to your relief downstairs." Then in a softer tone he asked, "How is my wife? Is she okay?"

"She is resting in the bedroom, sir."

Raliat could not miss the devotion in his eyes as he mentioned Rola. The way Group Captain Ishaya looked at his wife when his wife wasn't looking, when he let down his guard completely, it was like rivers of molten tenderness. Perhaps his wife hadn't even caught that particular look yet because he seemed to "package" himself a bit more when he was aware he was being observed.

The fact that Raliat was on duty and should be focused on observing security issues didn't blind her to the constant emotional exchange, the obvious devotion. Ordinarily, a look like that from any man would melt any woman but coming from the handsome Group Captain Ishaya...

Raliat sighed, some women were just blessed. Someday perhaps, someone would love her like this too. Raliat was devoted to Rola. Rola was fair, sensitive to her needs and so kind. However, her commitment to Rola had another dimension to it: the fact that someone like Group Captain Ishaya who Raliat admired, that so many millions admired, in turn obviously adored Mrs Ishaya to such a degree made Raliat more determined than ever to protect Mrs Ishaya, with her life if need be. If this was the only thing Group Captain Ishaya who sacrificed so much required of her, she vowed in her heart to do it. If anything happened to Mrs Ishaya, if he lost her on Raliat's watch, she knew she couldn't live with herself. She had been too late to help today, but she vowed to herself it would never happen again.

Rola was groomed and seated in bed, her back to the padded headboard as she watched Kaniz come in and couldn't fathom the look on his face. He walked briskly to her on the bed and threw his cap on the ottoman at the foot of the bed. Sinking to his knees by her bedside, he didn't say a word, he just held her for what seemed like forever. Then eventually, he sighed.

"I smell of blood and gunpowder," he said and rose up. He quietly moved around the room, taking off his watch, his shoes, his uniform which he threw in the laundry, not saying a word. Then he showered. She didn't know what to think. She felt after such a traumatic incident he should say more, talk it through. The way she saw it, men didn't seem to talk things through much. He slid beside her in bed, and only then did he speak again. He was looking at her, his hands framing her face.

"He had a gun to your head." His expression was a mixture of incredulity and rage. His voice was trembling, and his hands on her face were trembling. "I wanted to kill him. I wished I could just kill him."

He was trembling with repressed anger. Breathing hard.

"Morola, what would I do if anything happened to you?" His eyes were boring into her soul. His brow was furrowed with deep concern. "I promised to protect you..." his voice trailed away. "I am done with this, Morola. I am done. I have told Funso that the council gets my resignation in the morning. They can get a new chief of staff and run their country on their own. We don't know who to trust anymore."

As he confronted that thought, he moved even closer and embraced her, whispering softly, "Hold me, my love. Just hold me."

He buried his face in her chest. Her arms went around him spontaneously, and she held on to him. She held him close and then closer still with tenacity in her embrace, cradling his head to her cheek not just because he asked to be held but because in these debilitatingly uncertain circumstances, they needed each other's comfort. What would she have done if Abubakar had killed Kaniz tonight? Kaniz was actually the one his ADC had been after, and yet Funso, his most intimate friend, had appointed Abubakar his ADC. Who could they trust?

What was on her Kaniz's mind? What was he thinking? He was silent; he wasn't speaking. His hair was still slightly damp from the shower, but he smelt so good now that the sulphuric smell of the gunpowder was gone.

She lifted his head and kissed his furrowed brow. "What would I have done if anything had happened to you, my Amir? What would have happened if he had snuffed out the light of my eyes?" She kissed his eyes. "Your eyes are wet," she whispered.

He needed her comforting arms more than he had the words to express adequately tonight, but it wasn't a matter he could even broach for fear of being misunderstood. Morola was just getting to understand his needs and she wouldn't know that he needed reassurance. He needed *her* comforting reassurance that he had taken good care of her. He needed to know that she approved of how he had handled the crisis. Deep within his soul, he needed to be convinced that he hadn't lost her respect. He wanted her to demonstrate to him that she still admired him. He wanted her to show him he was still in charge and that he had proven it. He needed her to prove to him that she still trusted him to keep her safe and secure. He had almost lost her tonight and he wanted to feel assured,

that the notion of losing her was an unfounded fear,

that she was going nowhere,

that she was here with him for his lifetime.

Words, the spoken word, may convey the message adequately to Morola, but mere words wouldn't adequately and effectively communicate the message to his soul tonight. Only possessing her completely would convey to his inner being what he needed to know deep within him at a time like this. But if he approached her tonight, in her state of mind, the danger was that she would think, "On a night when we were almost killed, this is all you can think of? Don't you ever have anything else on your mind?"

His needs were not as important as losing Morola's carefully earned trust and respect. He needed her tonight more than ever, but he couldn't risk a rebuff. The rejection would hurt deeper. So he tried to distract himself, lowering his head again. His eyes caught the rose gold and diamond heart pendant he had given her the night of his first proposal.

"You wore it tonight," he smiled.

She smiled back at him, her eyes warm with love.

His lips brushed the pendant resting in her bosom.

"I wore it especially tonight because you are a man of your word. You keep your promises, Kaniz. You promised to love me, and you do love me. Even when you should be mad at me, you take the higher path. You decide to treat me like your baby sister, and you take the decision to be the mature one. You promised to cherish me and you actually pamper me. You make me feel so loved. And tonight, you showed me you *can* protect me. First you picked the danger up in your spirit and then physically, you acted to save me from the danger. I honour you, Ademi. I truly respect you."

She tilted his face up once more and said, "Thank you, Amir." Tenderly with both of her soft hands on his face, she kissed him with such gratitude and longing that he was left in no doubt as to what she expected his response to be. As he felt everything within him respond to her touch, he wondered how she knew.

She was shaken and wanted, perhaps, to be cuddled in his arms, while he spoke his reassurance to her. That was all *she* needed, but she put her own needs aside for now and decided to focus on him and carry him with her love past this crisis. Why was she so sensitive, so responsive to his needs? What had he done to deserve such a gift?

"My heartbeat. I will protect you with my life," he whispered, covering her face with kisses. There was an aura of dominion in his passionate touch tonight.

"My Amir," she breathed and at her whisper in his ear, he was like one intoxicated.

"My Amir." My king, my warrior-husband.

At that moment, Kaniz felt a surge of reassurance, a tsunami of boldness. He felt that he could take on the entire world. His wife admired him, he was a king in his beloved's eyes, he was a conqueror in her eyes, she respected him. At this instant, it mattered only what Morola felt. Those who hated him, betrayed him and wanted him dead ceased to matter. Those who sent the assassin faded from his consciousness. Those who criticised him relentlessly were inconsequential. In this moment, they were in their own cocoon, safe from the hostile world. He possessed his Morola completely. No other man could compete with him for her love in this moment; no man on earth had ever been with her like he, Kaniz had. She belonged to him alone. Kaniz's heart soared. He never knew love could be this encompassing and validating; that he could draw such strength from celebrating their love as he did in this minute.

"Hold me, my heartbeat," he whispered in her ear. "Hold me close, my love."

It was almost dawn. Morola was by Kaniz's side as she woke him up gently, rubbing his bicep. His eyes flew open but no sudden reaction followed, and she breathed a sigh of relief.

She was kneeling on the bed side rug. "My Amir, I couldn't sleep much."

"I am sorry." His hand lightly stroked her cheek. "And I slept so soundly. I didn't know you were awake at any time. It was the therapy you gave me, Morola." He smiled faintly. She was quiet as he gazed at her with a smile of deep appreciation.

"Morola, my heartbeat." He was still slightly drowsy so he spoke slowly, measuring his words. "Touch your heart."

She raised her right hand and touched her chest.

He shook his head slightly and smiled. "That's *mine*, you gave me willingly. Under God it's mine, Sarauniya."

He placed her hand on his chest, and she could feel his heartbeat. "This is *your* heart, Sarauniya." He drew her closer, her hand still over his heart. "Under God *this* is yours."

"Don't resign," she said gently.

The last vestiges of slumber cleared from his eyes at that remark.

"That's too late," he said briskly, frowning, his mood changing suddenly. "My mind is made up." His eyes were shuttered, brooking no argument, but she pressed on.

"But did you ask for guidance on the decision?"

"What are you talking about, my love? He had a gun to your head!" He was still lying down with his head on the pillow, but his hand flew to his left temple again. Morola took the hand away and kissed the scar gently. A jolt of arcane electricity went through him.

"More grey, Ademi," she said wistfully, looking at his temple. "And why do you think God spared us both?" Why do you think He let you know something was wrong all day yesterday? Why did you pull your gun out right on the doorstep? Then walk into the living room? You never do anything without guidance, and I prayed Amir. You shouldn't resign."

"You know she speaks the truth."

"What would I do without her? What if they actually get her next time? What if I am not with her?"

"I never doze, I never nap, I never sleep, I can keep you both. I kept you both didn't I?"

Kaniz was finding this meeting even more revealing than he had hoped. Prior to communicating the assassination attempt to the entire transition council, the Quartet was meeting.

Jude's strident insistence that Funso should take full responsibility for the debacle was insightful. Funso was in charge of intel and security and therefore, Jude was right that it was within his purview, but something told Kaniz there was more to this than meet the eye.

All Kaniz knew was that Funso had invited Jude to join the Quartet and at the time he came on, Jude was already firmly ensconced. So why was Jude going on in such a way that Funso would have no other honourable option than to resign?

"If our Quartet has no confidence in my ability to handle my role any more, then I have no choice than to tender my resignation to the NTC," Funso announced flatly.

Kola and Jude looked at Kaniz immediately. It was his call. He had the formal authority and in this case, more importantly, he had the moral authority. It was his life and his wife's life that had been in danger. Kaniz knew what he had to do.

"Funso, that won't be necessary. We will both get to the bottom of this matter. I have complete trust in you. We will start first with how my ADC was chosen. Then Jude, you want me to believe that a man I handed over to you at about 10:30 p.m. last night for questioning died in custody under your watch? Funso was with me. You were in charge and he died."

Jude hadn't expected that Abubakar Saleh's death would even become an issue. He spluttered. "He died from injuries sustained during the attack."

"I shot him myself," Kaniz said. He was barely restraining his anger. "I shot him thrice, and I avoided hitting any major artery. I will need a full investigation into his death, Jude. Funso, I need a report on Abubakar's death on my desk in the next forty-eight hours."

It was clear someone wanted to silence Abubakar before he could speak.

Rola looked at her husband seated across the desk from her. Was this Kaniz? Was he really the one she was seeing in daylight? She had started to call him "Kaniz the Owl" to which he replied by tweaking her nose and calling her "Morola the Bat". Then they both laughed sadly at the truth in their words. She had said in passing last night that their marriage was now a nocturnal marriage and this was his response – visiting her today in daylight. Even if she tried not to, she couldn't but love Kaniz. How many things did he leave behind this afternoon just to be here?

Kaniz was grateful that Morola understood so well the sacrifices they both had to make for leadership. She never complained about how their young marriage had been taken over by his service as chief of staff at the NTC barely three short weeks into their new life together. If she had let that "nocturnal marriage" comment slip, it was Freudian and he needed to address it. He told himself it was all very well. He also wanted to see what she looked like at work, what her clients saw of her and who her team were. He thought he should also assess the security at her office himself after the incident two days ago. Raliat and the security detail were stationed there with her, but he had decided to visit himself. He was impressed. The structure, the decor, the organisation; it was impossible to know it was a recent start-up. Morola had made him proud. The income was already coming in, that much he knew.

He had tried to inquire subtly in the first month about how things were going, thinking he would have needed to transfer some funds from an offshore account to assist her but instead, she had thanked him profusely and didn't give him an answer one way or the other. The next day when he got home at night, he had seen a large A4 size brown envelope on his pillow. He opened it and there was a deed of assignment in it. Two plots of land in one of the good sites and services estate schemes retailed for about $130,000. The deed was for Mr Kaniz and Mrs Morolawe Ishaya. Morola had bought land in both their names. He gave her $100,000 and in that same month, instead of coming back to ask for help, she invested $130,000 in real estate. She didn't buy jewellery? Not a bag? If he died tonight, he was sure she could handle his assets. If they had children and he passed and left them behind, his children would be taken care of. His name would survive. He had been watching how she took decisions, and he really respected his wife. She was so full of surprises, and he never knew what she would be up to next.

"I am so sorry to keep you waiting, Kaniz." Morola was trying her utmost best to cut off in the middle of the working day and accommodate Kaniz, but she already had her whole day planned.

Kaniz was in no doubt that what his wife was doing here was not only important to her but also was bringing a lot of value to so many businesses globally. He was secure enough to be proud of her. He wasn't going to admit openly to not minding the moderate wait for a worthwhile cause, but he was proud of her.

"I will take the conference call on my cell phone. Send me the number and the code I need to join in. Anything else?" She was speaking to her assistant, Tracy. As she got up, she was wondering what Kaniz had in mind. Her own mind had been clouded by thoughts of the horror of two nights ago.

Kaniz could tell. She had supervised the cleaning and repainting of the anteroom, but it was as if the blood had soaked not just into the rug which she had insisted was disposed but also into her consciousness. When she didn't know he was watching, she shivered involuntarily, from flashbacks no doubt.

He couldn't just stand by and watch Morola suffer like this, no matter how she tried to put up a bold front for his sake. Yet he still had to find a way to tell her what Funso had found out: that Abubakar had not died from his injuries at all but was an obvious victim of some foul play. Foul play that had taken place under Jude's watch. Funso had been so thorough in his investigation that he had Abubakar's hurriedly buried body exhumed and the autopsy had found a single bullet wound behind his skull, execution style. Someone had silenced Abubakar. Someone close to Kaniz. Things were not safe for Morola and himself. But he didn't want to alarm her.

"I am taking you out," he announced. They were in the lift on their way out.

"Can't you see how all the women were staring at you, Kaniz? I am sure they are not going to do any work in this whole building today," she quipped. She said that to compliment Kaniz, but it was true. They were staring. Not just because he was more handsome in person than on TV but because of who he was; someone they saw on local and international news strolling along with just one officer behind him. What they were used to was a shutting down of the entire building due to "presidential movement". He didn't shut down the building and blare sirens all over town.

Social media was agog with the news five minutes after Kaniz and Morola stepped into the car. *Chief of Staff, National Transition Council, visits Synergy Group.*

The speculations were rife, every blog had its own guess – they were going out on official assignment; he just stopped to visit her. There was a lot of buzz about how in love they were, but not one journalist alluded to work hours wasted, which had been Kaniz's only reservation. Rola and Kaniz seemed to be well-loved.

It had been a feat pulling this stunt, but Kaniz was determined. He had to show Morola that she mattered and her sacrifice mattered. Funso hadn't found out until Sierra Charlie, as they called Security Control (SC), had communicated that "the Lion was on the move", and they had pulled security and traffic reports for the route to Synergy Lagos. The whole building had been swept from top to bottom within thirty minutes and even now as they left, they left the canine unit of the bomb squad behind. Kaniz didn't care right now. Leadership meant personal sacrifice, but the hardest part had been giving up normal life with Morola so soon. He had never planned to be the chief of staff at the NTC or to be the one in the enemies' cross hairs and though he was a combatant and had signed up for a dangerous life, Morola had not. She didn't deserve this. Her only fault had been to love him back. Somehow in the midst of being the face of the nation's leadership today, something had prompted him not to forget to be her lover.

"So where are you taking me?" she asked.

"To heaven and back," he said with a coy smile.

"Oh," she cooed knowingly, returning his smile.

He knew where he had misled her thoughts. "Why are you so besotted with my body, my love?" he teased with his impish grin. "Focus!" he added with mock seriousness.

Kaniz and his mischief! If she could blush, she would have been beetroot red.

Kaniz loved the way Morola made him feel. He had been high on a lot of things in his early days, but the high her love gave him was a stimulant like no class A drug had ever been. He knew he was addicted; he had stopped denying it even to himself. She left him in no doubt that he was attractive to her. As shy as she still was, she paid him compliments, she praised him. No matter how everyone else praised him, he searched in her eyes for that look of admiration. They were watching the State of the Nation broadcast together exactly two weeks ago, and he was speaking instead of General Adewale who was on a state visit to Germany. She was uncharacteristically quiet after the address. He had turned to her for validation. He couldn't ask her directly of course, so he said, "Do you think that it was clear in that broadcast that the Electoral Commission must be ready for elections in four months and the state of readiness is being monitored daily by the NTC?"

"The whole address was a failure," she said.

He started in shock. He felt like she had just dropped a bucket of ice over his head. She had never given him such scathing feed back before. She would first praise him and if there were a few points to work on, she would tell him but "the entire address was a failure"? He was crestfallen, and it showed in his voice. "What went wrong?" he asked.

He always put a lot of work into communicating with the nation because he could remember how disgusted he was in the past when leaders in the country would come up and jumble speeches as if they didn't get a written copy before facing the camera. He had promised himself that if for any reason he was ever in a position to give such speeches, he would never be like that. Now, Morola, whose opinion he set such stock by, was telling him he failed dismally.

"For most women in this country, tonight that was a completely wasted address. The purpose of the address was to communicate information right?"

He nodded in agreement, quite concerned.

"It's a waste."

He was now really disturbed.

"I didn't hear a word you said, Amir. I was just busy checking you out." She licked her lips exaggeratedly and winked at him. "No woman heard a word you said in that broadcast, Kaniz. I assure you." She laughed as he threw a throw pillow at her, finally understanding her joke.

She responded with her own counter-attack, proving her mettle as the erstwhile captain of her school's volleyball team. At that, she got another volley of pillows thrown at her for teasing him that badly, and a full-scale pillow fight soon ensued.

Paul, who was tidying up in the anteroom downstairs, was smiling as he heard the peals of infectious laughter from the "combatants" on the first floor escaping down the staircase. He was happy with the way these two got along. His madam was always so considerate, sending money to his kids. She was already paying the school fees for Rachel, his eldest, who was of school age. Good woman. He smiled again.

They had negotiated a ceasefire.

"Seriously though, if you don't want to lose 51.8% of the audience from now on, get someone else like Jude who likes the camera to take the broadcasts when General is not around. That is, if you want the women to hear anything the NTC has to say. We are 51.8% of the population you know," Rola quipped.

She had to dodge yet another pillow for that remark.

"Ahn ahn! In the middle of a ceasefire?" She moaned as he scooped her into his arms.

If only he didn't have this job, he sighed as he recollected the lighthearted fun. If only they had more times together like that. He encouraged himself, the six months was almost up anyway.

Rola rounded up her conference call. They were in the car and the tint on the bulletproof Lexus LX570 SUV that Funso had delivered yesterday morning was so dark, Morola could hardly see out of the window. She worried that Kaniz would find the car interior too dark, but he didn't seem to be bothered. They turned in to their destination from what she gathered from the radio chatter of the security detail riding up front. As Bamidele opened her door, she saw they were at the Lekki Hangars, where quite a few private jet owners preferred to park their jets instead of the hangars on the mainland.

Kaniz took her by the hand towards a Gulfstream G650 parked on the tarmac. They were expected. She didn't bother wondering where they were going any more. They got into the plane, and he turned towards the cockpit.

"You fly commercial planes?"

"Morola, this was one of my side hustles." He smiled. "And yes, I am licensed to fly a Gulfstream G500 and a G650."

"Whose jet?" was the question he knew his wife was going to ask next. She wouldn't want him taking any favours from people, which might compromise his integrity – not even a flight. They both knew those who usually could afford these "toys" and how they came about the money.

"Alhaji has had private jets since I was a child," he said. "The exchange rate was strong remember? Fifty million dollars was really fifty million back then. Now, if you have a head start like that, it's easier to get things like jets. If we could just get headed in the direction of fixing things instead of a few appropriating all that belongs to the many.

"It just sets me thinking sometimes how unnecessarily difficult things now are for younger people just because of some people's greed. If every dollar stolen from this country was returned, everyone, every single person would be a dollar millionaire. No one in this country has any business being poor," he said.

She was still surprised and on her own tangent. "I never knew Alhaji had a private jet..." Her voice tapered off.

"You never asked." He smiled. "Aminat was actually one of the flight crew on the Lear jet he had back then. That is how they met."

As soon as they reached a cruising altitude, Alhaji's pilot flying with Kaniz as the co-pilot, Captain Adeaga, came to fetch her so she could sit by Kaniz.

"It's actually on autopilot. The weather is particularly beautiful today. I know I don't have to say don't touch anything," he said, smiling as she stepped into the cockpit. "I wanted to bring you here, share this with you. I want you to see my perspective. Abubakar and whoever sent him can't come here with us. Let him drop out of your mind, Morola."

She gasped. "The view is really something else from the cockpit. There's no end to the azure view, it's like an immersion. It's a never-ending horizon. I can't describe it. Just an oasis of peace. There's something so healing about it."

She really could feel the dark clouds of Abubakar's attack and his death rolling away from her mind just like that awful carpet soaked with blood the maintenance men had rolled away and burnt.

"This is my world, my love," he said as she looked out at the endless vista. "Before I met you, Morola, this was my escape. Peace would fill my heart as I came here and I left the ground and its gravity behind."

"And now??" she asked quietly, turning from the horizon and looking in his eyes.

"Whenever I am in your arms, Morola, I am at peace," he said softly, looking at her with unmasked love. His hand found hers and held it gently to his lips.

Chapter Thirty-Two

"For there is nothing hidden which shall not be revealed, nor has anything been kept secret but that it should come to light."

Mark 4:22

Kaniz reflected on his situation as Bamidele drove him home. The week had been tough, really tough. Emotionally and mentally rough. First came the report from Funso on Abubakar. Kaniz's four years in Colombia with its sophisticated drug money trails served him well. "Follow the money," he had told Funso. Funso had a court order in hand within hours to access Abubakar's entire family's accounts. Abubakar's wife had two lodgments of $50,000 made into her account two weeks ago. The forensic accountants and the bankers traced the inflow back to an account belonging to a shell company in the Isle of Man and apparently, Jude's cousin who had been implicated in the drug scandal in Indonesia was a director of the company, DMZ & Sons. Something about the way Abubakar kept saying, "Kill me," struck Kaniz as odd. There was more to it.

"Get his medical records," Kaniz instructed. The records were promptly obtained. Just as he thought, something was wrong. Abubakar had a terminal inoperable brain tumor, and he had been given less than six months to live. He had then asked that the three candidates who had been shortlisted by Jude for the role of his ADC be investigated further and sure enough, the other two had terminal diseases. Neither of them had been given more than six months to live. One had stage four cancer and the other had Lou Gehrig's disease. Jude had shortlisted men on borrowed time, men with nothing to live for susceptible to coercion. It was obvious that the deal was to carry out the assassination for $100,000 that would be paid to their families. This week had been shocking. Funso and Kaniz were yet to determine the scale of the danger and yet, they couldn't move too fast without alerting Jude.

It was difficult to determine if the worst threat was the internal or the external ones. The NTC's drive for resource control and federalism was being badly received in some specific quarters. This alone had put three different imminent targets on the leaders' backs according to the reports they were getting. The drive to make the centre unattractive before the elections was being fought tooth and nail by those who had made it their sole source of income.

The NTC was proposing a referendum for textbook federalism and Kaniz was quite vocal about it. What surprised him the most was how confidential council proceedings kept leaking to the public, such that it was clear what stand he took. These were joint decisions taken with due process. Now some disgruntled elements had sworn to assassinate him before a referendum could be held. Even his father had heard the rumours. Alhaji had been to the house to warn him to let the drive for federalism go, but Kaniz, Kola and Funso, with General Adewale's and AVM Woriabam's full backing, had brought the rest of the NTC on board. They were convinced that apart from conducting the freest and fairest elections in the history of the nation, this was the one "reset" with the farthest reaching gains they could leave the country with in their six months.

The pressure to stay beyond six months was also mounting massively. What use were elections, the populace was saying, when the pool of candidates were still the same rent-seekers and beneficiaries of nepotism? Kaniz was consistent in his reply on behalf of the NTC: "Democracy is a process. The NTC only stepped in with the full backing of the international community to stop a total slide into anarchy." Six months was it for Kaniz. He had his own life to resume and Morola to think of.

The evening before was one of those very rare times Morola ever pushed back on anything that came under the "security" heading. Funso had ordered the replacement of Paul, their cook. Morola had balked at the decision. She had asked Kaniz rather calmly why the decision was taken and when he had briskly replied that it was for security reasons and not something she should question, she had asked what the decision was predicated on. He was ashamed of himself for snapping at her. She made sense, and he wasn't angry at her at all. The tension over security had just become overwhelming. He himself was basically just aligning with orders. He had found his way to her that night when she retired to their sofa in the family living room, which had been witness to so many loving moments, and gently lay down, nestling his head on a throw pillow in her lap.

"It's just so tense these days, Saraun iya. I don't want something to go wrong, and Funso then says we ignored security reports," he said softly.

He buried his face in her belly. She was a strong woman, but he knew how to disarm her. She was a strong woman, and she could only fight strong men. She wouldn't fight her baby. With his head in her lap now, he was her baby. He was avoiding future trouble this way. No need being the man of the house and dying from stress. He preferred peace. He acknowledged that she knew how to deal with him, and it wouldn't be by shouting.

"I can't take it if anything happens to you," he said.

"Just find out the basis for the decision, Amir, hmm?"

"The role of our cook is a sensitive position. We need someone trusted. It's so easy to..." She couldn't even bring herself to say the words "poison you".

"Paul is Uncle Samson's blood nephew. He is Aunty Ruth's first son. You have known Aunty Ruth for as long as you have known Uncle Samson. Almost your entire life. We can't do this to Uncle Samson's nephew for no good reason."

Kaniz felt reproached and ashamed of himself. He was the one who should be fighting for Samson's nephew. This role was turning him into someone he didn't like.

She knew he was apologising underhandedly. He had been under so much stress on these security issues, and she could tell he was more worried for her than for himself. She cradled his head closer and kissed him on the forehead.

"You know I am concerned about you, Amir? Right? It's all for you," she said.

His heart melted at her words.

This morning at the HQ, he had asked Funso why Paul was to be replaced and apart from the cliché security reasons, Funso had no cogent reason. He insisted on a reason and after an hour, Funso had reverted to him that it was because Paul's surname was flagged as not being from the country. That was true, but Paul's late father who was from the neighbouring country had died since he was six. Father and son had lived in Lagos all their lives.

"Is that all?" Kaniz asked. Apparently Morola was right. It was baseless.

"Well it also seems HR wants to give you a more qualified cook."

"It would be destabilising for now. I decline."

Kaniz thought the whole thing smelt fishy. And now Jude wanted to see him urgently.

Jude had never requested an audience with Kaniz. Though Kaniz was younger, he still outranked Jude, and Kaniz was not sure if this had now become a problem.

Jude saluted Kaniz. Kaniz was his superior in rank and, by virtue of his position in the NTC, was way his senior in power. Kaniz watched Jude keenly for any signs of resentment. There didn't seem to be any. Jude was carrying two files in his hands which he placed on Kaniz's desk.

"Group Captain Ishaya, I have been very uncomfortable with the investigations on the assassination attempt. I can't get over the fact that whichever way we look at it, it happened on our watch. I really would like to have left Major Ajayi alone to investigate but from the point of view of checks and balances, it would appear you have requested Major Ajayi to investigate himself." He paused to let this sink in.

Kaniz could not fault his argument. Truly, the lapse had been in Funso's portfolio and under his oversight and therefore, it should never had been Funso who carried out the investigation. Kaniz was genuinely conflicted. The allusion Jude was making was clear and was just basic investigation protocol. It shouldn't have been Funso investigating himself. This now called into question everything Funso had "discovered". Kaniz had merely trusted his oldest and closest friend. But who else was he to trust when Rola's life and his life were at stake?

"I decided to conduct my own investigations." Jude slid the file on the desk towards Kaniz.

"The papers from HR on the candidates," he said.

Kaniz scanned through quickly wondering what he was supposed to see in the papers, then his eyes caught it. The original memo shortlisting the three candidates had been signed by Funso. He apparently had shortlisted them. Funso had shortlisted the candidates? That was Funso and not Jude?

He rallied. There could be another explanation. Funso may have been acting on someone else's recommendations.

He looked at the next memo and saw that HR had recommended three other candidates, listing some cogent reasons for their own recommendations – war experience, superior performance in courses and promotion examinations, and on the job appraisals. But Funso in the reply to HR's memo had overruled and in his own fresh memo, had insisted on his own picks. Why then had Funso picked out the ones with terminal illnesses?

So, granted, Jude had not shortlisted the candidates. How about the wrongful death of Abubakar under Jude's custody?

He decided to ask Jude directly. Jude pulled out yet another file. "When you asked me what happened to Abubakar under my watch that day, I was shocked because it was truly under my watch and I had entrusted him to Lieutenant Bako, one of my most trusted men to watch him while I stepped out for less than an hour. I didn't know what to say because it was an indiscretion, a rather frivolous escapade with a girl I met in questionable circumstances. Not all of us are lucky to be married, and we still have needs," he said, looking embarrassed. "I couldn't give my alibi in front of everyone, but Kaniz, that's what happened."

Kaniz noticed that Jude had reverted to calling him by his first name, no doubt invoking their friendship to forge a bond. So was that why Jude had spluttered and looked so uncomfortable that day? He was with a woman? When he should have been in the interrogation room with Abubakar?

"This is the report of the autopsy on Abubakar's death. I actually had asked already that an autopsy be done, but I couldn't speak to it on the day because the report wasn't ready yet. It takes these government labs forever, not like what we see in the crime series on TV." He managed a weak smile. "As soon as the report was ready today, I collected it from the lab and came directly to your office."

Kaniz read the autopsy report. Abubakar had died of exsanguination. Blood loss. Well this proved nothing, Kaniz thought. It was still possible that the exsanguination had been from the bullet wound to the head. He looked through the autopsy again and saw the wounds he knew he had personally inflicted on Abubakar documented. In the autopsy, his right tibia, right scapula and left phalanges were noted as sustaining gun shots, however, the autopsy had not mentioned the bullet wound to the base of the skull.

Where had Funso gotten the corpse with the head wound to the base of its skull? Or was Jude's autopsy report fake? Who was he to trust? They were all in the Quartet. Funso had brought Jude on board precisely because he said he was trustworthy.

Jude had more to say. "The events of that night of the assassination attempt were precisely why I was so vehemently against your getting married, but I have seen you and Mrs Ishaya together and . . ." He nodded. "I would have returned to the Quartet and had exactly the same discussion you had with us if I was ever lucky enough in this lifetime to have found what you have found in her. I just wanted us to be cautious. I wanted to avoid precisely the type of threat that we ended up having on Mrs Ishaya's life. We could have lost you both." He spread out his hands in dismay.

Kaniz's consternation escalated. Funso was his closest friend and Jude had also watched his back in the past. Who was he to trust? Is that why Funso had wanted to replace the trustworthy Paul with his own plant? He now truly knew you keep your friends close and your enemies even closer. Dangerous as it was going to be, he was now keeping his enemies as close to him as a second skin.

He decided that Kola should take over now and look into the money trail again. Where did the money in Abubakar's wife's account come from? Kola had returned within forty-eight hours to report that it was from a domiciliary account here in the country. The account had been shut down as soon as the transfers had been concluded and the account holder didn't exist. Where then did the telex and documents which, according to Funso, showed that the offshore company had transferred the two tranches of $50,000 to Mrs Saleh's bank account come from? Kaniz didn't know who to trust any more. Funso was still in charge of the NTC's intelligence. Should he suggest to General that he be replaced? Should he wait until there was unquestionable proof? Funso was his closest friend. How could he even contemplate replacing him? Who could he trust? A disproportionate number of the external conspiracies and foiled attempts were targeted at him. Who was he to trust?

At first, General Adewale felt Major Jude King represented a voice of balance in this sea of like minds but recently, he was beginning to wonder. The meeting two days ago was one such day as he listened on several levels to Jude. He listened not just with his auditory organs but was really observing Major King.

What exactly was Jude's rationale? He seemed to have none but that didn't deter him from speaking. The NTC had suspended the constitution. It had become apparent that the Quartet's strategy document was gold. The NTC couldn't make any impact in the systemic issues that beleaguered the country with the constitution being what it was. Those meant to administer it were the real bane of the system. Developing a strategy to institute a unicameral system of government was under consideration this morning. The facts were clear: the federal houses of assembly took up 28% of the nation's recurrent expenditure, more than what it took to run the actual federating units. This was just on the face of it without taking into account the money spent bribing the houses to pass the budget and so many unspeakable practices happening in two separate houses. What was the value added for this huge cost? How many bills were passed a year? What was the justification for such waste? Was it necessary to have two houses? The NTC now had a clear position following the excellent work the chief of staff and Head of Strategy Dr Kola Toriola had done.

"We must be aware that we will be upsetting the status quo which was not without antecedents in the first instance," King was saying.

Major Funso Ajayi seemed embarrassed for Major King.

"Major King, that is why we are running a change agenda to upset the status quo where it needs to be upset."

"It's a way of life for many, Major Ajayi. People have built careers around it. Their families' livelihood depends on this."

"So, we should have more personnel than is efficient? In effect, more redundant politicians living off the taxpayers money because a defective constitution which doesn't bear in mind present economic exigencies has condemned us to it? We should run into debt as a nation trying to fund our lawmakers because their families depend on the money they make?" the Chief of Staff interjected.

"Let's be aware that we would come against considerable resistance, and the credible threats we are already facing collectively and individually would escalate," Jude said.

Just before he left HQ, Kaniz had gone in to see General for briefing. Kaniz saluted General Adewale briskly.

"At ease," General said. "Sit, please, Kaniz."

Adewale was already fond of this serious and brilliant young man. Besides, his role demanded that his superior took him into confidence. "Kaniz, look at this," he said, setting what seemed to be four or five sheets of paper in front of Kaniz.

Kaniz looked. It was a report alleging Jude was being bribed by legislators to ensure the bicameral structure was not tampered with. Kaniz was aghast.

"How did they even know what we are discussing in the NTC?"

"We have a mole," Adewale said. "Look at those sheets."

They were bank statements, hundreds of thousands of dollars from an account to Jude's.

"The journalist, Tunde Asewa, claims they are bribes. He is publishing this tomorrow, Kaniz, and I am not going to attempt to stop him. He is just letting me know out of respect for me."

Who were they to trust?

The week had been interesting. He had two female secretaries removed this week alone. He also had to contend with the women outside his office throwing themselves at him. He had been dealing with such nuisances since he was nineteen after all, but it was just an unfair waste of time to have to deal with secretaries who became a bother. Kaniz reflected on how those who thought women liked rich men only knew half the truth. He could tell that women were attracted to power: to men who others respected, admired and obeyed.

They were attracted to leaders; the powerful who could solve their problems and had others doing their bidding. And as money could buy the trappings of power, it would appear that money was what they were attracted to. But it wasn't really money that attracted them, it was actually *power*. They were attracted to him like moths to the flame. Morola didn't seem to be bothered and that only made Kaniz respect her more. She just seemed so focused on what she was doing and had such faith in him that he had better sense than to fall for women cheap enough to throw themselves at him. He couldn't help but respect her. To resolve the issue, HR had sent him a male secretary.

As he rode in the silent convoy of three cars home, Kaniz reflected on how easy it would be to slip back into normalcy after this was over. It was the paraphernalia of office like sirens and motorcades that made it so difficult for some to live a normal life after office and make them hold on to power like a do or die affair. They also didn't have a wife like Morola to keep them grounded, he thought, smiling to himself.

"Morola," he said as he got into the family living room. Paul had told him Amaka and Alhaji had just left and his wife was upstairs.

Morola gave him a warm embrace and as he bent to give his wife a kiss, her response made his effort worth his while. She was working on her MacBook as Kaniz began to take his shoes off in the family living room. He was angling for a foot rub.

"Wow, my feet. They are definitely swollen," he announced.

Silence.

"Morola, my love, that foot rub you gave me the other day, I wonder? Could you just, haba!" Wrinkling his nose, he spoke in his father's language for added drama as if the feet hurt unbearably as he took the shoes off. "Can you just see to these feet for me again today? Kai! They are swollen," he added for good measure.

Morola looked up from her MacBook, "Aww, my love," she cooed. "Kaniz dear, these feet are so swollen, a foot rub would make them worse. Ah. Look at that swelling! No hands should touch them. You need a spray. What you need now is Deep Heat. It's on the bathroom shelf. The red can on the left, just spray it lightly on your feet. Pele, it's not easy sitting that long," she said, with a look of concern. "Are you still here? You need to hurry and spray the Deep Heat on before the feet get worse."

"Yes," Kaniz thought, "those who weren't grounded don't have a wife like Morola." He respected himself, carried his shoes gingerly and went in to their bedroom to change.

"Foot rubs *on demand*?" Rola thought as soon as she knew where Kaniz was going. "Nah! We are not going that route."

"Kaniz dear."

"Hmm?" he cooed. He knew it. He knew she found him irresistible, she was calling him back for that foot rub.

"You left a sock behind."

Kaniz changed into his pyjamas. For the few hours he had to rest, he intended to rest.

"Amir." It appeared Kaniz had managed to survive without the foot rub and remain in good health. "Amir, Alhaji just left before you arrived home."

"Hmm?" This was not one of Kaniz's nice "hmms" which were more of a coo. This was an "and what?"

"Well, his sources tell him Quantumtech's contract with the Ministry of Defence will not be renewed."

"Hmm?"

"That can't be right."

"Why not?"

"Why should their contract not be renewed? Have they failed to perform?"

"I don't want to be accused of swinging a contract of hundreds of millions of dollars my family's way."

"That contract was existing under the politicians and Mamane Group are the biggest defence contractors in this country."

"I will *not* be accused of nepotism."

"Then recuse yourself from the decision-making and allow a level playing field. We are not encouraging nepotism now, but we shouldn't be victimised because we are related to you either."

"What do you know about these things? Are you the one people will criticise in the newspapers and call names? Is it not I?"

"So, for fear of what people would say, Amir, you would throw Mamane Group under a bus? Is that it?"

"Look at the rest of the country suffering. The Mamane Group is wealthy enough, Morola, and its wealth came about because of unequal access to opportunities."

"So you are overcompensating for your guilt for being born into privilege."

"Privilege that I lived without for most of my adult life, Morola. That's such an unfair thing to say."

"Amir, do the right thing."

"Morola..." he began to say but as he watched, her legs seemed to give way. She went straight down on to the carpet and landed in a heap.

Kaniz sprang to her side and knelt on the carpet. "Morola, what is it?" The concern in his voice was palpable. All thoughts of nepotism, Mamane Group, anything at all but Morola and her well-being were gone out of his mind.

Chapter Thirty-Three

"I will say unto God my rock, why hast Thou forgotten me?
Why go I mourning because of the oppression of the enemy?"

Psalm 42:9

It was the longest thirty seconds of his life, but she finally spoke. "Were we having our first argument?" She smiled weakly.

"You blacked out."

"It appears so." She tried to get up. "I am dizzy, Kaniz," she said weakly, her head falling back on the carpet.

"I am calling Dr Abe." He instantly speed-dialled Dr Abe. The NTC had appointed Dr Abe Kaniz's official physician as Kaniz had recommended.

Dr Abe was playing golf when Kaniz got him, but he was instantly on his way. He was genuinely fond of Kaniz and respected the young man and in spite of his military reserve, Dr Abe could still pick up the distress in his voice. The golf course was close by and Dr Abe was in their bedroom in less than thirty minutes.

Morola was lying down in bed.

Kaniz was pacing in the bedroom. Since they met, Morola had never been ill. What had he done to her? Was it the argument? He hadn't even been shouting. Nothing could happen to Morola under his watch.

Dr Abe had arrived with a paramedic and drawn blood samples and a host of other samples for diagnostics. Kaniz stood by attentively as she was pricked and examined. It was obvious that she hated needles, but he liked that she put on a brave face.

It was clear to Dr Abe that her blood pressure was low, a result of her patchy eating habits, which would account for the dizzy spell and blacking out. He would revert within the hour with the other results and the cultures would take seventy-two hours.

Dr Abe called back within an hour. "Mrs Ishaya, you have malaria."

"I thought so. The hypotension didn't help too right?" Rola said.

"However, because of your condition, we have to be careful the kind of antimalarial medications we prescribe."

"Some antimalarial medications make hypotension worse?" she asked.

"Well, malaria also causes some anaemia, but I am actually referring to the fact that some antimalarial medications are contraindicated in pregnancy," Dr Abe was saying.

He was still speaking, but the last thing Rola heard was "pregnancy". She took some time to digest the news. "Please don't say anything to my husband yet," she said. Dr Abe assured her patient-doctor confidentiality precluded that.

During the week, on Wednesday precisely, she saw Dr Abe again. It was confirmed she was eight weeks pregnant. She had to be sure and asked to be tested again, and Dr Abe got Dr Folarin to give her an internal ultrasound scan. Talking to Mrs B later, she couldn't describe the awe and joy she felt when she saw Kaniz's child swimming and tumbling in her womb looking like he - or she, (she reminded herself it could be a girl) - was having the most amazing time ever. It was true. She was really pregnant. She could see their child. It was alive. A protective instinct swept over her. She felt like she would defend this life within her with her very own life. So, this was how a mother's love felt? A child that had done nothing yet but induce in her some rather flu-like symptoms, a tiny being that looked nothing like a human yet, and yet, she loved it so fiercely already? Love was a mystery indeed. "God is love." With this baby, she seemed to have been given a glimpse into another dimension of love.

Wednesday meetings were a relic of the political era which the intransigent civil service just couldn't shake. The reports coming in from various sectors encouraged hope but at a heavy price. The decisions of the Council were extremely well received by the populace but resented by the few who felt disenfranchised by the transformations which benefitted the many. Those who had the wealth and means to harm them were the ones they were offending daily by their "wind of change" policies. The upper class never encouraged a change in status quo, failing to see that they couldn't continue to live in a country where the middle class had been virtually eradicated. They remained obdurate in their failure to see that critical changes had to be made. In spite of the recent disastrous events, some of them stayed oblivious to the fact that when the poor have nothing to eat, they eat the rich. If things did not change soon, they were soon to be on the menu.

Kaniz and the NTC did not have the luxury of that level of ignorance. A disturbing report they got showed the scale of the problem. A forty feet container with 661 pump-action guns had just been seized from the ports and contrary to the spin the comptroller of customs had tried to put on it, it was actually not dutifulness at all but a betrayal that led to the seizure.

The clearing agent had refused to "settle" the men at the port gate with the customary $125 bribe. He was being made a scapegoat for his "greed". If the agent had paid $125 for the container, no one would have cared if he was importing toxic waste like some had actually done in the past. He would have been waved past. They were all stunned, imagining the state of insecurity if several of these shipments had already made their way into the country as was now being reported had happened. Who was arming themselves and what for? Was there a parallel army in the country? Reports like this were just the tip of the iceberg.

It was clear to the entire NTC and those in the know in the nation that the road map from Quartet was what was in play. It was no secret who the architects of the document were. Eliminate them and their major supporters in the NTC, and by and large the agenda could be derailed. From the NTC's point of view, things were going swiftly and according to plan. They had six months to reset a nation and they would do it. An extension was not even being discussed at all. These were career soldiers who really had no appetite for tangling with civilian intrigues which they now had to encounter daily. The military wasn't designed to govern. They were designed to defend the governing and the governed. People like Kaniz in the NTC were openly counting down to the end of the six months.

The process of restructuring was on course; the memos were being prepared and town hall meetings were held in the eight political zones to guide the terms of the impending referendum on restructuring. The Quartet, when they were drafting the memos, had completely underestimated the resistance the politicians were putting up to the abolishment of the bicameral system of government in favour of a unicameral system. Those who benefitted from the system had begun to resist very strongly and in insidious ways. With the intel he had seen pointing to the fact that money was changing hands, there were bound to be fault lines where one would expect them the least.

Kaniz and Rola were talking as they did every night before they prayed and went to bed. There was so much he wanted to say but couldn't.

That morning, there had been yet another incident, the *fifth* attempt on his life so far. At the opening of a new mega power station where he had been called to step in for General Adewale, as the little girl who was to hand him the bouquet made her way towards the dais, something about her awkward gait had caught his attention and he had motioned to Jude to get the canine unit to sniff her.

"Just ask her to pat the dog. Don't scare her," he had said to Jude as he withdrew to the back of the dais. Jude swung the canine unit into action. The dogs went into a frenzy as they sniffed her. She had one kilo of c4 on her, hidden in the bouquet on a timed device. The explosives unit only managed to defuse the bomb with seconds to spare. The bomb was certainly meant for him.

General had handed him the assignment to open the power station at a full meeting of the Council. Only the Council had foreknowledge that the chief of staff and not General Adewale, was going to attend the opening.

When the threats on the leaders of the NTC escalated, he hadn't been concerned about himself. After Darfur, he had lost all fear or dread of death. He had died that day to all intents and purposes. Morola was his focus. How would she cope? Even if he wasn't bound by the oath of office, he couldn't discuss the latest incidences with Morola, and this in itself was a point of great tension. He loved Morola too much to worry her. In the last couple of weeks, it had become clear that danger was indeed imminent. He shouldn't have married her if he knew this was his path, but it was now too late to spare her.

He had tried to console himself by rationalising that it was not how long he was around to love her, it was how well he loved her while they were together that counted. He had told himself he would make the short time count, and he had dared to hope. Indeed, he still hoped that there would be a way out, but he had to put his affairs in order and he was preparing her too.

With the constant threats to his life, his rationale was collapsing in the face of the reality of his imminent departure, and he just wanted more time with her. He wasn't afraid of death, he just didn't want to let go of Morola, not yet. He couldn't tell her about this morning or the other incidences, so he decided to make small talk instead.

"Mrs B said to say hello to you," Kaniz said. "I passed by Lekki on the way home."

Kaniz couldn't have "passed by" Lekki on the way from Ikoyi to VI. He had to have taken a detour. As busy as he was? Rola was impressed at the way Kaniz extended the love he showed her – to her parents. As for Olaotan, she jokingly called him her rival for Kaniz's affections.

Mrs B had just returned from settling Isa and Olaotan in school and that evening, while Kaniz was on his flying visit to his father and mother-in-law, Mrs B was openly wondering why TK had put on weight in her absence. TK had put it down to "peace of mind" with a straight face, and Kaniz, his accomplice and perennial cupcake supplier, had maintained a deadpan expression.

Kaniz was lying down and looking into her eyes. He held the card Morola had just given him in his left hand. He would open it as soon as they finished praying.

"Thanks so much, my love," he had said, receiving it and holding her hand to his lips.

She lightly brushed the hair at his temples with her fingertips. "More grey." She sighed. "But it makes you look even more distinguished," she said, kissing his temples.

"Amir, how do you cope with carrying most of the burden while someone else is seen as the head of the NTC? You are the de facto head. We all know; even the streets know."

"Sarauniya, no, that's not an accurate picture. I work hard, yes, but we wouldn't have stability without General Adewale's leadership. We would be dealing with perennial coup threats. The CDS and Joint Chiefs and all the GOCs defer to him. He provides stability to the NTC. And without Kola joining me in the strategic planning, we wouldn't move forward. Servant leadership is not about who takes the credit, anyone can get the credit once we get the desired results," he said.

What he really wanted to say was, "Morola, who gets the credit is not even the problem right now. The problem is that since even the streets believe they know who the key man is, and they believe it's me, I am a marked man and I don't even know who to trust anymore. The vultures are circling." But he couldn't burden her. Instead, he gave her good news.

"Morola, I recused myself from the defence contract evaluation and when due process went through, Mamane Group had their contract renewed."

"Thank you, my Amir, thank you." She kissed his forehead.

"You were right. When you make sense, why would I not accept? To prove I am a man?" He shook his head.

He was rather pensive these days, and his speech had this hint of wistfulness, which was beginning to bother Rola.

"You are a gift to me, Morola. The time we have spent together has been my happiest ever. I want you to know how fulfilled loving you has made me."

There it was again, a valedictory speech. He paused as his mood changed.

"Sarauniya, have I failed you?" He exhaled." We barely got married and this happened. We haven't really spent time together. This isn't what I promised you. Morola, do you still love me?" he blurted.

Rola looked into his eyes. He looked up at her with an expression she didn't quite understand – sadness? Regret? Yearning? Was he missing her? That couldn't be, she was right here lying by his side.

"My Amir, how can you even ask such a question?" She shook her head. "I didn't know I could ever love any man the way I love you Kaniz," she said quietly, factually.

He reflected on her words but his eyes still had the sad expression.

"Ademi, what can I possibly do to reassure you?" She was almost distraught.

"Have my baby, Morola. Have our child." His voice was husky, imploring her. "If something happens to me, there will be someone to remember me by, to remind you of how completely I loved you." His voice caught in his throat at the words, and he swallowed.

"Kaniz, read the card I gave you."

"I will, my love." His eyes were so sad.

"Amir, read it now."

"Oh, right now." He opened the card. A photocopy or fuzzy black and white photo of something dropped out of the card. It was definitely a medical document, like an x-ray of sorts. He stared at it a bit, and then he looked at the card.

"Congratulations Dad!" it said and, "I love you more each passing day My Amir." She signed, "Your Sarauniya."

His eyes were wide with wonder. "Does this mean what I think it means?" His tone was incredulous.

"Kaniz, we are pregnant!" she announced with joy. "We are going to have a baby and nothing will happen to you, we—"

Kaniz's kiss cut off her speech. "Oh God, I prayed and You answered so swiftly."

"Our child..." He touched her belly tenderly. "The scan says eight weeks already?" He said to himself, "You are carrying my child. Now you won't forget me even if..." He found it difficult to continue the painful thought, "even when you marry again."

He needed to get used to the idea that it was "when" and not "if". He said aloud, "My love, if anything happens to me, you should..." His hand went to his left temple again. His long fingers covering his forehead, his eyes closed in his characteristic manner and with a rasping breath, he finally spoke as if he had been battling with himself, "You should marry again, Morola. Be happy, you deserve... you deserve to be happy."

Morola looked him in the eyes and shook her head slowly. How did he even think she could ever love any man like she loved him?

His baritone voice was stressed. "I have left everything I have to you, Morola. You won't lack the means to take care of this child. Promise me you will take care of my child."

He held her by the shoulders and looked into her eyes. She had never seen him so serious.

"Promise me, my love," he said. His voice softer now but more insistent.

"Nothing will happen to you, Kaniz." Tears were welling out of her eyes at his tone. Why was Kaniz speaking this way?

He brushed her tears away with his lips. "Look at me Morola and promise me," he said calmly.

"I promise, we will both take care of our children."

He smiled ruefully and sighed. He held her close, kissing her forehead and stroking her hair as he muttered in Hausa. She could tell he was praying, but his voice was breaking. Somehow, she didn't need an interpreter to know what he was saying. He was praying for the woman he loved with his whole soul and their unborn child, praying for their preservation when he was gone. "Thank you for loving me back, my heartbeat," he whispered, "thank you."

Chapter Thirty-Four

"Set me as a seal upon thine heart, as a seal upon thine arm;
for love is as strong as death."

Songs of Solomon 8:6A

"Take any one of those with you, Kaniz," General said, motioning to the pile of white A4 envelopes in his "out" tray. "You won't need any explanation." Kaniz had just gotten up from his seat to leave after a meeting.

Kaniz took the top envelope. There were three others.

"May I see what it is right away, sir?"

"Go ahead."

They were bank statements for a certain John Kazeem, and the others were for Jane Ahmed and Ada Immaculate. Kaniz wondered why that should be of interest to him.

He looked closer. John Kazeem had significant inflows coming in regularly. However, he swept his account almost completely clean every week and paid just two beneficiaries. He looked closer at both beneficiaries – one was Jane Ahmed and the other was Ada Immaculate. Every Tuesday in the case of Jane Ahmed and every Thursday in the case of Ada Immaculate, they both paid Jude King everything, but... "Lets see," he said and did a quick calculation. That was it. They paid Jude King everything but five per cent of what was in their account. He looked at the summary; it was hundreds of thousands of dollars. But Jude didn't seem to have this type of money anywhere. With the exception of a garish gold Rolex, he hadn't bought anything new Kaniz could see.

Kaniz was crestfallen.

"I just didn't want to bother you, Kaniz. The other two envelopes are more of the same. Can you begin to make sense of Jude's line of reasoning at council meetings now?"

"Yes sir," Kaniz said slowly in a low voice. Demoralised, he felt partly responsible. Funso and himself had pushed for Jude to join the NTC.

"The last set of media reports were very embarrassing for the NTC. I got calls from all over. I will be speaking to the others about an investigation. I am just letting you know."

Rola had tried to keep still for as long as she could but she needed to get up to avoid an "accident".

"Kaniz, you and this baby are still at it. It doesn't understand English, Yoruba or Hausa now. It just hears sounds, that's all."

"You are on your own. My child understands what Daddy is saying, don't you, baby?" His lips were next to her belly.

"I need to get up and use the bathroom now. The doctor says my kidneys are functioning more efficiently because of the baby and you are an engineer, so do the math. I am currently doing bathroom duties for two. C'mon take your head off my belly," she said, teasing.

"Oooohhh this jealous woman!" he said. "I was talking to my baby. Why are you so possessive, Sarauniya? I love you too, a bit, but let me talk to my child."

Rola jumped off the bed. Their conversation would just have to continue later.

Kaniz had a point though. He and their baby seemed to be holding conversations. Around the fifteen-week mark of her pregnancy, something strange had started happening. She felt flutters, like butterflies, under her navel. The flutters weren't strange; that could happen as early as thirteen weeks for some. What was strange was that though the flutters could come at other times, regardless of whenever else the flutters happened, they *always* happened when Kaniz was speaking to his child. *Always*. Three weeks on now and Rola had no doubt that their baby knew Kaniz's voice or perhaps, it was reacting to her own excitement. But why didn't it react at other times when she was excited? Why didn't it respond to other people's voices? Why only Kaniz's?

General Adewale had a grave expression on his face as he dropped the papers on the mahogany conference table with a loud thud. The NTC had been called in for an extraordinary session. Funso had been given the task of following up on the investigations on Jude, and the evidence he returned was damning. Jude had also been tailed for weeks and his phones had been bugged. Jude had several conversations with two senators and though nothing damning was caught on tape, he definitely had links to those who were paying the money. The evidence was incontrovertible, except Funso had fabricated aspects of it, which was Jude's claim – that it was all a set-up and he was being framed in a most dastardly manner.

Kaniz was hoping Jude wouldn't claim he was being marginalised – it was such a well-worn cliché – but he did. Kaniz shook his head. Wrong move. Now, General Adewale would finally speak.

"Major King, you are here today because of Major Funso Ajayi and Group Captain Ishaya. Major Ajayi's portfolio as head of security, was the reason he was asked to investigate. That and the fact that he fought tooth and nail to get you here today. Why would he be the one working against you?" General Adewale was disgusted and it showed.

AVM looked at Kaniz solemnly, his mentee could be too principled, too unselfish. Why had he pushed for Jude King to join the NTC? What did it matter if he hadn't been part of the Quartet?

Woriabam was on the disciplinary committee, so he spoke now. "We will be making our recommendations to the NTC and looking into all the evidence. You will have the right to defend yourself, Major King."

Twenty-four hours later, Kaniz and Woriabam were in General Adewale's office, being shown a set of photos of Tunde Asewa in a pool of his own blood in his car, a black Hyundai. The car and his body were riddled with bullet holes, the beige fabric seats of the Hyundai was dark crimson with blood, what was left of the windshield was streaked with blood splatter, shattered glass all over him. The incident was being treated as an armed robbery by the police but not even his wallet had been stolen. His car had not been taken. Two men on a motorcycle had pulled up to his car as it stopped at a traffic light and shot through the window several times. It had happened about an hour ago.

The three men looked at each other. They knew Asewa had been on his way to meet Funso to hand over decisive evidence on Jude's case. The only thing the robbers had taken was the brief case in the boot of the car, where the papers he was handing to Funso was. The NTC was going to let the police treat it as an armed robbery attack as anything else would be too potentially embarrassing.

General Adewale reached into his drawers and set down another briefcase. "A young lady walked in here thirty minutes ago. She said Asewa told her if anything happened to him, she was to bring these directly to me."

He opened the case and brought out the documents. They were in neat files.

Kaniz and Woriabam looked at the papers and photos. The evidence against Jude was worse than they thought. This was enough for a court martial.

Kaniz sighed and got up from his desk in his study. He was tired, mentally and physically. He couldn't concentrate on any work again tonight. Asewa had been killed just yesterday and now this?

General Adewale's driver had been assassinated fifteen minutes ago. Funso had just called to tell him. For logistics and convenience, General Adewale had relocated temporarily from his own house in Ogudu on the mainland for the six months he had to run the NTC, to a house on Toju Teniola close, barely three minutes from the Ishaya's house. Going back to his VI home from HQ, because of the latest security briefing, he had taken a discreet precaution at the very last minute and stepped into the escort car in secret. No one knew that his driver, Michael, was alone in the decoy car driving with the tinted windows wound up. It was impossible to see the General was not inside. At the traffic light, the convoy of three cars without sirens had stopped for the red light. General was ahead in the escort car with the security personnel, when a hail of bullets from pump-action guns had come from the opposite lane in traffic. The bullets had failed to penetrate the bulletproof LX570, but an IED had been thrown under the car by a hostile on foot on the pedestrian walkway. It detonated with a horrific blast, and the car turned over instantly, the tons of steel lifted in the air by the deafening explosion. Michael had been instantly killed by the blast meant for his boss. What was going on? Only the five of them in the NTC knew General's route that evening – the Quartet and General himself. What was General sensing that made him keep his plans from even the Quartet and change the vehicle he was meant to be in?

Kaniz now ruled out General as the sponsor of the failed attempt against his life at the power plant. General himself was a target it seemed. The danger was closing in. Which one of the Quartet wanted General and himself dead?

Now that the end seemed near, he was suddenly obsessed with a deep desire not to fade from Morola's consciousness. He didn't mind dying, but the thought that she could move on and forget him was too much for him to bear. He went back to their bedroom and just sat on the rug beside Rola, placing his head on the bed by her sleeping form.

Rola woke up after midnight and she could hear Kaniz's familiar voice, praying and wondered why he wasn't asleep. She listened closely and he wasn't praying. He was soliloquising it seemed. He was seated or kneeling – she couldn't tell which it was with her eyes closed – by the edge of the bed on "her" side of the bed, talking to his child. As usual, his lips were close to her belly. Her sleepy mind remembered she had teased him earlier in the day that to him she was now just "the body carrying his precious baby". It struck her that this was an opportunity to get a glimpse into his mind. Something was going on but she could perceive that beyond the duty of confidentiality he had towards the NTC, he also felt obliged to protect her and was not sharing all his thoughts. Now, perhaps she could catch what he was saying when he thought she wasn't listening. She closed her eyes, pretending to still be asleep, his voice was low because he didn't want to wake her up.

"Take care of your mother, she's Daddy's heartbeat. Don't let her ever forget me." He paused. "Your father loves you; I love you so much." He sighed. "But I didn't have the time I had wanted with you." His voice sounded hoarse. He sighed again and brushing his lips gently against the slight swell of her midriff said, "Remember me, my heartbeat. Remember I loved you with all I am. Remember I loved you with all I have. Sarauniya, never forget your Amir."

Hearing his baritone voice so thick with sadness broke Rola's heart. She wanted to speak, but decided against it. It was his private moment. He was entitled to his space. This was apparently way more serious than she thought. Kaniz was obviously depressed. He was always so strong. He would never speak this way if he knew she could hear. He wouldn't want to worry her. What was all this morbidity about? She needed to have a talk with him about this. Depression was real and, in this society, under-diagnosed, especially amongst leaders and those with high-pressure jobs like his. What with all Kaniz had been through in the past, and the present stress he was now under, depression was a clear and present danger and they needed to watch out for it. There was nothing to be ashamed of.

As their baby fluttered in response to Kaniz's voice, her eyes flung wide open. It was so uncanny but real. It never failed – Kaniz's baby always responded to him.

"Amir, I will be having a meeting with Tega at home at about 6 p.m. Tega got us an impressive list of volunteer lawyers to provide pro bono services to the women in prison. We even have some celebrity lawyers on board. He has done well." She smiled.

It was dawn and she was dressed for work as was Kaniz. She in a pinafore-like, sleeveless, grey shift dress worn over a crisp white cotton shirt. Black Mary Janes clad her feet. Their baby was hinting at its presence by the slightest of bumps visible to only the very observant.

Rola cast another surreptitious glance at Kaniz. He was looking stately in his uniform. His broad shoulders and his washboard abs giving the jacket the right configuration. The grey that seemed to keep spreading on his temples only made him more attractive to her.

"Maybe I have 'Daddy issues', perhaps that's why I like him more with this grey," her rational mind chimed in, and she laughed at herself. They were in their bedroom, ready to leave for work though they were actually way too early as usual – Kaniz could never abide lateness.

He caught her scrutinising him, left the chest of drawers he was rummaging through and walked over to her as she stood by the closet door. She watched as he strode over and she couldn't believe his feline gait still "tripped" her till now.

Wrapping her in his arms he said to her, "Is it just my imagination or are you looking even more beautiful these days? It's the glow of motherhood, right?" He had a faint but proud smile on his face.

He held her close still, as he looked out of the window and observed it was still dark outside. Years of military training had made him an early riser and though Rola had been a confirmed owl from force of habit developed through years spent writing code overnight, she had rightly concluded that the only way she would get to see her husband during the day since the NTC was inaugurated was to sync her body clock with his. So she had struggled and adapted and now, she had joined him in the corps of early risers. He had a busy day ahead today. Besides his usual heavy schedule, he had a late meeting with General Adewale, and then, yet another meeting with Funso who wanted him to approve some new weapons. Still, it was too early to start out.

He sighed. He really felt strangely and deeply reluctant about letting her go this morning.

"I wish we didn't have to part today. I wish we could just spend the day together." He seemed to really mean this. Rola looked up at him.

"Amir, I am concerned. You have been different lately. I am not sure we shouldn't look into it more seriously, professionally?" Her voice was soft as she looked into his eyes.

Kaniz smiled to himself, he knew she was reacting to the fact that for some weeks now, he had been subtly preparing her mind for the inevitable. He was just being a realist. He knew the assassination attempts he had escaped and he saw the daily intelligence reports. The NTC was preparing too and was attempting to put measures in place. They weren't just going to be sitting ducks but who could they trust? That was the only issue – who to trust. Were they planning their protection with their assassins? He knew what she meant but he made light of it.

"My Queen thinks I am just being morbid?" He smiled sadly. "Please, cheer me up then, Morola," he muttered, drawing her closer and touching her forehead with his. He inhaled deeply, she smelt so good. Her skin was like the smoothest alabaster and she had this ethereal glow. Everything about her was exhilarating, irresistible.

"You know how happy I am when I am with you," he breathed. "Stay with me just a little longer."

"I am serious about your mood," she said.

"So am I," he said. "So let's do something about it?" he added, half teasing, his voice husky as he pulled her even closer and she felt his muscles ripple under his shirt.

"Am I hurting you, my love?" he whispered as he relaxed his hold a bit.

She shook her head silently. It felt comforting when he held her so close, he smelled so... delectable. His steady heartbeat was so comforting when he held her that way, her head gently against his shoulder. She could feel his heartbeat and when the pace of his heartbeat picked up, as it was doing right now, it did strange things to her.

Kaniz wondered at how Morola never ceased to thrill him, how there was always another dimension to discover with her. These days, she was just so attractive with this incandescent glow. Now she was no longer just his bride but the mother of his child, and there was just something so potently irresistible to him about the fact that she carried a part of him, growing within her.

"My love now lives within you, Morola." He touched her belly lightly.

His words tugged at her heartstrings, and she melted into his arms. "My Amir, the father of our child." He groaned as he bent his head and his lips found hers.

"Morola, promise me you won't ever forget me, remember how completely I loved you," he whispered, his voice hoarse. She felt him shudder. His touch had a definite urgency to it, his eyes filled with an unfathomable emotion.

"Stop talking like this, please," she whispered imploringly.

He just smiled sadly, knowingly, as he lifted her off her feet and laid her gently on their bed and kissed her tenderly. "Stay with me a while, Sarauniya. Please."

They left for work later than they had both planned, and he still insisted on dropping her off at work instead of going straight to his office at HQ. She had changed into a teal damask mandarin collar dress with nude piping and nude shoes and he had simply just picked out a fresh uniform from the several he had hanging in his closet. They were at her office, driving through the estate manager's private entrance they insisted she also used for security purposes. She was about to alight from the SUV, Raliat was already holding the car door handle ready to let her out when Kaniz suddenly said, "Bamidele, give us a minute."

He then asked his ADC too to disembark. They were alone in the LX570 with its heavily tinted windows, in their cool, soundproof, bulletproof capsule.

"I just don't want to leave you yet, Morola," he said wistfully. And as he held her hand against his heart, she could feel his heart throb under her palm.

He pointed at his heart under her palm. "Thank you my heartbeat, you have loved me beyond my pain." He gazed at her contemplatively. "I don't regret loving you with such abandon from the very first day." His voice was just above a whisper in that deep baritone. He shook his head. "No regrets."

"Amir, see you in the evening. Tega can join us for dinner? Okay?" She smiled, trying to lighten the mood. He bent his head and pressed his lips into her palm. Quite unlike him, he didn't respond to her chirpy banter about the evening plans.

He spoke slowly and his voice stayed low. He was shaking his head, trying to control his emotions. He looked away from her as he spoke, looking into oblivion. Something was up today; he could feel it.

"I don't know how to do this, my love, I just don't know, how to say good. . ."

His hold on her hand tightened, then he lowered his head and closed his eyes gently as he switched to Hausa. He poured forth a river of words in a cadence that sounded like a prayer or an invocation. Her heart felt like it could burst at the passion with which he spoke. As suddenly as he had started, he stopped and raised his head.

"Forgive me, my love, I should handle this better."

He shook his head as if to clear his thoughts, his voice was quieter, calmer. He was making an effort to maintain control, breathing in deeply, steadily, as he was trained to do. He turned his head back to her and looked into her eyes and his eyes were red with emotion.

Her heart went out to him in that moment, seeing him look at her with such a mixture of love and longing. She flipped the car's arm rest out of the way and rushed into his arms, holding him tight, her head on his shoulder. She could feel his artery throbbing against her left cheek. Reaching up, she kissed the throbbing artery on his neck, and as he shuddered, she kissed his lips tenderly.

"My baby," She whispered. "Ademi, I love you so much."

She always knew what to do to reach Kaniz – placate him when he was angry, calm him when he was stressed, make him laugh when he was melancholy – but not this time it seemed; this was defying her wisdom. Her heart broke at his pain. What could she do to take this weight off him?

At the touch of her lips, his pent-up emotions broke loose and he responded to her kiss with a passion that took her breath away. Her heart was racing when he paused, his lips still against hers.

"Promise me. Promise me you and our son will be fine, Sarauniya." His voice was hoarse and low.

She nodded slightly. What did he mean?

"I need to hear you *say* you will be alright, Morola. I need to hear you *say* it so I can leave in peace," he whispered, his lips were still touching hers.

"We will be fine, my Amir," she whispered. "Our baby, you and I; we will all be fine."

He exhaled and held her even tighter. "Set me as a seal upon your heart, my love." He relaxed his hold on her and laid his right hand gently over her heart. "It is mine, it is all mine," he said wistfully. "I never shared you with anyone."

"My Amir, you are my *first* love. I have never loved any man *before* you; I cannot love any *beside* you."

He groaned and she felt him shudder again as he kissed her again with more urgency.

""Morola, my love for you is as strong as *death* remember... always." He sighed, lifting his head up slightly and resting his forehead against hers. "I need to let you go now." His hand was still intertwined with hers, his right hand gently cradling her cheek.

He finally exhaled and let go of her hand as a tremor passed through his hand to hers. She didn't understand why, but a pall fell on her at that moment. She mentally shook off the morbid shroud and without another word, hopped down from the car's high seat. Once she was on the ground, she turned back and looked at him. He hadn't moved a muscle. He sat perfectly motionless, just gazing at her with that inexplicable sadness.

"See you later, Amir," she said cheerfully.

"Goodnight, Sarauniya," he replied, barely audible. "Goodnight, my heartbeat."

Good night? It was barely 8 a.m. He was still staring at her with that alloy of sadness and longing. He still hadn't moved.

"We need to ask Dr Abe who to see about this depression," she thought, blowing him a kiss. And that was the last time she had seen her Amir alive.

Chapter Thirty-Five

"What are these wounds in thine hands? Then he shall answer, those which I was wounded in the house of my friends."

Zechariah 13:6

Though the detour to Synergy had meant taking a totally different route to the HQ, Kaniz had arrived at work in good time. The HQ was housed in a repurposed five-storey office block on a good-sized plot. The Quartet – Kola the Head of Strategy, Funso in intelligence, and Jude, who General Adewale had thought best to be in "Special Duties" – and General Adewale, were all stationed in the HQ to enable easy communication and nimble decision-making.

The Joint Chiefs were stationed in the Defence HQ and were on retreat. Every Wednesday, they all met as the NTC but today was not a Wednesday. It had been an extremely busy Friday, and he was billed to have a meeting with General Adewale at 5:00 p.m., but it was 4:55 p.m. already and General's principal assistant had just informed him that Adewale had not yet arrived from his external meetings. General never missed a meeting without prior notice, so, perhaps he had also tried to reach him unsuccessfully.

He also had been trying to call Morola all day, but it seemed there was something wrong with his phone, the network couldn't be that bad. That was probably why General hadn't been able to reach him. The meeting with Funso to approve the new generation RPGs was at 6 p.m. To be honest, why he had to approve was not too clear to Kaniz but in an attempt to ameliorate the tension the recent findings on Funso was causing their relationship, he agreed to meet with his friend.

At 5:05 p.m., his secretary called him. A very efficient older man in his late forties, HR had sent him over a month ago. Kaniz's secretary boomed over the intercom to announce the arrival of Major Ajayi. *Why was Funso here almost a whole hour early*? He wondered.

"Tell him to come in."

Funso came in and saluted. Funso was being really formal these days. He motioned to his friend to sit and Funso took his seat in one of the two black fabric visitors chairs in front of Kaniz's desk.

Behind Funso came four burly NCOs carrying two rather long wooden boxes, over six feet long, Kaniz estimated the lengths at about 6'6'. Interesting. The new generation RPGs couldn't be this long, or could they? Perhaps they were arranged in a double bank? That had to be it. Why show him two sets? There had to be two different models.

"You should inspect before we approve and order," Funso was explaining. "You are the expert. You dealt with all the hardware for *Operation Shield*."

His intercom buzzed again and Kaniz took his eyes off Funso for a few seconds as he leaned to pick up the hand piece. He felt the needle prick on his neck before he even saw it and instantly, paralysis spread through his limbs even as his eyes remained wide open. He could hear and see, but he couldn't make a sound nor move a limb. The payload discharged, Funso began disassembling a hypodermic needle. He threw the needle into Kaniz's trash can and kept the syringe in his pocket.

"So sorry I had to do this Kaniz, my brother. Really sorry, but there's no other way," he heard Funso say. He sounded like he was speaking from a mile away and as if Kaniz was hearing him through a tunnel.

So Funso really felt "there was no other way," but to kill his friend? Even as the paralysis spread through Kaniz's body, his anger at being called "brother" by this traitor also spread through his being. So his suspicions were right – Funso had indeed turned traitor. But to this level?

Funso motioned quietly to the two officers carrying the first box, and they prised open the cover easily with a pen knife. The box was empty and padded with foam. Both officers then picked up Kaniz's crumpled form and dropped him in the box, shutting the lid tight. Kaniz was in a box again in pitch darkness. Panic set into his very soul, but he was numb and unable to make a sound or move. Mercifully, whatever substance Funso had injected him with took full effect and he blacked out.

"Well done," Kaniz's secretary replied as the four men with the two heavy boxes greeted him as they departed. They had apparently left Major Funso Ajayi behind in the meeting with Group Captain Ishaya. When "they" called to ask whether the Group Captain and Major Ajayi were still in the office, he could confidently say they were still in HQ. "They" had been particularly interested in Group Captain Ishaya's movements today. It appeared that his coming in later than usual today was an aberration they hadn't planned for.

He had discharged his assignment of reporting on his boss's movements faithfully since he resumed. He was under strict orders to do so from these men who knew where he lived and even where both his sons were studying outside Lagos; in secondary schools in Enugu and Ibadan. He had never been under such duress in his life. His wife had reported that she saw strange men tailing her even to the market; the same two men now for four weeks running. He had no doubt that "they", the people who had called him on an unidentified number when he started this job and threatened him to comply with their instructions or lose his family, "they" were watching and waiting for any lapses on his part. "They" had extremely accurate details on everyone and even when he tried to make adjustments to his family's movements, "they" reported back to him on every step he had taken. When he tried to move house, "they" told him where he was planning to move to and even which estate agents he had been speaking with. It was pointless. He had to comply. He had been warned not to even consider resigning so he was well and truly stuck.

The two boxes were loaded in the back of the army green truck, covered with green tarpaulin. The back of the truck was loaded to capacity with similar wooden boxes, a cargo of RPGs bound for the armoury in Ikeja.

The truck trundled to the gate of the HQ burdened by its load. The sentries had recently been charged "to tighten security" with all the intelligence reports on imminent threats coming in. Those on duty this morning were particularly efficient but new to the HQ gate. No one went through or came in without a full check, absolutely no one. That was part of the reason for the change, to ensure that familiar faces did not get a free pass and everyone passed through equal scrutiny. The Chief Security Officer manning the post looked at the truck. A consignment of RPGs. He consulted the log. It was billed to pass through at 18:00 hours, this was 17:25 hours. It was early but that wasn't significant.

"Officer!" he shouted, "this consignment is passing early?"

The driver, a war-hardened NCO, replied, "We load am quick, no need to dey waste time. Traffic fit hook person if we no move now."

He made a solid point, the CSO thought.

"Wait," he called out. He had to check the consignment at least.

He moved to the back of the truck, motioned to the passenger riding in the front cab of the truck. The passenger promptly disembarked as the CSO pointed to a random box.

"Open am!"

The NCO looked taken aback for a split second. These were weapons with a tamper-proof chain of custody but he had seen the tension around HQ rapidly mount in the last months. This week was especially tense with all the changes in staffing, so he complied.

"Yes sir!"

He pried open the box with his Swiss army knife to reveal two rows of RPGs glinting in the sun.

The CSO seemed satisfied that everything was kosher.

"Pass!" the CSO commanded.

"Permission to exit!" he said to the sentries manning the gate barriers.

The NCO got back into the truck. The driver got the huge truck out of gear. The truck was passed through and was on its way to Ikeja.

Chapter Thirty-Six

"Many waters cannot quench love, neither can the floods drown it."

Songs of Solomon 8:7A

"Morola."

The voice pulled her back from her memories, jolting her rather rudely back to the present and back to the fetid dark dungeon and its horrors.

"My Amir's voice again." She smiled. Rola was convinced that if she didn't die soon, insanity would be the only coping mechanism she had. She had been fleeting in and out of consciousness for... for how long? In this dark hole, she had no way of measuring time. She opened her eyes and saw that the door to her dungeon was ajar and light filtered through.

"Dr Abe! She is here! In here, sir. Hurry!" Kaniz's voice again and now coming from an apparition.

She felt a flutter in her belly. Perhaps excited at "hearing" that voice, the body couldn't distinguish between fake and real stimuli. She could hear footsteps, not in soldiers' boots as she had heard the night she got here, but now it seemed in softer-soled shoes. She heard another voice saying, "Oh God." It was Dr Abe's voice.

Was she hallucinating now? And why was Dr Abe here with Kaniz in her delirium? She smiled. Her rational mind was still striving to order her madness, but this was insanity and it had a life of its own. It was fluid, creative, and it could take any form. Anyone could barge in uninvited in her delusion. Latex-sheathed hands were examining her now and a light of sorts was shining down on her, disorienting her. Her eyes were watering, shocked by the sudden light after days of pitch-black darkness.

"Oh no!" a third voice said, and it sounded like Funso's voice but muffled, like his mouth and nose were covered.

This delusion was now getting rather crowded; everyone wanted to feature in it. She was drifting back into her dark hole which obviated her pain. She felt strong arms pick her up and wet drops of warm liquid on her face.

"Hurry doctor, her clothes are stiff with blood," Kaniz voice was saying. "My love, what did I get you into?" He sounded distressed. She was on a stretcher. He was by her side and his eyes were wet. "Kaniz?"

It was a delusion, but she could play her own part too. Everyone else was doing what they wanted and what she wanted to do was touch her Amir's face, so she lifted her blood-encrusted hand and reached for his face but couldn't quite muster the strength. Her arm dropped, and she touched his arm as the stretcher raced ahead, strong hands propelling it. The forearm she touched felt solid. It felt like the familiar ripple of her Amir's muscles. It was a splendid and welcome delusion. She smiled as she sank again into the black hole, dead to the world and to the delusion.

She came round gradually. First the smell. The fetid stench was gone and in its place, was the pine-like smell of disinfectant and a leathery spicy fragrance, very comforting and familiar, stirring nostalgic emotions within her.

The heat had given way to coolness. She was no longer lying on a gritty slimy floor but on a cool, soft surface, feeling refreshingly clean.

The silence had given way to the gentle melody of one of her favourite songs – "Your grace abounds in deepest waters".

"Spirit lead me where my trust is without borders," she croaked, echoing the song. Her voice was hoarse, but she must have been audible because she heard Kaniz's voice above her head break as he said ever so softly, "My love."

She felt the drops of liquid on her face again. She felt the flutters in her belly at his voice.

The darkness had given way to light and the first face she saw was Kaniz's as he just held on to her hand and pressed it desperately to his lips.

He kept shaking his head as the tears poured down his face silently. But how? How was he alive? It didn't matter for now. For now, she would just enjoy him. Even if it was still a dream.

She managed to breathe out the word. "How?"

"Just get stronger first," he said. "No secrets."

"No secrets," she repeated weakly.

She saw Dr Abe come into her field of vision.

Kaniz turned to Dr Abe. "Doctor, she's awake."

Dr Abe. Their baby. Sadness swept over her. She had failed. She had promised, but she had failed Kaniz.

"Ademi, our baby died," she said. "He died," she repeated, crying as sadness swept her soul at the loss of their child, at her failure.

"They beat me. The men hit me all over. I tried to protect him, but they handcuffed me. I bled. So much blood. And pain..." Anguish swept her soul.

Perhaps the burden of her failure, the fact that she couldn't protect such a precious trust was too much for her mind to grapple with just yet. Kaniz was alive - but his cherished baby was dead. She had *failed*. She slipped into the blackness again.

Kaniz couldn't believe the state in which they had found Morola. The fact that she was alive was nothing short of a miracle. There was nothing to indicate that any attempt had been made to give her any form of nutrition or even water in the time she had been incarcerated. Her face was swollen from blunt force trauma. Her lips were cracked and swollen, and the blood, the blood seemed to have been everywhere. The heat and the stench in the dungeon had been intolerable and to Morola who was so sensitive to smell and heat, it must have been a living hell.

She had been locked up in complete darkness. No wonder she kept slipping in and out of consciousness. She was allowing her mind to rest, avoiding facing the pain. What had he gotten her into? Would she ever forgive him? Would she ever pardon him for this avoidable suffering that his choice to serve had exposed her to?

Kaniz could vividly recall the events of the day or at least the times when he had been conscious. He had come to in a bed in a rented house in Lekki. The first face he saw was Funso's and as he saw the traitor's face, he instinctively reached for his Glock in its holster, but his fingers were not working well yet. His right hand fell to his side and off the bed. Gradually, his muscles started working again. Funso was by his side, holding a glass of water, concern on his face.

"The drug can be very dehydrating. You need to have some water, Kaniz."

Kaniz wasn't going to take water from this beast. What did he know that his frenemy had laced the water with? He knocked the water out of Funso's hand with an unsteady swipe. His tongue was not cooperating yet so he didn't try to say a word.

General Adewale's face swam into his view and he smiled. "Ah! Kaniz, you are now with us. Good. Funso, I must confess, I had my doubts that this plan would work," he said.

Kola came into the room too and by this time, Kaniz could sit up properly. He sat up on the bed. It felt weird being in bed, fully clothed in his uniform and with his shoes on.

General drew a chair up to the bed and briefed him.

Major Jude King had seen the writing on the wall. He had killed a civilian to cover his corruption. Funso was gathering conclusive evidence that would trace at least three assassination attempts to him. There were not enough falsified autopsy reports in the world to get him out of this mess. Death by firing squad was inevitable, no matter what the outcomes were, and he opted to go down fighting.

Jude had a coup underway as they spoke, he had taken over HQ at 6 p.m. This was a time when all the principals were usually at the HQ. Jude had studied the patterns and knew the best time to strike. At 6 p.m., the guests and external meetings would have been dealt with and the foot traffic subsided so he could take HQ with fewer men.

Major King was working with mercenaries. Kaniz was right in alluding to the fact that Jude hadn't started spending ostentatiously. He had squirrelled about 7.5 million dollars of the money away in accounts from what Funso had been able to trace successfully, but he had also invested several millions of dollars into the coup. It was not yet clear how much. Investigations were ongoing, but the scale hinted at, was enough cause for concern. Mercenaries and weaponry were not cheap.

General was departing from his meeting at Defence HQ with Dr Kola Toriola and the NSA, General Chukum, when Major Funso Ajayi had intercepted them with the news of the coup. They had been immediately diverted to the safe house. The Joint Chiefs had almost arrived at the retreat venue when the soldiers sent by Funso, reached them and diverted them. Jude's mercenaries were still lying in wait at the venue. The disinformation they had been fed through the venue management was that the Joint Chiefs were still in transit. Major King had limited troops. Because General and the NTC had too many loyalists, he had been forced to work with soldiers of fortune. By tying down his men at various locations with decoys, they were already derailing Jude's logistics.

Kaniz's case was special. He was meant to have been the first casualty because of the definite loss of morale his death would cause, nationwide. The assault squad had laid in wait for him just 300m after the last checkpoint out of Toju Teniola close from 06:30 hours till as late as 07:30 hours.

Another squad had laid wait for him on his route to work from 06:30 hours to 08:00 hours. Both squads had laid in wait and had only departed when he had not shown up. Kaniz, without fail would have encountered both squads on the way to HQ in the morning but bizarrely, he hadn't shown up at the usual time this morning, and the route he then took from home to work was different. He hadn't been anywhere he should have been today at his usual set times. He had completely deviated from his routine.

General looked at Kaniz quizzically at this point. What had happened today? Kaniz remembered what had happened. Who he had been with at the time when he would have been felled by a hail of bullets. "Stay for a while please," he had said that morning, and the fact that his wife had stayed back and let them share that magical moment together had saved his life. He had insisted on dropping her off at the office afterward. He was missing her already and it just seemed like the right thing to do after that beautiful morning. His heart was so heavy even when he was to drop her off; he just couldn't let her go and therefore, he had spent even more time at her office.

His movements would have seemed deliberately evasive to those stalking him, but it was not deliberate. It was all because he wanted to be with his wife for as long as he could because he felt he was saying a final goodbye. He could see the question in General's eyes but offered no explanation.

"General, my wife!" Had he indeed been saying a final goodbye? "Is she safe? I haven't been able to reach her all day." He spoke for the first time and sat bolt upright, his expression animated with grave concern. If anything had happened to Morola...

Funso replied, "She is okay. She is not even on the list of targets. We have reliable intel. You couldn't reach her because network services have been suspended since 9 a.m. Jude has taken over the GSM companies. They couldn't achieve complete nationwide shutdown immediately but right now in Lagos, we have no network and nationally, we have no fibre optics. You may have noticed that your emails too weren't sending. We are communicating on the few secure radio lines we have.

"You arrived at HQ this morning and from the time you arrived, your every movement was being watched by that new secretary of yours," General continued. "You were not to be allowed to leave HQ before the full assault started at 6 p.m., by which time, I was also meant to be in there with Dr Toriola and Major Ajayi. You couldn't even leave if you tried to, because Jude's man was already manning the ingress and egress at the sentry post."

He shook his head. "I thought putting him in Special Duties without any specific portfolio would render him harmless, but he managed to take over HR and staffing."

Funso had to arrange to evacuate Kaniz in the empty RPG boxes. Funso himself had been carried out by the NCOs in the second box because the head of the new sentries had been warned not to let General, Kaniz, Kola and Funso through. The boxes were the only way to smuggle themselves out. Kaniz didn't trust Funso anymore and even if he did, he wouldn't ever willingly get into another dark box. The only way was to immobilise him.

"So sorry I had to do this, Kaniz, my brother. Really sorry, but there's no other way." That was why Funso apologised – for immobilising him.

Funso had endangered his life by venturing into HQ that evening to spring Kaniz. The truck carrying the boxes had now been driven to the Mainland for the sake of those waiting to see if it arrived, but had discharged four precious boxes; two of which harbored Kaniz and Funso on a slight detour along the way. The van which the truck had discharged its precious cargo into had then turned into this rental safe house Funso had prepared for such a day as this.

Jude and his mercenaries had taken over HQ now, but there was no member of the NTC there.

Jude's men had control of the radio stations, the TV houses and the HQ. He could announce his takeover, spread disinformation but hadn't captured the key personnel he needed to silence to take over power. The communications blackout was to ensure he had sufficient time to take over.

The counter-coup was on. The least of their worries was the media stations. They would get to those later that night. They were each being held by about four mercenaries who had taken the broadcasters and technicians hostage. They were mercenaries, likely to give up once Jude was taken. The focus was to capture Jude and the two military officers he had managed to persuade to join this ill-advised attempt – Colonel James Prince and Major Ezekiel Wisdom.

Jude and Major Wisdom were holed up in the HQ with eighteen mercenaries and the staff. The GOCs had been mobilised and GOC 6 under Brigadier General Akpata had engaged the HQ. GOC 8 had sent a company to Camp Daniel, where the retreat was to have taken place. A battalion would have been excessive. There were just twenty mercenaries there under the rebel Colonel Prince's command.

The counter-coup was proceeding swiftly and so far, very well. The tide was turning at the battlefront at the HQ.

Jude sat on Kaniz's chair, his feet on Kaniz's desk. He dropped his AK 47 on the desk in front of him and looked around the spartan office of the chief of staff. His thoughts were racing. Chief of staff? He hissed. The Quartet was Kaniz's brainchild but where was he when the others were the boots on the ground? The entitled idiot was on another plush assignment, defence attaché in Colombia, never mind that everyone he had asked had said Colombia was a serious "hardship" posting. Hardship or not, where had he, Jude, ever been posted to? Entitled brat.

His face was a grimace as he considered the situation, going by the steady sound of gunfire outside. There was no way of getting out of this alive. No way. He at least should have delivered on his task of eliminating Group Captain Ishaya and General Adewale and he would be sure to have derailed the NTC. Dr Toriola and Funso would have been a real bonus, and AVM Woriabam and the Joint Chiefs would have been the icing on the cake. But those four, those first four were the moral compasses of the NTC, and somehow, they had escaped. He had a mole. He shook his head. Or perhaps, he just didn't have enough loyal men. Mercenaries were mercenaries after all. They fought for money.

Was *he* a mercenary? No. He was fighting for his own life. He was about to be eliminated militarily, which made him better than these mercenaries in his own eyes.

Jude was resolved. He would die, but he would inflict incalculable pain on this holier-than-thou Kaniz. This boy who had everything going for him but still wanted to be everything. Who has such a rich father and joins the air force? When he, Jude, had been abandoned by his father since he was nineteen? Kaniz had a doting wealthy father. Kaniz had his father's vast wealth and still, from all indications, he had gone to a university abroad on an air force scholarship. He, Jude, put himself through polytechnic, selling anything he could sell, including his body.

He had joined the Quartet because he thought this was finally his chance to make a name for himself, for the abandoned boy to become the celebrated hero... how did he end up the villain, with Kaniz, the boy with everything, becoming the celebrated folk hero of *Operation Shield* fame?

Kaniz had massive respect in everyone's eyes. General Adewale said Kaniz fought for him, Jude, to get on the NTC. Shouldn't he have been there on merit? That was such an insult that day. How could one man have everything? While he, Jude, didn't even have a father.

The same Kaniz decided he would get married. And see who he married. That beautiful, intelligent, well-bred girl. One who didn't even need Kaniz's money, not like the girls, he picked up who were such a drain on his resources. Kaniz had a truly lovely wife, one that was the light of his eyes. While he, Jude, had to make do with a procession of paid girls he could barely afford on the measly pay he got.

Then they started investigating him for collecting money from his benefactors. How much was his pay? Was Kaniz living on his own pay? Jude laughed sardonically as he remembered how Kaniz transformed radically around his wife. His body language shifted and his eyes took her in as if there was no one else around. It didn't matter what the setting was, Kaniz would find an excuse to touch Mrs Ishaya. He softened, he smiled easily. That was it. *That* was the key.

"Kaniz, you may have lived through this, but I will make sure you pray for death before this is over," he said aloud.

He spat on the carpet with a look of utter disgust. "Chief of staff," he hissed.

He picked up his radio. "Charlie—Fox—tango," he said and gave the men their orders.

The eight men stationed three hundred meters away from the checkpoint at Toju Teniola close started their trucks and drove towards the Ishaya's residence. They drove their first bulletproof truck straight towards the checkpoint and sprayed a hail of gunfire at the sentries. The sentries rallied and cut down one of them. The second truck ran through the breach the first had created in the checkpoint. The element of surprise had taken the sentries off guard. The men had their orders – get to the Ishaya's residence and extract Mrs Ishaya to the location they had received. Do not kill her yet. Death would be too easy.

Kaniz and Funso arrived at Toju Teniola barely ten minutes after the men left with Rola. Kaniz was intent on securing the house despite all remonstrations that it was unnecessary. From the sentry station at the entrance to the close, it was clear that security had been breached. Wounded sentries were radioing for backup. They got to the house with the squad he had intended to put in charge of securing the house following behind and found the huge front door ajar. A captain, a survivor from the sentry station stood guard. They went in.

The glass table in the anteroom was shattered by gunfire. A dead soldier of fortune was in the anteroom – felled by Raliat's bullet. A blood trail led to the study where Kaniz had found Paul, palpably shaken, trying to clean the gory mess on the study desk. Tega's corpse lay on the floor. Raliat had roused but had done so too late, to pursue the men.

Chapter Thirty-Seven

"...also He has put eternity in their hearts, except that no one can find out the work that God does from beginning to the end."

Eccelesiates 3:11B

Daybreak on Saturday ushered in victory, and jubilation took over as the disinformation of Kaniz's death was disproven. Jude was captured alive, as was Colonel Prince and Major Wisdom. Many of the mercenaries were "wasted", as the military boys said later. They seemed to despise these soldiers of fortune who fought not for principles, loyalty or country but for dollars.

The NSA had advised that the news of Mrs Ishaya's capture should not be made public if the chances of finding her alive were to be maximised. But it took two more harrowing days, in which Funso and the NSA painstakingly gathered intel and followed every lead to find Rola in the disused prison; abandoned, alone and locked in. Funso's men had followed the lead provided by one of the men at the location where Mrs Ishaya was brought in that night. Her face was too bruised for him to recognise her from the photo, but he knew they had taken a woman in that night and had then been ordered to leave the location and not return. They had cut off the power and left the building.

Kaniz was heartbroken at the intel – his Morola had been dumped in a facility without power, water, nothing, for two days and nights as she lay severely injured.

The soldiers had searched high and low and were about to leave the location when shouts of "Mrs Ishaya!" had received no response as they proceeded through the disused facility overgrown with weeds and other vegetation. They had stepped back into the daylight outside the prison, about to set off in their truck when a little boy had come up to them and insisted that he saw a lady being dragged into the derelict prison and he could hear her screams.

Somehow, the war-hardened soldiers had listened to the boy and radioed for an ambulance immediately. Then they resumed their search with renewed zeal and started knocking down every door. They were about shattering the lock on the metal door of the solitary confinement cell Rola was in when Kaniz, Dr Abe and Funso had arrived with an ambulance and paramedics.

When they came out of the dark prison into the daylight, with Mrs Ishaya safely on her way in the ambulance to the hospital, accompanied by Kaniz, Funso asked the soldiers why they had heeded the little boy and one of them had said, "There was just something about him." He sounded embarrassed as he admitted, "His voice filled me with hope." Kaniz insisted they had to find him. He had to reward him in one way or the other; give him a scholarship or something. So, the new search was for the little boy. They had combed the neighbouring village, but didn't find him. No child matched that description.

That had been two days ago. Morola had slipped into unconsciousness after she had come round for a few minutes and told him their baby was dead.

What would he tell Mrs B and TK who were outside, waiting, sitting with his father, if today passed and she still didn't wake up? Mrs B was calmer, but TK seemed worried to distraction. What would he say to Morola's parents? They had given him their daughter's hand for less than a year and see what had happened. TK had said to him in Yoruba on the day of the traditional wedding, "I am giving you a living daughter. You won't bring me back a corpse."

And he had answered, "Amen, sir, by God's grace."

This wasn't a disease or infirmity or an inevitable incident that had cruelly snatched her away from him. This was the result of his own decision to serve. His own colleague had done this to his wife.

Jude knew how precious Morola was to him and had decided to obliterate Kaniz in every way. Not only kill him, but wipe out his legacy. Jude knew that as long as Rola was still living and breathing, she was too strong a woman to let Kaniz be forgotten, so he had gone after not only Kaniz, but Rola also. The plan was to use her as leverage, if need be, while she was alive and when she was no longer useful to his cause, to let her die a slow, painful death in that disused prison; abandoned to die in the hole. Jude was a master of irony. He had chosen to throw the advocate of women in prison into a disused prison to die.

Rola didn't stir at all anymore. He moved closer to her and whispered into her ears. "Come back to me, Morola. I know you can hear me. You promised. You promised you would never leave me, but now you are not even trying anymore. Stay with me, Morola. Only God knows how much I need you."

After two long days and two long nights, sleep deprivation was messing with his mind, but he didn't want to doze in case she woke up and needed him. The fatigue from the sleepless nights was breaking Kaniz down. He wasn't ready to go out of this room and face another barrage of questions from the parties waiting outside. As for Amaka, she was no help at all. She was worse than the three elders. She was distraught and beside herself. Only the nurses kept them at bay.

Deep within him, he believed she would wake up, but his faith in a positive outcome didn't stop his emotions from spilling over.

He was physically and mentally tired, absolutely fatigued. Conflicting emotions clashed within him – relief and the tension of the last few years with the risky venture he had committed to. Then meeting Morola and struggling with the idea that he was free to love and be loved in return. The tension he had felt loving her when it became clear it was going to be short-lived, committing to heaven that he would fit a lifetime of loving into the few months. Loving her like a man who knew his days were numbered. The struggle. The conflict. Should he restrain himself and rein in on expressing his love for her so she would miss him less when he was gone? Or should he love her without holding back so she would always remember him and hold him in her heart, regardless of who would come after him? Was it really selfish of him to want her to never forget him? Was it not kinder to release her to a new life free of his memory?

Every time he thought of his Morola bearing another man's name, his heart twisted in pain. He hurt at the thought of his child growing up under another man's protection, calling another man "Daddy". How long before her first love, Kaniz, became a faint memory, subsumed in the shadows of time? He had battled the conflict on long nights, lying awake, holding her in his arms and yet missing her in advance. The assassination attempts and then the short-lived relief that he had more time with her. The daily dangers he faced that he hadn't been able to share with her, escalating dramatically every week after, till death became a certainty and the only uncertainty was exactly *when* and *how* he was going to be killed.

He had dealt with dutifully tidying up his will, his affairs, trying to prepare Morola for the inevitable. That Friday morning, as she started to get dressed all over again, it was all he could do to put on a brave face as he finally let her out of his arms. He was certain that was the last time he would hold her and feel the warmth of her embrace. He had seen her off to work that day and the tension had come to a crescendo. While trying to say goodbye, something inside him had rebelled at leaving her, and he had burst out praying in Hausa that the pall of death should lift.

Had he not been told his season of rejoicing had just started? How could he leave his best friend behind as a widow? Bereft? That Friday in the car, he wasn't concerned about himself but for Morola. She loved him with a love that compassed him. His thoughts inexorably strayed back again to their time together earlier that morning. He relied on her love. Morola would be shattered at his death. Devastated.

"Oh Lord, only You know the depth of my love for Your daughter. Spare us this pain," he had prayed. "Only You understand what we feel for each other. Have mercy. This doesn't have to be our last moment together. You can intervene. Oh God, it doesn't have to end this way. Let the plans of the wicked fail. Let them be caught in the snare they have set for me." And his prayers that morning had been spectacularly answered.

Then the tension created by Jude's ill-fated moves soon followed. Right now, he was relieved that she was alive, that Funso's frantic search led them to her eventually. And just for seeing her alive again, he was infinitely grateful, but at the same time, he was sad that she was still lost to him, unconscious.

Why did everyone think he was so strong? Why did everyone think he was a rock? He was glad that he was alone with her, hiding out in her private ward. He broke down and sobbed silently. He was overwhelmed. He now understood why Jesus wept at Lazarus' grave. The Lord knew fully well He would still raise His friend Lazarus up from the dead but confronted with all the pain from Mary and Martha whom He loved and the crowd grieving, he empathised with those who mourned and His emotions flowed over.

If Jesus could cry, Kaniz could too. He sat in the chair by her bedside alone as his shoulders shook with silent sobs. He was tired on every level. Gradually, the racking sobs gave way to silent tears. His mind needed to rest a bit, so he laid his head on her pillow, placing his head right beside his wife's head as he whispered again fervently, "Come back to me, Morola. Please, please. Father... please."

The room remained silent and the only sound in it was the hum of St Paul's state of the art medical equipment in the VIP ward.

"Amir? Kaniz?" Rola's voice broke the silence.

It had been a struggle to comfort Rola. Within minutes of her coming round, she remembered Tega's death. Raliat's survival was a consolation but she struggled with the loss of Tega.

"Was it my fault Kaniz? He was helping me. Tega... What will Jolomi say? How will Jolomi cope?"

The doctors couldn't sedate her, not so soon after she just woke up, so she struggled with the pain.

Kaniz held tightly on to her, reassuring her.

"Jolomi is coping, we have been to see her, she is under our watch. It wasn't your fault, my love, you didn't shoot him. He was there by choice."

Finally, he just held her head close to his chest and rocked her gently as she sobbed as if her heart would break.

When the doctors came back two hours later, Rola was calmer. Kaniz had that effect on her as she seemed to have on him too.

Dr Abe was happy to see Mrs Ishaya stable and coherent. She had now taken some water and liquid nutrition orally and the prognosis was good. She looked set for a full recovery. She was young, twenty-nine last November, her body healed fast and the swelling was subsiding. The chief of staff too was looking much better. At a point, he was almost getting as worried about him as he was about his wife. He remembered the "tribe" waiting outside the door, ready to burst in any moment, but he had a few things to discuss with her first.

"Mrs Ishaya, Dr Folarin is also here." He observed her to see if she could recollect properly and saw the light of recognition in her eyes. Dr Folarin had done that first intrusive scan. She wrinkled her nose and Dr Abe smiled.

"The bleeding was from a threatened miscarriage. You bled pretty badly and the muscular pain must have been from the same trauma that caused the threatened miscarriage – the beating you received. You were covered in bruises on your lower back and lower abdomen, Mrs Ishaya." He shook his head. "You went through a lot, but your baby is fine. Your baby is fine, Mrs Ishaya," Dr Folarin repeated for emphasis. "This is the ultrasound scan from this morning."

A file flipped open in her peripheral vision and a fuzzy scan was held in front of her face.

"His heartbeat is strong. You have a brilliant one. He seems to recognise daddy's voice already." Dr Folarin was smiling widely.

"We took the liberty of checking the baby's gender. Although I suspect you may have already guessed you're expecting a son? The chief of staff does not look surprised."

"But the contractions, the pain," Rola said. Her rational mind was trying to make sense of her experience.

"They weren't true contractions, Mrs Ishaya. You just had severe muscular pains from the beating." Dr Abe winced at the thought of all the bruises they had seen resulting from the injuries his young patient had sustained. "But your child survived and is fine. Amniotic fluid is at a good level. No leakage. Your cervix is closed. No infection."

Morola was dumbfounded. Kaniz was alive? Kaniz's child was fine? Was she now dead and in heaven?

Mrs B knew without a doubt that her daughter would be found alive. She had prayed fervently before she supported Rola and Kaniz's relationship and she knew that if it was going to end in such an unmitigated disaster, she couldn't have felt the measure of peace she felt at the time she took the decision to back them both. She looked at her daughter. She had lost weight but the bruises had faded and the cut at her temple from the gun butt was mercifully close to her hairline.

Rola had pointed to the slight scar a few minutes ago and said to Kaniz. "Are we twinning?" She smiled, her eyes dancing.

Could Morolawe not even be serious for once? Mrs B smiled.

They both now had scars on their left temples. But Rola's own scar would fade in mere months. Mrs B hoped the memories too would fade. The birth of her grandchild should help replace the dark memories with joyful ones.

Jude's ill-fated coup and the cruelty he had subjected Rola to after attempting to eliminate her husband had brought Rola and Kaniz incredible social capital. Strangely, human beings empathised with suffering and seemed to find suffering an endearing trait in leaders. Perhaps it made them find the powerful human more relatable.

The NTC had less than two months to go and the elections were still on course in spite of Jude and his collaborators' best plans. Kaniz had put in his resignation from the air force to coincide with the end of the NTC's six-month tenure. He was well and truly done.

Rola had insisted that the best homecoming gift Kaniz could give her was not any type of celebration, especially not in the light of recent events. She sighed as she recollected. She was grateful Raliat had survived. Her bulletproof vest had stopped the coup plotter's bullet, but Tega's death had taken a lot to get over.

She was grateful for her husband's understanding. He had proposed to General Adewale that an endowment be made for Jolomi and General had approved. General had impressed her with his care; as soon as she came round, he had been to see her in the hospital and he came back three other times. He teased her for "fighting for the cause" and half-jokingly promised her a medal. Sincerely though, he respected her for all she had suffered and survived. AVM too had been so caring. It had been a surreal hell, but she had survived by God's grace. All she wanted and had asked for now was what Kaniz and herself never seemed to have enough of. She wanted them to have *time* with each other. She suspected he had called everyone to keep away at least till evening. The call she got from Amaka seemed to suggest they were all straining to keep away.

Their house was peaceful and quiet. The attentiveness of the hospital staff and the incessant checks were enough to make a well person fall sick.

Rola was just glad to be back home as they sat in "their" sofa in the family living room. The TV, though on, was on mute to allow Kaniz sleep as she read rather than listened to the news – reading the headlines as they scrolled on the screen. Which one of these headlines could any human being have predicted accurately a year ago? She certainly could not have guessed in her wildest imaginations the events of the last year or so in her own life. She could not believe how much had transpired between then and now. Was it not just about a year ago she had been celebrating Di's birthday with friends at dinner in Bryant Park? When she had popped back into Manhattan for a week to see to Synergy? Thoughts of returning home for what was left of her youth service were the closest hint she had of the events that had now unfolded.

Fifteen months ago, she had just met him and she genuinely couldn't stand him. She smiled. She looked down, her gaze going beyond the gentle rump of her midriff to the father of her child and the enigma who had become such a joy to her. "My Amir," she whispered to herself, "my crown, my king." She contemplated his handsome features – his head on her lap, his long frame stretched across the rest of the sofa. He was breathing gently in deep sleep, his expression completely relaxed.

Her friend, her husband, her lover. Kaniz, whose words pulled at her heartstrings. She smiled and as if inexorably drawn, her fingers brushed his scar and his greying left temple, and he stirred in his slumber. The grey creating a striking contrast to his ebony black skin. He needed and deserved the rest. She gazed at his serene face and her heart melted with compassion for him. She respected how hard he strived to do right. It was a paradox to her how one man could be her baby and her Amir at the same time, but she felt so protective of him at moments like this.

At the touch of her fingers on his temple, he subconsciously snuggled closer to her, with his face nestling closer to her belly. A year ago, she could never have believed any man could love her so passionately, so sacrificially, so unabashedly. She sighed. She would never have believed any man could make her love him back so much. Sometimes, her heart actually ached thinking about him. Kaniz. Even at the beginning, she had known this one wouldn't be "managed" and as he had declared, he had gotten what he wanted. He had said with certainty that day he dropped her off at camp, "You can't run away from me, Morola. It won't work." And at that joint, "I want you, Morola, all of you. Nothing held back."

And Kaniz kept on plying her with flagons of pure love until she was totally intoxicated. Kaniz had cocooned her completely with his love and he now truly had all of her.

It had been rough recently, but that part of their lives was coming to an end. She was happy. She exhaled as she turned back to reading the news. She had been recovering so Kaniz hadn't been able to fill her in yet. She had shown scant interest in the politics that had begun to take over the atmosphere with six weeks to go for the elections to hold. This was a three-horse race with none of the three parties sure to win the presidential elections. The populace really had had their fill of the jaded politicians.

People were now made more politically aware. They had tasted focused and expedient, no-waste and efficient leadership under the NTC for almost five months and the scramble to field candidates as credible as the electorate had seen demonstrated in the NTC had proved futile. The strongest candidate had also come under the pall of suspicion with whisperings of having a hand in Jude's putsch. Nothing was proven, but the streets believed what the streets believed. The "Big 3", as they were called, had been "in talks" all week to consolidate their position and map out the way ahead. They were yet to announce any headway in their talks but they were set to make a statement of sorts today.

Big 3 round up talks, issue communiqué adopting Kaniz Ishaya as a consensus presidential candidate. The scrolling words caught Rola's attention and she gasped. It went on to explain that the "Big 3" recognised the figure Kaniz Ishaya cut in the mind of the people and after weeks of consultations, the three presidential candidates had stepped down and decided to adopt Kaniz as the consensus candidate for the presidency only.

"What?" she shouted. "Not Kaniz." Kaniz stirred, startled awake at the sound of his name. "It's nothing, Amir." She soothed him but he was already rousing.

"No way. Not again," she mouthed silently. She calmed herself down. No one had spoken to Kaniz about it. By announcing it publicly this way, they were trying to make the decision a fait accompli. Everything would be alright. Consensus candidate for the "Big 3"? That meant he would effectively be president-elect if he accepted. Already, she could see both their phones which were on silent mode by her outstretched legs ringing incessantly but she studiously ignored the frantic calls.

The pressure to accept was about to start, no doubt. Kaniz was done with all these public roles, wasn't he? He would turn down the offer. He was awake now and wondering what the noise was for. They would sort it out. He wouldn't accept. Would he?

Acknowledgement

I am sure this attempt at acknowledgements will land me in trouble if I forget someone I shouldn't have.

So, I will try to be chronological and hope to stay on track. First to my editor, Enajite, who believed in this book as soon as she heard my story and demonstrated a rare dedication and devotion to the project by handing me a publishing contract. Enajite, I truly appreciate you.

To my classmate from university and collaborator, Muhtar Bakare, Director of Kachifo Limited, who went way beyond the call of duty to ensure the project was kept on track. Thank you for believing so much in me and helping me add yet another dimension to a life that is already multifaceted.

To Pastor Agu Irukwu for getting my perspective right on this book. Indeed, without your encouragement, I would probably never have signed the publishing contract. Thank you, PAI, for reading a pretty rough first draft that I couldn't even read myself! Thank you for always believing that I can deliver value, regardless of the task.

To Toluwaloju, my son, for saying, "Mum, go for it! All your other books are nothing like this one will be." Even when I despaired about the very serious me writing fiction, you assured me, "Mum, I am sooo proud of you." Without your support, I certainly wouldn't have felt I should write a work of fiction.

Thank you, Toluwalase, Mrs A's son and friend, for your unrelenting faith in me. Always, no exceptions.

Thank you, Mr A, for condoning my constant typing and complete absorption in my writing while I worked on this book.

To my dear BJ, you read the manuscript on your laptop, your phone

and listened to the audio. You kept me writing chapter after chapter. I had to write and send the next chapter to BJ. You have no idea how incredibly motivating your expectant calls were. It was not a breeze writing hundreds of thousands of words myself, but the fact that I had to send the next chapter to you kept me punching away at my MacBook. Thanks for your sincere and positive feedback.

To "my sis", Olutola Omotola, it takes a special woman and great client to attempt to read a work of fiction your very serious architect who delivered on your project less than a year ago wrote. You took me seriously, which attests to your amazing character. Thanks for your truly, awesomely, encouraging feedback, even on a badly punctuated first draft. You know how highly I regard your discretion and good taste; you are my favourite client and that explains a lot. Your feedback meant the world to me!

Thank you, Tola Odeyemi, for your encouragement and sincere, positive feedback, for the real inspiration you were, reading the draft, hanging in there with me as I tweaked various things. You are a blessing Tola! I truly appreciate you.

Rhema! Your millennial biases helped me see what the challenges we are facing are and helped me address and set out issues we all would have taken for granted. Thanks for the fresh eyes you brought to reading the draft. I sincerely appreciate you.

Emmanuel Oyeleke, what do I say? You are a gem. You always answer when I call. Thanks for believing in my cover concept and coming through brilliantly as always.

It has been really hard work, but a lot of fun writing a story I had carried within me since I was sixteen. I never knew I could type 180,000 words in under a month.

I am almost tempted to write a second novel...

Acknowledgement

I am sure this attempt at acknowledgements will land me in trouble if I forget someone I shouldn't have.

So, I will try to be chronological and hope to stay on track. First to my editor, Enajite, who believed in this book as soon as she heard my story and demonstrated a rare dedication and devotion to the project by handing me a publishing contract. Enajite, I truly appreciate you.

To my classmate from university and collaborator, Muhtar Bakare, Director of Kachifo Limited, who went way beyond the call of duty to ensure the project was kept on track. Thank you for believing so much in me and helping me add yet another dimension to a life that is already multifaceted.

To Pastor Agu Irukwu for getting my perspective right on this book. Indeed, without your encouragement, I would probably never have signed the publishing contract. Thank you, PAI, for reading a pretty rough first draft that I couldn't even read myself! Thank you for always believing that I can deliver value, regardless of the task.

To Toluwaloju, my son, for saying, "Mum, go for it! All your other books are nothing like this one will be." Even when I despaired about the very serious me writing fiction, you assured me, "Mum, I am sooo proud of you." Without your support, I certainly wouldn't have felt I should write a work of fiction.

Thank you, Toluwalase, Mrs A's son and friend, for your unrelenting faith in me. Always, no exceptions.

Thank you, Mr A, for condoning my constant typing and complete absorption in my writing while I worked on this book.

To my dear BJ, you read the manuscript on your laptop, your phone

and listened to the audio. You kept me writing chapter after chapter. I had to write and send the next chapter to BJ. You have no idea how incredibly motivating your expectant calls were. It was not a breeze writing hundreds of thousands of words myself, but the fact that I had to send the next chapter to you kept me punching away at my MacBook. Thanks for your sincere and positive feedback.

To "my sis", Olutola Omotola, it takes a special woman and great client to attempt to read a work of fiction your very serious architect who delivered on your project less than a year ago wrote. You took me seriously, which attests to your amazing character. Thanks for your truly, awesomely, encouraging feedback, even on a badly punctuated first draft. You know how highly I regard your discretion and good taste; you are my favourite client and that explains a lot. Your feedback meant the world to me!

Thank you, Tola Odeyemi, for your encouragement and sincere, positive feedback, for the real inspiration you were, reading the draft, hanging in there with me as I tweaked various things. You are a blessing Tola! I truly appreciate you.

Rhema! Your millennial biases helped me see what the challenges we are facing are and helped me address and set out issues we all would have taken for granted. Thanks for the fresh eyes you brought to reading the draft. I sincerely appreciate you.

Emmanuel Oyeleke, what do I say? You are a gem. You always answer when I call. Thanks for believing in my cover concept and coming through brilliantly as always.

It has been really hard work, but a lot of fun writing a story I had carried within me since I was sixteen. I never knew I could type 180,000 words in under a month.

I am almost tempted to write a second novel...

Acknowledgement

I am sure this attempt at acknowledgements will land me in trouble if I forget someone I shouldn't have.

So, I will try to be chronological and hope to stay on track. First to my editor, Enajite, who believed in this book as soon as she heard my story and demonstrated a rare dedication and devotion to the project by handing me a publishing contract. Enajite, I truly appreciate you.

To my classmate from university and collaborator, Muhtar Bakare, Director of Kachifo Limited, who went way beyond the call of duty to ensure the project was kept on track. Thank you for believing so much in me and helping me add yet another dimension to a life that is already multifaceted.

To Pastor Agu Irukwu for getting my perspective right on this book. Indeed, without your encouragement, I would probably never have signed the publishing contract. Thank you, PAI, for reading a pretty rough first draft that I couldn't even read myself! Thank you for always believing that I can deliver value, regardless of the task.

To Toluwaloju, my son, for saying, "Mum, go for it! All your other books are nothing like this one will be." Even when I despaired about the very serious me writing fiction, you assured me, "Mum, I am sooo proud of you." Without your support, I certainly wouldn't have felt I should write a work of fiction.

Thank you, Toluwalase, Mrs A's son and friend, for your unrelenting faith in me. Always, no exceptions.

Thank you, Mr A, for condoning my constant typing and complete absorption in my writing while I worked on this book.

To my dear BJ, you read the manuscript on your laptop, your phone

and listened to the audio. You kept me writing chapter after chapter. I had to write and send the next chapter to BJ. You have no idea how incredibly motivating your expectant calls were. It was not a breeze writing hundreds of thousands of words myself, but the fact that I had to send the next chapter to you kept me punching away at my MacBook. Thanks for your sincere and positive feedback.

To "my sis", Olutola Omotola, it takes a special woman and great client to attempt to read a work of fiction your very serious architect who delivered on your project less than a year ago wrote. You took me seriously, which attests to your amazing character. Thanks for your truly, awesomely, encouraging feedback, even on a badly punctuated first draft. You know how highly I regard your discretion and good taste; you are my favourite client and that explains a lot. Your feedback meant the world to me!

Thank you, Tola Odeyemi, for your encouragement and sincere, positive feedback, for the real inspiration you were, reading the draft, hanging in there with me as I tweaked various things. You are a blessing Tola! I truly appreciate you.

Rhema! Your millennial biases helped me see what the challenges we are facing are and helped me address and set out issues we all would have taken for granted. Thanks for the fresh eyes you brought to reading the draft. I sincerely appreciate you.

Emmanuel Oyeleke, what do I say? You are a gem. You always answer when I call. Thanks for believing in my cover concept and coming through brilliantly as always.

It has been really hard work, but a lot of fun writing a story I had carried within me since I was sixteen. I never knew I could type 180,000 words in under a month.

I am almost tempted to write a second novel...

Author's NOTE

I love my country passionately and, as you may have guessed, this is a book about leadership and its nexus with relationships. The basic character of a leader determines the type of leader (s)he would be – a transformational, selfless servant-leader, one with integrity; or a transactional, corrupt leader, one who bends the rules.

The character of a leader is formed within the family unit and parenting is one of the largest determinants of outcomes in the family unit. Knowing this fact, how do we choose our spouses - the persons who would be co-parents with us? How do we choose these spouses who would have to bear the burden of our leadership journey with us? Are the traits that the journey and task ahead call for even considered at all? Or are we more concerned with ephemeral issues when choosing our spouses? We moan about not having good leaders, but the leaders we have weren't flown in from alien planets; they come from our society.

What we obviously lack is a critical mass of people ready for leadership. We lack a pipeline of potential leaders. The family, school and other recognised matrixes of character are just not producing leaders in the quantity and at the rate that our society demands.

It is my hope that *Beyond My Dreams* will raise awareness in the reader about the power our choice of partner has in affecting not just our individual but corporate futures.

I started writing *Beyond My Dreams* when I was sixteen, in a notebook I should have dedicated to ARC 302 or some other school course. I was in the third year of my architecture programme at the time. My older friend, Mrs Sunmbo Campbell, would read the chapters as I produced the work, and she really liked it! So, I was encouraged, but I stopped abruptly when the events in the story, as written at the time, began to uncannily come to pass at a national level.

I must state here, though, that even in this reincarnation, the events in the novel are entirely fictitious. If anything, they serve as a warning to deter us from the romantic but naive notion that a revolution is a panacea for positive social change. In the decades since starting this book, I counselled so many women and men, and the need for the book became increasingly apparent.

I struggled with continuing the book because as a polymath I get upset when asked by people who cannot fathom that someone can do several things, "Do you still practise architecture?" I still practise daily and I love architecture. I will never stop practising architecture. I am passionate about architecture. I hope that settles the question forever even as *Beyond My Dreams* gets published.

As a practising architect with my own firm, AD Consulting, founded in 1994, and in my capacity as an Aposotolic Leader in service in Awesome Treasures Foundation, I see the struggle the contemporary Christian woman of African descent faces straddling traditional expectations, current socio-economic realities and her aspirations. I was consulted by so many who had been hurt and wounded. I proffered solutions that were common sense and worked like a miracle. The counselees returned to me in wonder and I began to see that the counsel I took for granted wasn't common knowledge.

The story I conceived as a teenager never left me and when I finally began to write again – thirty-four years later under the guidance of the Holy Spirit – my fingers flew over the keyboard. My editor says I wrote 180,000 words in the first three weeks (even with my two full-time day jobs). I didn't notice this! Time flew while I was writing. It's my hope that you, also, won't notice the pages fly by as you read and that this book won't be "just another book" but will impact you positively.

Except for my Lhasa Apso, Jay Z (who I still miss so badly), all the characters in *Beyond My Dreams* are not real persons. They assist us to discuss some issues that are pertinent and recurrent, and the guidance they represent is tested and proven. The scripture passages/quotes at the beginning of each chapter invite us to find out more about God's intention for relationships, love and marriage.

All proceeds from the sale of *Beyond My Dreams* will go to Awesome Treasures Foundation, which I founded out of my passion for leadership in 1999, to raise transformational leaders.

I pray that this book will help you forget what lies behind and press forward towards the mark of the High Calling (Phillipians 3:13-14).

About the Author

Olajumoke Adenowo (Arc) is a multiple award-winning architect with over three decades of industry experience. Described as Africa's "starchitect" and trailblazer when profiled by Cable News Network (CNN) and British Broadcasting Corporation (BBC), she is one of Africa's most outstanding architects and the only female in this elite category. Christened the Face of Architecture in Nigeria by *The Guardian*, she has been featured in the world's foremost architectural journal *Architectural Record*, *ForbesWomen* and *Fortune*. In 2013, she was instituted into the Hall of Fame of Personalities of Black Ancestry by the University of West England, Bristol, among other global personalities of black heritage.

Adenowo gained admission into Obafemi Awolowo University Ile-Ife at the age of fourteen, and she acquired the first distinction in Masters of Science in Architecture in the University's history. She is also an alumnus of a number of prestigious institutions including the Harvard Kennedy School of Government, the Yale School of Management, the IESE Business School amongst others. She is a member of the Institute of Chartered Arbitrators, United Kingdom, and a fellow of the Nigerian Institute of Architects.

Adenowo started her career at Femi Majekodunmi Associates, where she had the privilege of designing the Federal Ministry of Finance Headquarters in Abuja. In 1994, she founded her own multi-award-winning architecture firm, AD Consulting, which specialises also in master planning of eco-sensitive developments. AD Consulting is Nigeria's most internationally awarded firm. She has been the principal partner from inception to date.

In 1999, Adenowo's passion for raising transformational leaders led her to establish the faith-based philanthropy, Awesome Treasures Foundation, recognised by the United Nations and affiliated to the Edmond De Rothschild Foundations' Family Philanthropy platform. Awesome Treasures Foundation is established on three continents with initiatives impacting millions.

Adenowo is the pioneer recipient of the New African Women in Business Award and has been recognised as one of Africa's Top Ten Most Powerful Women in Business, one of Nigeria's Most Inspiring Women, one of Nigeria's 100 most Influential Nigerians, the International Alliance for Women World of Difference 100 Award, as well as one of the Most Inspiring Women in Nigeria amongst other honours. Adenowo was the recipient of the 2019 Leadership Award by the Constituency For Africa, Washington DC. In 2019, Olajumoke Adenowo was appointed a visiting professor at Germany's Leading Architecture program, Technische Universität München (TUM) in Germany. She was honoured as a laureate and guest scientist at the Chair of Theory, History of Architecture and Art & Design.

Adenowo is a speaker of note at summits and conferences and has spoken at several global platforms including the Global Women's Forum, Harvard Business School's Africa Business Club, Cambridge University's African Society and SOLVE MIT's flagship Conference for Global Thoughts Leaders and Innovators. She is a minister of the gospel and member of The International Coalition of Apostolic Leaders. She hosts her own syndicated radio program, Voice of Change, on leadership.

Adenowo has served on the juries and panels of global initiatives such as The Cartier Initiative for Women Awards and authored several books including *Life Spring*, *The Mysterious Seed* and *Appointment with Destiny*.

She is married to Olukorede and they are blessed with two men.